1 MONTH OF FREE READING

at

www.ForgottenBooks.com

By purchasing this book you are eligible for one month membership to ForgottenBooks.com, giving you unlimited access to our entire collection of over 1,000,000 titles via our web site and mobile apps.

To claim your free month visit:
www.forgottenbooks.com/free854932

* Offer is valid for 45 days from date of purchase. Terms and conditions apply.

ISBN 978-0-666-83092-0
PIBN 10854932

This book is a reproduction of an important historical work. Forgotten Books uses state-of-the-art technology to digitally reconstruct the work, preserving the original format whilst repairing imperfections present in the aged copy. In rare cases, an imperfection in the original, such as a blemish or missing page, may be replicated in our edition. We do, however, repair the vast majority of imperfections successfully; any imperfections that remain are intentionally left to preserve the state of such historical works.

Forgotten Books is a registered trademark of FB &c Ltd.
Copyright © 2018 FB &c Ltd.
FB &c Ltd, Dalton House, 60 Windsor Avenue, London, SW19 2RR.
Company number 08720141. Registered in England and Wales.

For support please visit www.forgottenbooks.com

Technical and Bibliographic Notes / Notes techniques et bibliographiques

ute has attempted to obtain the best original able for filming. Features of this copy which bliographically unique, which may alter any of es in the reproduction, or which may tly change the usual method of filming are elow.

□ ured covers /
verture de couleur

□ ers damaged /
verture endommagée

□ ers restored and/or laminated /
verture restaurée et/ou pelliculée

□ er title missing / Le titre de couverture manque

□ ured maps / Cartes géographiques en couleur

□ ured ink (i.e. other than blue or black) /
re de couleur (i.e. autre que bleue ou noire)

□ ured plates and/or illustrations /
ches et/ou illustrations en couleur

□ nd with other material /
é avec d'autres documents

□ edition available /
e édition disponible

□ t binding may cause shadows or distortion along
ior margin / La reliure serrée peut causer de

L'Institut a microfilmé le meilleur exemplaire qu'il été possible de se procurer. Les détails de cet plaire qui sont peut-être uniques du point de vue ographique, qui peuvent modifier une image repro ou qui peuvent exiger une modification dans la m de normale de filmage sont indiqués ci-dessous.

□ Coloured pages / Pages de couleur

□ Pages damaged / Pages endommagées

□ Pages restored and/or laminated /
Pages restaurées et/ou pelliculées

☑ Pages discoloured, stained or foxed /
Pages décolorées, tachetées ou piquées

□ Pages detached / Pages détachées

☑ Showthrough / Transparence

□ Quality of print varies /
Qualité inégale de l'impression

□ Includes supplementary material /
Comprend du matériel supplémentaire

□ Pages wholly or partially obscured by errata
tissues, etc., have been refilmed to ensure the
possible image / Les pages totalement
partiellement obscurcies par un feuillet d'errat
pelure, etc., ont été filmées à nouveau de fa
obtenir la meilleure image possible.

copy filmed here has been reproduced thanks
he generosity of:

> McMaster University
> Hamilton, Ontario

images appearing here are the best quality
ible considering the condition and legibility
e original copy and in keeping with the
ing contract specifications.

nal copies in printed paper covers are filmed
nning with the front cover and ending on
ast page with a printed or illustrated impres-
, or the back cover when appropriate. All
r original copies are filmed beginning on the
page with a printed or illustrated impres-
, and ending on the last page with a printed
ustrated impression.

ast recorded frame on each microfiche
contain the symbol ⟶ (meaning "CON-
ED"), or the symbol ▽ (meaning "END"),
hever applies.

, plates, charts, etc., may be filmed at
rent reduction ratios. Those too large to be
ly included in one exposure are filmed
ning in the upper left hand corner, left to
and top to bottom, as many frames as
red. The following diagrams illustrate the
od:

L'exemplaire filmé fut reproduit grâce
générosité de:

> McMaster University
> Hamilton, Ontario

Les images suivantes ont été reprodu
plus grand soin, compte tenu de la co
de la netteté de l'exemplaire filmé, et
conformité avec les conditions du con
filmage.

Les exemplaires originaux dont la cou
papier est imprimée sont filmés en co
par le premier plat et en terminant so
dernière page qui comporte une empr
d'impression ou d'illustration, soit pa
plat, selon le cas. Tous les autres exe
originaux sont filmés en commençant
première page qui comporte une emp
d'impression ou d'illustration et en te
la dernière page qui comporte une tel
empreinte.

Un des symboles suivants apparaitra
dernière image de chaque microfiche,
cas: le symbole ⟶ signifie "A SUIV
symbole ▽ signifie "FIN".

Les cartes, planches, tableaux, etc., p
filmés à des taux de réduction différe
Lorsque le document est trop grand p
reproduit en un seul cliché, il est film
de l'angle supérieur gauche, de gauch
et de haut en bas, en prenant le nomb
d'images nécessaire. Les diagrammes
illustrent la méthode.

1	2	3

1
2
3

MICROCOPY RESOLUTION TEST CHART

ANSI and ISO TEST CHART No. 2

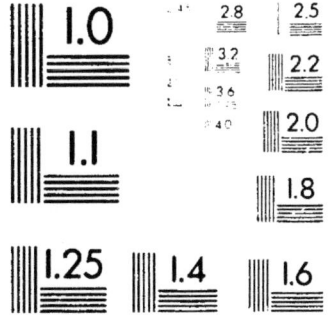

APPLIED IMAGE

1914-18

JULY, 1916

The Durham Forces in the Field
1914-18

By
Captain Wilfrid Miles
(Late 13th Durham Light Infantry)

Volume II
The Service Battalions
of the
Durham Light Infantry

With 17 Illustrations and 34 Maps and Plans

Cassell and Company, Ltd
London, New York, Toronto and Melbourne
1920

To

THE OFFICERS, WARRANT OFFICERS,
NON-COMMISSIONED OFFICERS AND PRIVATES
OF THE
SERVICE BATTALIONS OF THE
DURHAM LIGHT INFANTRY

WHO DIED ON THE FIELD OF HONOUR

*They shall grow not old, as we that are left grow old :
Age shall not weary them, nor the years condemn.
At the going down of the sun and in the morning
We will remember them.*
                                LAWRENCE BINYON

I am glad that the history of the different units of the Durham Light Infantry, both pre-war and new battalions, is to be written. I know that such a history must provide a record of which all Durham men for all time will be rightly proud.

Haig

Field-Marshal

PREFACE

This volume appears in advance of that which will carry forward the History of the Durham Light Infantry (68th and 106th Regts.) through the Great War and will also include the War History of the First Line Territorial Battalions of the Regiment. The explanation is to be found in the regrettable decease of Colonel the Hon. W. L. Vane while engaged upon this task which was to form a continuation of his earlier Work.

The following pages deal with the eleven Service Battalions of the Durham Light Infantry in such a manner as to bring them all within the compass of a single volume.

I am deeply indebted to those who have put themselves to much trouble in assisting me with their personal knowledge of events, they number far too many for me to mention them all by name. My grateful acknowledgments are also due to the courteous staff of the Historical Section (Military Branch) of the Committee of Imperial Defence and I have to thank the Durham Territorial Force Association for their advice and assistance on many occasions.

W. M.

November, 1920.

CONTENTS

The Birth of the New Battalions	1
Training at Home	6
First Months in France, 1915	11
The Battle of Loos, 1915	20
Trench Warfare: October, 1915—June, 1916	25
The Battle of the Somme, 1916	45
Trench Warfare: July, 1916—March, 1917	105
The Battle of Arras, 1917	132
Trench Warfare: April—June, 1917	150
The Battle of Messines, 1917	159
Trench Warfare: June and July, 1917	167
The Third Battle of Ypres, 1917	171
Trench Warfare: August—November, 1917	208
The Battle of Cambrai, 1917	218
Italy: November, 1917—February, 1918	230
Trench Warfare: December, 1917—March, 1918	239
Italy: March—September, 1918	250
The German Offensive, 1918	260
Holding the Line: May—August, 1918	307
The Last Campaign, 1918	321
The Victory in Italy, 1918	362
Conclusion	369
Index	371

ILLUSTRATIONS

July, 1916. By Adrian Hill . . . *Frontispiece*	
	FACING PAGE
Lieut.-Col. F. H. S. Morant, D.S.O., 10th Durham Light Infantry	4
Lieut.-Col. K. J. W. Leather, C.B.E., 20th Durham Light Infantry	4
Lieut.-Col. H. Bowes, 18th Durham Light Infantry	12
The late Lieut.-Col. C. B. Morgan, D.S.O., 22nd Durham Light Infantry	12
Private (afterwards Coy.-Sergt.-Major) T. Kenny, V.C., 13th Durham Light Infantry . .	32
Private M. Heaviside, V.C., 15th Durham Light Infantry	112
The late 2nd Lieut. F. Youens, V.C., 13th Durham Light Infantry	168
The 13th Durham Light Infantry before their advance on Sept. 20th, 1917 . . .	184
The 11th Durham Light Infantry moving up on July 31st, 1917	204
The late Capt. A. M. Lascelles, V.C., M.C., Durham Light Infantry	228
Aeroplane Photograph showing Poelcappelle-Westroosebeke Road; Vicinity of Goudberg Sector	238
Lieut.-Col. D. H. Clarke, D.S.O., M.C., 13th Durham Light Infantry	320

xi

Illustrations and Maps

PAGE

THE LATE LIEUT.-COL. C. E. R. HOLROYD-SMYTH,
D.S.O., M.C., 15TH DURHAM LIGHT INFANTRY . 320

GENERAL VIEW OF THE PIAVE. THE MONTICANO
RIVER 364

SENTRY OF THE 51ST DURHAM LIGHT INFANTRY:
HOHENZOLLERN BRIDGE, COLOGNE . . . 370

MAPS

(At End of Book)

1. FLANDERS TO SOUTH OF BÉTHUNE AND EAST OF TOURNAI.

2. LENS, ARRAS AND CAMBRAI BATTLEFIELDS TO SOUTH OF HEBUTERNE AND MARCOING.

3. CAMBRAI BATTLEFIELD AND BATTLEFIELDS NORTH AND SOUTH OF THE RIVER SOMME.

4. THE LAST CAMPAIGN, 1918, ILLUSTRATING:

    ADVANCE OF 15TH DURHAM LIGHT INFANTRY FROM OCT. 22ND.

    ADVANCE OF 13TH DURHAM LIGHT INFANTRY FROM OCT. 9TH.

    MOVEMENTS OF 11TH DURHAM LIGHT INFANTRY IN EARLY NOVEMBER.

5. THE LAST CAMPAIGN, 1918, ILLUSTRATING:

    ADVANCE OF 18TH DURHAM LIGHT INFANTRY FROM NOV. 9TH.

    ADVANCE OF 19TH DURHAM LIGHT INFANTRY FROM OCT. 31ST.

    ADVANCE OF 20TH DURHAM LIGHT INFANTRY FROM NOV. 1ST.

THE DURHAM FORCES IN THE FIELD, 1914—18

THE BIRTH OF THE NEW BATTALIONS

The mobilisation of the British Army which followed the Declaration of War with Germany on August 4th, 1914, brought an immediate call for recruits. In his letter of August 7th Lord Kitchener asked the counties to provide 100,000 men for the New Armies, and these were forthcoming in a fortnight—at the time when a German wireless message proclaimed the failure of his appeal. Men continued to offer themselves in numbers far greater than could be dealt with by the military authorities, and in no part of the kingdom was the response greater or more spontaneous than in the county of Durham. Newcastle-upon-Tyne, in which are the Depôts of the Durham Light Infantry and the Northumberland Fusiliers, was thronged with recruits, who filled all the public buildings which could be utilised for their accommodation and crowded the Town Moor and every open space to learn the rudiments of drill.

On August 22nd 500 men left the Depôt of the Durham Light Infantry for Woking, Surrey, to form the Tenth (Service) Battalion of the Regiment. Lieut.-Col. H. H. S. Morant, a Regular officer of many years' service with the 1st Battalion, was there to receive and command them. Other detachments followed so quickly that by the end of the month over 2,000 men were assembled, and the surplus became the Eleventh Battalion.

No less than 2,180 recruits were despatched from Newcastle on September 16th to Bullswater Camp, near Pirbright, in Surrey. These men were divided into the

The Durham Forces in the Field

Twelfth and Thirteenth Battalions. Five days later 710 men came south to billets in Aylesbury, Buckinghamshire, and a further contingent of 100 joined them on September 24th to complete the Fourteenth Battalion. The Fifteenth assembled at Halton Park, near Aylesbury, 800 men starting from the Depôt on September 26th and 240 on the first day of October.

Thus within two months of the beginning of the War six strong battalions of Durham men had been contributed to the New Armies, though it were more correct to style them the raw material out of which the battalions were made. They had everything to learn and the path of learning was beset with difficulties, as will be related.

Recruits continued to come in at a rate that promised easily to make good the wastage of war when the new battalions should take the field. But Durham was doing more even than finding the men. As the result of a suggestion of Major F. T. Tristram contained in a letter to Colonel R. Burdon, V.D., it was decided to raise and completely equip a battalion free of all expense to the Government. An influential committee, over which the Earl of Durham presided, was formed early in September for this purpose. Durham City, Darlington, the Hartlepools, Middlesbrough, Stockton, Sunderland, Bishop Auckland and a host of smaller places hastened to provide their share of the men and money required. More than £10,000 was subscribed and recruiting began at various centres in the county, while some men enlisted at the Depôt. From an unsympathetic War Office Colonel Burdon had wrung official sanction for the scheme. The question of housing the recruits would have been both difficult and expensive to solve had not Lord Durham lent Cocken Hall, where, on September 24th, the men assembled to form the County Battalion of the Durham Light Infantry soon to be known as the Eighteenth—the only battalion, in Durham or any other county, raised and equipped free of expense to the Nation. Three other battalions were raised and fitted out by Durham, but the cost incurred by each was refunded by the War Office.

The Birth of the New Battalions

At the beginning of December, 1914, the Durham Parliamentary Recruiting Committee was formed, with the Earl of Durham as president, Mr. C. R. Barratt of Pelton Fell as chairman, and Mr. A. B. Forsley as treasurer. The duties of secretary were shared by Mr. J. Corrie of Newcastle, Mr. F. W. Slater of Durham and Mr. T. W. Dawson of Crook, who represented respectively the Liberal, Unionist and Labour parties.

As a result of a prolonged correspondence with the War Office official sanction was given on January 13th, 1915, for the Committee to raise the Nineteenth, one of the first of the " Bantam " battalions. Recruits had to be not less than 5 feet or more than 5 feet 3 inches in height, and the minimum chest measurement was 34 inches. Many eager applicants, stout of heart if small of stature, hastened to enlist at the first opportunity. There was some difficulty with regard to accommodation, as a new battalion was not allowed to concentrate in the Coast Defence Area or, indeed, within ten miles of the coast; but special permission was given to assemble not more than 500 men at West Hartlepool and " Bobs' Durham Bantams " commenced to arrive there on March 3rd, 1915. They were quartered in the Co-Operative Society's buildings and Lieut.-Col. W. Thomlinson, V.D., assumed command.

In June, 1915, the War Office approached the Mayor (Alderman Stansfield Richardson) and Recruiting Committee of Sunderland as to the possibility of raising an infantry battalion in Sunderland and district. The Wearside folk had just contributed to the New Armies a complete brigade of field gunners, but they accepted the new commission and in July authority was given to raise the Twentieth Battalion. Recruiting commenced on August 19th, after Major K. J. W. Leather—then second-in-command of the 4th (Extra Reserve) Battalion of the Regiment—had been secured as commanding officer. The men began to assemble at St. John's Wesleyan Schools, Sunderland, on August 23rd.

On August 6th the County Recruiting Committee was asked by the War Office if it could provide a battalion of Pioneers. Enlistment for the 3rd County Battalion, the Twenty-Second of the Regiment, eventu-

The Durham Forces in the Field

ally opened on October 1st, and the first contingent of recruits went into billets at West Hartlepool ten days later. The ranks filled steadily, though Lord Derby's Group System of attestation was rather a hindrance, many men preferring to await the calling up of their groups instead of enlisting at once. Lieut.-Col. W. Thomlinson, who had supervised the early training of the Nineteenth to such excellent purpose, now performed a similar task as commanding officer of the Twenty-Second.

The Twenty-Ninth, who did not come into being till 1918, need not claim attention at this juncture, but there existed many reserve formations who supplied drafts to the Service Battalions in the field.

The 16th Battalion of the Durham Light Infantry were formed in November, 1914, by men from the 3rd (Special Reserve) Battalion, who were soon joined by a draft of recruits from the Depôt. In the same manner and at about the same time the 17th sprang from the 4th (Extra Reserve) Battalion. These new units were located at Rugeley, Staffordshire, in June, 1915, when the 89th Brigade, to which they belonged, became the 2nd Training Reserve Brigade for the supply of reinforcements. The 16th and 17th Battalions added " (2nd Reserve) " to their titles, but they lost their County names on September 1st, 1916, when they were re-christened, respectively, the 1st and 2nd Training Reserve Battalions and with the 10th North Staffordshire Regt. (re-named the 3rd T. R. Battalion) formed the 1st Training Reserve Brigade. The 1st Training Reserve Battalion was disbanded at the end of November, 1917.

The 21st (Reserve) Battalion of the Durham Light Infantry dates from July 29, 1915. When the Nineteenth left Cocken Hall their reserve companies were left behind and joined with the reserves of the Eighteenth to form this unit. The battalion were afterwards stationed at Wensleydale, Richmond and Hornsea, but while at Wensleydale they lost the reserve companies of the " Bantams " at the end of October, 1915.

The latter formed the nucleus of the 23rd (Reserve) Battalion who moved to Scotton Camp, Catterick, early in November. In January, 1916, it was decided that

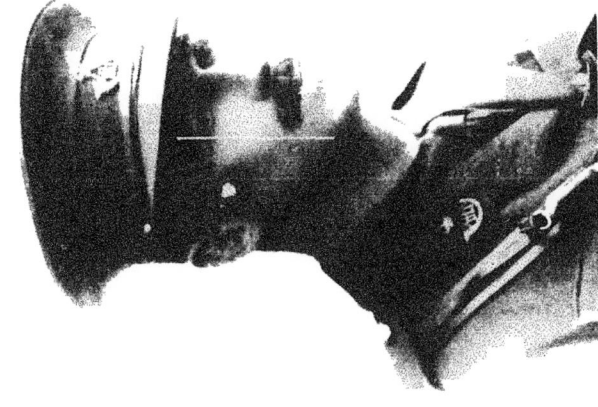

LIEUT.-COL. K. J. W. LEATHER.
20th Durham Light Infantry

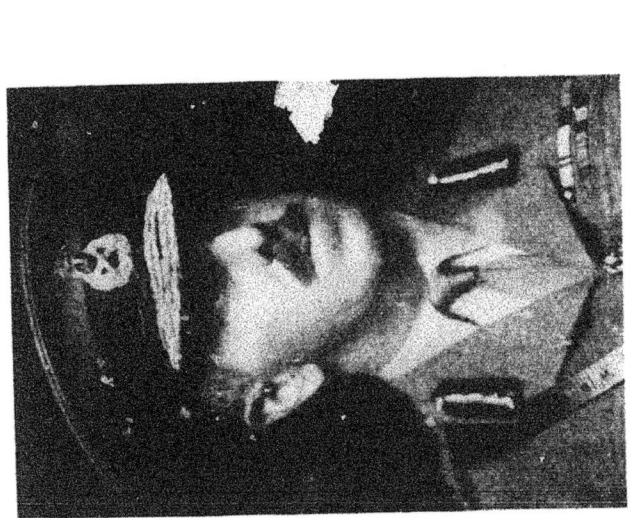

LIEUT.-COL. H. B. S. MORANT, D.S.O.
10th Durham Light Infantry
(afterwards G.O.C. 3rd Infantry Brigade

The Birth of the New Battalions

this battalion should supply drafts to the Twentieth. They moved to Atwick, near Hornsea, in April, 1916, for coast defence work.

The reserve company of the Twenty-Second, though intended to form the 24th (Reserve) Battalion, joined the 16th (2nd Reserve) Battalion at Rugeley when the Pioneers went to France.

The 25th (Works) Battalion was simply a labour depôt raised for the Northern Command in May, 1916. No arms were carried and no military training was done.

When the 16th and 17th (2nd Reserve) Battalions lost their county designations at the beginning of September, 1916, all reserve battalions raised during the War were treated in similar fashion and renumbered. The 11th (Reserve) Battalion, North Staffordshire Regt., and the 31st (Reserve) Battalion, Northumberland Fusiliers, became respectively the 4th and 86th Training Reserve Battalions. In July, 1917, when there was a further re-organisation of the Infantry, the Training Reserve Battalions were divided into four classes according to the category, age and training of the recruits posted to them. The 4th Training Reserve Battalion were re-numbered the 258th and the 86th the 273rd. Then in October, 1917, it was decided to affiliate all such units to Line Regiments, and the 258th and 273rd became the 51st and 52nd (Graduated) Battalions of the Durham Light Infantry.

The 53rd (Young Soldiers) Battalion of the Regiment came into being in October, 1917, from the 2nd Training Reserve Battalion, who were originally the 17th Durham Light Infantry.

The Young Soldiers Battalion received recruits of 18 years and one month (later the age was increased by one month) and, after training them for four months, sent them on by companies to one or other of the Graduated Battalions. Seven months more of training then rendered these lads fit for active service as they attained the age of 19 years. In March, 1918, boys of 18 years and six months were sent overseas and thenceforward the 53rd Battalion acted merely as a collecting station for the young recruits, who were passed on to the 51st or 52nd Graduated Battalion almost at once.

TRAINING AT HOME

It is hardly an exaggeration to say that the first six Service Battalions of the Durham Light Infantry began their training under the worst possible conditions. In common with the remainder of the " First Hundred Thousand " the Tenth had some advantages over the other battalions. Their Commanding Officer, Adjutant, and Regimental-Sergeant-Major were all Regulars, and this alone counted for a great deal. But there was a general lack of competent instructors, and officers, non-commissioned officers and men all had to be trained at the same time.

Many of the camps turned into quagmires when the fine weather of the early autumn of 1914 was followed by rain; and winter arrived while several of the battalions were still in tents. The food supplied was good and sufficient, but unskilled cooks, working with improvised kitchen arrangements, were at first unable to give the men the full benefit of their rations. The Tenth had little difficulty in getting their men clothed in khaki, though greatcoats and caps were more difficult to procure; but the men of most of the battalions had to wear their old civilian attire until blue serge uniforms were issued, and the fit and quality of the latter left much to be desired. Khaki was more generally available in the spring of 1915.

It was long before arms and equipment reached the new battalions, though in this particular the Tenth were again better served. Drill was done with the old long rifle and even with wooden dummies, range practice—except with miniature weapons—being mostly out of the question for the first six months, though much theoretical instruction was imparted.

In the autumn of 1914 there was a medical re-examination of the troops, and many men who had been passed by the doctors on enlistment were found to be

Training at Home

unfit for active service. They were discharged, and their places were filled by new drafts from the Depôt and the Reserve Battalions.

In spite of these handicaps good progress was made towards the attainment of the high standard of efficiency which had prevailed in the Regular Army. Training was on the same lines, so far as time and opportunity permitted, but more digging was done and the men had some practice in bomb throwing. Although exercises in relieving trenches were carried out, the arts of trench warfare remained to be learnt by actual experience after arrival at the Front.

Much credit is due to the Regular officers who commanded and directed the training of the new battalions; devoted work was also done by temporary officers with some military service and other experience in the handling of men; but the truly admirable spirit of the recruits commands our greatest admiration. They had confidence in their officers, they endured hardships and monotony with patience and cheerfulness, and they were always eager to learn.

The men of the locally raised battalions, who bore themselves equally well, started their military career in better circumstances. For the most part they did their early training within the County and local enterprise was able to do more for them than the military authorities could do for their comrades who were concentrated in the south of England.

When the Tenth assembled at Woking in the last week of August, 1914, they went under canvas on the recreation ground, the barracks being occupied by the 6th King's Own Yorkshire Light Infantry. The two battalions, together with the 6th Duke of Cornwall's Light Infantry and the 6th (Prince Albert's) Somerset Light Infantry, formed the 43rd Brigade of the 14th (Light) Division.

On September 23rd the Tenth marched to Aldershot, where they went into tents at Berkshire Copse. Training was hurried on, as it was understood that the division were to go overseas before Christmas. While at Woking 500 service rifles and about the same number of sets

7

The Durham Forces in the Field

of equipment had been issued, but most of the rifles and all the packs were gradually taken away to replace wastage in France. Then the old long rifle was used, both arms and equipment being handed from man to man, as there were not sufficient for all.

Rain set in after the Tenth moved to Witley Camp on November 23rd. The huts there were unfinished and leaked and no roads or drains existed, with the consequence that there were many cases of sickness. In December 400 men from each battalion in the 43rd Brigade were warned to move at three hours' notice in case of invasion. Complete battalions could not be used owing to lack of arms and equipment, and the transport was to consist of farm carts.

When the Tenth moved to Aldershot on February 21st the transport was complete, and each man had a service rifle and new leather equipment. The battalion now shared Corunna Barracks with the 8th K.O.Y.L.I., and brigade and divisional training was carried on. New service rifles were issued in March and the shooting of the Tenth proved to be the best in the brigade.

By the time that the division were ready to proceed overseas Colonel Morant considered that his men were quite up to the standard of pre-war training in the Regular Army with the exception of their musketry.

Under the command of Colonel G. M. Davidson the Eleventh began their career at Woking and remained there until the end of November, when they moved to the camp at Pirbright which the Guards battalions were wont to use when at musketry. The Durhams found huts in process of building, but they were not finished before the battalion moved again.

The Eleventh were in the 61st Brigade of the 20th (Light) Division, but in December, 1914, the War Office decided upon the formation of pioneer battalions as divisional troops. Early in January, 1915, the Eleventh were replaced in their brigade by the 12th King's Regt. and became the Pioneer Battalion of the 20th Division. This involved some reorganisation. A number of men were sent to the Tenth in exchange for others who were considered to be of suitable pioneer type, skilled arti-

Training at Home

sans being much in request as the duties of a pioneer battalion were intended to be many and various. Some officers of special training and experience joined the Eleventh in March.

In February, 1915, the Pioneers moved to very comfortable billets at North Chapel, the division concentrating at the big camp at Witley, where the Durhams arrived a week later. One company then put in three weeks very necessary work on the roads and drains.

While here the battalion were gradually fitted with equipment, but khaki clothing was not received till after removal, on March 26th, to Larkhill, their last station before going overseas.

The Twelfth and Thirteenth, at Bullswater, formed, with the 10th and 11th Northumberland Fusiliers, the 68th Brigade of the 23rd Division. These two Durham battalions were commanded respectively by Lieut.-Col. L. E. C. Elwes, D.S.O., and Colonel C. A. Ashby, C.B. The whole brigade continued under canvas at Bullswater until the end of November, by which time the rain and mud and cold had tried all ranks severely. Marching into Aldershot, the Twelfth and Thirteenth shared Malplaquet Barracks and continued here till the end of February, though a fortnight was spent by the Twelfth in billets at Sandhurst, while the Thirteenth went to Wokingham for the same period. The next move was by rail, the Thirteenth going into billets at Ashford, in Kent, while the Twelfth were located just outside the town. The men now received their khaki and some musketry was done, while brigade exercises and the instruction of specialists were features of a period of hard training. On May 23rd the 68th Brigade entrained for Bramshott, a large new camp off the Portsmouth Road between Hindhead and Liphook. The ranges at Longmoor were utilised for musketry, and then came the final weeks of preparation for active service. The Twelfth, like the Tenth and Eleventh, were taken to France by the officer who had commanded them throughout their training; but Colonel Ashby, to the regret of all ranks, vacated the command of the Thirteenth on July 8th. He was succeeded by Major

The Durham Forces in the Field

J. R. O'Connell, but the battalion eventually went out under Major N. T. Biddulph, a former officer of the 2nd Durham Light Infantry, who had been second-in-command since September, 1914.

The Fourteenth moved from their Aylesbury billets on October 3rd to Halton Park, where they joined the Fifteenth. With the 9th and 10th King's Own Yorkshire Light Infantry the two battalions formed the 64th Brigade of the 21st Division. During the ensuing weeks preliminary training was carried out under wretched weather conditions, which caused much sickness. Until the middle of October the men were still in their civilian clothes and there was a great shortage of officers. The move to comfortable billets in High Wycombe and the vicinity at the beginning of December, 1914, was an immense improvement.

Training now made steady progress, with Colonel R. Eccles in command of the Fourteenth, and with the Fifteenth under Lieut.-Col. R. A. Smith. During the fourteen weeks spent here the despised dummy rifles were replaced by weapons of service pattern and the men were issued with khaki clothing. The 64th Brigade marched back to Halton Park early in April, 1915, and found a vastly improved camp of huts. Battalion, brigade and divisional exercises along the wooded slopes of the Chiltern Hills continued until July, when the 21st Division marched to Witley Camp, a distance of 75 miles which was covered in five days. Lieut.-Col. A. S. Hamilton, 4th Notts and Derby Regt., was now commanding the Fourteenth. At Witley the battalions worked very hard in hot and dusty weather during the remaining weeks before embarkation. In August Lieut.-Col. E. T. Logan, D.S.O., 3rd Cheshire Regt., was gazetted to the command of the Fifteenth, replacing Colonel Smith.

The Eighteenth, located at Cocken Hall, were recruited to full strength early in October, 1914, and two companies moved into billets as further accommodation became necessary. Lord Southampton, the first commanding officer, was soon succeeded by Lieut.-Col. H.

Training at Home

Bowes. The committee now arranged for the building of huts, so that Cocken Hall soon became a comfortable and well-appointed camp. By the middle of November the battalion had made great progress in training and organisation; the men were all in uniform and much equipment had been received. On the 16th of the month two companies, under the command of Major F. T. Tristram, went to Hartlepool for coast defence duties. They provided guards at various points, improved the existing trenches and continued their training.

A month later, on December 16th, the bombardment of the Hartlepools by a squadron of German warships gained for the Eighteenth the distinction of being the first of the Durham Service Battalions to come under fire. As infantry their rôle was a passive one and the story of the fight very properly belongs to the Durham Royal Garrison Artillery; but the Eighteenth lost 5 killed and 11 wounded by the enemy shell fire, and the cool and gallant bearing of the two companies was beyond all praise. Sergt. W. E. Heal and Corpl. M. Brewerton went down to the beach during the bombardment and rescued an injured fisherman.

In December, the Eighteenth with the 16th, 18th and 19th Northumberland Fusiliers were brigaded to form the 122nd Brigade of the 41st Division. Early in 1915 the Hartlepool detachment rejoined the battalion, who were called upon to strengthen the Middlesbrough defences in the following April. This provided a week's outpost duty for three companies. On May 3rd the 122nd Brigade concentrated under canvas at Cramlington, but later in the month the Eighteenth were posted to the 93rd Brigade of the 31st Division and joined them at Ripon. The other battalions of this brigade were the 15th, 16th and 18th West Yorkshires.

The Eighteenth derived great benefit from their training at Ripon and in August the War Office took over a very fine battalion indeed. The next move was to the unfinished camp of Fovant, near Salisbury, on September 23rd. Here musketry was done and other training carried out in bad weather. At the end of November advance parties of the 31st Division crossed the Channel, but orders for the Western Front were

The Durham Forces in the Field

cancelled and sun-helmets were issued. Early in December the Earl of Durham inspected the Eighteenth and bade them farewell in the name of the County.

Recruiting for the Nineteenth had to be temporarily suspended when no more men could be accommodated at Hartlepool, but in May, 1915, the Cocken Hall camp became vacant. The battalion moved there in the middle of the month, and were then 1,100 strong. On June 22nd they went to Masham, in Yorkshire, and in July came south to Perham Down on Salisbury Plain. Lieut.-Col. W. Thomlinson had been succeeded in the command by Colonel A. W. Newbold, and in September the latter handed over the Nineteenth to Major L. S. Stoney, 4th Royal Irish Fusiliers, who took them to France in January of the following year.

The raising of the " Bantam " battalions was, of course, in the nature of an experiment, but all inspecting officers who saw the Nineteenth on parade or at work reported them a very valuable addition to the Armies. Lord Durham inspected them in August and again in December, 1915, and expressed his complete satisfaction on both occasions.

It cost the County upwards of £11,500 to raise and equip the battalion, this sum being refunded by the War Office. The Nineteenth, with the 17th West Yorkshire Regt., the 17th Royal Scots and the 18th Highland Light Infantry, formed the 106th Brigade of the 35th Division. All the infantry of the division were " Bantam " battalions.

The Twentieth soon removed from their billets in Sunderland. On August 28th, 1915, the battalion entrained for Wensley, in Yorkshire, where tents had been pitched in pleasant surroundings. No rifles or equipment were available at this period, but Colonel Leather was able to get his men disciplined and physically fit while officers and N.C.O.'s were being trained. In October, when the weather changed very much for the worse, the Twentieth moved to billets at Barnard Castle, and here the battalion made rapid progress as equipment of all kinds arrived. In November, 1915, the

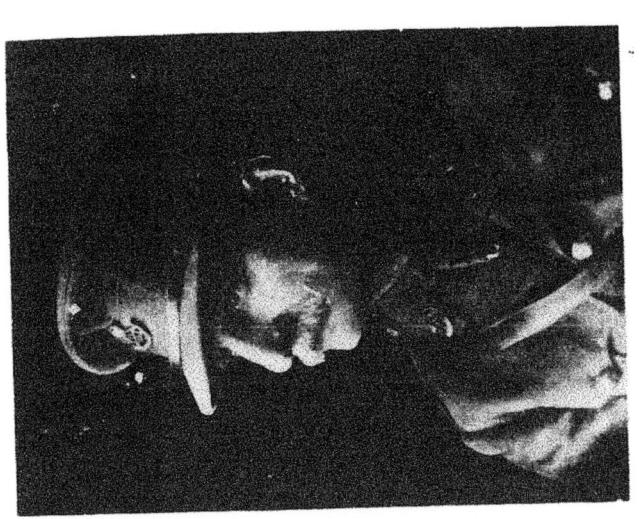

LIEUT.-COL. H. BOWES
18th Durham Light Infantry

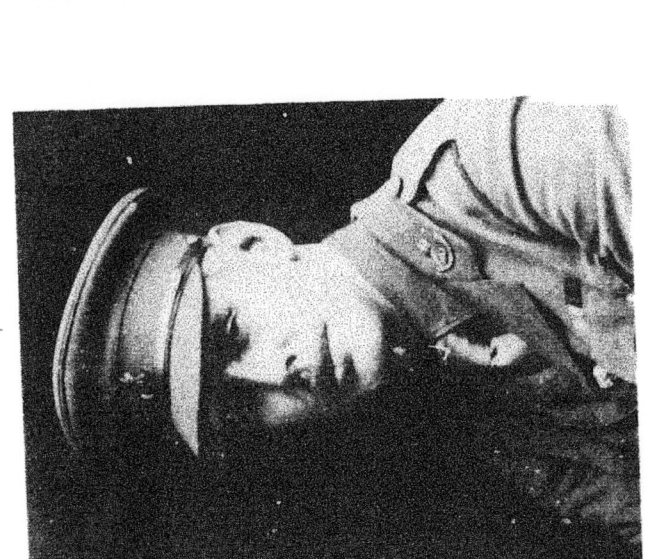

The late LIEUT.-COL. C. B. MORGAN, D.S.O.
22nd Durham Light Infantry (Pioneers)

Training at Home

Wearsiders were posted to the 123rd Brigade of the 41st Division then forming at Aldershot, but they did not come south till the War Office took over the battalion from the Sunderland Recruiting Committee at the beginning of January, 1916.

On arrival at Aldershot the Twentieth found themselves brigaded with the 23rd Middlesex, the 11th Queen's and the 10th Queen's Own (Royal West Kent Regt.). Without delay the battalion were completely equipped in every detail for service overseas, but training—varied by frequent inspections—continued till the end of April.

The Twenty-Second, who were taken over by the War Office on March 9th, 1916, remained at West Hartlepool until March 21st. Colonel Thomlinson ably directed the training throughout this period and he was justly proud of his Pioneers when he reviewed them on the 20th before handing over the command to Lieut.-Col. C. B. Morgan of the West India Regt. Next day the Twenty-Second moved to Scotton Camp, Catterick, their last station before proceeding overseas. As Pioneers they were not attached to any infantry division in England.

THE FIRST MONTHS IN FRANCE

MAY TO SEPTEMBER, 1915

The Tenth left Aldershot on May 21st and crossed from Folkestone to Boulogne the same night. On the 25th they left by train for Cassel and marched to billets at Volkerinckhove, eventually reaching Bailleul on the last day of the month. Here work was done on the local defences till the battalion moved to Dickebusch, after which parties were employed at St. Eloi.

The first experience of trench duty commenced on June 12th, when the Tenth were attached to the 46th Division and went into the line, first by platoons and then by companies, west of Wytschaete. During this tour there were 21 casualties, including 2nd Lieut. G. E. Fairbairn, mortally wounded. A few days in billets near Poperinghe followed, and then on June 24th the battalion took over the line astride the Menin Road opposite Hooge. The trenches here were in a bad state after a successful British attack. Next morning Capt. C. James was killed, and on June 27th the Germans shelled the support position occupied by A company, killing Major H. R. Chapman and wounding 2nd Lieut. C. E. Sewart. Capt. J. T. Saunders was also wounded before the battalion were relieved and casualties in the ranks amounted to 50.

Now came a few days rest near Vlamertinghe and an opportunity to fraternise with the 2nd Durham Light Infantry before the Tenth moved into reserve at Ypres ramparts. On July 22nd the battalion took over the Railway Wood sector on the left of the line previously held. A night of rain gave some indication of what winter in the trenches would be like, but this tour was quieter than the first had been. The Tenth were relieved in peace on the night of July 26th and returned to their camp near Vlamertinghe.

First Months in France, 1915

At 3 A.M. on July 30th came orders to move at half an hour's notice. It was on this morning that the Germans introduced a new weapon—the flame-thrower—in an attack on the battalions of the 41st Brigade holding the line before Hooge. The Rifles had had to give ground after losing heavily, and a counter-attack was now in preparation. The Tenth were hurried forward towards Ypres and reached the ramparts soon after 2 P.M., to learn that the counter-attack had failed. At night they went forward to unfamiliar ground south of the Menin Road and relieved the Rifle men as best they could in the darkness.

The trenches were filled with killed and wounded, who lay as they had fallen. Soon after midnight both British and Germans began a terrific bombardment, each anticipating an attack. Shells tore into Zouave Wood, and the troops holding the front edge appeared to have retired. The division asked Colonel Morant if this line were lost and said it must be held, so D company, who had been in reserve, went forward. They found the trenches empty and occupied them without much trouble. At dawn Major J. S. Unthank was wounded, and the growing light revealed a terrible scene of slaughter. Zouave Wood suffered from the German snipers, and here Capt. R. W. Braithwaite was killed. There were no orders and the Tenth spent the day rescuing wounded and striving to improve the line. At night the enemy poured in a storm of heavy trench mortar shells, but the Durhams held on to their damaged trenches. Capt. H. M. Atkinson, Lieut. W. B. Marchant and 2nd Lieuts. Ritchie and Earley were all wounded, and in these two nights and a day the Tenth lost 170 men.

On August 1st A company were relieved and withdrew to the western edge of Sanctuary Wood, but before the rest of the battalion did likewise next day a good support line called Durham Trench was dug in the wood. The Tenth and the sappers now worked hard to strengthen the front, and the whole line was wired under the direction of Lieut. C. E. Pumphrey, who won the Military Cross for his activity on patrol. The 2nd Durham Light Infantry came in on August

The Durham Forces in the Field

5th, and the Tenth moved back in the rain to Vlamertinghe.

They came up again on August 9th and took over the battered line in the Y Wood salient. The trenches so gallantly carried by the 2nd Durham Light Infantry earlier in the day were now occupied by neither British nor German, but were a target for the artillery of both. Unfortunately the British heavies dropped some shells among the Tenth, killing several men. On August 13th some machine-gunners were buried by our own fire, but were promptly dug out under the direction of Lieut. J. B. Rosher. Colonel H. H. S. Morant was wounded on this day, Major the Hon. R. T. St. John assuming command until the return of Major J. S. Unthank a fortnight later.

The Tenth were relieved and withdrew to Ypres ramparts on the night of August 14th. Here they were subjected to a bombardment by 17-inch guns, but casualties were not heavy. Nine days were spent at Watou, west of Poperinghe, before the month ended. During September the battalion had a fairly quiet tour in Railway Wood trenches, a week in reserve and much work on the defences.

When Bellewaarde ridge was attacked on September 25th, " with the object of distracting the enemy's attention and holding his troops to their ground," the Tenth did not participate; but they had one exciting experience during the preliminary bombardment. They were heavily shelled while coming up by train in open trucks toward Ypres and lost 40 killed and wounded. Parties of the battalion assisted to dig assembly trenches for the attack, and Lieut. A. Parke, with 32 of the best bombers, was lent to the 9th Rifle Brigade, who led the assault upon the left.

At 3.15 A.M. on the 25th the German redoubt just south of the Roulers railway was blown up, forming a vast crater. The infantry advanced about an hour afterwards and, though all went well at first, the line was not strong enough to resist the vigorous German counter-attack which followed. Losses were heavy, and the whole of the ground gained was relinquished as the morning wore on. Lieut. Parke, who had led

First Months in France, 1915

his bombers into the crater on the left, was wounded and did not get back and only 12 of his men returned. They had held on alone in the German third line till nearly noon.

In the evening the Tenth came up through pouring rain to take over the line on the left. The trenches were now just heaps of earth and tumbled sandbags, and all next day the Durhams laboured to improve them. The rescue of the wounded was completed by nightfall, when a bright moon arose and Germans sniped incessantly from the crater. Suddenly at midnight the Germans attacked the 3rd Division, further south, and a fierce bombardment swept the trenches of the Tenth, but few casualties were caused.

On September 28th an informal truce resulted in the rescue of two British wounded lying outside the crater, and at night the Tenth were relieved. Casualties were not so heavy as might have been expected. Capt. W. T. Wyllie, Lieut. Stobart and 2nd Lieut. Jordan were among the officers wounded.

Lance-Corpl. Chicken won the Distinguished Conduct Medal on September 26th for taking out food and tea to several wounded who lay between the lines. He attempted to bring one in, but the German fire killed the man before he could do so.

The Eleventh crossed to France on July 20th by the Southampton-le Havre route. Several days were then spent at Esquerdes, but before the end of the month the Pioneers were engaged in cleaning ditches and repairing roads near the forest of Nieppe and in making brushwood hurdles. On August 3rd C company were employed upon strong points behind the 8th Division front at Fleurbaix.

The 20th Division soon took over the line, south of the 8th, in the flat lands north of Neuve Chapelle, and three companies of the Eleventh worked on the trenches. C company were still making hurdles in the forest and continued to do so when the rest of the battalion assembled at Estaires in readiness for the operations of September 25th. On this day the advance of the 20th and Meerut Divisions was attended with

The Durham Forces in the Field

heavy loss and no gain of ground, so that the Pioneers were not called upon; but three days later the Eleventh were wanted to hold a portion of the line taken over from the Indian troops on the right. The battalion relieved the 9th Gurkhas in trenches which were, for the most part, very wet and muddy. There was little enemy action, but the weather hindered the work of draining the trenches, repairing the parapet and strengthening the wire in front. At this time several platoons were away working with the tunnelling companies at Fauquissart.

The Twelfth and Thirteenth, being both in the 68th Brigade, had similar experiences on proceeding to France. Arriving at Boulogne in the early hours of August 26th, the former entrained, later, for Watten and reached billets at Houlle. The Thirteenth followed by the same route some hours afterwards and were located in the neighbouring village of Moulle—situated on the Calais-St. Omer road—by August 27th. Training was carried on till September 6th, when the whole brigade marched to Hazebrouck and on the following day to the vicinity of Steenwerck.

On September 9th both Twelfth and Thirteenth marched south, and were attached to troops of the 20th Division for instruction in actual trench duties. Each battalion suffered a few casualties while in the line. A move to the vicinity of Erquinghem was made on September 17th, the Twelfth going to l'Hallobeau and the Thirteenth to Petit Moulin, near the river Lys. The other brigades of the 23rd Division now took over the line from the vicinity of Bois Grenier to Armentières, and the Durham battalions provided working parties for the construction of strong points and the improvement of trenches in preparation for the Flanders winter. On September 24th six men of C company of the Thirteenth were wounded in their bivouac by a German anti-aircraft shell.

The Twelfth and Thirteenth stood to arms when the British offensive began upon September 25th. On the afternoon of the next day a German counter-attack was feared on the front held by the Meerut Division,

First Months in France, 1915

who had suffered cruel losses, so the two battalions marched down through Estaires and were billetted for the night on the la Bassée road. On the 27th they made the return journey, only to be brought back to Estaires again on the following day and placed under the orders of the 20th Division. Large working-parties were now provided and assistance was given to the tunnellers.

On the night of September 28th Pte. Jameson of the Thirteenth fell into the river Lys, which contained quite eight feet of water. In darkness and heavy rain Lance-Corpl. R. Boagey promptly jumped in and rescued him, winning thereby the bronze medal of the Royal Humane Society.

THE BATTLE OF LOOS, 1915

The Fourteenth and Fifteenth left Witley camp on September 11th and crossed from Folkestone to Boulogne the same night. They entrained on the 12th for the St. Omer district, where most of the new divisions were sent to prepare for service in the line. The Fourteenth went to Nielles-lez-Ardres, some miles east of the forest of Eperlecques; the Fifteenth to Nordausques, further down the Ardres—St. Omer road.

A week later the 21st Division commenced their forward march into as tragic an experience as troops can be called upon to endure. Moving mostly by night, the Fourteenth came by Arques and Lambres and Ecquedecques to Noeux-les-Mines, where they bivouacked on the afternoon of September 25th. The Fifteenth, moving in similar fashion, had reached Houchin on the 24th and were near-by. The concluding march of both battalions was particularly wearisome by reason of the frequent delays at level crossings.

At 7.15 p.m. on September 25th the 64th Brigade moved off through Mazingarbe in the rain, passing divisional headquarters at Vermelles about an hour later. All that the battalions knew was that they were following in support of the 63rd Brigade. The men were wet, tired and hungry, for all had been sacrificed to get the division into the battle with the least possible delay.

At 9 p.m. the 64th Brigade halted in the darkness. It took three hours to prepare for the advance to the line. Orders had to be issued, and it was necessary to unload Lewis guns, ammunition, bombs and tools before the transport could be withdrawn clear of the troops. There was no time to reconnoitre the ground, but the 63rd Brigade were presumed to be somewhere in front.

At midnight the 64th moved forward on a front of

The Battle of Loos, 1915

two battalions in line of companies in column, the Fourteenth and Fifteenth leading. The rain had stopped when the old British front line was passed at about 1 A.M. on September 26th. Some of the trenches could be jumped, others were bridged by planks or narrow causeways; but the checks and delays in order to reform after negotiating each obstacle seemed interminable. It was moonlight now. On the left a column of wagons was seen following a track which, if its existence had been known, would have saved the brigade much valuable time in the advance. Now and then shells burst near. Soon after 2 A.M. the old German front line was reached, and about an hour later the brigade halted. Patrols went out but could find no trace of the 63rd.

The Fourteenth were sent forward to occupy a deserted German battery position which had been discovered, while one company were located on the Loos-Hulluch road. The Fifteenth settled down in a trench about a quarter of a mile in rear, but there was not room for all of them, so one company fell back to the la Bassée road, on the northern outskirts of Loos, where they were in touch with the right of the K.O.Y.L.I. A field company of R.E., with the horses and pack-animals, were in the old German front line.

The whereabouts of the enemy and the dispositions of the British troops in this portion of the field were as yet unknown; but, soon after dawn, touch was obtained by the K.O.Y.L.I. with the 24th Division, further north, and the 63rd Brigade were found to be holding the Lens-Hulluch road, north of Bois Hugo. The transport, which had been ordered to move to Loos by road and rejoin the brigade at daylight, was looked for in vain. The congestion of traffic during the night was the cause of the delay, and when the sun dispersed the morning mists the German shell-fire stopped all movement on the road. The enemy batteries soon began to take their toll of the brigade, casualties including Lieut. V. B. Odhams, of the Fifteenth, who was mortally wounded about this time.

Orders had been issued for an attack by the 24th and 21st Divisions, the latter having for their final ob-

The Durham Forces in the Field

jective the town of Annay, some four miles east of Loos. But this was on the supposition that Hill 70 was in British hands, and now it appeared that a redoubt on the north-eastern slope of the hill was to be taken before the 63rd Brigade attacked north of Puits 14 bis at 11 A.M.

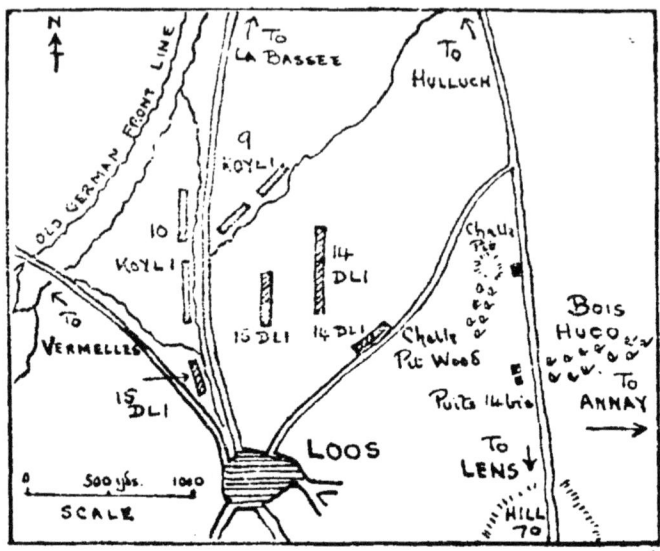

Position of 64th Brigade: Daybreak, Sept. 26

At nine o'clock the 64th Brigade watched the troops on the right go forward from Loos and up the slopes of Hill 70. About fifty minutes afterwards the 63rd Brigade, who appeared to be facing a hostile counter-attack, asked for a battalion to reinforce their right in Chalk Pit Wood. The Fourteenth were selected for the task and were soon advancing steadily. By half-past ten, when they were nearing the western edge of the wood under considerable shell and machine-gun fire, troops of the 63rd Brigade began to retire on their left. Perhaps these troops mistook the Durham men in

The Battle of Loos, 1915

their overcoats for Germans. To observers in rear they seemed to change direction, as though to take the Fourteenth in flank, and then to discover their mistake. They soon continued to withdraw, involving the Fourteenth in the process. At this time, too, British troops were leaving Hill 70 and the retirement became general, though carried out in good order. No Germans were seen to advance, but the line came back over the Loos-la Bassée road and rallied behind the three remaining battalions of the 64th Brigade.

Then at 11 A.M. the 24th Division advanced according to orders, and the whole line followed suit. The Fourteenth, with the Fifteenth in support, now linked up the right of the 63rd Brigade with the troops advancing from Loos. Keeping touch on the right the Durhams were pulled round towards Hill 70, and suffered heavily through enfilade machine-gun fire from Chalk Pit Wood. Lieut.-Col. E. T. Logan, D.S.O., had already fallen, mortally wounded, while gallantly leading the Fifteenth. Declining all aid he handed over the command to the adjutant, Capt. Babbage, and urged forward the advance. Soon the troops on the right of the Durhams began to retire, and by 12.30 P.M. the whole line was in retreat. Followed by heavy shell fire, the troops came back over the Loos-la Bassée road again.

It was intended to launch another attack, but before 2 P.M. came a spontaneous advance, in which the survivors of the Durham battalions joined the K.O.Y.L.I. of the 64th Brigade. Heavily punished in flank by shrapnel and machine-gun bullets, and unsupported by the British gunners who had not been warned of the attempt, the infantry had no chance of success. The inevitable retreat was conducted under intense shell fire, and the German bombardment continued till dusk on the 64th Brigade position. Many of the severely wounded had to remain where they fell. The exhausted survivors, suffering tortures from thirst—they had no chance of refilling their water-bottles—remained in the old German trenches till they were relieved by the Guards in the early morning of September 27th.

The losses of the Durhams were very heavy. In the

The Durham Forces in the Field

Fourteenth, Lieut. W. T. Thompson and 2nd Lieut. F. E. Burkett were killed, and Lieut.-Col. A. S. Hamilton, who had led his men well, died of his wounds. Capts. F. W. Eastcott, P. C. Blackett and M. Mackenzie; Lieuts. Moss-Blundell, C. F. Stringfellow, J. F. Edwards, F. Hatch and C. Hodgson, 2nd Lieuts. T. R. Cox, R. Raynes, E. J. W. Cray and C. Hyden, were all wounded. Losses in the ranks amounted to 277.

Besides the officers already mentioned, the Fifteenth had Major R. B. Johnson; Capts. L. A. de V. Carey, F. Wardell and C. T. Fitzgerald; Lieut. E. M. Carter; 2nd Lieuts. J. W. L. Birkbeck, E. Partridge, F. A. Boulton, C. F. Readman and O. de Putron wounded. There were no less than 450 casualties in the ranks.

Capt. Fitzgerald kept his Lewis guns in action after being wounded. C.-S.-M. Herbert and Sergt. Bushell, also of the Fifteenth, did good and brave work, the former rescuing ten wounded men. The stretcher-bearers of both Durham battalions worked with great gallantry and perseverance, while Capt. Bourchier, the chaplain of the Fourteenth, displayed great courage in tending the wounded under fire.

The 21st Division soon moved north again. Entraining at Noeux-les-Mines for Berguette, on September 29th, the Fourteenth reached billets at Flêtre on October 2nd. The Fifteenth had arrived at Berguette even earlier, and were located at Caestre by October 1st. They reached Armentières nine days later.

TRENCH WARFARE

OCTOBER, 1915—JUNE, 1916

The Tenth relieved the 6th Dorset Regt. in the line at St. Eloi on October 4th. Trenches were bad and the wire poor, but there was little German activity. Nine days later the battalion withdrew to rest at St. Jan-ter-Biezen, behind Poperinghe. Soon after arrival here Lance-Corpl. George Alderson was fatally wounded by the accidental explosion of a bomb. He had gallantly taken a great risk in order to preserve his comrades from injury, and was awarded the Albert Medal of the First Class.

The battalion were now employed building huts of wattle covered with mud, which would not harden in the wet weather—neither could the mud floors be dried. A detachment was sent to the King's inspection at Abeele on October 27th. Drafts received brought the strength of the Tenth up to over 1,000, though casualties, since coming to France, already amounted to 25 officers and 586 men.

On November 11th the Durhams moved up to the line which ran north-westward from Wieltje, and were in and out of these trenches—really a chain of isolated bits of breastwork—until the end of the month. The weather was wet, then cold and frosty, and the prevention of trench-foot was an important problem. Capts. Jerwood and Rogers and Lieut. Celham were all wounded by shell fire. December was a wet month. On the 12th the battalion took over the line to the right, which included the village of Wieltje, and had to submit to a heavy German bombardment two days later, which killed 2nd Lieut. A. Fines, wounded 2nd Lieut. Canney, and caused 24 casualties in the ranks. Before Christmas the Durhams went back to St. Jan-ter-Biezen, with the prospect of leaving France for another theatre of war.

The Durham Forces in the Field

All ranks were disappointed when it became known that they were to stay in the salient.

The sector occupied on December 29th formed the left of the divisional front, astride the Langemarck road. Here the line was held by bombing and Lewis gun posts, which were isolated during daylight. The tour was quiet, but when the Durhams came up again, after staying in filthy huts on foul ground at Vlamertinghe, a bombardment of the front line killed 4 men and wounded 10. The recognition of the soldierly qualities of popular R.-S.-M. A. Noble, D.C.M., gratified everyone about this time. He was awarded a bar to his medal.

Before January had passed, the Tenth had to endure further intense shelling, which killed and wounded 20 men. Other losses included 2nd Lieut. C. F. Batty (killed), and Lieut. Crause (wounded), and on January 31st, 2nd Lieut. W. F. Butland died of his wounds.

A heavy German bombardment started on the morning of February 2nd, and lasted for over two hours. The enemy infantry came forward with great determination, but the leading groups were dispersed by rifle and Lewis gun fire. Larger bodies in rear were broken up by the British artillery, and the snipers of the Tenth shot many Germans crawling in the long grass of "No Man's Land." Several honours were won on this day. Lieut. G. L. Wood was completely buried by a shell and on being dug out coolly directed the repulse of the Germans who had reached his wire. He was awarded the Military Cross. Corpl. W. Blenkinsopp crossed open ground several times under the German bombardment to visit an isolated bombing post, and Corpl. R. W. Charley, of Kirkby Stephen, went out under fire to rescue a wounded man. Each of these N.C.O.'s received the Distinguished Conduct Medal.

On February 12th, when the battalion held the front astride the Pilckem road, the German trench mortars concentrated upon them. No infantry attack developed, but for four hours and a half the bombardment continued. Losses amounted to 22, including R.-S.-M. Noble, who was killed. "He was beloved by all," wrote Colonel Morant. Corpl. J. Edwards and Pte.

Trench Warfare, Oct., 1915—June, 1916

W. Lalley won the Distinguished Conduct Medal for carrying messages under heavy fire on this day.

The Tenth were relieved early next morning, and withdrew to Poperinghe, reaching Houtkerque later in the day. Their long tour in the Ypres salient was over, and after inspection by the Commander-in-Chief they entrained at Cassel. The 14th Division were about to relieve the French at Arras and the Tenth occupied support positions at Agny and Achicourt by the beginning of March. The weather was wintry and hindered work on the trenches, which were in urgent need of repair, but the deep dug-outs in this chalky soil were a great comfort after the crazy shelters in the salient. Colonel H. F. S. Morant rejoined the battalion on March 9th.

The enemy was very quiet at first, but his shell fire increased later, without, however, doing much damage. Out of the line the Tenth worked hard improving the trenches, and supplied parties to bury cable. Fine weather came with April. On the 3rd the mistake of a sentry, who mistook a wiring party for Germans, cost 2nd Lieut. F. C. F. Dorell his life. Trench mortars were now active on both sides and the Tenth soon appreciated the value of the Stokes gun. Towards the end of the month another case of mistaken identity resulted in 2nd Lieut. Dawes being wounded.

The soil was very favourable for mining operations and the Tenth supplied many parties to assist the New Zealand tunnellers. At the end of May the award of the Distinguished Conduct Medal to C.-S.-M. J. Slater was announced. As signal sergeant he had done consistent good work under heavy fire in the salient.

In June the grass was so tall in " No Man's Land " that sentries could dispense with periscopes and observe from the fire step during daylight. Artillery fire—both British and German—was heavier now, and continued to be so until the 14th Division were relieved by the 55th on June 20th. The Tenth withdrew to Arras and continued to help the tunnellers.

On October 1st Lieut.-Col. C. M. Davidson relinquished command of the Eleventh and was succeeded

The Durham Forces in the Field

by Major A. E. Collins, D.S.O. The battalion took their turn in the trenches near Laventie, and continued their pioneer work when out of the line until the Guards relieved the 20th Division about mid-November. Casualties were light during this period, but the weather was wet and the trenches, into which all the ditches seemed to drain, were in an awful state.

The 20th Division did not go out of the line, but relieved the 8th further north. Drainage and road-making were now the principal occupations of the Pioneers, though there were generally some men working with the tunnellers. In the early part of December the river Layes was cleaned, widened and deepened as far forward as the front line; the duckboards in the trenches were raised above the mud and the collapsing dug-outs were restored. In the New Year pumping operations became of great importance, for the weather did not improve. Soon the 8th Division relieved the 20th, and the Durhams moved back on January 12th. Several weeks of training and recreation followed, first in the area west of Morbecque and then at Zermezeele, north of Cassel. The division subsequently relieved the 14th in the Ypres salient, and the Eleventh arrived at Elverdinghe Château on February 12th.

The alternate frost and rain provided plenty of work on trenches and communications during the ensuing weeks. The enemy mortars caused much damage and destruction, and his guns harassed the working parties by day and night. About April 10th the 6th Division took over this sector, and a week later the Eleventh were concentrated at Oudezeele, in the area north of Cassel, for training.

On May 20th—when the division came in on the right of the 6th Division—the Eleventh arrived at Brandhock, about midway between Poperinghe and Vlamertinghe. From here 300 men were sent up every night to work in the forward area—reclaiming and repairing trenches, heightening parapets and putting out wire. C Company were soon moved up to cellars at Ypres in order to be nearer their work. Nothing could be done on June 26th owing to the heavy German shelling of Wieltje, Potijze and St. Jean in reply to a suc-

Trench Warfare, Oct., 1915—June, 1916

cessful raid of the 59th Brigade. Next day 2nd Lieut. E. R. B. Clough was killed by shrapnel on the St. Jean road.

The Twelfth left Estaires on October 2nd and took over trenches beyond Bois Grenier in the evening. This was a quiet part of the line and incidents were few, but later in the month Lieut. N. A. B. Neligan did not return from patrol. At this period life in support and reserve was, perhaps, more uncomfortable owing to the large working parties which were required. The weather was very wet, and the trenches suffered accordingly. On December 4th C company were shelled in their billets at Rue Marle—near Armentières railway station—and lost six killed and seven wounded. Lieut. F. C. A. Golden was killed on December 26th while handing over a machine-gun post on relief by the Thirteenth, and a month later battalion headquarters were shelled and 5 men were killed in the signal dug-out. During February some of the Tynesiders of the 34th Division came in with the Twelfth for their first experience of the trenches. There was one day of severe bombardment which caused 20 casualties and Capt. J. P. Day was wounded on February 19th. Snow fell before the Twelfth departed from this front on the 25th. Three days were spent at Norbecque before moving to the mining town of Auchel and on March 2nd the battalion reached billets at Estrée Cauchie, on the old Roman road to Arras. The 23rd Division eventually took over the line in the colliery towns nearer Lens and the Twelfth moved to support positions in the Cité Calonne on March 17th. Lieut. N. L. Smith was wounded on this day. Four days later the battalion relieved the Thirteenth in the front line, which, on the right, ran through the houses. The reserve billets were back over the hill in Bully Grenay. The Twelfth occupied the front line on April 10th, when a hoax attack was carried out. The divisional artillery had cut the enemy wire and now, reinforced by the Corps' heavies, they opened on the Germans in Cité des Champs Grenelles, Cité de Rollencourt and Liévin. Smoke was liberated from the front trench and indications given of an impending

The Durham Forces in the Field

infantry attack. The barrage then lifted from the enemy front line and returned when it was calculated that he had fully manned his trenches. Casualties in the Twelfth were very small, and the losses inflicted on the Germans were not known; but the infantry of the 68th Brigade were used to sitting in trenches in front of severely rationed guns, so they were much heartened by the volume of the British bombardment.

The last tour of the Twelfth in the trenches of this sector ended on April 18th and working parties were then supplied while in reserve. On one of these Lieut. Summerhayes was wounded. The manœuvre area was reached on May 5th and the battalion occupied billets at Matringhem, on the river Lys, during the period of training which followed. The next move forward was on May 17th, and at dusk of the following day the battalion occupied support positions on the slopes of Notre Dame de Lorette. On May 25th the Twelfth took over trenches in the Souchez sector, on the left of the brigade line. Next day Colonel Elwes was invalided home and Capt. Arnott, 2nd East Lancashire Regt., soon assumed temporary command. There was much rifle-grenade and trench-mortar activity until May 30th, when the battalion withdrew to reserve in Bois de Noulette. Major W. W. Macgregor, Gordon Highlanders, the new commanding officer, joined them here. On June 3rd the Twelfth turned out in response to the S.O.S. signal sent up by the Thirteenth, who were heavily shelled in their trenches, and next evening the Thirteenth were relieved in the badly damaged line. The trench communicating with the "island" posts on the left was completely obliterated, but the enemy's wrath—he had been raided by the Thirteenth on June 2nd—was not yet appeased. Until the relief of the Twelfth, by the 10th Duke of Wellington's, on June 9th the steady destruction of their trenches continued and the experience was shared by a company of the Royal Naval Division sent in for their first experience of trench warfare in France.

The Twelfth moved to huts at Bouvigny Wood and then to Reclinghem, in the training area. The whole brigade now practised trench-to-trench attacks, and there was one big divisional day. On June 21st the

Trench Warfare, Oct., 1915—June, 1916

ribbon of the Military Cross was presented to Lieut. J. B. Jaques, and that of the Distinguished Conduct Medal to Pte. F. James. Three days later the Twelfth marched to Aire and entrained for the Somme.

The Thirteenth were detained at Estaires until October 4th, and then returned to their old bivouacs near Erquinghem. On October 7th the Twelfth were relieved in the trenches and a quiet tour followed, though there were some casualties from sniping fire. Lance-Corpl. W. Claire and Pte. R. Hickson won the Military Medal during the next tour of the Thirteenth in the line. In a successful sniping expedition they shot two Germans and brought in valuable information. On October 19th 2nd Lieut. G. H. Bailey was mortally wounded, and at night 2nd Lieut. C. T. W. Sauerbeck led a bombing attack upon an enemy working party, but was accidentally wounded on the return journey. Towards the end of the month the weather was so wet that some working parties had to be cancelled and the trenches were in a deplorable condition when the Thirteenth went into the line again early in November.

About 9 p.m. on November 4th Lieut. P. A. Brown left the trench to visit a party working on the wire in front. He was accompanied by his observer, Pte. Kenny. The fog was very thick, and they over-ran the wire and were lost. After going a considerable distance they sat down to listen for some sound to guide them and as they rose again a rifle shot rang out close by. Lieut. Brown fell, shot through both thighs, and Kenny took his officer upon his back to carry him away. Heavy rifle fire was now opened by the Germans and Kenny had to crawl through the mud with his burden. Sometimes he had to lie still until the fire slackened. Lieut. Brown ordered him to go on alone, but he refused to do so, and for upwards of an hour he struggled along until at last he found a ditch he recognised. Here he made Lieut. Brown as comfortable as possible and started for the British line to get help. It was after 11 p.m. when he came upon Capt. G. White and two men in a listening post. Stretcher-bearers were summoned and, although Kenny was very exhausted, he endured until he had guided the party to the wounded man. The return journey was made under rifle fire at close range, and some bombs were thrown, but Capt. White got everyone back without further casualty. Lieut. Brown —a very good and popular officer—died before he could be carried to the dressing-station, but the self-sacrifice and endurance of Thomas Kenny won him the Victoria Cross.

When the battalion was holding the left of the line, near the Lille road, on December 5th, Lance-Corpl. W. Hornby and Pte. J. C. Worton carried out a daring and valuable reconnaissance at the enemy salient known as German House, and each was awarded the Distinguished Conduct Medal. At Christmas time the trenches were about at their worst and life in and out of the line was very uncomfortable. On the 27th and 28th, when some of the 15th Royal Scots (34th Division) were in the trenches with the Thirteenth for instruction, a German bombardment did much damage, though few casualties were caused. At 9.15 P.M. on January 29th Capt. J. A. L. Downey and his company attempted a raid, but the enemy was on the alert, and after waiting very patiently and making many efforts to get forward unseen the party had to withdraw when the moon rose.

Before leaving this sector the Thirteenth had to endure one bad bombardment. This was on February 13th, when 5 men were killed and 14 wounded. The battalion moved to Sailly in wintry weather on February 25th, reaching Morbecque next day and Auchel just before midnight on the 29th. Rain, hail and snow were experienced here, but the weather improved when the Thirteenth moved to Hermin, where nine days were spent. On March 17th the battalion moved to trenches in Calonne. The enemy soon became aggressive and some men were wounded on the 19th, bringing the casualties since arrival in France up to 132. Probably few battalions had spent over seven months on the Western Front without suffering more heavily. On the afternoon of March 26th rifle grenadiers and mortars joined with the artillery in a bombardment of the enemy line. As time went on the German gunners became more active, and much damage was caused to the

PRIVATE (afterwards Coy.-Sergt.-Major) T. KENNY, V.C.
13th Durham Light Infantry

Trench Warfare, Oct., 1915—June, 1916

trenches. A company, whose right adjoined Pit Prop Corner where a slag heap was always smouldering, received most attention, but on April 6th all the occupants of a C company dug-out were killed, the body of one man being blown over into the wire. When the hoax attack was delivered on the 10th the Thirteenth were occupying the cellars of Calonne, in support. There were two more days of heavy shelling, and little retaliation from the British guns, before the Thirteenth moved back. The brigade had worked hard in the Calonne sector on the support line of trenches and on fortified houses. Communication trenches forward over the hill from Bully Grenay had been deepened and much improved.

The Thirteenth arrived at Pernes on April 26th and on May 5th they moved to Redinghem to continue training, Capt. C. White now being in command of the battalion. A fortnight later came a return to the line, the Thirteenth taking over part of the Souchez sector on May 20th. Ceaseless war was waged in these trenches with rifle grenades and trench mortars, the artillery of both sides joining in as occasion seemed to demand. Lieut. E. A. P. Wood was wounded on June 1st. The night of the 2nd was light but moonless when Lieuts. J. F. Clarke and N. A. Target, with 23 men, raided the German trenches. At 1 A.M. the artillery opened an intense bombardment of the enemy front line, and a minute later lifted to barrage his support positions. The raiders were across " No Man's Land " and in the trenches before the alarm was given, and the officers headed a party which worked 40 yards along to the left, killing 8 Germans and bombing two deep dug-outs. Others worked to the right for the same distance, erected a barricade and bombed the trench beyond it, after killing several of the enemy and bombing four dug-outs. All withdrew without difficulty after ten minutes had been spent in the German trenches and the only casualties were three men slightly wounded by British shrapnel. The enemy next day retaliated by half an hour's bombardment of battalion headquarters, and in the evening came a terrific shelling of the whole line. All communications were cut and an attack was

The Durham Forces in the Field

suspected, so the S.O.S. signal was made; but it was cancelled when no German advance was observed. June 4th was also a day of hate and the Twelfth took over very damaged trenches in the evening.

About this time the awards were announced of the Military Cross to Capt. C. White and of the Military Medal to Lance-Corpl. Robinson.

The Thirteenth now did a tour in support on the Notre Dame de Lorette spur and then moved back to Delette, which was reached on the 15th. Before this date Major R. V. Turner, of the 2nd Durham Light Infantry, had joined and assumed command.

On June 21st the divisional commander presented the ribbon of the Military Cross to Lieuts. D. F. Clarke and N. A. Target and that of the Military Medal to Sergts. R. Boagey and R. B. White; Lance-Corpls. W. A. Bowran and E. Hetherington; Ptes. C. Barker, J. Dodds, W. Hart, R. Hedley, J. Keenan, T. Middleton, J. Moyle, W. Orr, A. Stephenson and S. Williams. These decorations had been won in the Souchez raid. On June 24th the Thirteenth marched to Aire and entrained for the Somme area.

The Fourteenth came to Flanders by train at the end of September and reached Armentières on October 10th. They entered the trenches for instruction with troops of the 50th (Northumbrian) Division and took over a portion of the Ploegsteert line on October 19th.

The 21st Division soon relieved the 50th in the sector east of Armentières, between the Lille road and the river Lys, and the Fourteenth went into the front line here on November 12th. But before the end of the month the battalion left the division and were replaced by the 1st East Yorkshire Regt. The Fourteenth arrived at Herzeele on November 28th, taking over the billets vacated by the Yorkshire men whom they succeeded in the 18th Brigade of the 6th Division. The other units in this brigade were the 1st West Yorkshires, the 11th Essex, and the 2nd Durham Light Infantry. The latter extended a warm welcome to their young brothers of the Service Battalion and a temporary exchange of 4 officers, 8 sergeants and 32 men was afterwards

Trench Warfare, Oct, 1915—June, 1916

arranged. This was the beginning of a close friendship which endured until the Fourteenth were disbanded.

The right of the 6th Division sector in the Ypres salient was on the Zonnebeke road, and part of the Fourteenth moved up to occupy the Potijze defences on December 11th. Five days later the battalion went into the front line on the left and on Sunday, December 19th, they bore the brunt of an enemy gas attack. At about 5.30 a.m. a greenish-yellow cloud swept forward, south of the village of Wieltje, over the trenches of the Fourteenth. No infantry attack developed, but a heavy bombardment of gas and high explosive shell continued all day. A company had to wear their gas helmets for three hours and D company, being on lower ground, for one hour longer. The German fire was almost as fierce during the night and next day, but in the evening the Fourteenth were relieved and withdrew to Poperinghe. Casualties in the ranks amounted to 149, but would have been lighter if there had not been so many defective gas helmets. 2nd Lieut. L. N. Hickson and Lieut. N. Beatty were gassed and Lieuts. O. W. C. Mann and R. L. Eyre were wounded. Capt. G. A. Richardson, who refused to leave his company after being wounded, was awarded the Military Cross.

The Fourteenth had another and quieter tour in the line before the end of the year, by which time losses to officers were increased by 2nd Lieut. F. A. Cormack (gassed), and Lieuts. J. F. Iveson and A. D. Rawlins (wounded). When in support the battalion lived in or near Ypres and worked on the trenches in the common endeavour to minimise the ravages of the rain and frost. Training and recreation were possible when in reserve at Poperinghe.

On January 27th two Germans surrendered to the Fourteenth, who were then in the line, and a wounded German was brought in by a party under Lieut. Harris and Corpl. Robson. The battalion had 40 casualties during this month, including 2nd Lieut. G. Auten (wounded). The 14th Division, further north, were heavily shelled on February 12th and the working parties of the Fourteenth were wisely cancelled, but on the morrow 6 men were killed and 13 wounded by

The Durham Forces in the Field

a single shell. 2nd Lieut. E. W. Stewart was wounded on February 19th.

In the middle of March the Guards relieved the 6th Division and the Fourteenth went back to Proven. After ten days of training and inspections the battalion left for Calais and went into tents at Beaumaris. Training continued, and the French rifle-range on the seashore was used, but this interlude would have been more appreciated if the weather had been kinder. On April 5th the Fourteenth began a three days' march back to the salient.

Nearly a week was spent at Kickenput, near Wormhoudt, and the battalion took over the line between the Pilckem road and the Yser Canal on April 18th. The trenches were bad and the German snipers active. During the next tour the enemy guns and mortars caused a lot of damage, and 2nd Lieut. R. J. C. Leader was killed. 2nd Lieuts. J. W. Gamble and W. Robertson were wounded on May 21st and the former died later.

On June 2nd the dispositions of the Fourteenth were changed. For weeks past the front line had consisted of short lengths of breast-work, and now Capt. J. B. Rosher was placed in command of the whole front and support positions held by the battalion. The awards of the Distinguished Service Order to Lieut.-Col. G. F. Menzies and of the Military Cross to Lieut. C. A. V. Newsome were announced about this time. Sergt. (afterwards C.-S.-M.) Pearson, well known at Seaham Harbour, was given the Distinguished Conduct Medal for his good work while in charge of the snipers and for his gallantry in digging out men who had been buried by shell fire.

The Guards came in again on June 16th and the 6th Division withdrew. Four days later the Fourteenth arrived at Bollezeele and remained there training for the attack until the end of June. The last six months in the salient had cost them 260 casualties in the ranks.

The Fifteenth reached Armentières early in October. On the 11th they were distributed among the units of the 50th (Northumbrian) Division for instruction in

Trench Warfare, Oct., 1915—June, 1916

trench warfare, B, C and D companies working with the 9th, 6th and 8th Durham Light Infantry. A portion of the line further north was taken over on October 19th, and two days later 2nd Lieut. A. A. Gray carried out a daring reconnaissance and returned with a valuable report. 2nd Lieut. E. J. Gray was killed during this tour.

On November 10th the battalion relieved the 8th and 9th Durham Light Infantry and thenceforward were in and out of the line between the Lille road and the river Lys. Capt. A. D. L. Campbell was killed on November 18th, but casualties were not heavy: the Saxons opposite were as busy as the Durhams in the endeavour to make the wet trenches habitable, and had no time or inclination to be aggressive. The left of the line, near the swollen river, was in the worst state. 2nd Lieut. R. M. Nicholson was wounded on patrol on the night of December 10th, and Sergt. J. Broderick and Pte. Middleton displayed great gallantry in bringing him back. The sergeant was awarded the Distinguished Conduct Medal.

Armentières was shelled frequently, but there was a general bombardment by the enemy on December 30th which killed Capt. G. F. Fitzgerald and 2nd Lieuts. J. W. Arkless and C. E. A. Pullen.

January passed without incident until the 10th K.O.Y.L.I. raided the German line on the night of the 23rd. Next morning the Germans retaliated with a fierce bombardment which fell to a great extent upon the trenches of the Fifteenth. Lieut. N. F. Smith and 10 men were killed, and Capt. G. Taylor-Loban and 40 others wounded. This shell fire continued till the afternoon of the 25th, causing still more casualties. There were three awards of the Distinguished Conduct Medal for gallantry during this ordeal. Pte. W. Stout repaired a telephone wire, remaining out over two hours under heavy fire to do so. Ptes. J. W. Coates and E. Hope—the latter a Pelton Fell boy only 17 years of age—kept their telephone wires repaired under violent shell fire, and when their signal dug-out was blown up they took turns in delivering messages over the open.

In February, when the battalion were holding that part of the line which contained the crater known as

The Durham Forces in the Field

the Mushroom, snow fell on three successive days and patrols went out dressed in white.

The 21st Division left this part of the front in March, and the Durhams reached Outtersteene, in the "rest" area, on the 19th. On March 30th they left by train for the south. From Longueau station, outside Amiens, they marched to la Neuville, a little village on the Ancre river opposite Corbie. Training occupied the days spent here and when the 64th Brigade took over the line the Fifteenth were in reserve at Méaulte. The right of the new divisional front was in the valley of a stream running from Fricourt to the river Ancre; the centre and left traversed a spur north-west of Fricourt. "No Man's Land" was for the most part 200 or 250 yards wide, but on the right, at the Tambour salient, the Germans were less than 100 yards away.

About the middle of April the 64th Brigade returned to la Neuville, where the Fifteenth were employed on gun positions and tracks for the Corps' heavies in preparation for the offensive. On the 22nd they moved to Méaulte to work on the trenches and went into the front line opposite Fricourt on May 2nd. Corpl. T. Lavery, of Stanley, found his wiring party was repeatedly annoyed by German snipers and after three nights of this he went forward alone and silenced the enemy with bombs. Half an hour later he repeated this performance, with the assistance of another corporal, and then the work on the wire was completed without further trouble. Corpl. Lavery was awarded the Distinguished Conduct Medal.

After ten days in the trenches the battalion withdrew to la Neuville and then to Bois de Tailles. In these woods near Bray a pleasant time was spent, and then on June 1st the Durhams moved up to support positions, with two companies in strong points and two in Bécordel.

Five days later came another tour in the line and June 13th found the Fifteenth at Huire, on the river Ancre.

The Eighteenth were the only Service Battalion of the Durham Light Infantry to see service in the East.

Trench Warfare, Oct., 1915—June, 1916

They left Fovant Camp for Liverpool on December 5th, and embarked next day upon the S.S. *Empress of Britain*. She was a crowded ship, as the whole of the 93rd Brigade were on board besides the 12th K.O.Y.L.I. divisional pioneers. The voyage began on December 7th, with an escort of two destroyers. Attack by submarines had to be expected, so the vessel steered an erratic course, and heavy weather was experienced in the Bay of Biscay. Gibraltar was passed after the sixth day out. The men were in crowded quarters and were none too well fed, but the passage was uneventful until the night of December 13th, when a shock was felt throughout the vessel and the engines stopped. The troops, thinking of torpedoes and submarines, "stood to" in their quarters with perfect calm and discipline. The ship had collided with the French S.S. *Djurdjura*, from Salonica, cutting her almost in halves and killing two of her firemen. Throwing out flares and using her searchlights the *Empress of Britain* stood by till all had been rescued from the sinking vessel.

Malta was reached on December 14th and the transport berthed in Valetta harbour before nightfall. Damaged bow plates caused a stay of two days for repairs, but no shore leave was allowed. The voyage was resumed in the evening of the 17th and about noon next day an enemy submarine was sighted. The 6-inch gun mounted aft fired three rounds as soon as it could be brought to bear, but the transport escaped by hard steaming and skilful seamanship. Two torpedoes were discharged at her and she passed between them.

In the evening the mountains of Crete were sighted, and the impression grew that the division were bound for Salonica. Early next morning another submarine fired a torpedo at the transport, but she reached Alexandria safely at night. No one was allowed to land and the vessel left on the afternoon of the 20th, arriving at Port Said next morning. The S.S. *Shropshire*, which had brought the transport from Devonport, was already here and disembarkation began on December 22nd. It was a slow process, but the Eighteenth eventually found themselves in tents south of the town, where a few days were devoted to drill.

The Durham Forces in the Field

Bathing, in a very warm sea, became popular, but the Christmas dinner was hardly a success, for none of the seasonable supplies arrived and the troops had to be content with hard rations.

On December 28th the battalion entrained in open trucks for El Kantara. This village lies chiefly on the eastern bank of the Suez Canal and was defended by field works. There was much work to be done at El Kantara in reconstructing and improving the defences and unloading material from barges. Light railways were to be pushed out to the forward posts in the desert east of the canal, and on January 3rd Capt. Hutchence took D company to Abu Raidhar and established a post there in order to cover the construction of a line from Ballah.

The canal defences were divided into sections and in January the El Kantara section—from that village to the Mediterranean—was held by the 31st Division on the right and the 13th Division on the left. The policy of pushing the lines defending the canal further eastwards into the desert was now being carried out. The front line was sited about 11,000 yards from the canal, with the intermediate line 6,500 yards in rear of the former, while the old canal defences formed a third line. It was estimated that so long as the intermediate line was held there could be no serious shelling of ships passing through the canal. No continuous trenches were dug, but fortified localities were in course of construction. The protection of water supplies was, of course, very important.

Before the end of January the Eighteenth commenced on this work in earnest, two companies being at Hill 108, in the forward line on the right of this section of the front, while the other two remained at El Kantara. Digging trenches in the loose drifting sand proved hard and tiring work, and sandstorms occasionally filled up excavations in a most annoying manner. The army shovel was not a very suitable tool, and hurdles and grass matting had to be securely wired to pegs by way of revetment. Water and material were carried forward by camels and the escorts had trying times when, as often happened, the loads broke away.

French Warfare, Oct., 1915—June, 1916

Still, much was accomplished before February 18th when two companies and battalion headquarters moved to Spit Post, three miles north of El Kantara. The Spit was a narrowing tract of land which ran northeastward into the inundated country near the sea. A road and railway were started from the canal to the outpost positions five miles forward, and a pipe line for water was also commenced. Bathing parades were always a feature of the routine and when the Eighteenth left Egypt non-swimmers were few in the battalion. A warning order for a move to Mesopotamia was cancelled about this time and towards the end of February the Eighteenth withdrew to El Kantara—now a much larger and busier base. The old camp at Port Said was reached on March 2nd, with the battalion under orders for France.

The Eighteenth had spent just over two months in Egypt during the best season of the year. Sea-bathing, heavy marching, heavy digging and rather Spartan fare had made officers and men very fit and the time had been interesting and enjoyable.

The Eighteenth embarked upon the S.S. *Ivernia* on March 5th, and left next day for Marseilles. The weather was bad for most of the way, but there was no crowding on board and the food was better than on the previous voyage. Marseilles was reached safely on March 11th, and no time was lost at the French port. D company started at once and the rest of the battalion were in the train the same night. The journey through France was slow, but the French authorities thoughtfully supplied rum and coffee to the troops at regular intervals. At Pont Rémy the battalion detrained, on March 14th, and marched to Citerne, a small village about twelve miles from Abbeville. Snow fell and the bitter weather was very trying after the Egyptian sun. Most of the training done here was route marching, as the desert sand had left the feet of the men in no condition for the pavé roads of France. On March 25th the Eighteenth began to move towards the line.

The stages were long and heavy rain was only varied by showers of sleet, but the spirit of officers

The Durham Forces in the Field

and men was splendid. Eventually Beaussart was reached, by way of Flesselles and Beauquesne. In the evening of March 30th the battalion moved on through Mailly-Maillet and Auchonvillers in a snowstorm, and took over trenches north-west of Beaumont Hamel. Capt. W. G. Hutchence was wounded soon after the relief was complete. The trenches were waterlogged and the German trench mortars were active, the most satisfactory feature of this first tour being the success of the battalion snipers under Lieut. Hawdon. On April 3rd the 12th York and Lancasters relieved the Eighteenth, who withdrew to Beaussart and then to a hut camp near Bus-les-Artois for a fortnight's training in the cold and rain. The Eighteenth went into the trenches again on April 20th when the weather improved. There was an explosion in one of the British mine galleries during this tour and Pte. W. J. Warwick did gallant rescue work in spite of the smoke damp. After a few days in the support line the Eighteenth resumed training at Bertrancourt and Bus-les-Artois. During May they only did one tour in the trenches, and this was in a new sector just north of the Serre-Colincamps road where the British line was commanded by the enemy on the higher ground at Serre and his sniping and trench mortar fire was somewhat trying.

On June 4th the Eighteenth arrived at Colincamps, which was becoming a favourite target of the German gunners, and thenceforward the battalion were engaged in digging assembly trenches, making dug-outs and aid posts, burying cable and in other preparations for the great offensive.

On the night of January 31st, 1916, the Nineteenth left Perham Down for Southampton and crossed to le Havre. They reached St. Omer on February 4th and marched to billets at Campagne and five days later, when on the march for Thiennes, were inspected by the Commander-in-Chief and Prince Arthur of Connaught. Some officers and N.C.O.'s had already left to pay an instructional visit to the trenches of the Guards. Lord Kitchener inspected the whole of the 106th Brigade at Boeseghem on February 11th in cold

Trench Warfare, Oct., 1915—June, 1916

and wet weather and a week later the Nineteenth arrived at Merville for ten days' training. On the last day of the month the Durham "Bantams" went into the trenches for instruction with the 57th Brigade of the 19th Division, north of Neuve Chapelle. On March 8th they withdrew to billets at Pont de Hem and on the 11th, though still attached to the 19th Division, they went into the line as a battalion. On the 14th the enemy blew up a mine, on the right of the Nineteenth, and shelled their trenches with gas and high explosive. Casualties only amounted to 17, but the little men found that repairs to the parapet and the clearing of the all-important drains taxed their strength to the utmost. Next day they were relieved and they occupied support positions on the 27th, when the 35th Division replaced the 8th in the line south of Bois Grenier.

Early in April the Australians took over this sector and the Nineteenth held the line further to the south. It was a quiet month, but the trenches were still very wet and provided ceaseless occupation for the "Bantams." The battalion spent most of May at Richebourg-St. Vaast and in the line in front of that village, but had a week's rest before the end of the month.

On June 1st they took over trenches near Festhubert, where the grass was two feet high in "No Man's Land" and there was much dead ground in front. Here a company of the 2/4th Gloucesters came in for instruction. The division moved away soon afterwards and the Nineteenth reached Gonnehem, by easy stages, on June 16th. A journey southwards commenced on July 2nd, by train from Chocques, and the Durhams marched from Frevent, by le Souich, Bois de Warnimout and Bresle, to Bois des Tailles, west of Bray-sur-Somme. On July 15th they reached the trenches behind Montauban.

In high spirits the Twentieth left Aldershot on May 4th and crossed to le Havre at night. Three days later they reached Strazeele, about four miles east of Hazebrouck, where they put in nearly three weeks' training, which included visits to the trenches. On May 29th

The Durham Forces in the Field

the battalion relieved the South Africans near le Bizet, on the Belgian border just north of Armentières. They were the first unit of the 41st Division to appear in the line and earned the compliments of the divisional general during this tour. Casualties were few, but on the night of May 30th one man was killed and one wounded while working on the wire. Lieut. J. Thompson-Hopper made two journeys and brought them both in under heavy fire, thereby winning the Military Cross. Lieut. J. F. Barker was wounded on June 2nd.

The following weeks contained little of incident, the Wearsiders providing large working parties when out of the line. Capt. N. Wayman was wounded on June 29th and on the following night 2nd Lieut. E. W. Britton and 12 men attempted a small raid, with the assistance of gas and smoke. But the Germans had manned their trenches and put down a barrage while the party was in "No Man's Land," so there was no prospect of success. Lieut. J. Thompson-Hopper, M.C., and 2 men were killed, and 4 others were wounded, while Capt. A. Pumphrey was also hit but remained at duty.

The Twenty-Second left Catterick Bridge on June 16th for Southampton, and arrived at le Havre in the early hours of next morning. The train took the battalion straight to the Somme area, Frechencourt, about two miles north of the Albert-Amiens road, being the site of their first camp. On June 20th they moved northwards to Bavelincourt. The Pioneers were busy unloading ammunition and repairing roads until they marched forward to Millencourt, on the last day of the month.

THE BATTLE OF THE SOMME, 1916

CHAPTER I

WITH the battle of the Somme, which opened, so far as the infantry were concerned, on July 1st, 1916, came the supreme test of the Service Battalions of Durham. The Tenth had endured the horrors of Hooge, but had never been called upon to attack; to the Fourteenth and Fifteenth Loos was the tragic memory of a single day; the other battalions entered the great offensive with experience of nothing but trench warfare behind them.

Where the British line turned northward, at Fricourt, the 21st Division held the front. The Fifteenth were in reserve at Buire, upon the river Ancre, in the middle of June, and worked for a whole week carrying battle stores into the trenches. When the British bombardment opened, on June 24th the battalion had little to do but wait for the day. News from the front line was good. Prisoners described the horrors of the British gunfire, which kept rations from the Germans who held the line and made the relief of troops all but impossible. The Durham men held concerts while our field guns and trench-mortars systematically cut the enemy wire and smoke clouds threatened him with attack which did not come.

On the morning of June 28th packs were stored in the cinema hall at Buire in preparation for the move, in fighting order, to the assembly trenches. The attack was to be on the morrow, but the fair weather changed to rain which caused two days' delay. So the Fifteenth continued to wait, while the bombardment went on, varied by intervals of intense gunfire and the discharge of clouds of gas and smoke. The 21st Division were to advance from the front they held,

The Durham Forces in the Field

with the 64th Brigade upon the left and the 63rd upon the right. The two K.O.Y.L.I. battalions, leading the 64th, had the Fifteenth and 1st East Yorkshire Regt. in support. When the front line system of German trenches had been over-run, and the sunken road between Fricourt and Contalmaison reached, the support line was to pass through and take Crucifix Trench, Shelter Wood and the redoubt called the Quadrangle, 1,000 yards beyond.

On the evening of June 30th Lieut.-Col. A. E. Fitzgerald led his battalion up to the assembly position. Casualties were few upon the way and by 3 A.M. on July 1st the Fifteenth were ready to advance behind the 9th K.O.Y.L.I., who led upon the right. Day broke beautifully fine, and the German reply to our terrific gunfire was of no great strength. At twenty-five minutes past seven the heavy artillery lifted from the German front line, and the eager Yorkshiremen began to climb out of their trenches and advance into the smoke as the shrapnel barrage came down. The Fifteenth followed in their turn, with A and B companies in front. German machine guns hastily hoisted from deep dug-outs which were little damaged by our hurricane of high explosives opened on the Durhams, who covered the 200 yards of "No Man's Land" without a pause and entered the shattered German line. Men in field grey came out of the earth and surrendered, but others were fought with bomb or bayonet where they resisted in shell craters and bits of standing trench. So the Fifteenth won their way until they joined the Yorkshiremen in the sunken road and what had been Round Wood upon the left.

More prisoners were gathered in the dug-outs under the bank, but the men of the Fifteenth went on over the open and before half-past eight had taken Crucifix Trench, which ran out beyond. The shrapnel barrage moved ahead, but the ground in front was swept by machine-gun fire from the right, where the Germans still held Fricourt, and from the left, where they lay in Birch Tree Wood. Colonel Fitzgerald assumed command of the whole position. Besides his own battalion he had Yorkshiremen and Lincolns and some of the

The Battle of the Somme, 1916

34th Division, who were fighting on the left of the brigade. The sunken road and Crucifix Trench were put in a state of defence, and in the road at the entrance to one of the dug-outs—now all filled with British and German wounded—headquarters were established. The brigade had gone far ahead of the troops on the flanks, but with Lewis guns in Round Wood and Lozenge Wood all was in readiness for the German counter-attacks which were bound to follow.

At twenty minutes to two came orders to try for Shelter Wood, even if the advance were carried no

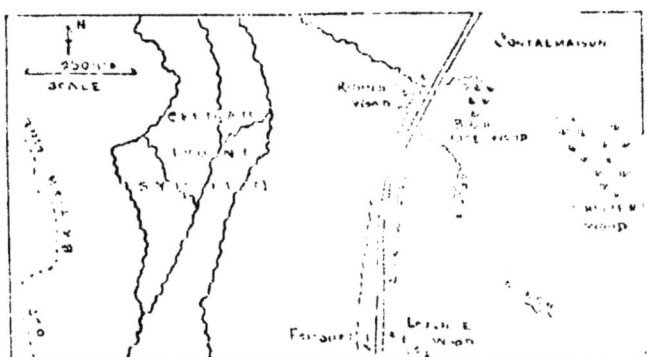

further; but the protective barrage had come down ten minutes before, so that the venture had to be made without artillery support. Fighting patrols went forward to gain what ground they could, and in this advance Capt. D. H. J. Ely, already wounded in the foot, was killed by a German sniper. Pte. J. Jolley spied the slayer as he prepared for a second shot, and British and German fired together. A bullet grazed Jolley's nose, but he got his man through the head. 2nd Lieuts. F. J. Cartman and A. S. Morley, who had each replaced a fallen company commander, thrust forward with their men until shell holes only 40 yards from the wood were reached. In these positions the Durhams sniped at such of the enemy as could be seen and, despite repeated attempts to dislodge them, held

The Durham Forces in the Field

on until relieved eight hours later. Both officers eventually received the Military Cross.

As the afternoon wore on the captured area was heavily shelled, while machine-gun bullets whipped along the sunken road. At five o'clock Germans were seen assembling near Birch Tree Wood, and a party of 300 advanced but were dispersed with heavy loss by Lewis gun fire. While watching this affair Colonel Fitzgerald received a machine-gun bullet in the thigh and was carried to his headquarters. Fourteen hours passed before he could be conveyed to the rear and, though he reached a London hospital, he died there on July 12th.

In the evening two companies the 10th Yorkshires arrived in Crucifix Trench to establish touch with the 63rd Brigade upon the right. It was much later when the Lincolns and Middlesex appeared to take over the positions held by the Fifteenth, a long and difficult operation which was not completed till dawn. At six o'clock on the morning of the 2nd parties were still arriving in the original British front line, where the Fifteenth assembled under Major R. B. Johnson.

Grievous losses had been suffered. Among the other officers killed on July 1st were Capts. J. East and L. F. Sanger-Davies, and 2nd Lieuts. R. O. Cormack, C. S. Haynes, J. M. Jones and M. L. Huddleston. Capt. F. P. Stamper was among the wounded and casualties in the ranks numbered 440. For their gallantry Sergts. E. Willison and T. Jones; Corpls. F. Connor and J. B. Lauder; and Ptes. J. Gray, J. Robinson, J. W. Robson, C. Tait and S. S. Dennis were awarded the Military Medal. The captures of the brigade—it is impossible to say what fell to each battalion—were 200 prisoners, one field-gun and numerous machine-guns.

On July 3rd the Fifteenth carried up water, ammunition and bombs to the 62nd Brigade, who had taken Shelter Wood.

Near the left of the British line, and opposite the German trenches, which were backed by the ruins of Serre upon higher ground, lay the 31st Division. D company of the Eighteenth formed part of the assault-

The Battle of the Somme, 1916

ing troops and had had a week of special training before the opening of the battle, the postponement of which was unfortunate for the division. It was afterwards learnt

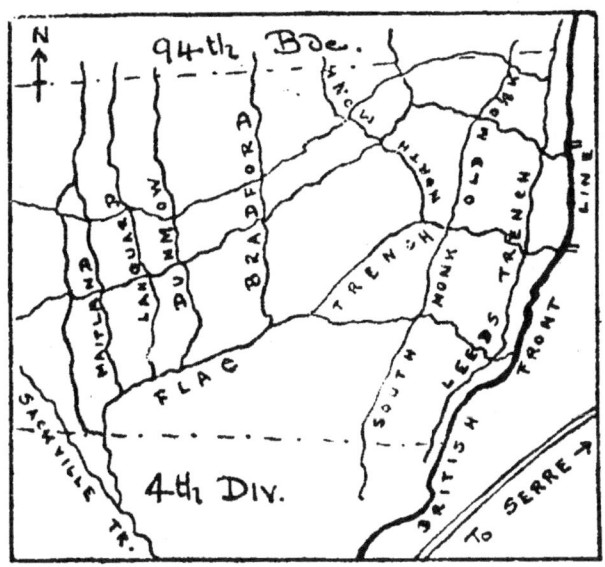

93rd Brigade.

Front Line & Leeds Trench – 15 W. Yorks.
S. Monk, Old Monk & Bradford – 16 W. Yorks
Dunmow & Languard – 18 W. Yorks.
South Monk – D Coy. 18 D.L.I.
Maitland – A, B & C Coys., 18 D.L.I
Saps thus =

from captured German documents that many batteries of heavy guns were brought up to this part of the enemy line during the last two days of June.

The Durham Forces in the Field

At 8.45 p.m. on June 30th) company moved up to their assembly position. The remainder of the Eighteenth left Courcelles later and, giving a wide berth to shell-stricken Colincamps, arrived before five o'clock next morning in Maitland Trench.

The position of the different battalions of the brigade may be seen upon the map. By zero hour the assaulting lines were to be formed on tapes laid outside the wire—D company, and then the 16th and 15th West Yorkshires from right to left. In support were the 18th Battalion of the same regiment, with the three other companies of the Eighteenth in reserve. The advance was to go south of Serre and then swing to the north-east, with the right flank facing south-eastward from Pendant Copse.

During the night casualties had been few, and when day broke the manifest superiority of our aircraft and artillery heartened everyone. At twenty minutes past seven was heard the explosion of the great mine by Beaumont-Hamel, and the British rate of fire increased. But now the German artillery opened in earnest upon our trenches, dealing death and chaos among the infantry already climbing out to form for the assault. In the ten minutes which followed the fate of the day was decided. Though every effort was made to advance, few men lived to pass beyond the hostile curtain of fire which barred the way across "No Man's Land." Some there were who struggled on and reached the German parapet, now alive with machine-gunners and riflemen; we know, too, that a gallant handful of) company reached Pendant Copse, a mile inside the German front.

At 9.30 a.m. the three companies of the Eighteenth were ordered forward to Monk Trench. Into the German shell fire, which seemed greater than our own, A and B companies moved up in succession. The other battalions had each lost their colonel and most of their officers, and the remnants of the Yorkshiremen were crowded, with the dead and wounded, in what remained of the front assembly trenches. As a counter-attack was now probable much depended upon the Eighteenth. Capt. Ince had reorganised B company, who lay west

The Battle of the Somme, 1916

of Monk Trench, A company were distributed by platoons in Flag, Maitland and Monk Trenches, with C company also in Maitland. Such was the situation at noon. B company were afterwards ordered to hold Sackville Trench in conjunction with the 4th Division, who had also suffered heavily and made little progress. Colonel Bowes reported that Monk, Languard and Dunmow Trenches could still be held and undertook to do so.

All the afternoon and evening the work of reorganisation went on under the German fire. Wounded and dead were removed, and some attempt was made to improve the shattered trenches. The front line no longer existed as a fighting trench and all the forward communication trenches were nearly obliterated. It was known, too, that although a few men had been seen to enter Serre, the 94th Brigade were in no better case than the 93rd, and all thoughts of a fresh attempt to advance were abandoned.

The Eighteenth, with the prospect of a counter-attack ever present, took over the front line before nightfall, C company holding with a series of posts what was probably the remains of Leeds Trench. Bombing parties were established in the saps; in Languard Trench were a company of the 11th East Yorkshire Regt., and West Yorkshires held Dunmow. A and B companies of the Eighteenth were in Maitland Trench with the few survivors of D company.

The firing died down towards evening and the night was quiet. At 1 A.M. B company relieved C company, who went back to Old Monk Trench.

In the afternoon of July 2nd the Eighteenth were ordered to hold the front with one company and four Lewis guns by day and to double this strength at night. The remainder of the battalion were to occupy South Monk Trench and these dispositions were soon completed. In the evening the British gunners maintained intense fire for half an hour to mask an advance further south, and this drew retaliation on C company, who lost 2 officers and 10 men. At eight o'clock the enemy drenched North Monk with tear shells, but the Eighteenth went on with their task of wiring the front

The Durham Forces in the Field

posts and collecting the wounded, of whom 40 were rescued by C company alone.

The dead, too, could not be allowed to lie in weather so damp and hot, and as many as possible were buried. Before midnight came a report that the enemy was carrying up gas cylinders in readiness for an attack.

In the early hours of the 3rd a visitation of high explosive and tear shells had to be endured in retaliation for our bombardment in support of troops further south. The Eighteenth, at full fighting strength when the battle began, now numbered, with reinforcements, only 14 officers and 357 men.

There was rain before dawn on the 4th, and at 4 A.M. red rockets went up and machine-gun fire opened from the British line to the right of the battalion, whose own front was immediately deluged with shell and machine-gun fire. The enemy barrage lifted to Monk and Maitland Trenches and then returned to Monk, but our artillery retaliated and the German fire weakened. During the morning Lieut. F. W. Tait, who had been lying in "No Man's Land" since July 1st, was rescued by a party under Sergt. Cross.

Now the ordeal of the Eighteenth was drawing to an end. News of the coming relief was received before noon, and at night a battalion of Worcesters (144th Brigade) arrived. By 5 A.M. on July 5th the Eighteenth were assembled at Louvencourt, back beyond Bus-en-Artois. Twelve officers were killed or wounded, and 58 per cent. of the rank and file, but this sacrifice was adjudged to have served its purpose. The Corps commander, Lieut.-Gen. Sir Aylmer Hunter-Weston, in a characteristic message to the troops said:

"We had the most difficult part of the line to attack. The Germans had fortified it with skill and immense labour for many months, they had kept their best troops there and had assembled north, east, and south-east of it a formidable collection of artillery and machine guns. By your splendid attack you held these enemy forces here in the north and so enabled our friends in the south, both British and French, to achieve the brilliant success they have. . . . You and our even more glorious comrades who have preceded us across the Great Divide have nobly done your

The Battle of the Somme, 1916

duty. . . . I salute each officer, N.C.O., and man of the 4th, 29th, 31st, and 48th Divisions as a comrade-in-arms, and I rejoice to have the privilege of commanding such a band of heroes as the VIII Corps have proved themselves to be."

Durham's youngest battalion, the Twenty-Second (Pioneers), were concluding their first fortnight of service overseas when the battle of the Somme began. On June 23rd all available officers had been sent up for their first experience of the trenches, visiting the line east of Albert. A week later the battalion arrived at Millencourt after a long march. A company remained here in reserve, but B, C and D companies moved forward through Albert: they were to consolidate the ground won, but the attack of the 8th Division round Ovillers and la Boisselle met with indifferent success. There was work to do on the following day, bringing up R.E. stores and carrying back wounded, and at night a party of 100 men established a dump in the captured German trenches near la Boisselle. Early next morning the Twenty-Second were relieved by the 5th South Wales Borderers and in the evening of July 3rd the battalion left Millencourt, the 8th Division being withdrawn from the battle. Five men had been wounded and the Twenty-Second, under fire for the first time, had worked steadily and well.

The 23rd Division came south to the Somme late in June and the 68th Brigade spent several comfortable days at Picquigny. The move forward commenced at the end of the month, but when the division relieved the sorely tried 34th Division the 68th Brigade were kept in reserve, and on July 3rd occupied trenches along the railway embankment south of Albert. On the afternoon of the following day all four battalions moved up in pouring rain to Bécourt Wood, which was crowded with guns and the cookers and reserves of the 69th Brigade, then fighting for Horseshoe Trench south-east of la Boisselle. The Twelfth were the only battalion to bivouac in the wood, the others returning whence they came by order of the division. All next day and night Colonel Macgregor's men worked hard for the 69th

The Durham Forces in the Field

Brigade, carrying up bombs, rations and R.E. stores and bearing the wounded away. On July 6th the 69th Brigade were replaced by the 68th, the Twelfth relieving the 8th West Yorkshire Regt. in the line. A company occupied Birch Tree Avenue, on the right; B and C companies had Horseshoe Trench; D company held a portion of the Triangle beyond. All trenches were deepened and improved, and further ground was then gained without active opposition, giving a front running, roughly, east and west on the line of the Triangle Losses from the German shrapnel were slight, 3 men being killed, and Lieut. M. Campbell-Jones, Lieut. C. Powell-Smith and 10 others wounded.

Before dawn on July 7th the 11th N.F. took over the position, and the Twelfth were withdrawn to a portion of the area won by the Fifteenth on the first day of the battle. The Fusiliers had orders to attack the German line, which ran eastward from the crossroads west of Bailiff Wood to the outskirts of Contalmaison. This advance was made at 9.15 A.M. On the right and in the centre the low ground was commanded by the Contalmaison defences, which had so far resisted all efforts of the 24th Brigade. At some sacrifice —for the Germans had put a barrage upon the whole valley—the objective was almost reached, but it was impossible to dig on ground dominated by the machine-guns in Quadrangle Trench, and by about 10.30 A.M. the Fusiliers were brought back, though two advanced posts were retained.

Meanwhile the Twelfth had pushed forward in support. B and D companies came up by way of the Triangle at 9.30 A.M., and were directed by Colonel Macgregor at the high ground which was really the objective of the 19th Division, on the left of the brigade. These two companies advanced over the open in the face of heavy rifle and machine-gun fire, and gained the trench running back to the la Boisselle-Contalmaison road, where a few wounded Germans were found. C company, who had experienced more difficulty in getting forward, strengthened the line here in the afternoon.

The Twelfth had now filled a gap, and the right

The Battle of the Somme, 1916

flank of the 19th Division was secure. Shortly after mid-day a platoon were required to join up the right of the Fusiliers to the left of the 24th Brigade, who were still struggling for Contalmaison. No. 3 platoon, under Lieut. Francis, reached Peake Wood, but could get no further owing to heavy shell fire; but Capt. F. St. J.

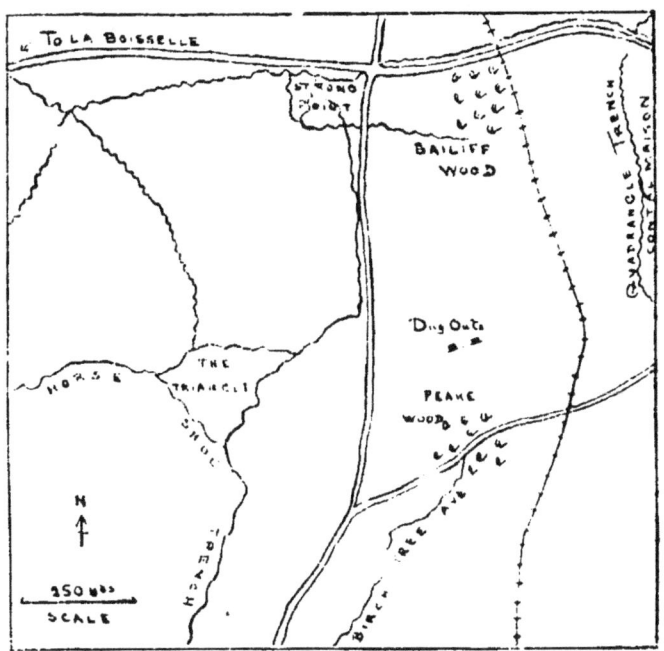

Carr-West brought up the remainder of A company and during the afternoon reached several deep dugouts situated about 200 yards north of the wood. Here 16 Germans were captured.

All these operations were carried out under very trying conditions. The men had had no sleep for 48 hours and the trenches were now knee-deep in mud and water, for rain had fallen heavily all day. More-

The Durham Forces in the Field

over, it was only with the greatest difficulty that rifles and Lewis guns could be kept free of mud and fit for action. B, C and D companies spent the morning of July 8th in consolidating their defences, after D had occupied the strong point on their right south-west of the cross-roads. This had been the scene of a fierce bomb fight until the Germans retired, leaving 5 dead behind them. The three companies handed over their line to the 19th Division during the afternoon and returned to Bécourt Wood, where A company rejoined next morning, bringing in 9 unwounded prisoners.

The Twelfth were soon called on again. At 4 P.M. B, C and D companies started through heavy shell fire for the line, D company, under Capt. H. E. Pease, being ordered to lead a fresh attack on Bailiff Wood and the road and trench beyond. This was timed for six in the evening, but the march up had been delayed owing to rumours of a break in the line of the 19th Division; consequently the artillery preparation was over before the infantry were ready.

By dark Capt. Pease's men were in position near the cross-roads on the left of the Thirteenth, whose line ran southward. The first attempt to gain ground failed, but the next attack—delivered with rifle and bomb upon a wider front—met with better fortune. The trench along the Contalmaison road was occupied as far as the remains of the German light railway and a block was made beyond; a platoon of C company reached the eastern edge of Bailiff Wood; and on the left flank to the north of the road Lieut. A. T. Price dug in with his platoon in front of three damaged German field-guns. During the morning of the 10th two platoons of B company, in support near the cross-roads, found much employment for their snipers, particularly when German infantry were seen advancing on the left. Later in the day Lieut. Price repulsed two counter-attacks by means of rifle and Lewis gun fire.

The task of the Twelfth was well accomplished, for the ground won was of great value when the 69th Brigade attacked Contalmaison on the morrow. Capt. Pease won the Distinguished Service Order for his hand-

The Battle of the Somme, 1916

ling of the operations, and Lieut. Price received the Military Cross.

In the afternoon of July 10th the new positions were taken over by the 69th Brigade, but the platoon from C company remained in Bailiff Wood and supported the attack on Contalmaison. The remainder of C company, who had been assisting the Thirteenth to consolidate their trenches, had already withdrawn to Albert.

Besides the losses already recorded, Capt. F. St. J. Carr-West and 2nd Lieuts. E. A. Nicholson, T. B. Duffy, J. F. Lowes and C. C. Longstaff were wounded, and there were 235 men killed, wounded and missing.

The Thirteenth moved up to Bécourt Wood again on July 6th and waited in reserve till 4 P.M. next day, when the battalion were sent for to take over the brigade line. It was dark when the leading company, nearly waist-deep in mud, arrived upon the scene. The guides were at a loss and the trenches were crowded with carrying parties and wounded, yet by the dawn of July 8th the Thirteenth occupied a line from Birch Tree Avenue, near Peake Wood, to the captured strong point before mentioned, though the position in the centre was by no means clearly defined. Attempts were made to improve upon this, but the mud was a terrible handicap and every sign of movement was visited by German shrapnel. In the afternoon came a report that Bailiff Wood, Quadrangle Trench and Contalmaison had been evacuated by the enemy, but patrols which were pushed forward found that such was not the case. During the day the Thirteenth lost 2nd Lieut. F. R. Wheatley and 21 men wounded and 7 others killed or missing.

By the morning of the 9th the battalion had dug in well from the cross-roads on the left to a point 500 yards south. A bombing party reached Bailiff Wood, but came under our own shell fire and that of an enemy machine-gun; later on another patrol, under the command of Lieut. N. A. Target, M.C., entered the wood, but the fire of our own guns made the position untenable. Losses on this day amounted to 80, besides 2nd Lieut. O. A. Kerridge, mortally wounded.

The Durham Forces in the Field

On the morrow at 4.30 p.m. the 69th Brigade advanced through the battalion front to the capture of Contalmaison. The left flank of the 69th finished on the line of the road beyond Bailiff Wood, and two platoons of A company of the Thirteenth were sent forward to fill a gap. Another party helped the Yorkshiremen to consolidate their captured ground.

Early on the 11th the 1st Cameron Highlanders of the 1st Division arrived to take over from the Thirteenth, who marched back to billets at Albert. Before relief Capt. G. M. Long and 2nd Lieuts. C. Wharton and A. Green were all wounded and there were 58 casualties in the ranks. Lieut. C. S. Kaye-Butterworth had replaced Capt. Long in command of A company, and for his good work was awarded the Military Cross.

The Fifteenth, after a few days' rest, during which drafts brought the battalion up to something like fighting strength, again moved forward on July 9th " to complete," in the words of the divisional commander, "the work so brilliantly begun." The 63rd Brigade had left the 21st Division and were replaced by the 110th Brigade of Leicester battalions.

At dusk on July 11th the division took over the line. On the right were the 38th Division, who had captured two-thirds of Mametz Wood; on the left the 1st Division had relieved the 23rd after the capture of Contalmaison. The Fifteenth arrived at Lonely Copse, north of Fricourt, on the afternoon of the 13th. It was the 110th Brigade who represented the division in the big attack before daylight on July 14th, when good progress was made along the whole line and the Leicester men took the village and most of the wood of Bazentin-le-Petit. On this day the Fifteenth lost 2nd Lieuts. H. J. Peck and H. P. Toou, killed by the same shell.

On July 15th the battalion moved up behind Mametz Wood in support of a fresh attack, but returned in the evening without being engaged. On the afternoon of the next day came orders to take over part of the front in Bazentin-le-Petit Wood. The Fifteenth assembled in the rain and reached the north-east corner of Mametz

The Battle of the Somme, 1916

Wood at dusk, but it was much later when Major Johnson arrived after a partial reconnaissance of the line. The position formed a pronounced salient, and gas shells, tear shells, high explosive and shrapnel tore into the wood all night long. It was a difficult relief in the darkness, but by six o'clock next morning the battalion held the west and north-west portions of the wood with the 10th K.O.Y.L.I. on the right. Touch was kept on the left with the 1st Division who were still gaining ground up the bare slopes to the west of the wood. At ten in the morning a party was sent forward to occupy a German strong point 50 yards away near the tramway running north to Martinpuich. Various trench mortars had fired upon this work during the night after attempts to rush it had failed, and the Durham men found no garrison but 20 German dead. Patrols worked in conjunction with the 1st Division during the day and at dusk it was found possible to hold an outpost line from the junction of the tramway and the Pozières road on the left to the village of Bazentin-le-Petit on the right. This line was taken up by one company with four Lewis guns.

The heavy hostile bombardment was unceasing, and contained enough gas-shell to make respirators necessary until relief came during the next night in the shape of the 1st Middlesex Regt. At 7 A.M. on the 18th the battalion bivouacked on familiar ground between Méaulte and Bécordel. Losses in the ranks during these days amounted to 8 men killed, 65 wounded and 19 missing.

CHAPTER II

THE 35th Division reached the Somme early in July and the Nineteenth, moving forward by easy stages, were disposed in trenches at Montauban on July 15th. Here they came under considerable shell fire, and Lieut. J. Phillips and 2nd Lieut. A. S.

The Durham Forces in the Field

Carroll were wounded. The battalion were under the orders of the 9th Division, then engaged in the struggle for Longueval and Delville Wood, but they were not called upon until the evening of July 18th. A large portion of the wood had been re-taken by the Germans and the "Bantams" now received orders to assist the 26th Brigade in a fresh attack.

The Nineteenth—commanded by Major E. F. Osler since Colonel Stoney had become the victim of an unfortunate accident—moved forward about half-past seven in the evening. Heavy shell-fire was encountered on the way and it was late when Longueval was reached.

Orders for the projected attack had been cancelled —a wise decision, for the Nineteenth did not know the ground and could only move slowly in the darkness under the heavy hostile bombardment. Moreover, the gallant 26th Brigade were already spent with the struggle and very weak in numbers. The "Bantams" remained in Longueval all next day assisting to consolidate what the gallant Scots had won and providing escorts for prisoners. The German shell fire continued and before relief by a battalion of the Royal Scots Fusiliers on July 20th the Nineteenth suffered many casualties. 2nd Lieut. W. Millar was killed, and Capts. J. W. Waller and R. C. Taylor and 2nd Lieuts. F. Featon, W. F. Reeve, J. Mundy and P. V. French were all wounded. The last-named officer died later.

The Nineteenth bivouacked at Caftet Wood near Carnoy and here Major S. Huffam, from the 17th West Yorkshire Regt., arrived and assumed command. A party of 800 men was provided to dig a communication trench forward from Trones Wood to Waterlot Farm, but in the early morning of July 24th the whole of the Nineteenth moved up to spend two days digging reserve trenches on the slopes south-west of Longueval. A heavy bombardment of high explosive and tear shells interrupted the work, killed 2nd Lieut. W. Braidford, wounded 2nd Lieuts. S. H. Smith and C. W. Pollock and caused many casualties in the ranks. After returning again to Caftet Wood the "Bantams" moved to Silesia Trench in the old

The Battle of the Somme, 1916

German front line south of Montauban where a draft of 100 men was received.

On the evening of July 29th the whole of the 106th Brigade assembled in the vicinity as reserve to the 89th Brigade, who were to attack on the morrow from the line Malzhorn Farm to Guillemont. Gas and tear shells caused much discomfort during the night.

As the 89th Brigade advanced, the "Bantam" battalions had to follow in succession, occupying the positions in front as they were vacated. But this plan of moving to the assault up communication trenches caused great congestion and delay. Progress was always regulated by the battalion in front and the Nineteenth, who only got as far as a sunken road south of Bernafay Wood, did well to secure good cover and avoid casualties. At night the battalion marched back to Caftet Wood and moved to Sand Pit Valley, near Méaulte, on the last day of the month. For a full fortnight the "Bantams" had worked under heavy shell fire, their powers of endurance being taxed to the utmost. Losses amounted to 12 officers and 250 men.

The 34th Division had been thrusting forward from the south towards the high ground on which stood the remains of Pozières. On July 15th the 68th Brigade, having spent a few days in billets at Albert and suffered some casualties from shell fire there, were placed at the disposal of this division. The day was one of inaction for the Twelfth and Thirteenth, but an attack on Pozières by the 112th Brigade failed before a heavy hostile artillery and machine-gun barrage and the fatal obstacle of uncut wire. On the evening of the 16th the Twelfth moved up and relieved the 10th Loyal N. Lancashires in the line before the village. Near the Bapaume road on the left two companies found continuous trenches, but the position on the right consisted of a chain of posts in shell holes. One company proceeded to connect these, while the rest of the battalion dug assembly trenches for the attack. The work went on throughout the next day. At 10.30 A.M. a smoke barrage was put out, but the Germans did not disclose their machine-guns or indulge in rifle fire.

The Durham Forces in the Field

though their shelling increased in volume. At 8 P.M. the Twelfth were to advance upon the enemy trenches which crossed the road to Contalmaison south of Pozières and extended to the Bapaume road. The Thirteenth were to occupy the line vacated by the Twelfth, and the remainder of the 68th Brigade were to take the village when the first objective was gained.

The Stokes mortars, which were to deal with the German machine-guns, dropped their shells 50 yards short, but at the appointed hour the Twelfth left their trenches and went forward under the barrage. C company on the right covered 100 yards before the enemy machine-guns opened. Then further progress could only be made by crawling forward and another 100 yards was gained in this fashion. Capt. R. C. Woodhead was killed soon after, in the act of rising to lead his men on. No. 9 platoon managed to get near enough to engage the enemy with bombs and, though 2nd Lieut. J. Harrison fell, Sergt. J. Hughes and the devoted few who survived continued the unequal fight for three-quarters of an hour. The wire at this point was found to be 20 yards wide and uncut by our artillery. B company in the centre had advanced only 70 yards when a hail of machine-gun bullets swept through them. Capt. C. S. Wolstenholme fell dead leading a rush forward, which on the left of the company reached the German trench; but uncut wire and the deadly machine-guns held up every other effort. A company on the left had a shorter distance to cover and some of them climbed the German parapet. Lieut. T. S. Warren was killed here and few survived to return to the British trenches. Two platoons of D company, following in support, also suffered very heavily, their leader, Lieut. T. W. Hetherington, and 2nd Lieut. R. Pearce-Brown being among the fallen.

Eventually the attackers withdrew, bringing most of their wounded with them. Losses in the ranks amounted to 130 and among the wounded were Capt. S. Holmes, Lieut. E. W. Lafone and 2nd Lieuts. A. G. Francis and F. H. Casson.

The Thirteenth and the 10th N.F. relieved three companies of the Twelfth without delay and twenty-

The Battle of the Somme, 1916

four hours after the attack the battalion were back in Albert. The brigadier said: "I am satisfied that not only did they do their best, but that their best was most gallant," and the commander of the 34th Division sent the following message: "I consider the 12th D.L.I. attacked most gallantly and did all that soldiers could have done under the circumstances." Sergt. Hughes was awarded the Military Medal.

The Thirteenth had taken over trenches from the 6th Bedford Regt. on July 16th near Contalmaison Wood. A digging party, sent up at night to help the Twelfth, made a painful progress to the line under heavy shell fire. When the attack of the Twelfth failed on the following evening the battalion took over the trenches astride the Contalmaison-Pozières road. The Germans shelled this position steadily and the battalion lost 50 men in two days, including Lieut. E. Thompson, wounded. Early on July 19th the line had to be readjusted in order to join with the 1st Division on the right. In the evening the Australians arrived to take over and the battalion withdrew to Albert through a barrage of gas shells.

The 68th Brigade now spent nearly a week in Franzvillers, where drafts were received, inspections held, and the ribbon of the Military Medal presented to Sergt. I. Fitzpatrick and Ptes. W. Hutchinson and I. Suddes of the Thirteenth.

On July 26th, when the 23rd Division relieved the 1st on the high ground beyond Contalmaison, the Thirteenth occupied support trenches in that village. Australians were on the left and troops of the 70th Brigade on the right. The battalion took over the front line next evening in the German trench system running south-east from behind Pozières now in the grip of the Australians. These two trenches were known as O.G.1 and O.G.2. Linking them up with the German Switch Line beyond ran Munster Alley, where several unsuccessful attempts to advance had already been made. When the Thirteenth came in no British troops were further forward than the point called 41 on the map.

The Durham Forces in the Field

Before the morning of July 28th A company under Lieut. G. S. Kaye-Butterworth, M.C., assisted by a company of the Twelfth, had gained ground on the right by digging Butterworth Trench, 200 yards in length and almost parallel to the German Switch Line. Ten men were wounded in doing this and Lieut. Kaye-Butterworth was also hit, but remained in command.

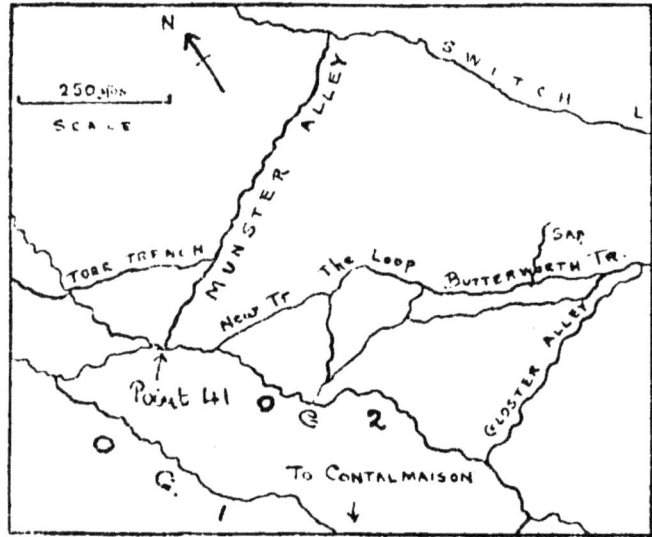

Meanwhile Lieut. C. I. W. Sauerbeck with his bombers had pushed up Munster Alley for 70 yards and was erecting a barricade. Before 8 o'clock in the morning he was heavily attacked and had to give ground, though the fight continued. Lieut. Sauerbeck was wounded and 2nd Lieut. C. I. O'Callaghan, who afterwards received the Military Cross, carried on the struggle till he too fell, badly hit in both legs. C.-S.-M. Morton, assisted by Sergt. Carling whose Lewis gun opened upon the Germans as they scrambled across Lieut. Sauerbeck's barricade, then

The Battle of the Somme, 1916

conducted the defence until the enemy withdrew soon after half-past eight. 2nd Lieuts. Johnson and C. H. Robins with the bombers of C company held our end of Munster Alley until the evening. Then, as a result of two daring reconnaissances by Lieut. N. A. Target, M.C., the enemy forward block was bombed and our left barricade advanced to a better position.

The 10th Duke of Wellington's (69th Brigade) relieved the battalion that same night. Heavy shell fire wounded 2nd Lieuts. C. H. Robins, A. G. Dugdale and W. G. Charlton before the Thirteenth were clear of the trenches, and losses in the ranks now amounted to 50.

The last days of the month were spent in Albert. Lieut.-Colonel R. W. Turner, owing to ill-health, was now obliged to leave the battalion and Major G. White, M.C., assumed command.

On August 1st the Thirteenth moved to Peake Wood and were back in the front line again on the evening of the 2nd. During the night a sap was dug from Butterworth Trench out towards the Switch Line, and the bombing post in Munster Alley was strengthened and wired. On the following day the British shells were falling short so that D company had to evacuate this hardly-won position. When in the evening the battalion were relieved and withdrew to dug-outs near Contalmaison casualties amounted to 29, including 2nd Lieut. I. C. Saint, wounded.

On the afternoon of the 4th the Thirteenth moved up again in readiness for the attack on Torr Trench and its junction with Munster Alley. This was entrusted to D company, who occupied New Trench. A company held Butterworth Trench; B company were at point 41 and the barricade in Munster Alley; C company with C company of the 10th N.F. were in Gloster Alley. The attack, which was to be accorded lavish artillery support—a difficult problem with the Germans so near—had been fixed for 9.16 P.M. If Munster Alley and Torr Trench had received the full effects of the fire of the British heavies all might have gone well. But these trenches were practically untouched by the artillery, and the advance of D com-

The Durham Forces in the Field

pany across Munster Alley, exposed to enfilade machine-gun fire at close range, assumed the character of a forlorn hope. In two waves the men went forward. Capt. A. H. P. Austin with a gallant few actually reached Torr Trench and, it is to be presumed, died there.

It was not till the second wave had crossed Munster Alley that the bombers could get to work, but the attack up the trench was then pressed with vigour. Sixty yards were won and 5 Germans taken and then the Durhams were faced by a strong barricade heavily wired and defended by a machine-gun. About 18 yards from the enemy a block was made and held against repeated counter-attacks. 2nd Lieut. F. L. F. Rees won his Military Cross here, and Corpl. H. Craddock his Distinguished Conduct Medal.

The brigadier called upon the Thirteenth for a further effort. Shortly after midnight Lieut. Kaye-Butterworth was ordered to come round the Loop with A company and form up for an attack, but our own shells were falling short here and this could not be done. The bomb fight still raged in Munster Alley, where Lieut. Target, M.C., now commanded and later died most gallantly with many of his men. All that could be done was to defend the block already made until, at nine in the morning, the fighting died down and a party of Fusiliers came up in relief.

In the evening of August 5th the 8th Yorkshire Regt. took over the position, and the Thirteenth moved back to Albert. Losses in officers had been very heavy. In addition to those already recorded, 2nd Lieuts. W. L. Oakes, F. L. F. Rees, M.C., E. W. Atkinson and J. C. Batty were wounded, and 2nd Lieut. N. Thompson died of his wounds. The death of Lieut. G. S. Kaye-Butterworth, M.C., was a great loss to English music, as well as to the Thirteenth who knew him as a gallant and efficient officer. He was killed by a German sniper in the early morning of August 5th. Casualties in the ranks amounted to 126. Sergt. W. Calley, Corpl. T. Bellerby, Lance-Corpl. W. Claire and Ptes. J. Anderson, M. Brough, H. Dickenson, R. Hickson, T. O. Kerr, W. Luke, W.

The Battle of the So**m**e, 1916

Vaughan, W. Si**mm**s and J. J. Wilkinson were all awarded the Military Medal for gallantry displayed during these operations.

The Twelfth spent July 26th in reserve and then occupied trenches at Contalmaison. Bécourt Wood was reached again on the evening of the 28th and next day 200 men carried bombs to the front line under heavy fire. On July 30th the Twelfth were shelled in their bivouacs, and sustained 7 casualties, including 2nd Lieut. C. A. Heppell, who was wounded. Carrying parties were still in demand, the battalion now coming under the orders of the 70th Brigade. On August 2nd the Twelfth took over the front line eastward from the scene of the fighting at Munster Alley. There was much work to do, both digging and wiring, while patrols and snipers were busy. Two days later came a move to support trenches and the battalion withdrew altogether on August 7th, being relieved by troops of the 15th Division. The German shell fire had never ceased and the Twelfth lost 68 men during this last tour in the line.

Lance-Sergt. H. E. Hitchin, Lance-Corpls. P. Mitchell and J. Moore, and Ptes. I. C. Bamborough, E. Jones, S. Shanks and W. E. Watson were all awarded the Military Medal for their gallantry during the operations of July.

Early in August came the 14th Division to bear a part in the battle. The Tenth reached camp at Dernancourt upon the 8th and Colonel Morant and the company commanders visited the line on the following day. Rain fell, but the weather had improved when the battalion moved up on August 12th to Pommiers Redoubt, an old German work just south of the Maretz-Montauban road. The front was taken over that night at a cost of 24 casualties. Hostile shelling had obliterated most of the tracks leading to Longueval, but before morning the Tenth were established in trenches to the north of the village with the right of the line in Delville Wood. It was a scene of great horror and desolation, for the British and German

The Durham Forces in the Field

dead all lay as they had fallen during the fierce fighting of the past four weeks. Even now the enemy held a part of the wood despite the valour and sacrifice of the 9th, 18th, 3rd, 2nd and 5th Divisions.

The Germans shelled the line throughout the 18th while the Durhams improved their defences and dug much needed communication trenches. 2nd Lieut. J. N. Jackson was wounded on this day, and on the morrow Capt. C. E. Pumphrey was so badly hit in the arm that he had to lose the limb. Many casualties were caused by German snipers. When the Tenth were relieved on the night of August 15th losses in the ranks amounted to 70.

The 43rd Brigade attacked in conjunction with the 41st on August 18th, the Tenth being in support; but they had to send up C company and some bombers at night to strengthen the line as the attempt upon the last German positions in Delville Wood had failed. The battalion lost 2 killed and 26 wounded.

Five days' rest at Fricourt followed and then on August 25th the Tenth relieved a battalion of the 42nd Brigade now a little further forward in the wood. The Durhams took over Inner Trench eastward from Cocoa Lane with B company under Capt. J. C. Parr and C company bombers. D and A companies occupied Devil's Trench, and C company were in reserve. Part of Edge Trench was free of Germans, but they still held the eastern portion and it was the task of the Tenth to drive them out.

The attack was fixed for 7.30 P.M. on August 26th and then postponed till 5 A.M. next morning, when a further delay ensued as the Stokes mortars were not ready. Colonel Morant determined to do without them. At 5 P.M. on August 27th a shrapnel barrage came down, and 2nd Lieut. E. E. Canney led a strong party of bombers across the open from Edge Trench and entered New Trench. While some of his men erected a barricade in the rear he directed a vigorous attack with bombs towards Edge Trench from the north. Meanwhile Sergt. E. Chicken, D.C.M., and Lance-Corpl. Sherrif headed a similar assault along Edge Trench from the west. Lieut. J. R. Paris had led an

The Battle of the Somme, 1916

advance from Devil's Trench through the wood, and arrived at the junction of Edge Trench and Ale Alley where the German wire was too thick to be negotiated. Though many casualties were suffered the Lewis gun and rifle grenade fire of this party was of great assistance. Edge Trench was soon taken, together with 60 prisoners, and the capture of Delville Wood was thus completed. 2nd Lieut. Canney built a block

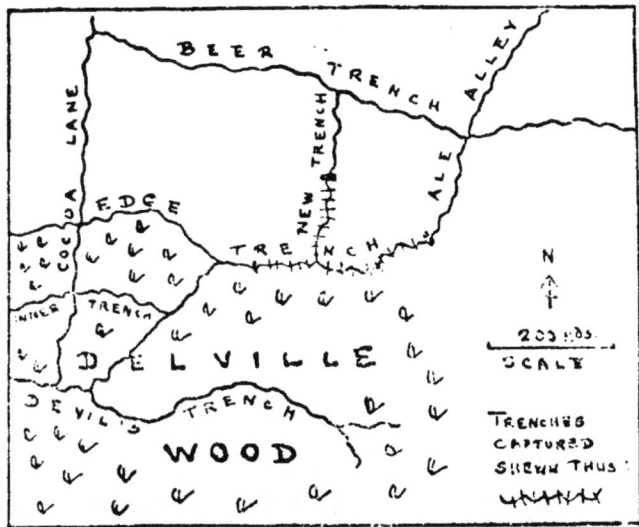

nearly 50 yards up Ale Alley, and work was begun upon a trench from this point to the barricade in New Trench, and thence north-westward to link up with the 6th K.O.Y.L.I. upon the left.

Capt. Parr, who had ably directed the whole attack and subsequent consolidation, was awarded the Military Cross. Lieut. Paris and 2nd Lieut. Canney received the same decoration, which was also conferred upon Lieut. A. Todd, the bombing officer of the battalion, who had not spared himself. Sergt. Chicken has already been mentioned. Despite a wound in the leg

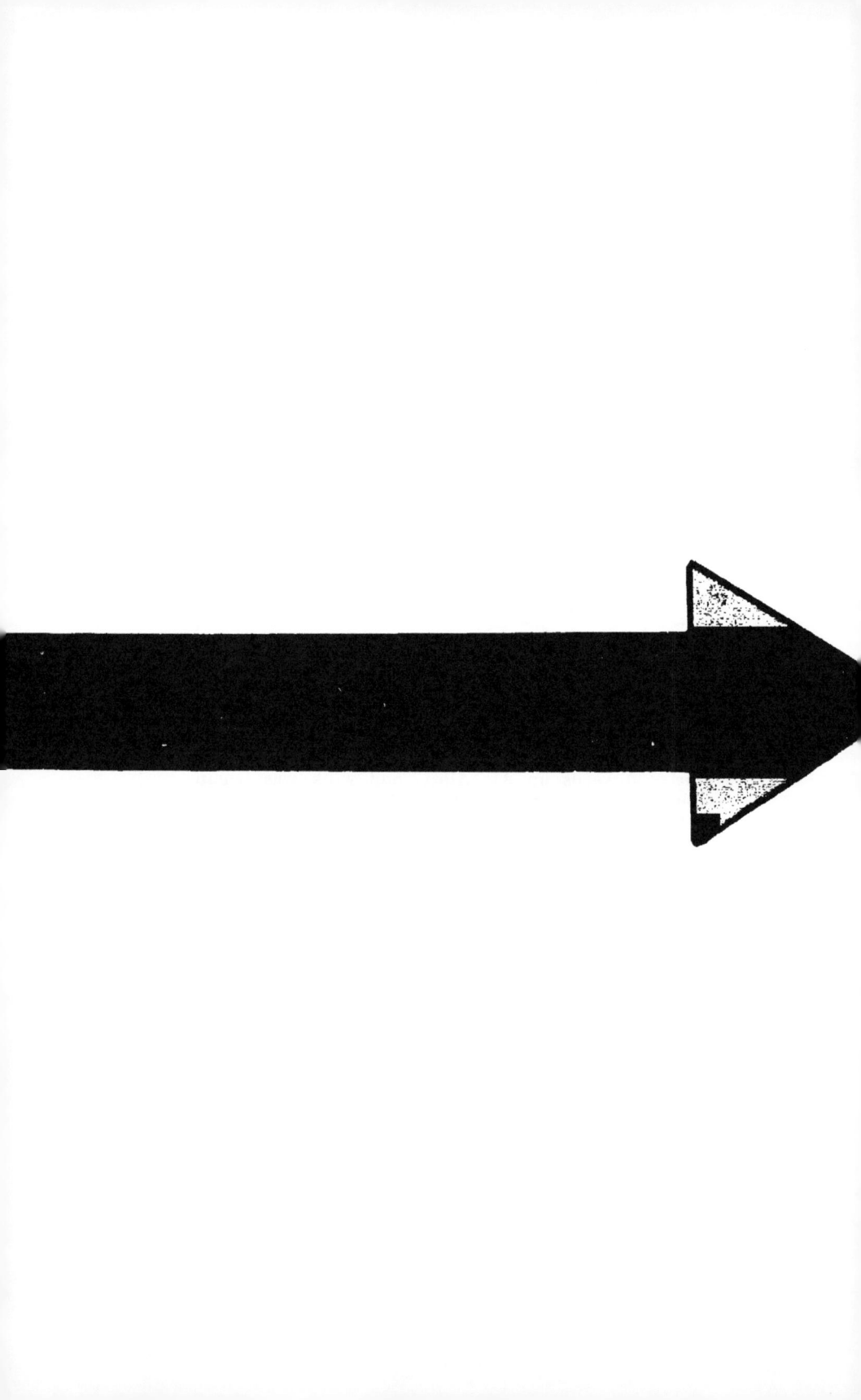

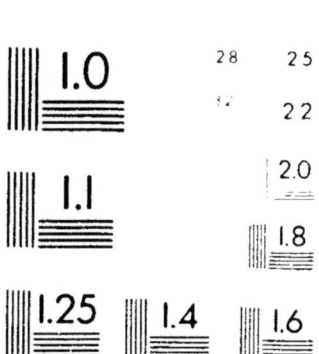

The Durham Forces in the Field

he showed great dash and spirit throughout the fight and is alleged to have "enjoyed every moment of it." Lance-Corpl. Sherrif, who so ably supported him, was badly wounded, and unfortunately fell into the hands of the Germans at the farthest point reached in Ale Alley.

Another attack was ordered for the evening of August 27th with the object of clearing Ale Alley as far as Beer Trench. Lieut. Todd arranged to co-operate with the 1st Royal Welch Fusiliers upon the right, but the infantry were not ready when the barrage came down at five o'clock. The gunners ceased fire, and the brigade then named a later hour and eventually cancelled the operation. But this last order was not received in time, and the Fusiliers led off without artillery support. The Tenth joined in, but only 15 yards of the trench was taken, and that at great cost.

Under heavy shell fire the Tenth were relieved the same night and returned to Fricourt, casualties amounting to 6 officers and 203 men. At the end of the month the battalion moved back to rest at Hornoy.

The "Bantams," who had spent most of August training at Norlancourt and Foudrinoy, moved up on the 20th to Sand Pit Valley. Two days later they were in trenches on the slope of Malzhorn ridge, north of Hardecourt, where the British line joined the French. The advance of the Allies in this part of the field was still stubbornly contested and ceaseless shell fire caused the Nineteenth many casualties. The front of the 35th Division ran from Hardecourt to the Trones Wood-Guillemont road and faced almost due east. An attack was projected for August 24th, but this was cancelled and the action of the Nineteenth was confined to patrol work under fire of the German snipers. That night the division commenced to hand over to the 5th Division, and the "Bantams," whose losses amounted to 3 officers and 110 men, withdrew from the line.

About August 22nd the 20th Division came in on the left of the 35th, taking over the sector in front of

70

The Battle of the Somme, 1916

Trones Wood, including the remains of Guillemont station to the north. The Eleventh had arrived at Morlancourt on August 20th and marched next day to the Citadel, where the men made their own bivouacs from empty shell-boxes. Three companies reached the front line on August 23rd, and commenced work on assembly trenches north of the railway and in front of the extreme left of the divisional line. The enemy shell fire was heavy, and at 10.30 p.m. a German counter-attack was delivered and repulsed further south. Before midnight the Pioneers resumed their interrupted work, but half an hour later a heavy bombardment came down and digging had to be abandoned. The Eleventh continued the task under heavy fire on the following night after another German counter-attack had failed. Thus the preparations for the attack were pushed forward, and the casualties of the Eleventh were light considering the conditions under which they worked. By the end of the month the assembly trenches north of the railway were complete and good progress had been made with those in front of Arrow Head Copse for the Brigade on the right. There was a day of rain which made the roads and tracks all but impassable and the journey to and from the front line difficult and wearisome in the extreme. The British guns began the preliminary bombardment on August 30th which provoked a vigorous reply, and every day the Eleventh suffered casualties, including Lieut. J. H. Marples, gassed on September 1st.

The weather was fine again when on the morning of September 3rd the Pioneers marched up to play their part in the capture of Guillemont. Three times already British troops had entered the ruins of the village, but had never been able to stay. Now the 20th Division—using the 59th Brigade and one Brigade of Irish troops—were to capture it in a general advance of the Allies. A company of the Eleventh were attached to the 59th Brigade on the right and assembled in Liverpool Trench running south from Trones Wood; on the left behind the Irishmen D company were in Dummy Trench. The remainder of the battalion were in reserve behind Bernafay Wood.

71

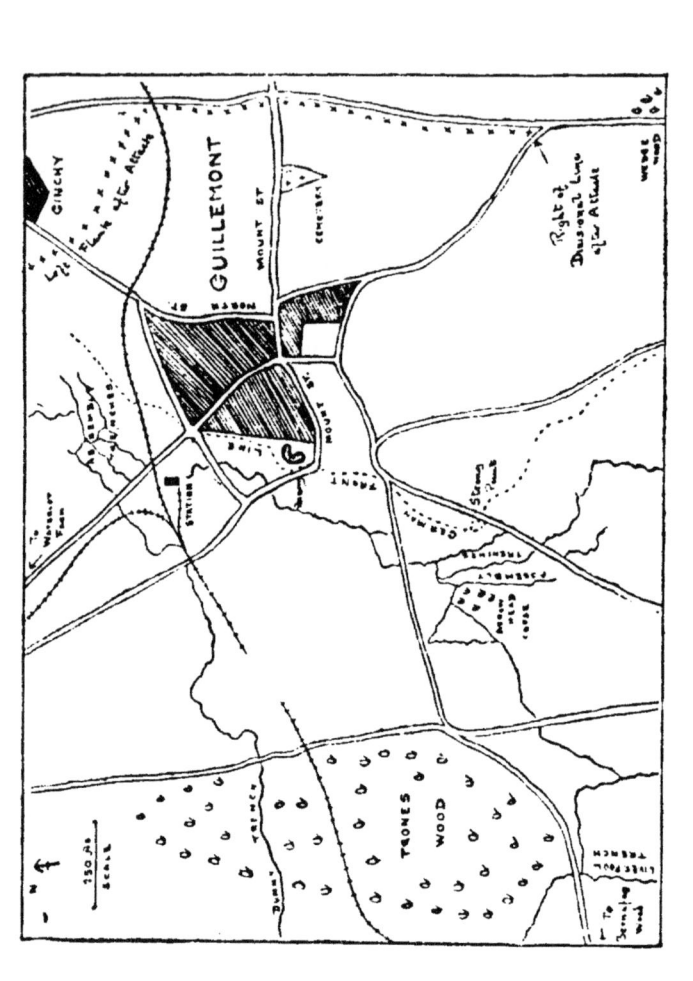

The Battle of the Somme, 1916

At ten minutes after mid-day the assaulting battalions anticipated the appointed time by a few moments and began to advance. On the right a platoon of A company followed the leading wave, which reached its first objective by half-past twelve. The 47th Brigade on the left had met with similar success, and two platoons of D company were then entering the village. A hostile barrage came down on Troncs Wood, but in an hour the advance had passed through Guillemont and did not stop till the line of the Ginchy-Wedge Wood road was reached. Under heavy hostile shelling the work of consolidation went on. Mount Street, which ran through the centre of Guillemont, was blotted out and only a few pieces of railing marked the site of the cemetery. D company helped the Connaught Rangers to put North Street in a state of defence; most of A company were employed at the ruins of the German strong point in front of Arrow Head Copse. In the evening B and C companies began work with the sappers. They carried up wire, which was put out in front of the new line, and they commenced to make communication trenches through the village.

As the divisions to left and right had made little progress, the flanks of the 20th Division were in danger. Towards Ginchy, whence there was most fear of a counter-attack, a defensive line was established and here D company toiled during the night. A company were now employed in consolidating the southern portion of Guillemont, which they were detailed to hold in conjunction with the 7th D.C.L.I. At dawn on September 4th the Eleventh were withdrawn to Carnoy, but came up again in the afternoon through heavy shell fire to continue their labours. B and C companies were diverted to la Briqueterie, south of Bernafay Wood, and were brought forward later to Arrow Head Copse. They were intended to relieve troops of the 59th Brigade in the new front line, but the journey up through the village under the storm of high explosive was difficult and took hours. Few, if any, of the 59th came out before the relief of the whole brigade, which was accomplished by dawn of Sep-

73

The Durham Forces in the Field

tember 5th. During these two days and nights the Eleventh lost Lieuts. W. A. Cunningham and Robertson and 2nd Lieuts. Stubbs and Wood, all wounded. Capts. Pollock and Pemberton were evacuated sick and losses in the ranks amounted to 87, nearly all of whom were wounded.

CHAPTER III

At 6 a.m. on September 12th a general bombardment began in preparation for a big combined attack of the British and French which was to start three days later. The British battle front, which extended from the region of Leuze Wood—east of Cuillemont—to the vicinity of Martinpuich, eventually absorbed no fewer than seven of our Service Battalions. The fortunes of each up to the end of the month will be followed in turn, commencing on the right of the line where the Fourteenth were making their first appearance in the Somme battle.

The 6th Division took over the front east of Guillemont on the night of September 11th. On the following day the Fourteenth moved up from Sand Pit Valley to the Citadel, south of Fricourt. They were in reserve with the rest of the 18th Brigade and did not come into action on September 15th when the division made a hurried and unsuccessful attack on the Quadrilateral, a German work about 1,000 yards east of Ginchy.

Later on the same day the 18th Brigade were put in to rush the Quadrilateral from the flanks and the 2nd Durham Light Infantry entered the trench called Low Road, bombed down it for 100 yards and held on. The Fourteenth had waited in Guillemont during this fighting, but were sent forward at night to consolidate a position where the railway crossed the Ginchy-Leuze Wood road. The battalion arrived upon the scene in darkness and found the trenches full of dead and wounded Norfolks and Suffolks. After working hard until dawn, improving the position and getting the

The Battle of the Somme, 1916

wounded away, patrols were sent out to establish touch with the troops on the flanks. Sherwood Foresters were located on the left just east of Ginchy, and on the right were the 1st King's Shropshire Light Infantry of the 16th Brigade.

During the day there was fighting further to the north, where the Guards were attacking in the direction of Lesbœufs; the Fourteenth waited till dusk and

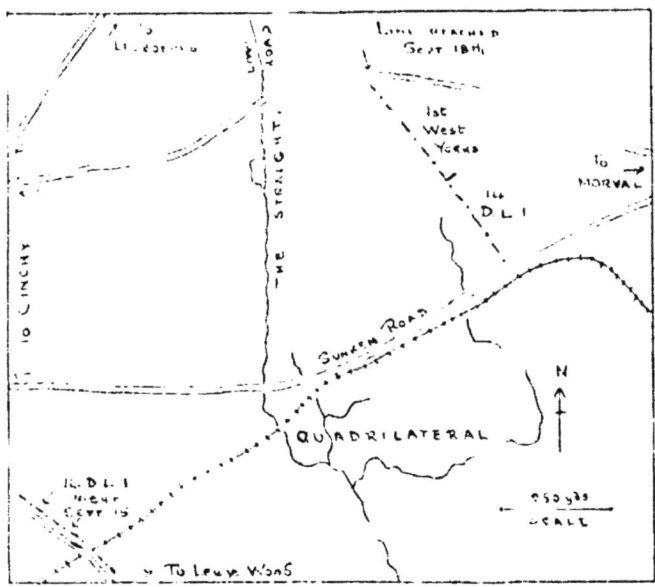

then began work on an assembly trench in front of their position, for another attempt was to be made upon the Quadrilateral in the early morning of September 18th. Soon after midnight a heavy hostile barrage came down. The Durhams dropped pick and shovel and, rifle in hand, lined their trenches in readiness for the counter-attack; two hours passed and it did not come, so work was resumed until dawn. Another day of waiting followed. The 1st West

The Durham Forces in the Field

Yorkshire Regt. were now in position on the left and at dusk the Fourteenth went to work on a fresh assembly trench 70 yards further forward.

The battalion had lost 24 wounded, including Capt. S. R. Streatfield and 2nd Lieuts. E. W. Tuffs and C. P. Hart, before the attack started. First came an intense bombardment of the German positions by the British heavy artillery. Rain began to fall before 5.50 A.M. when the Fourteenth climbed out of their wet trenches and plodded forward through the mud behind a creeping barrage. The right of the battalion was on the railway, and A and B companies on this flank and in the centre of the line made good progress. On the left German machine-gunners had survived both high-explosive and shrapnel and maintained a galling fire. The advancing line paused and engaged the enemy with rifle grenades, but the success on the right took the Germans in flank and the machine-guns were soon in our hands, together with the whole of the trench called the Straight and the battered Quadrilateral. The advance pressed on. North of the railway the Fourteenth took prisoners and bombed dug-outs in the sunken road, and reached the forward slope within view of the ruins of Morval on the other side of the valley. Here the battalion dug in, the Yorkshire men prolonging the line to the left. Patrols pushed on down the hill and found the enemy still in force in front of Morval, but no infantry counter-attack developed, though the German gunners opened upon the new position.

At night the whole brigade were relieved with some difficulty and the tired, wet and muddy Fourteenth reached billets at Méaulte in the course of the following day. Capt. C. M. Hodgson, Lieut. A. Milne, 2nd Lieuts. F. Cutler, A. Wild and 31 men had been killed; Lieut. G. E. Stringfellow, 2nd Lieuts. W. D. Anderson, A. Rothfield and A. M. Lascelles and 161 were wounded. A few of the 32 men reported missing afterwards rejoined. Between them the Fourteenth and the West Yorkshires had captured 106 unwounded Germans and six machine-guns. The number of wounded prisoners was very large.

The Battle of the Somme, 1916

A draft of 80 men was received before the battalion moved forward again on September 21st. The 18th Brigade were relieving the 1st Guards Brigade in front of Lesbœufs, and the Fourteenth spent the night in reserve between Trones Wood and Bernafay Wood. The awful state of the ground delayed the renewal of the attack, but on the evening of September 23rd the Fourteenth moved forward and relieved their brethren of the 2nd Durham Light Infantry and also the 11th Essex, thus taking over the whole of the brigade front. D and B companies held the line with C and A companies in sopport. The position was just south of the Ginchy-Lesbœufs road and the 16th Brigade were on the right. Cow Trench on the left beyond the road was still occupied by the Germans.

Hostile shell fire continued all night, and at dawn of September 24th the German infantry advanced under cover of a fiercer bombardment. They did not reach the trenches of the Fourteenth and the 16th Brigade line, though penetrated, was soon restored. The British gunfire undoubtedly prevented further enemy attacks, but many shells fell short into the trenches of the Fourteenth, and one killed Capt. O. A. Ferd. Later in the day on the front of the left company 2nd Lieut. Hellier effected the capture of 4 Germans on patrol, and at night the battalion were relieved by the 2nd Durham Light Infantry and the 11th Essex. Losses in the ranks had only amounted to one man killed and 10 wounded.

Next day the two battalions in the line participated in the general attack along the whole Allied front from the Somme river to Martinpuich. The 1st West Yorkshire Regt. had to make good the village of Lesbœufs, and A and D companies of the Fourteenth were to assist in this operation. The weather was fine and the attack was so successful that these companies were not called upon. The Fourteenth sat in reserve positions all day under a heavy German bombardment, which killed 2nd Lieut. T. N. Robinson and 2 men and wounded Capt. P. A. Trechman, 2nd Lieut. J. G. R. Pacey and 32 others. On the evening of the 26th the Durhams relieved the Yorkshiremen on the

The Durham Forces in the Field

ground that had been won. All four companies were put in the front line, which ran just east of the ruins of Lesbœufs, and here the battalion remained until the early morning of September 29th, when the 2nd Sherwood Foresters of the 71st Brigade took over the position. During this period the German shell fire never ceased and losses amounted to 13 killed and 2nd Lieut. R. E. Bryant and 29 wounded. On the 28th an enemy aeroplane flew over the trenches and was driven off by Lewis gun and rifle fire.

In the evening of September 29th the Fourteenth arrived at billets in Méaulte again, and moved on the following day to Ville-sur-Ancre to reorganise and prepare again for battle. Lieut.-Colonel G. F. Menzies, D.S.O., had gone back for a much-needed rest and Major J. B. Rosher, M.C., was now in command.

The 20th Division did not occupy a portion of the battle front on September 15th, but were there ready for action and on the following day lent the 61st Brigade to the Guards, who were following up their initial success. The Eleventh left Méricourt on September 12th for Sand Pit Valley, and did some road-making before moving to the Citadel for the night. On the 15th the battalion marched up in battle order to Talus Bois, in a ravine east of Carnoy, and waited there during the whole of the following day. Then the Guards pioneer battalion were relieved at Bernafay Wood, the division taking over from the Guards the line on the left of the 6th Division. There was much work for the Eleventh to do in preparation for the next advance. After repairing roads and tracks going forward through Troncs Wood, 440 men were employed for two nights on the assembly trenches needed west of Lesbœufs. It was a long journey to and from the line and the weather was very bad, but neither officers nor men spared themselves, and the task was finished by September 20th. The battalion moved back to Sand Pit Valley, but 150 men had to spend the night in digging a new trench under the noses of the enemy in order to straighten the front line. When the Guards came in again next day preparations for the attack

The Battle of the Somme, 1916

were practically complete. The Eleventh had lost less than 30 men, which speaks volumes for the skill and discipline with which their dangerous tasks had been performed.

After a few days' work on roads and R.E. dumps the Eleventh came forward to the Malzhorn valley and began the unpleasant task of cleaning trenches. A track from Ginchy towards Morval was repaired, but the division were now handing over this sector to the French and the battalion marched back in the rain on the evening of the 27th to rest in the open at Talus Bois. On the following day a draft of 45 men arrived. A move was made to shell-holes and trenches in Troncs Wood on September 29th and next day, when the 20th Division relieved the 21st beyond Gueudecourt, the Pioneers marched up by platoons and occupied third-line trenches with two companies. C and D companies were located at Waterlot Farm.

The Tenth had a pleasant time at Fornoy during the early days of September, and the kindly French villagers were sorry to see them go. Bivouacs at Dernancourt were reached in heavy rain on September 12th.

The 14th Division had a share in the big attack of September 15th, being on the left of the Guards and on the right of the 41st Division, who were opposite Flers. The 43rd Brigade were in reserve and the Tenth moved to the vicinity of Fricourt on the night of the 14th. Here battle stores were distributed, and next morning the battalion moved up to the familiar Pommiers Redoubt and on to Bernafay Wood. In the afternoon the Tenth were ordered to occupy trenches east of the Longueval-Flers road. The way led through Delville Wood, and although 8 men were killed by one shell there were no other casualties from the persistent fire of the enemy until the position was reached. But gun-pits for British batteries were being dug between the trenches of the two front companies and the rest of the Tenth, and the enemy artillery concentrated accordingly. Lieut. J. C. P. Barkas was killed here, together with a company-sergeant-major and several others.

The Durham Forces in the Field

The 42nd Brigade were now leading the division and it appeared that the advance had been checked with heavy losses at Bull's Road east of Flers. Orders were received for the Tenth to take over the line on the left in touch with the 41st Division where Bull's Road met the road from Gueudecourt. On the right the 6th Somersets were to join with the left of the Guards. The Tenth moved off at midnight in artillery formation and, though there were a few casualties from German shrapnel on the way, the relief was easily accomplished. At dawn of the 16th one could see down the slope to Gueudecourt beyond Gird and Gird Support trenches, and considerable movement of the enemy near the village was observed. By Bull's Road stood four field guns abandoned by the Germans.

Orders were received to attack at 9.25 A.M. with the object of breaking through the Gird defences, clearing Gueudecourt and establishing a line beyond. The enemy was very quiet when the British heavy artillery opened, but the bombardment did not seem to trouble him much. Some Germans even disdained to take cover. The shrapnel barrage came down 600 yards in front of the trenches of the Tenth and was weak and scattered; nevertheless the Durham men went forward at the appointed hour, though as soon as they appeared in the open there came heavy machine-gun fire from the front and from the right. On they went, paying dearly for every yard, but when nearly a quarter of a mile had been gained the survivors had to seek cover in shell-holes and stay there. Before midday parties of Germans were seen coming forward to the Gird line from the direction of le Transloy, but no counter-attack was attempted. The afternoon passed and then came orders for another attack to be delivered at 6.55 P.M. Colonel Morant collected about 100 men, which included all employed at battalion headquarters; his only remaining officers were the adjutant, Lieut. F. A. Stewart and the bombing officer, Lieut. Todd.

The bombardment was now better, though still not heavy enough considering the area to be covered and it had the effect of shelling out most of the survivors

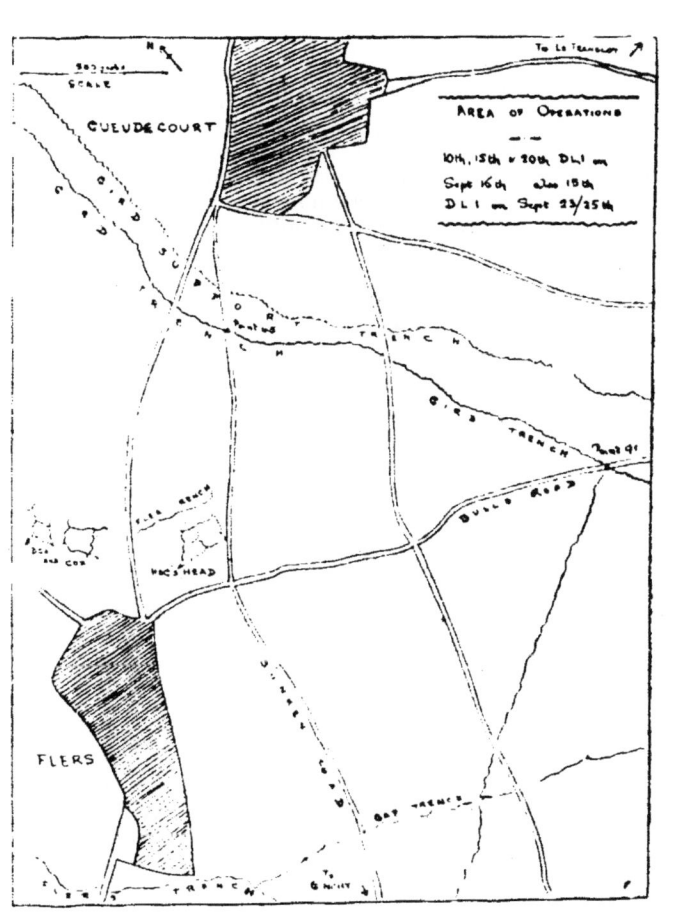

The Durham Forces in the Field

of the first attack still holding on in front. But C.-S.-M. C. Wakeham and the remnants of C company stayed till the evening attack came up to them. It got no further. The creeping barrage was again negligible and the German machine-guns were as active as before. With no troops in immediate support and both flanks unprotected a withdrawal was inevitable, and after dark the survivors of the battalion fell back and put Bull's Road in a state of defence. Many of the wounded were then brought in.

The position of the Somersets on the right was not known. Sergt. J. Donnelly* was sent across with a message to their commanding officer, and in the dark encountered a German outpost. "Are you the Somersets?" he asked, and received a bullet in the arm. Nevertheless he eventually delivered his message and volunteered to take a reply.

The 21st Division were coming up in relief and the Tenth handed over the position before dawn. A very weak battalion reached Pommiers Redoubt during the morning of September 17th. Losses in killed, wounded and missing amounted to 381, besides Lieuts. W. R. James and P. A. Stewart, 2nd Lieuts. A. D. Whittle and J. Graham killed; 2nd Lieut. W. J. Clappen mortally wounded; and Lieut.-Col. F. F. S. Morant, Major B. J. Bryant, Capt. J. G. Parr, Lieuts. G. G. S. Fitzgerald and G. t;. Wornum and 2nd Lieuts. A. E. Turner, J. N. C. Watt, N. H. Watson, H. Storey, F. J. Richards and Maitland all wounded. The commanding officer was able to bring the Tenth out of the line, and after about ten days at Rouen came back and assumed command again.

2nd Lieut. A. E. Turner, who had led his platoon with conspicuous skill and courage, was awarded the Military Cross. C.-S.-M. Wakeham and Sergt. Donnelly received the Distinguished Conduct Medal,

* Later on, when at home convalescent and serving with the 16th (Reserve) Battalion, Sergt. Donnelly " deserted " and mysteriously re-appeared with the Tenth. Enquiries were made about twelve months afterwards regarding a " deserter " called Donnelly, said to be deficient of a great deal of kit. By this time he was a company-sergeant-major with D.C.M. and bar and M.M. Before the end of the war he was given a commission and won the Military Cross.

The Battle of the Somme, 1916

as did Lance-Corpl. W. Hoole, who carried messages and brought in a wounded man under heavy fire. Pte. Dixon also displayed great gallantry. He was wounded while tending Lieut. Stewart in the open, and afterwards walked about under heavy machine-gun fire fetching bandages and water. C.-S.-M. W. Cooper was awarded the Distinguished Conduct Medal. With two others he dug for two hours under heavy shell fire in order to rescue a man reported buried.

The 64th Brigade of the 21st Division concentrated near Poiziers Redoubt on the afternoon of September 15th, and came under the orders of the 41st Division that evening. The brigade were to be used for a fresh attack on the Gird system of trenches west of Gueudecourt.

At two o'clock on the morning of the 16th the Fifteenth started for the line. Progress in the dark along tracks and roads congested with all the traffic of battle was very slow. Instead of being in position by dawn of September 16th, it was 5.30 A.M. by the time the place of deployment was reached. The 9th K.O.Y.L.I. were then in the sunken road east of Flers which led back to Ginchy; but the 1st East Yorkshire Regt., better served by their guides than were the Fifteenth, had arrived in front of the Durhams and occupied Flers Trench. Colonel Pedley's men were in shell-holes just behind, but as they had to form the right of the attack it was considerably later before the assaulting troops were in position east of the southern side of Flers village. Very little was known of the whereabouts of the troops of the 41st Division or of the enemy.

At 8.45 A.M. C and D companies moved forward to get into closer touch with A and B companies, who were to lead the way. Half an hour later the shrapnel barrage came down nearly three-quarters of a mile beyond the battalion, who then advanced to the attack. A storm of German high explosive burst behind them, but shrapnel and machine-gun bullets smote them almost from the start. After covering about half a mile the Lesbœufs road was reached and the line re-organised. Troops of the 41st Division were found to

The Durham Forces in the Field

be in the vicinity. The Fifteenth, with the 9th K.O.Y.L.I. on their left, went on again into an ever-increasing hail of shell, machine-gun and rifle fire. When at last the survivors of the two battalions came to a halt in shell-holes some of the Fifteenth were within 70 yards of the German trenches. The Yorkshiremen were not quite so near, but had overrun a few advanced posts of the enemy and collected a few prisoners. The men lay in the mud at the limit of the advance throughout the afternoon, every incautious movement drawing German fire. They could not indicate their position, for the red flares they carried were too damp to ignite and the British barrage fell alike on friend and foe. Orders for another attack were issued, but there was no chance of success and it was never made. At dusk came a withdrawal, the Fifteenth first occupying Flea Trench, and at dawn on the 17th the sunken part of the Ginchy road. There was great congestion in all the positions around Flers and when the Twentieth began to arrive later in the morning the Fifteenth moved back again to a position south of the village, where the rest of the day was spent under heavy shell fire. The battalion were now only 260 strong. 2nd Lieuts. G. H. Wesselhoeft, C. K. O. Graham, E. B. George and G. A. Garland and Capt. E. R. Welch had fallen. 2nd Lieut. A. R. Jacob died from his wounds. Among the wounded were Capts. J. K. L. Cockburn, G. C. Bell and F. J. Widdowson; Lieuts. C. L. Bleaden, M.C. (adjutant), W. C. Warren and W. Edmondson; 2nd Lieuts. J. Key, M. B. Jopling, J. F. Leys and M. R. Pease. Three other officers, 2nd Lieuts. A. S. Morley, M.C., A. H. Grant and H. Royley, were missing, presumably killed, and losses in the ranks amounted to 119. These casualties, the heaviest in the brigade, bore tragic witness to the determination with which the Fifteenth had gone forward. In the words of the brigadier, " Success was beyond the power of the very best troops. All did excellently."

2nd Lieut. M. B. Jopling was awarded the Military Cross for his cool courage and fine leadership during the attack. There were numerous other recommendations for gallantry, including 2nd Lieuts. F. J. Cartman,

The Battle of the Somme, 1916

M.C., E. B. George (killed), M. R. Pease (wounded), and E. W. Pritchard; C.-S.-M. C. Croom and C.-Q.-M.-S. A. Small; Sergts. J. T. Booth, F. Bushell (killed), J. Catnach, J. Cregg, C. McPherson, E. Lloyd and J. C. Walton (killed); Lance-Sergt. T. Funton (wounded) and Corpl. C. Dixon; Lance-Corpls. M. Bretwood and T. A. Needham; Ptes. J. F. Gardner, T. Leonard, R. Nattress and W. Richardson.

The Fifteenth were withdrawn to Pommiers Redoubt upon the evening of September 17th and moved to tents at Bécordel next day to rest until the 22nd. The 21st Division had now taken over the 14th Division front, where the Gird trenches and Gueudecourt were still in German hands.

The 64th Brigade relieved the 62nd in the front line before dawn of September 23rd. Now about 350 strong, the Fifteenth occupied the left of the line. Aeroplanes had reported no sign of the enemy in Gird Trench opposite, but patrols who tried to effect an entry were fired on and fell back. On the night of the 24th the Fifteenth gave way to troops of the 110th Brigade, and were in reserve during the attack on the following afternoon. The enemy wire was still strong and his machine-guns were unsubdued, so that the assault made no headway but cost many lives. When the Fifteenth, coming up by way of Gap Trench, replaced the 1st Lincoln Regt. in the front line at night the other units of the 64th Brigade were withdrawn, and the Leicester troops on the left were relieved by fresh battalions. The attack was to be resumed next day, employing different methods which offered greater prospect of success and at a smaller price. Point 45 on the map was in British hands, and point 91 on the right was held by bombers of the Guards. At a quarter past seven on the morning of September 26th a female tank spurting machine-gun bullets came lurching down the enemy line from Point 45, followed by bombers of the Leicesters. Low overhead flew an aeroplane with active Lewis gun, and those of the affrighted enemy who were left alive soon surrendered. Nearly 400 Germans, including several officers, were thus taken.

Advancing over the open about nine in the morning,

The Durham Forces in the Field

the Fifteenth occupied the captured trench and pushed forward patrols. Before mid-day Gird Support trench was reached and passed, and the advance still continued. During the afternoon the Durhams got well forward on the ground east of Gueudecourt, with the 10th K.O.Y.L.I. on their left and the Leicesters through and beyond the village, where the tank had continued to render good service till her petrol was exhausted. In the evening the 64th Brigade were relieved and the Fifteenth spent the night back on the Gueudecourt-Lesbœufs road. The task of the division was now ended, and the battalion found themselves at Poizières again by the end of the month. The last eight days had increased the casualty list by 54, besides Lieut. E. N. Carter and 2nd Lieut. N. B. Jopling, M.C., wounded, the latter accidentally, and 2nd Lieut. J. F. C. Schofield wounded and missing.

On September 10th the 41st Division began to come into the battle line. The 123rd Brigade took over the front on that night, the Twentieth relieving the 7th King's Regt. in support trenches west of Longueval. Beyond Delville Wood were the 23rd Middlesex and the 11th Queen's, confronted by the Switch Line which was the outer defence of Flers.

As soon as darkness fell upon September 11th the Wearsiders were busy. Capt. C. McNicholl took forward C company and two platoons of A company, who passed through the Queen's in the front line and dug a chain of posts in "No Man's Land." When daylight prevented further movement C company with their Lewis guns remained in occupation. On the next night the Twentieth relieved the Queen's and the posts were linked up, communication trenches being dug to the old front line. The West Kents had performed a similar task on the right, so the whole front was thus advanced by 100 to 150 yards without opposition—a gain of ground which proved very valuable to the attacking troops. Capt. McNicholl was given the Distinguished Service Order for his skilful handling of the operation.

The Twentieth were relieved in their turn on the

The Battle of the Somme, 1916

night of the 13th and arrived at Pommiers Redoubt early on the following morning. Casualties caused by the enemy's harassing fire included 4 men killed and Lieuts. A. F. Collins, J. A. Struthers and 30 more wounded. That same evening the Wearsiders moved up to the Check Line behind the crest of the ridge where stood the ruined villages of Bazentin-le-Grand and Longueval. Hostile shell fire accounted for 25 killed and wounded on the way. At 6.20 a.m. on September 15th the other brigades of the 41st Division went forward with the tanks, broke the German line and entered the village of Flers, keeping pace with the New Zealanders on the left. Following the advance the Twentieth came up through a heavy enemy barrage and by evening occupied the old front trenches astride the Longueval-Flers road. Losses in the ranks on this day amounted to 44 and 2nd Lieut. F. C. Arkless was wounded.

All was not well beyond Flers. More ground had yet to be gained, and the other brigades of the division were spent and not even in touch with each other. It has already been related how the 64th Brigade were brought in, made a fresh advance on the morning of September 16th, and failed with bloody losses. The Wearsiders were sent for during this action and had to negotiate a heavy German barrage on the southern side of Flers. During the morning the Twentieth began to arrive at the forward positions, where there was much confusion, for it was difficult to collect and reorganise the men of the many battalions now involved. By noon, however, C company were established in the trenches called Box and Cox on the north side of the village, filling a gap between two companies of the Queen's. Colonel Hills with the rest of the Twentieth occupied the sunken road leading to Ginchy, from which position the gallant remnants of the Fifteenth had been withdrawn. During the rest of the day, the night and all next day the work of consolidation went on under heavy and increasing shell fire. The afternoon of the 17th was particularly trying for the Twentieth, who had to endure an intense bombardment of high explosive and tear shells. At night a counter-

The Durham Forces in the Field

attack was expected but did not come, and troops of the 55th Division managed to effect a difficult relief. The companies of the Twentieth marched back through pitch darkness, pouring rain and considerable shell fire. When in the early morning the Montauban line was reached, the men were glad to lie down and sleep in the mud. The last two days had cost the battalion 103 casualties, besides Capts. P. Spencer (adjutant), J. E. Jessop and H. Risdon; Lieut. C. E. Hopkinson and 2nd Lieuts. T. M. Fletcher, W. Mitchell and F. Wayman, who were all wounded.

The Twentieth now reorganised and spent eight days in attack training near Bécordel. On September 27th the battalion moved up by Montauban and relieved the 8th King's in reserve trenches near Flers next day. The enemy shell fire had died down here, but carrying parties to the front, which was now beyond Guendecourt, cost 3 killed and 10 wounded. In the afternoon of the 30th two companies relieved two companies of the Queen's in the line. This daylight operation was over-bold, for the watchful enemy shelled D company to some purpose. In the evening the other two companies completed the relief by occupying support positions and the night was spent in improving the new line which had been dug beyond Gird Support trench. Losses amounted to 38, including Lieut. C. E. Hopkinson, wounded again, and the commanding officer, who sustained a nasty wound in the wrist. Lieut.-Col. J. W. Hills, M.P., had led the Twentieth with great courage and coolness during their first big experience of active warfare, and his departure was regretted by all ranks.

The 23rd Division returned to the battle mid-way through September, when the Thirteenth were at once lent to the 47th Division, then attacking the German positions east of High Wood. Reaching Bécourt Wood from Millencourt on September 15th, the Thirteenth marched up at night to trenches behind the Londoners near Bazentin-le-Grand. The task of the battalion was to furnish carrying and working parties by day and night for the 140th and 141st Brigades, who were

The Battle of the Somme, 1916

fighting hard and losing heavily. On the night of September 17th 2nd Lieut. V. L. D. Beart was in charge of a party taking bombs to the 6th Londons in the line. A hostile barrage came down in the darkness, killing and wounding many of the men. To collect the survivors was no light task, but 2nd Lieut. Beart got together about fifty before he fell mortally wounded. Sergts. H. Craddock, D.C.M., and Fittes did not know the way, and the guide could not be found, but they managed to get the party to its destination. For this good work each received the Military Medal.

Rain fell steadily throughout the 19th. In the morning the 140th Brigade reported that all objectives had been captured, but that the Germans had counter-attacked and gained the junction of the Flers line and the communication trench called Drop Alley. The Thirteenth were called upon to assist in regaining this point, and Colonel Lindsay lent B company under Capt. D. H. Clarke, M.C. The scene of the fight that followed was rather less than a mile north-east of High Wood. At 6.45 P.M., after a preliminary bombardment by Stokes guns, two bombing attacks were made, one up Drop Alley and the other up Flers front line. On the right the New Zealanders joined in up Flers support trench. 2nd Lieut. A. Hudspeth led the advance up Drop Alley, and went 70 yards before reaching a heavily wired barricade held in strength by the enemy. Mills bombs were fired over the heads of the stormers, but a strong party of Germans counter-attacked over the open and the Durhams had to fall back to their starting point. After a ten minutes' struggle the other party, led by 2nd Lieut. Mitchell, won 130 yards of Flers Trench. Shortage of bombs stopped further progress, but a barricade was erected in the face of a heavy cross fire of German bombs. By some mischance the British guns were firing upon the captured portion of the trench and continued to do so for four hours. Twice the barricade was demolished by our own shells and another was eventually built 20 yards further back. This was held till relief came six hours later. B company rejoined the battalion, now back in Bécourt Wood, on the morning of Sep-

The Durham Forces in the Field

tember 20th, having sustained 30 casualties, besides 2nd Lieut. Hudspeth who was missing.

The 23rd Division had relieved the Fifteenth after the capture of Martinpuich, and on September 22nd the Thirteenth moved up to support positions. Colonel Lindsay was slightly wounded on the following day. On the 24th D company relieved a company of the 11th N.F. in the northern outskirts of Martinpuich, among the wounded on this day being 2nd Lieut. F. C. Allan and Capt. J. A. L. Downey, who was able to remain at duty. By the morning of September 26th the whole battalion were in the line, but at night the 70th Brigade came up and the Thirteenth withdrew to Bécourt Wood once more.

The Twelfth had also moved up from Millencourt to Bécourt Wood on September 15th. Three days later the battalion took over Gourlay Trench, beyond Contalmaison Villa, from the 11th Argyll and Sutherland Highlanders. The Twelfth were heavily shelled here, losing 2nd Lieut. C. Armstrong (killed), and Capts. H. A. Heyner and A. T. Price, M.C. (wounded) on September 21st. After submitting to the attentions of the official photographer next day, the battalion moved up through a barrage to the front line. The trenches taken over extended to the Bapaume road on the left. Prue Trench on the right ran eastward from the north side of Martinpuich and on this flank touch was obtained with the 50th (Northumbrian) Division. To the north of the village a sunken road, the ruins of a windmill and other trenches were in our hands, forming a salient which reached out to 26th Avenue. This was a fortified trench line which crossed the Bapaume road south of Courcelette and ran north-eastward down the slope till it linked up with the German defences just south of le Sars. The enemy was known to be in 26th Avenue, though reports varied regarding his strength.

The Twelfth lost several killed and wounded by shell fire on September 23rd. At night an officer and two men made a long and careful reconnaissance of 26th Avenue, which was found to be held in force.

The Battle of the Somme, 1916

Orders were received to capture this trench, and at 8 A.M. on the 24th two platoons and a strong bombing party advanced under cover of a thick mist. But as soon as the attackers topped a rise in the ground and came within sight of their objective, they were met with a deadly fire from rifles and machine-guns. Five men and 2nd Lieut. J. Bollon were killed and 28 wounded before a withdrawal was effected, and then the line held by the Twelfth was fiercely bombarded.

At 5 A.M. next morning the battalion were relieved, but had to return to the line in the course of the day on account of the heavy losses sustained by the 10th N.F. in another abortive attack. The enemy artillery was still active and when the British guns concentrated upon 26th Avenue next morning the Germans retaliated upon the village, the Factory (support) line and the sunken road, called Gun Pit Alley, which led from Martinpuich to Courcelette. In the evening a patrol of the Twelfth, under 2nd Lieut. A. T. Hunt, found much of 26th Avenue deserted, though German Very lights were discharged from two points in the trench.

Before dawn of September 27th the Twelfth were relieved, having sustained 35 more casualties. After a day of rest the battalion worked upon the repair of roads near Contalmaison, and R.E. stores were unloaded and grenades carried up to the dump at Martinpuich. Also assistance was given in digging assembly trenches east of that village.

CHAPTER IV

On the right of the British line strenuous efforts were made at the beginning of October to push the advance north-eastward towards le Transloy. Wet weather delayed operations and the enemy took advantage of the respite to strengthen his defences and move up fresh troops; consequently further progress was only achieved after hard fighting and heavy losses.

The 20th Division held the front between Lesbœufs and Gueudecourt and, on the night of October 1st,

The Durham Forces in the Field

gained a little ground. Groups of men from the 61st Brigade advanced under an intense barrage for about 400 yards, and dug a line of posts which it was the duty of the Pioneers to go forward and convert into a continuous trench. The manner of their going may best be described in the words of an officer of the Eleventh:

"At dusk parties were told off from each company to get pickets and wire and tools, and an officer was detailed to go in advance to the front line and lay out the task about 200 yards from the Boche. Then, when the battalion were well on the way, the Boche S.O.S. went up, and the stuff, consisting of a well-selected assortment of shells of every kind and calibre with a trimming of machine-gun fire, began to arrive. However, everyone slid into the nearest, newest shell-hole and waited. It passed, and we had few casualties. We pushed on, climbed over the front line, and were led on to the job. Whilst placing men on the task a Boche Very light fell behind the party, but the machine-gun fire which followed was rotten, and we carried on with the work. Although the soil was chalky in parts the trench was finished in five hours, and each company proceeded home carrying its own wounded and those of the units in the line. There were a good number of casualties that night. A memorable sunken road which received a very regular supply of shells took some negotiating. A company lost 15 men just crossing that road."

In such fashion the front line of the 20th Division was advanced and assembly trenches dug in preparation for the attack on October 7th. By that date the losses of the Eleventh amounted to 43, besides Lieut. A. Brown and 2nd Lieut. F. Pickering sent back sick.

The division did well on the day of the attack, carrying portions of Rainbow, Misty and Cloudy trenches on the spur west of le Transloy. C company, waiting in the valley south of the Gueudecourt-le Transloy road, came forward at 5 P.M. and began to consolidate Rainbow trench. B and D companies were employed in the construction of dug-outs. There was

The Battle of the Somme, 1916

much to do, for the divisions on either side had failed, and defensive flanks had to be established. On the left Rainbow trench was still held by the Germans. C company withdrew to Waterlot Farm in the early hours of October 8th and the other companies followed during the afternoon. Next day the Eleventh moved back to billets at Méaulte.

The Fourteenth came forward again on October 7th, the day before the battle front of the 20th Division was taken over by the 18th Brigade. On the evening of the 10th the Durham men came under heavy shell fire at their Trones Wood bivouacs, just before they moved up to a support position, and 17 were killed and wounded. Twenty-four hours later the Fourteenth moved into their assembly positions for the next attack. The battalion had to complete the capture of Rainbow Trench and Shine Trench. This done they would be in line with the West Yorkshire men, and both battalions could advance upon that part of Cloudy Trench still held by the enemy. Tapes were laid to assist the men to keep direction, as the Fourteenth had to attack from the immediate rear of the West Yorkshires and go half left.

At five minutes past two on the afternoon of October 12th the advance began, D company leading on the right, C company on the left. Almost at once the enemy barrage came down, but the Fourteenth went forward without a check and entered Rainbow Trench. Fifteen Germans were taken here, many were killed and few of those who fled escaped the rifle grenades of Lieut. W. A. Batty's party. At the sunken road on the left the Fourteenth joined hands with the troops of the 12th Division, who had come forward on that flank. B company had lost both officers—Capt. F. Hellier killed, and 2nd Lieut. Gillott wounded but before three o'clock the advance was resumed, bombers clearing the dug-outs in the sunken road. German shell and machine-gun fire was still heavy, but rifle grenadiers and Lewis gunners, boldly handled, helped to overcome the enemy resistance.

Moving up in artillery formation A and C companies

The Durham Forces in the Field

occupied Rainbow Trench with little loss, though 2nd Lieut. J. Swindell was killed and 2nd Lieut. W. F. Dunn was wounded. Leaving A company to his sergeant-major, Lieut. C. A. V. Newsome, M.C., hurried forward and assumed command of B company.

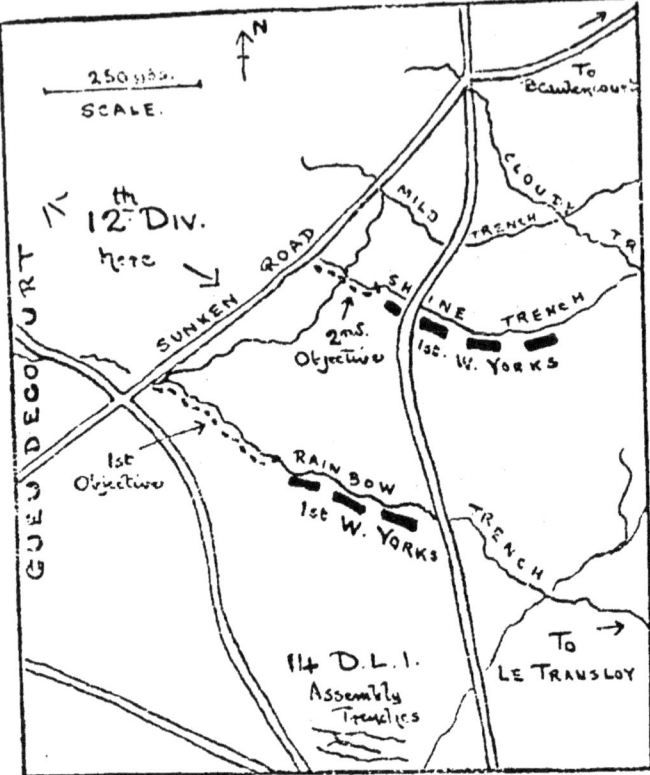

Shine Trench was soon won, and here Lieut. Batty was wounded. Bombing up a communication trench he had captured a German officer, and for his prowess on this day was awarded the Military Cross.

D company on the right were in touch with the

The Battle of the Somme, 1916

Yorkshiremen, but further progress was impossible, for the Germans were in great strength with many machine-guns and the troops on the left had not come forward. A defensive flank was formed under the direction of Lieut. Newsome, who was afterwards awarded a bar to his Military Cross. He was wounded on the following day when the Germans shelled their lost trenches persistently, but by the dawn of October 14th the battalion had handed over to the 11th Essex and retired to a position south of Gueudecourt. At night 80 men carried rations to the 2nd Durham Light Infantry, who had relieved the West Yorkshires in the line.

At 5.35 A.M. on October 15th, when the brigade attacked again, but without success, Lieut. A. Owles, 2nd Lieut. S. G. Highmoor and 60 men were in support to the 11th Essex. In the evening the Fourteenth, now only 200 strong, relieved the Essex men in Rainbow and Shine trenches. 2nd Lieut. Mellor was wounded on this day. Just after midnight Rainbow Trench was heavily bombarded, and during the 16th when the British gunners were busy, many of our own shells fell short among the men in Shine Trench. The Fourteenth were relieved that night and moved back to Montauban, where a draft of 185 men of the 21st Derbyshire Yeomanry was absorbed. During the October fighting the battalion had lost 7 officers and 182 men.

The 6th Division gave way to the 8th, who had to continue the attempt to carry, in spite of the rain and mud, the German defences on the spur running south-east in front of Beaulencourt and le Transloy. The Twenty-Second arrived at Citadel camp on October 14th, but D company were ordered to Montauban to work on the roads. The headquarters of the battalion and B company moved on October 20th to Waterlot Farm. One dug-out and a few cellars were the only habitable places at this ruin which had once been a sugar refinery. Next day B and D companies started work on a communication trench, but this had to be suspended in view of the attack to be carried out

The Durham Forces in the Field

on October 23rd when each company of the Twenty-Second were given a different task.

Capt. W. H. Perkins with C company reached brigade headquarters on the right of the line at 7.30 p.m. on October 22nd. Guides met them here but were uncertain of the route and it was not till after midnight that the company reached the place of assembly in Spectrum Trench astride the Gueudecourt-le Transloy road. At 2.55 p.m. next day the attacking infantry went forward and C company followed the second wave. The Pioneers found Zenith Trench opposite clear of Germans, except dead, wounded and prisoners, and started to dig two communication trenches back to our old front line. Heavy shell fire killed 5 men, mortally wounded 2nd Lieut. G. Fitzbrown and wounded Capt. Perkins and 14 others. Good progress was made by 3 a.m. next day when work ceased and the company tramped the weary miles back to Waterlot Farm. At night the guide who had to bring the company up again went astray, after the manner of guides, and it was nearly dawn when work was resumed. This meant an early withdrawal until dusk, but on the night of October 25th two communication trenches were finished, one 250 and the other 300 yards in length. The total losses of C company were 6 killed and 24 wounded.

B company, under Capt. A. H. Robson, reported to the centre brigade, and spent the night previous to the attack digging assembly places behind the front line. Just before the zero hour on October 23rd No. 5 platoon, under 2nd Lieut. Watson, were sent up with instructions to begin a communication trench forward to Zenith Trench as soon as the latter was captured by the assaulting infantry. But just before the 25th Brigade were timed to advance an intense bombardment swept the assembly and support trenches with fearful effect. Large numbers of men were killed, wounded, or buried alive, and the German fire did not abate till 5 p.m. Capt. Robson withdrew his men to the shelter of a sunken road and afterwards to a trench in the rear. Assistance was given in digging out men who had been buried, but all thoughts of attack

The Battle of the Somme, 1916

had to be abandoned till next morning. Then at 3.50 A.M. the infantry went forward, 2nd Lieut. Hartley following the second wave with his platoon to dig the trench already planned. The attack failed and this platoon rejoined the company on hearing that no further attempt was to be made. At 7 A.M. B company were ordered to work as stretcher-bearers. The front trenches were congested with wounded and the Pioneers worked with great devotion all day, carrying them back through the mud under heavy shell fire. B company eventually returned to Waterlot Farm on the morning of the 25th. 2nd Lieut. J. Cook had fallen and losses in the ranks amounted to 10 killed, 11 wounded and one missing. 2nd Lieut. Hartley set a very fine example to his men during these two days and nights. The gallant conduct of Sergts. Clifford and Rowe (missing) is also mentioned by their company commander. They assisted, very coolly, to reorganise the men when the company had sustained many casualties from two direct hits by enemy shells, and took great personal risks in supervising the work of getting the wounded away. Bandsman Tarn assisted to dig out 3 men who were buried by a shell, and then dressed their wounds under heavy fire. B company went forward again on October 25th and assisted to consolidate Zenith Trench on the extreme right of the line. Here 2nd Lieut. R. Watson and 9 men were wounded.

Capt. G. Dawson took D company forward on the evening of the 22nd to the left of the line. On the way the guide acknowledged that he was lost. By the aid of a very indifferent map the company eventually reached Bulford Trench, behind Rainbow Trench, about 7 A.M. on the morning of the 23rd. At zero hour No. 14 platoon was sent to Shine Trench and remained there till the early hours of the 24th, "standing to" the whole time. No. 16 platoon went to the British portion of Mild Trench on the extreme left of the line, and at 6.30 P.M. started to dig towards a strong point constructed in rear of the captured portion of Mild Trench south of the Gueudecourt-Beaulencourt road. Meanwhile the two remaining platoons deepened and

The Durham Forces in the Field

improved Bulford Trench. At 6.30 P.M. they were ordered to move up with a field company of R.E. to Mild Trench. No one knew the way, and in the darkness the adventures of these sappers and pioneers became obscure; it is alleged that they entered the German lines before arriving at their destination. Mild Trench was improved during the night and early in the morning D company came back to Waterlot Farm, a journey which occupied nearly five hours. Next day they helped B company to consolidate Zenith Trench upon the right of the line.

Commencing on October 23rd, A company had worked in reliefs night and day as stretcher-bearers, thereby earning the gratitude of the whole division. On October 26th they took pick and shovel again, and got to work on a new communication trench. In the evening, after a few hours' rest, C company joined them. Capt. A. Tait-Knight was mortally wounded on this day and Lieut. R. Thwaites was wounded on the 27th. Next day B and D companies, who had continued at work in the line, clearing and consolidating trenches, came back exhausted and wet to the skin, and A and C companies went up to replace them. B company became stretcher-bearers on October 29th and D company worked on the new communication trench. Now came the welcome news that relief was at hand. B company finished work in the evening. C company in the line lost Capt. S. W. Southwood, wounded, but both A and C companies came back next day and the Twenty-Second gradually withdrew to Montauban. They rested at the Citadel on November 1st, though A company had to be left behind to clear up the battlefield. The total losses of the battalion amounted to nearly 120 officers and men.

The dawn of October 1st found the Twentieth in the line north-west of Gueudecourt, and in the afternoon the troops on the right and left made a small advance. The Wearsiders had to push out patrols to discover if the German trenches opposite were held in strength. If this proved to be the case, posts were to be dug not nearer than 200 yards from the enemy. Three

The Battle of the Somme, 1916

parties went forward behind a barrage, and dug in as ordered despite heavy shell and machine-gun fire. They were relieved some hours later, and 2nd Lieut. R. N. Fulljames, M.C., who had directed the operation with great judgment, received a bar to his decoration. The battalion withdrew to Pommiers Redoubt at night, having lost 30 killed and wounded. Here Lieut.-Col. P. W. North, Royal Berkshire Regt., assumed command, and training was carried out until October 7th. On that day of battle, when, after the usual postponement due to bad weather, the British attacked along the whole line from Lesbœufs to le Sars, the Twentieth were in reserve. But the assaulting troops of the 41st Division made little progress, and the Twentieth moved forward in the evening to take over a portion of the front. The maps showing the position of the line were not correct; the communication trenches were blocked with returning wounded; the German shell fire was very heavy; the guides all lost their way. Thus it came about that battalion headquarters, having taken to the open, arrived before the companies. The battalion to be relieved had nearly all departed, and a large gap was left in the line. Colonel North got in touch with the troops on the flanks and some hours later B company and then A company appeared upon the scene and filled the gap which the Germans had not discovered. Just before dawn the rest of the battalion arrived and occupied a support line. Daylight showed the position of the Wearsiders to be a good one on the reverse slope of a ridge, with the German shells falling in rear of the battalion. A company on the right had dug a continuous trench and were in touch with the troops on that flank; the left of B company was only protected by the lie of the ground and two Vickers guns. There was no wire in front, and by the evening of October 8th the enemy were sweeping the top of the ridge with machine-gun fire. The night was clear, but an effort was made to get the front wired and A company actually succeeded in completing their portion before dawn through the gallant exertions of a party which consisted of 2nd Lieut. Brewer and 19 others, of whom all but one were

The Durham Forces in the Field

killed or wounded. On the following night B company dug through and joined up with the battalion on their left. 2nd Lieut. J. W. Butterworth was wounded before the Twentieth were relieved on October 11th. The Wearsiders reached Maretz Wood on the morning of that day.

In addition to the other honours won during the Somme battle, Lance-Sergts. Dazley and E. Winter; Corpl. F. R. Abernethy; and Ptes. I. McClumpha, J. I. Hardy (killed) and E. Anderson (killed) were awarded the Military Medal.

On October 3rd in rain and mud the Twelfth relieved the 5th N.F., and the Thirteenth the 8th Durham Light Infantry in reserve and support positions. The 23rd Division, slowly approaching le Sars, took over on this day that portion of the line held by the 149th Brigade of the 50th (Northumbrian) Division.

Rain fell steadily during the next two days, while there was fighting on both flanks and much German artillery fire. October 6th was fortunately fine and in the evening the two Durham battalions began to take over the front before le Sars. The Twelfth replaced the 10th N.F. on the right and, after the 11th N.F. on the left had had a try at the Tangle—a nest of enemy machine-gunners—and failed, they gave way to the Thirteenth.

Le Sars was to be taken in the big attack of October 7th. The task of the Twelfth was to seize the Tangle and the sunken road east of le Sars while troops of the 69th Brigade carried the south-western part of the village. Then the Thirteenth were to clear the rest of the ruins and establish a line beyond. Battalions were very weak in numbers—the Thirteenth had two small platoons per company—but every man knew what he had to do, and felt more than equal to the task.

At 1.45 p.m. the Twelfth advanced and A and C companies, who led the way, escorted a female tank. The conquest of the Tangle proved easy, but the sunken road was obstinately defended. The tank turned along the southern side of the road towards the village, but suffered a direct hit from a 5.9 shell. A company were

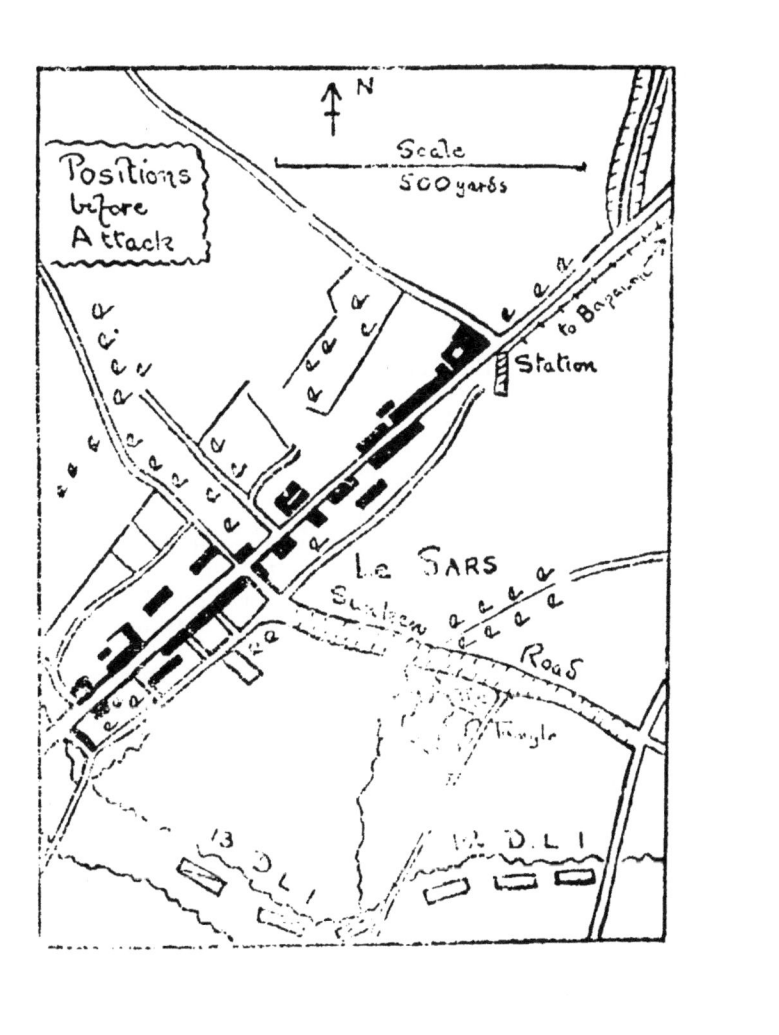

The Durham Forces in the Field

checked by machine-gun fire from the right, but nearer le Sars C company and two platoons of D company, under 2nd Lieut. A. T. Hunt, entered the road. 2nd Lieut. W. L. Hughes followed with the rest of D company and the Germans who survived surrendered. The position was speedily put in a state of defence, and heavy fire was brought to bear upon the enemy now retreating from the right. Then B company, under 2nd Lieut. Harris, came through and continued the advance until a chain of posts was established a quarter of a mile in front, protecting the right of the division. Seventy Germans were taken by the Twelfth, and the battalion lost 2nd Lieuts. W. H. Lockett and Telfer and 31 men killed; 2nd Lieuts. J. H. Law, A. T. Hunt, A. E. Hales, A. B. Wallace, J. C. Hugall and W. C. Leggatt and 86 wounded.

When the Twelfth advanced the Thirteenth kept in touch by means of a patrol, some of whom reached shell-holes from which they could fire at and bomb the Germans in the sunken road. But the heavy enemy barrage made it difficult to send back information, and it was not till nearly half-past two that news of the capture of the Tangle arrived. At the same time patrols in touch with the troops on the left reported that the 9th Yorkshires required support. C company, under Capt. H. F. Blake, were therefore directed straight at the village south of the cross-roads, while B company, led by Capt. D. H. Clarke, V.C., followed in close support, with orders to assist the Yorkshiremen if necessary by bearing left and clearing the houses on the near side of the Bapaume road. The German machine-guns in le Sars brought the leading wave of C company to a halt on the outskirts of the village and the fight continued with rifle and bomb. Here Capt. Blake fell dead, but when B company arrived the machine-guns had been silenced and all pressed forward together. Entering the sunken road C company bombed the dug-outs there, while Capt. Clarke led his men forward through the ruins of the houses, where Germans in dug-outs and cellars were taken or killed. All resistance was soon at an end and Durham patrols appeared beyond the village in open

The Battle of the Somme, 1916

country, where, in some places, they out-ran the British barrage. Soon after half-past three they reported that there were no signs of the enemy.

A company were sent up to work on the defences of le Sars, strong points being made and the sunken road consolidated. The whole of the captured area was now fiercely shelled by the enemy, but before eight o'clock in the evening these tasks were done and the defences manned, the rest of the battalion returning to the old trenches. But attacks to right and left of the division had not gone so well and the dispositions were soon afterwards strengthened, a company of the 11th N.F. and four Vickers guns coming under the command of Colonel Lindsay, while the sappers and carrying parties from the 15th Division helped to improve the defences.

The captures of the Thirteenth comprised 150 Germans, including one officer, besides another officer and 30 men found wounded in cellars and dug-outs. The death of Capt. Blake has been recorded. Lieut. H. R. Markham and 2nd Lieut. E. W. Atkinson were wounded, as was 2nd Lieut. E. Gray, but he remained at duty. There were 57 casualties in the ranks.

The German bombardment continued during the night and next day. All telephone wires were cut and the only communication was by runner. In the afternoon of the 8th a patrol of the Thirteenth got in touch with the enemy at a point on the Bapaume road well beyond le Sars. The battalion lost 15 more men killed and wounded before relief by the 15th Division at night.

Both Twelfth and Thirteenth withdrew to Bécourt Wood to rest after the greatest success they had so far won. Honours were bestowed upon many in each battalion. Of the Twelfth Pte. G. W. Kilburn received the Distinguished Conduct Medal for making a daring daylight reconnaissance and carrying messages under heavy fire after being wounded. Lance-Corpl. G. Slasor, who led successful patrols on three occasions and showed conspicuous courage during the attack, was awarded the same decoration. Among the recipients of the Military Medal were Sergts. C. C. Garvey and W. Monk; Corpls. I. Lackey and J.

The Durham Forces in the Field

Milburn; Lance-Corpl. C. Brown; and Ptes. N. R. Agar, J. Boulger, E. Halford, J. Harness, F. Johnson, W. R. Nessworthy, W. C. Watson, F. Wilson and W. Smith.

In the Thirteenth Capt. D. F. Clarke received a bar to his Military Cross for his capable direction of operations in le Sars and beyond. 2nd Lieut. E. W. Atkinson, who led his platoon well and gallantly and, though wounded, remained with his men until consolidation was complete, was awarded the Military Cross. Sergt. M. Brough, M.M., won a bar to his medal. Sergt. C. A. Stirling, Lance-Corpl. C. Cowland and Ptes. T. Y. Bowman, N. Brown, A. Constantine, D. Graham, J. F. Creen, T. Earle, T. Jackson, C. E. Newby, C. Nichol, C. O'Rourke, R. Purvis, J. Tonkin and J. E. Vipond all received the Military Medal.

TRENCH WARFARE
JULY, 1916—MARCH, 1917

THE Tenth went back into the line south of Arras on July 4th to find bad trenches and an alert enemy. They returned to Arras a fortnight later, and withdrew from this sector to do battle training at Beuzecourt, which was reached, after several trying marches, on August 1st. The battalion moved to Candas on the 7th, and went by train to Mericourt; later in the day they reached a camp north of Dernancourt ready to enter the battle of the Somme.

On September 18th the battalion marched back in pouring rain from Pommiers Redoubt to Ribemont, and arrived in French buses at le Souich and Brevillers four days later. Training and recreation filled the days till the Durhams embussed for Arras in time to take over trenches again on the night of the 27th. The line was thinly held by this sector and there was so much work to do that few men could be spared for patrols. But the enemy, apart from his trench mortar fire, was quiet. A regrettable accident happened on October 12th when Lieut. V. C. Clarke, coming in from patrol, was mortally wounded by a sentry.

The Tenth left the line on October 26th and arrived at Ambrines three days later. Drafts were received, but training was interrupted by bad weather which continued until November 8th, when congenial quarters were found at Sibiville. The country in the vicinity abounded in game, and there was plenty of time for football and recreation of all kinds. December 16th saw the battalion on their way back to Arras, where they occupied the cavalry barracks in the city. On Christmas Eve, when the Tenth took over very wet trenches in foul weather, no gum boots were available and cases of trench foot developed. After this tour a raiding party started training and the enterprise was carried out in daylight on January 11th.

Following an elaborate artillery preparation, the raiders crossed " No Man's Land " under a barrage at about 3 P.M. and entered the German line. Mills and phosphorous bombs were thrown into the dug-outs and the only German seen was shot by Capt. Berisford. Then the enemy bombed in on both flanks. Capt. Berisford conducted the fight on the left and Lieut. Todd, who had been detailed to lead an advance to the German third line, was involved in the struggle on the right. Some of his men had gone on over the top, but the bombing in their rear soon caused them to withdraw. Capt. Berisford saw them return and gave the signal to retire from the German trenches, but 2nd Lieut. Bell, with a small party, had now reached the enemy second line. Here five dug-outs were bombed and the advance was then continued until the third line was nearly gained. Lieut. Bell now realised that he was without support and commenced to withdraw. On reaching the German front trench he had to repel a bombing attack, but he got all his wounded clear of the German wire and into a shell-hole. Capt. Berisford and Lieut. Todd then took out some men to search " No Man's Land " for wounded of whom they found and brought in six.

No prisoners or identifications were collected in this raid, but, considering that many fresh men were brought into the affair at the eleventh hour and that plans were altered several times, the result was satisfactory. Casualties amounted to 2 officers wounded and 44 others killed, wounded and missing. 2nd Lieut. A. G. Bell who was only 19 years of age and had had but three weeks' experience of trench warfare—was awarded the Military Cross and six Military Medals were won.

Preparations for the Spring offensive were being pushed forward and the Tenth worked hard on the underground shelters and tunnels at Arras when not holding the line. On February 3rd 2nd Lieut. McCullough was killed by a sniper and Capt. Hopkin-

Trench Warfare, July, 1916—Mar., 1917

son was accidentally wounded on the following day. In the middle of the month a slow thaw followed a spell of frosty weather which increased the discomfort of life in the trenches. The whole front was very lively, for there were many British raids and the activity of artillery and aircraft, both British and German, increased.

On March 8th the Tenth withdrew to brigade reserve in Arras, now a much-stricken city, and on the 16th the battalion reached Grande Rullecourt to train for the coming offensive. The Germans were retreating to the Hindenburg Line and had already vacated their trenches south of Arras where the 14th Division were to advance. On March 23rd the Tenth moved up to Dainville.

At the opening of the Somme battle the Eleventh were still working in the Ypres salient behind Wieltje. July 14th was memorable for the visit of the Prince of Wales to the headquarters of the battalion at Brandhoek. The 20th Division now left the line after holding it for two months, during which period the Pioneers had lost 2 officers and 89 men killed, wounded, or sick. After several moves in Flanders, carrying out training when opportunity occurred, the Eleventh left Bavinghove by rail on July 25th for Doullens. Next day they marched to very filthy huts at Couin and spent a day cleaning them. The 20th were now relieving the 38th Division in the Colincamps-Hébuterne sector, and on July 28th the Pioneers took over, at the Dell, the dirtiest camp they had yet seen. In this portion of the line both sides were busy repairing the havoc wrought on the opening days of the battle and the Durhams were employed upon the support trenches and also in building deep dug-outs. Occasionally the German shell fire was very heavy. The Guards relieved the division on August 16th and four days later the Eleventh moved by train from Candas to Morlancourt in the Somme area.

The Pioneers had a breathing space at Méaulte and Ville-sur-Ancre from October 9th onwards, Colonel

The Durham Forces in the Field

Collins rejoining the battalion from sick leave. Although the 20th Division now withdrew to the " rest " area, the Chief Engineer of the X Corps claimed the services of the Eleventh, who moved to the Citadel at Carnoy on October 18th. The rest of the month was spent in repairing roads and unloading material and stores. The weather was vile, officers and men were often wet through, and work was delayed and rendered more difficult by the state of the ground. In their few moments of leisure the Pioneers had to repair their own leaky huts. " Seldom," writes an officer of the battalion, " had men more to grouse at, but a grumble without a grin was never known."

On the first day of November came orders to entrain for the " rest " area. The Eleventh went by train from Dernancourt to Saleux, bivouacked in the wet, and marched through rain and mud next day to billets at Bourdon on the river Somme. The battalion could now enjoy a little comfort and relaxation, the " Black and White " concert party, which was formed proving an immediate success. When they moved to Picquigny on November 8th the Pioneers had to clean out some very dirty billets but there was another week's respite before moving forward again.

Corbie was reached by bus on November 16th and the battalion marched to the Citadel in heavy rain on the 25th. The camp was deep in mud and there was little protection from the weather, nor were better quarters found when the battalion moved to Montauban. Work was done on the construction of a light railway till the 20th Division relieved the 29th in the front beyond Lesbœufs and Morval. Then parties were provided to carry up rations, water and trench boards to the line, and the cellars of Ginchy, Lesbœufs and Morval were explored and cleared. Two main communication trenches called Ozone and Flank Avenues were put in hand. The latter was taken up to the forward side of the ridge north of Morval, but further progress was impossible as the ground was so bad. The trench became a drain and the Pioneers spent much of their time " pulling out stuck infantrymen " and helping the stretcher-bearers, whose task was in-

Trench Warfare, July, 1916—Mar., 1917

describably difficult. One of the wounded died after being thirty-two hours on the way from the front trenches to the Lesbœufs-Morval road. These communication trenches were afterwards abandoned in favour of the duck-board tracks which had been originally suggested by the Eleventh.

On December 20th, when the division were relieved, the Pioneers remained at work. The extension of a light railway for the gunners, well beyond Guillemont, entailed the removal of piles of German dead. Weather conditions were as awful as they could be; it was a long journey to and from work; and bivouacs were very bad. All ranks were becoming thoroughly tired out and unfit and the climax was reached on December 29th when heavy rain flooded the camp at Montauban. As a result of the medical officer's representations the ... th were moved back to Ville next day, the Guards returning to take over the old camp which was certainly unfit for human habitation.

The Durhams worked under better conditions during January, while the 20th Division held the line in front of Sailly-Saillisel. Comfortable billets in Frégicourt and Combles were occupied by the battalion, who were employed on the defences of this sector and had to blast the frozen ground with ammonal before digging was possible. On January 29th the Eleventh withdrew to Méaulte, but after an interval of ten days the old Morval-Lesbœufs sector was occupied again. Work was done on dug-outs, camouflage screens and new trenches until the German retreat began at the end of February, when the Pioneers toiled hard on roads and railways as the British line was pushed forward.

About this time Sergt. Gardner was awarded the Italian Bronze Medal for Valour.

The Ginchy-Lesbœufs road was taken in hand by A company of the Eleventh on March 18th, the day after the enemy evacuated le Transloy. Before the 25th, when the Pioneers moved forward to that village, cavalry were encountered on their way to keep in touch with the retreating Germans. Ere the end of the month detachments of the battalion had reached Bus,

The Durham Forces in the Field

le Mesnil, Rocquigny, Ytres and Lechelle, and had made good progress in repairing the damage to the roads wrought by the German mines.

The Twelfth left the Somme area by train on August 11th, and reached Armentières a week later. The 68th Brigade went into the line north of the river Lys, but the battalion remained in reserve and supplied large working parties until August 25th, when they relieved the Thirteenth in the trenches. All was quiet until the Fusiliers on the left attempted a raid, when the enemy retaliation cost the Twelfth a dozen casualties.

During August the award of the Military Medal for gallant conduct on the Somme was made to Corpl. A. Long and Ptes. J. McCarthy, J. R. Dyson, W. Gill, I. Waistell, J. Pye, J. Harrington, W. Parrett and W. Peat.

On September 3rd the Twelfth were relieved by the 9th Royal Scots and marched to camp outside Bailleul. After a few days' training in the St. Omer area the battalion then returned to the Somme battle, arriving by train at Longueau on September 10th. They marched to Molliens-au-Bois and thence forward to Millencourt.

After being relieved on October 8th at le Sars, the Twelfth rested at Bécourt Wood. The 23rd Division were now destined for the Ypres salient and the Durhams, moving northward, detrained at Proven on October 15th. Their first tour, in trenches just south of the Menin road, was a quiet one.

For the next four months the routine of trench warfare continued. When not holding part of the line north of Hill 60 to the Menin road, the Twelfth were either in support at Zillebeke Bund or at the barracks in Ypres. When the 68th Brigade passed into divisional reserve, the battalion went back to huts at Montreal Camp near Ouderdom. Working parties were always busy. Before the end of the year there was much rain, and afterwards came bitter frost and some snow. The front was officially reported " quiet "

Trench Warfare, July, 1916—Mar., 1917

during this period, but with his excellent observation the enemy made a practice of bringing fire to bear upon all daylight movement and bombarded at intervals all vulnerable targets behind the British line.

In the New Year's Honours Major C. E. Cummins was awarded the Distinguished Service Order and many of the Twelfth were mentioned in dispatches. Soon afterwards was announced the award of the French *Médaille Militaire* to Pte. J. Harness.

On February 11th Lieut.-Col. W. W. Macgregor left the battalion, and was succeeded by Major R. Tyndall of the 1st Durham Light Infantry. The Twelfth lost a good officer on the 20th, when Capt. D. Y. Chambers was killed by a shell splinter.

At the end of the month the Durhams withdrew for three weeks' training in the Merckeghem area. This was carried on, first in bitter cold and snow and then in wet and misty weather. On March 21st the Twelfth relieved the 17th R.W.F. near Elverdinghe and worked hard for a week before withdrawing to Poperinghe, where large parties were in demand for burying signal cable in the forward area.

The experiences of the Thirteenth differed but little from those of the Twelfth. On arrival in Armentières, where billets were taken over from the Twentieth, Major N. E. Lindsay, 7th Dragoon Guards, assumed command of the battalion. The 23rd Middlesex were relieved by the Thirteenth in the trenches on August 17th and a quiet tour followed, although D company on the left lost a patrol. When the division went out of the line at the beginning of September, the Thirteenth stayed at Norbécourt for a few days before entraining for the Somme area. The battalion eventually reached billets and bivouacs at Millencourt on September 12th.

On arrival at Proven on October 15th the Thirteenth marched to Winnipeg Camp near Ouderdom. Wet weather was succeeded by frost when the battalion relieved the Twelfth in the line south of the Menin road. The ensuing months were spent between the front

The Durham Forces in the Field

trenches, Zillebeke Bund and the barracks in Ypres. When the brigade were in reserve the Thirteenth occupied Winnipeg Camp.

In the New Year's Honours Colonel Lindsay received the Distinguished Service Order and the Military Cross was awarded to the medical officer, Capt. G. M. Shaw, and to C.-S.-M. R. Richardson.

2nd Lieut. F. Hall and Sergt. H. Craddock, D.C.M., carried out a useful reconnaissance in the thick fog on January 14th. Early in February Sergt. J. Askew and Lance-Sergt. G. Bell were awarded the Military Medal. For the rest there is little to record except the patient and cheerful endurance of the rigours of another winter in the trenches. At the end of the month the Thirteenth moved back to the training area and were located at Bollezeele. They came up again on March 19th, and spent ten days at work in wintry weather around Ypres.

On July 1st the Fourteenth reached Houtkerque on their way back to the salient and moved to camp at Proven next day. Here they stayed for a fortnight, supplying regular working parties to bury cable and repair the dug-outs of the Ypres defences. Training was carried on with the numbers available till the division relieved the 20th in the line on July 15th. Then the battalion moved to support positions on the bank of the Yser canal. Three days later they took over trenches near Wieltje from the 2nd Durham Light Infantry. A quiet tour, during which 2nd Lieut. W. Michelson was wounded, was followed by a stay at Camp J on the Poperinghe road. Working parties were still called for here, but the 6th Division left the salient soon after. On August 2nd the Fourteenth entrained at Esquerdes, and on arrival at Doullens marched to huts at Acheux Wood. Attack training was assiduously practised both here and at Engelbelmer, where the 10th Cheshires were relieved. After occupying various billets and bivouacs and furnishing parties to work with the sappers, the Durhams went into the line north-east of Hamel on the evening of August 14th. The Germans were fiercely bombarding the trenches

Trench Warfare, July, 1916—Mar., 1917

and during the night the valley of the Ancre behind the British front was drenched with tear and gas shell. The enemy mortars were also busy and this activity continued until the Fourteenth were relieved after a tour of five days. They had sustained surprisingly few casualties.

In billets at Engelbelmer nightly working parties were the rule and a raiding detachment started training under Capt. J. B. Rosher. At 1 A.M. on August 25th an attempt to enter the German line failed in the face of an alert enemy, with a loss of Capt. Rosher and 11 others wounded. Next day the battalion began a move which brought them to Vignacourt on the 30th, where training consisted of musketry and practice in the attack. Losses in the ranks during August amounted to 44.

On September 6th the Fourteenth left for the Somme battle front. They marched by Coisy to Vaux-sur-Somme and thence to Sand Pit Valley.

The Fourteenth left Ville-sur-Ancre on October 23rd and reached Oisemont by train, being continually on the move until they arrived at Lapugnoy on the 29th. Here they settled down for a fortnight's training in good weather. The 18th Brigade now relieved the 6th in the Cambrin sector and the Fourteenth were set to work with the tunnelling companies, moving for this purpose to Nœux-les-Mines, Sailly-Labourse and Annequin. Major J. B. Rosher returned to the battalion about this time and took over command from Colonel Menzies, who was required at the First Army School. On November 24th the battalion moved to Lapugnoy, but were in brigade reserve at Annequin by the end of the month.

They relieved the 1st West Yorkshires in the front line at Cambrin—just south of the la Bassée canal—on December 6th. 2nd Lieut. R. H. C. Macdonald with 8 men attempted to enter the German trenches on the evening of the 10th, but the enemy was on the alert and opened fire. Most of the party were hit, the officer being mortally wounded. Sergt. R. I. Young and Corpl. T. Jaye showed great courage in attempt-

The Durham Forces in the Field

ing to recover him and both received the Military Medal.

The Fourteenth were in and out of this part of the line until the middle of February. In the New Year's Honours Major J. B. Rosher was awarded the Military Cross and C.-S.-M. J. Hunter the Military Medal. Casualties during January included Capt. R. E. Bryant and Lieut. J. H. Edwards killed, and Capts. R. le G. Eyre and A. G. de Bunsen wounded. The Germans shelled Annequin severely at times and several women and children were among the victims.

In the early morning of January 25th the 1st West Yorkshires carried out a successful raid and the Fourteenth promptly arranged to send over a party in the evening, hoping to catch the Germans repairing their trenches and dug-outs. Prisoners reported that a relief would be in progress. 2nd Lieut. S. M. Wilson and C.-S.-M. Nicholson each led a detachment of 17 men across " No Man's Land " when the barrage came down at about 11 p.m. On the flanks were small covering parties and Capt. G. A. Richardson, M.C., directed operations from the British front line. Lieut. Wilson jumped into the enemy trench upon two Germans, one of whom he shot. The other ran away, but some of the enemy were more aggressive, and delivered a bombing attack which wounded the officer before it was repulsed. C.-S.-M. Nicholson's men had seen only one German, who promptly fled, and, as the enemy mortars now began to fire on his own front line, the signal to withdraw was given. The raiders, who had identified a dead German as belonging to the 201st Regt., reached their own trenches with a loss of 7 men slightly wounded. 2nd Lieut. Wilson was awarded the Military Cross.

On February 13th the Fourteenth handed over trenches to the Fifteenth, and spent the remainder of the month at Busnes and la Miquellerie, where Colonel Menzies rejoined the battalion. Early in March the battalion came up by way of Béthune and Mazingarbe and took over reserve trenches in the Loos salient just north-east of the village on the 3rd. Colonel Menzies now definitely vacated the command and was succeeded

Trench Warfare, July, 1916—Mar., 1917

by Major J. B. Rosher. The Fourteenth did two tours in the front line before going into divisional reserve at Mazingarbe. At the end of March they were in the reserve or " Village " line, and casualties for the month had amounted to 8 killed and 2nd Lieut. W. Severs and 10 wounded. Corpl. J. W. Wilkinson was awarded the Military Medal.

The Fifteenth began to move away from the Somme on July 20th and before the end of the month were in trenches near Arras. The weather was warm, and the enemy inactive though alert. When in divisional reserve at Duisans early in August, Lieut.-Col. S. H. Pedley, C.B., Royal West Kent Regt., arrived and took command. Casualties during this month only amounted to 7, and the first ten days of September were spent at Izel-les-Hameau training in preparation for the return of the division to the Somme. The Fifteenth arrived at Frevent by train and reached Pommiers Redoubt on September 15th.

Fifteen days later the battalion arrived at Pommiers Redoubt on their way out of battle. They went by bus to Ribemont and after a few days' rest got on the move again, eventually reaching Béthune on October 11th. On the 14th the Durhams took over the line on the extreme left of the Cambrin sector. The German trench mortars were very active and 2nd Lieut. F. W. Good was wounded during this tour. When not in the front line the battalion now occupied keeps in the support line or were in reserve at Annequin. As the weather got worse the enemy became less aggressive, but two attempts in November, led by Lieut. V. A. V. Jessel, failed to procure an identification. In another expedition 2nd Lieut. R. Cudworth was wounded by a bomb while cutting the German wire.

Before the end of November the Fifteenth went back to billets at Béthune, and here Colonel Pedley presented to the battalion a banner of white silk backed with green. On the front was a green cross, with the legend " Saint Cuthbert of Durham." The colonel related

115

The Durham Forces in the Field

how in the days of Edward III the Queen had a banner made from an old silk relic of Saint Cuthbert in Durham Cathedral. This banner, borne by the men of Durham, rendered them ever-victorious against the Scots, and Colonel Pedley hoped the new flag would prove as full of virtue to his men in their struggle with the Teuton. This ceremony took place on December 6th and next day the Fifteenth moved to the Nœux-les-Mines area, where working parties were supplied until they went into the line in the Hulluch sector. Here there was every indication of a German attack, but Christmas passed with nothing worse than a gas bombardment of Annequin on December 27th. The Fifteenth now withdrew to Nœux-les-Mines, and in fine frosty weather nearly the whole of January was devoted to training and recreation. Before the battalion went into the trenches again, Colonel Pedley, appointed G.O.C. 3fth Brigade, was succeeded by Major N. R. Daniell, D.C.L.I. and Major J. Falvey-Beyts became second in command, replacing Major R. B. Johnson, who left to command a technical unit.

On February 12th the Fifteenth relieved the Fourteenth in the "Village" line and took over front trenches six days later. The thaw had worked great havoc and it was often necessary to take to the open ground with consequent casualties from the fire of the German snipers. The battalion reached Béthune on their way out of this sector on March 6th, and le Souich was reached on the 13th. Training was carried out here and Colonel Daniell, who left to command the 9th K.O.Y.L.I., was succeeded by Major Falvey-Beyts. Attack practice in preparation for the Spring offensive continued after the Fifteenth moved to Pommera. They arrived at Hendecourt on March 28th.

Leaving Louvencourt on July 7th the Eighteenth were on the move every day until they reached la Perrière in the area of the First Army. A week later they took the road again, and training was continued at la Fosse. On July 27th the battalion went into the line near Neuve Chapelle. That same night the

Trench Warfare, July, 1916—Mar., 1917

Germans fiercely bombarded the whole brigade front. Huge gaps were blown in the breastwork, communication trenches were practically destroyed and all telephone wires were cut. An hour later Germans entered B company's lines but, after a struggle lasting five minutes, Capt. Ince's men drove them out. Corpl. N. R. Pinkney, who shot three of the enemy with his revolver, won the Distinguished Conduct Medal in this affair. Meanwhile Lance-Sergt. F. G. Allison, who was on the extreme left of C company's front, enfiladed with his Lewis gun a party of about 50 Germans as they climbed the parapet. Most of these fell, killed or wounded, and the few who got into the trench were soon driven off. On the right A company had not suffered so much from the bombardment and, when the German barrage lifted, their Lewis gun fire easily checked the enemy advance. The only prisoner taken was discovered by D company in the ruins of Neuve Chapelle. It was estimated that quite 200 Germans were killed or wounded, while the losses of the Eighteenth from shell fire amounted to 79. At this time the British artillery was severely rationed as regards ammunition, but the support of the guns during the raid was admirable.

For the rest of the tour the Eighteenth worked hard repairing damages, and were able to do so without much interference from the enemy. When the battalion withdrew to la Fosse on August 4th, Colonel Bowes took leave of the Eighteenth and returned to England, being succeeded in the command by Lieut.-Col. R. E. Cheyne, 29th Lancers (Indian Army). The next turn in the line was in front of Festhubert, where the Eighteenth found that the breastworks had fallen into decay and could only be manned at intervals. The salient called Pope's Nose in the German line was the centre of strife in an otherwise quiet sector. During September the Eighteenth had one tour at Neuve Chapelle again in wet, cold weather. On the 21st the battalion took over the front at Givenchy, just north of the la Bassée canal, a centre of mining activity. Many men worked with the tunnellers here.

Capt. J. B. Hughes-Games was wounded while out

with a wiring party on October 1st. On the 5th the Durhams departed, spending one night in Béthune on their way to la Perrière. Orville, in the Reserve Army area, was reached on October 9th and training was carried on till the battalion started for the line again on the 17th. Four days later the Eighteenth arrived at the shattered village of Sailly-au-Bois, and took over support positions there. After five days of hard work, carrying, wiring and digging under heavy fire, the Durhams occupied the line near Hébuterne and found the trenches thick with slime. Heavy artillery fire had to be endured, but patrols found no signs of the enemy who never ventured into the expanse of water-logged shell-holes called "No Man's Land." At the end of the month the Eighteenth went back to billets at Rossignol Farm. Big working parties were provided while here and a detachment began training for a raid. On November 13th, when the 92nd Brigade took, but could not hold, the German trenches south of Serre, the Eighteenth provided a party to assist in putting out a smoke screen; but the battalion were not engaged and suffered no casualties.

At this time no place on the Western Front was worse than the Hébuterne sector. All roads to the trenches led through the village, which was kept by the Germans under almost ceaseless fire; the weather could not have been worse and the troops lived and worked under the most miserable conditions imaginable. Small wonder that the Eighteenth, in common with other units, evacuated many sick men.

By December 16th the Durhams were nearly ready to make their raid. When the British guns were bombarding the Gommecourt salient on that date, the German retaliation killed Capt. D. S. Phorson and 2nd Lieut. R. G. C. Busby, and slightly wounded 2nd Lieut. G. H. Lean. The raiders went over on the 19th, found the salient deserted and very much damaged by the British gun fire, and returned with a few men slightly wounded. Two days later the Eighteenth withdrew to rest at Famechon, where Christmas was spent.

Lance-Corpl. Lawson and Pte. Nesbitt both received the Military Medal for their gallant conduct during the

Trench Warfare, July, 1916—Mar., 1917

raid and in the New Year's Honours was announced the award of the Military Cross to Major W. D. Lowe and Capt. J. B. Hughes-Games.

The Eighteenth had another tour in the line—where they found the trenches worse than ever- before going back for rest and training, first at Frohen-le-Petit and Outrebois, west of Doullens, and then at Thievres and Marieux. On January 22nd the Durhams moved to Heuzecourt, where training and recreation continued in bright, frosty weather. It was nearly a month later when they came back into support positions in the Hébuterne sector. The enemy was known to be retiring, and when the Eighteenth occupied front trenches on February 25th fires were seen behind his line.

Early next morning six platoons, under 2nd Lieuts. Keith and Lean, were ordered to occupy the German first and second line trenches near Nameless Farm, but the enemy was shelling these positions and the advance was held up by his barrage in " No Man's Land." Meanwhile Lance-Corpl. Rigg and Pte. Lawer paid an unofficial visit to the Gommecourt salient, which they penetrated as far as the light railway, seeing no Germans. The British barrage prevented further progress, so they returned with their report.

In the afternoon an advance was made along the sunken road and by midnight positions were taken up as ordered. Further ground was gained by daylight of the 27th and at 5.15 p.m. two platoons, led by 2nd Lieuts. C. G. Findlay and J. H. Ruby, entered Gommecourt and established posts which were handed over next morning to the troops on the left of the 31st Division. Moltke Graben was occupied later and in the evening of the 28th patrols found that the Germans held First Garde Stellung in strength. At 6 a.m. on March 1st, 2nd Lieut. McConnell reported that he had attacked up Rom Graben—a water-logged communication trench—with one platoon, but could make very little progress. Attacks up Lehmann and Becker Grabens—both wide, shallow trenches much damaged by shell fire—also failed. As the Stokes guns were clogged with mud it was obvious that more artillery preparation was needed. During the afternoon patrols

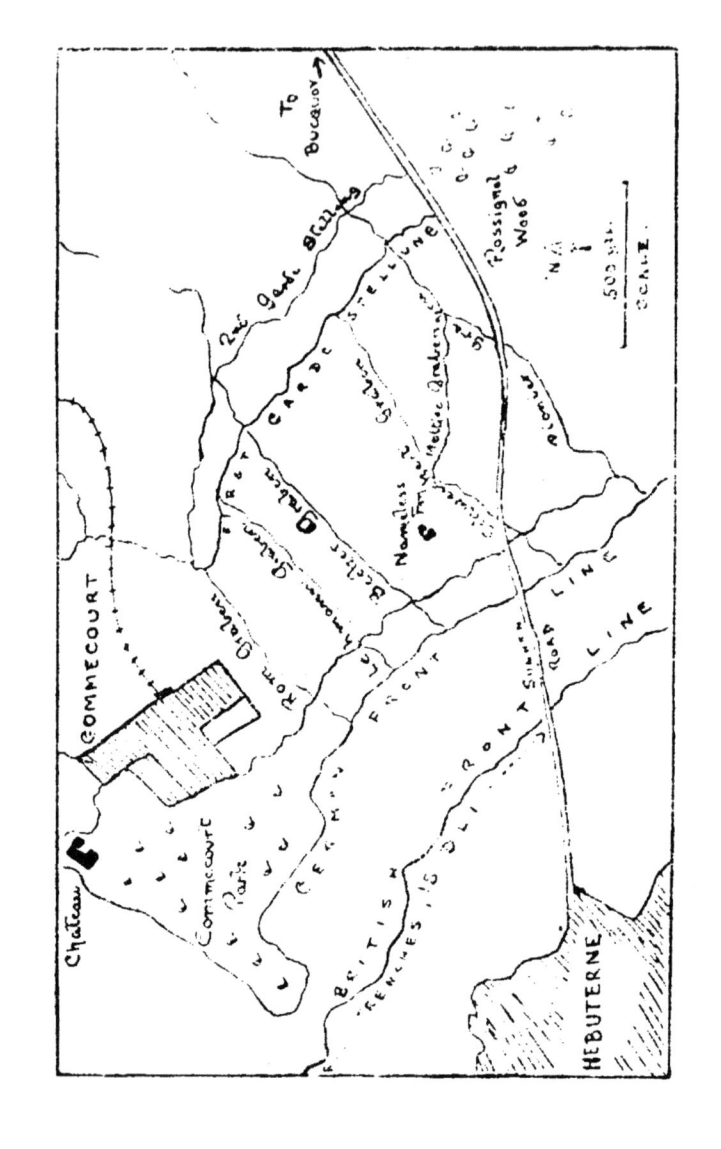

Trench Warfare, July, 1916—Mar., 1917

kept contact with the enemy and all next day the British guns cut the German wire in front of First Garde Stellung. At night repairing parties were reported to be busy and Corpl. Rigg found that between Becker and Lehmann the wire was undamaged. At 6 A.M. on March 3rd 2nd Lieut. H. E. Hitchin, M.M., led bombing attack up Pionier Graben, but although he did some damage a strong block with thick wire checked the advance. At 7.25 A.M. a platoon under Sergt. Reay worked up Lehmann and got a footing in First Garde Stellung, bombing right and left. Another attack was made up Becker and succeeded in joining hands with Sergt. Reay's men who were in touch with the troops on the left. During the afternoon repeated attempts were made to work south-east along First Garde Stellung, up Schweickert, which was full of water, and up Pionier Graben; but the wire and barricades were very strong, and defeated every assault. Our posts were then withdrawn while the heavies and mortars carried out a forty minutes' bombardment. This ceased at 5.10 P.M., when 2nd Lieuts. Hitchin and J. B. Bradford rushed the whole position and bombed the dug-outs. None of the garrison escaped and 25 Germans and two machine-guns were taken. A counter-attack from Second Garde Stellung followed but was easily repulsed and at night the Eighteenth withdrew on relief to Rossignol Farm. Casualties amounted to 15 killed, 28 wounded, and 3 missing. The battalion received the congratulations of the First Army commander and the Distinguished Service Order was conferred upon 2nd Lieut. F. E. Hitchen, M.M. 2nd Lieut. J. B. Bradford received the Military Cross and the Military Medal was awarded to Lance-Corpls. T. Rigg, F. W. Lawer, Laskey, Hutchinson and Fraser and to Pte. Vocknick.

After a rest the Eighteenth worked for several days on the broad-gauge railway from Colincamps to Serre across the old battle-ground of July 1st, 1916. They moved away on March 18th, and arrived in Béthune a week later. Here the Durhams stayed, attached to the 66th Division for defence purposes, until April 12th, when they came south again to work on the Arras-

The Durham Forces in the Field

Bailleul light railway in fine but cold weather. Their camp was near St. Nicholas, a northern suburb of Arras.

The Nineteenth left the Somme battle late in August, and were constantly on the move until the 106th Brigade went into the trenches at Arras on September 3rd. The battalion, now commanded by Lieut.-Col. B. C. Dent, remained in this sector till the end of November. After a discharge of gas on the night of October 8th, two raiding parties of the Nineteenth attempted to enter the German trenches, but the enemy was alert and his wire was not properly cut. 2nd Lieut. F. G. Smith was mortally wounded in this affair.

On November 26th the Germans blew a mine in the early morning, and then entered a crater in the battalion line. Before they were forced to withdraw Lieut. J. Mundy was fatally wounded and several men and 2nd Lieut. Harding were also hit. The Durhams were making a raid at about the same time, but the British barrage was short and fell among the men as they approached the German wire. Nevertheless the enemy trench was entered and several dug-outs were bombed before the party withdrew with the loss of 2nd Lieut. Welbourne wounded and 2 men killed.

On December 2nd the Nineteenth moved out of the Arras trenches but stayed in the city till the 29th, supplying workers for the tunnellers who were busy clearing the vaults and underground passages of the city. These were to be utilised in assembling for the big offensive in the Spring. Major W. B. Greenwell, from the 1st Durham Light Infantry, joined the battalion here. During the month the infantry of the division were all medically examined and, as a result, the authorities abolished the " Bantam " standard. The whole of January, 1917, was spent by the Nineteenth at Maisnil St. Pol, whence unfit men were sent away and replaced by new-comers of ordinary height. Thus the Nineteenth, in common with all the battalions of the 35th Division, ceased to be " Bantams." The original recruits had been men of wonderful physique despite their lack of inches—it was not uncommon to

Trench Warfare, July, 1916—Mar., 1917

find a man 5 feet in height with a chest measurement of 60 inches—but during the service of the division in France the ranks had been replenished by drafts containing a large proportion of striplings and men who were medically unfit. The new men now received were fine material and a divisional training battalion was formed to get the drafts fit for service as soon as possible. Colonel Dent commanded and Lieut. Jackson of the Nineteenth became quartermaster of this unit.

On February 7th the Nineteenth moved again and arrived at Vignacourt for training on the 9th. During these marches in frosty weather the little men still with the battalion were on their mettle and nothing could persuade them to fall out. After ten days' training at Vignacourt, the Nineteenth—now a splendid fighting unit—came south by train to Marceleave. The 35th Division were relieving the French in the Lihons sector south of the Somme river and the Durhams came into a support position on February 26th. The trenches were poor and very muddy and the enemy was known to be on the point of retiring; but when the Nineteenth took over the line the relief was interrupted by heavy shell fire. In the front trenches movement was almost impossible owing to the mud which prevented two attempts of another battalion to carry up trench boots to the Durhams. The sharp frosts caused trench foot and when the tour was finished fully 80 per cent. of D company, who had had the worst position to hold, were unable to march back to billets. They were conveyed by motor ambulances and the battalion limbers. This company were personally congratulated on their endurance by the divisional commander and Sergt. W. Wilson received the Distinguished Conduct Medal for his work during this tour in the line.

After the battalion moved back to Rosières, on March 6th, the last draft of the unfit went away. Working parties were now in great demand until the line was taken over again. When the Germans retreated on this front the 106th Brigade were in divisional reserve and the Nineteenth, following up the advance, occupied the old British front line near Chilly on

The Durham Forces in the Field

March 18th. Next day they moved forward over the railway track to Halhi for work on the roads, while Colonel Greenwell and his officers studied the German defensive system. The weather was still very bad when, on March 29th, the work was continued from Morchain.

During March the divisional training battalion was disbanded, but Colonel Dent went to the 16th Cheshire Regt., Lieut.-Col. W. B. Greenwell being confirmed in the command of the Nineteenth. The spirit and efficiency of the reconstituted battalion already owed much to him.

In July B company of the Twentieth, under Capt. D. E. Jessop, commenced to train for a raid. The battalion were still in the sector north of the river Lys and on July 22nd Colonel Leather was wounded while visiting the wiring parties. Major J. W. Fills, M.P., succeeded to the command.

The raid was to be on a large scale. Barbed wire gates for blocking the German trenches and ladders for scaling the parapet were part of the equipment, while a party of sappers were to carry demolition charges. Many of the men were armed with revolvers and knobkerries. The night chosen was that of July 26th. The raiders were to form up on tapes laid outside the wire, but as they did so a hostile barrage came down, causing heavy losses. Capt. Jessop went forward in the centre and then endeavoured to get in touch with the men on his flanks. He sent back Lieut. Carroll to reorganise and bring forward all the men he could find and, with this reinforcement, approached the German wire which was uncut by our bombardment. Eventually all were ordered to withdraw and did so, bringing the wounded with them. 2nd Lieut. Britton and his party on the left had been more fortunate. They found the wire cut, reached the German parapet, and had begun to bomb the enemy when the signal to withdraw was seen. On the right Sergt. Hanlon and 4 men lost direction when coming back and spent next day in the long grass of "No Man's Land." They got in safely after dark.

As nearly half the total men engaged were killed or

Trench Warfare, July, 1916—Mar., 1917

wounded by the enemy barrage which broke up the assembly, the raid was doomed to failure. 2nd Lieut. R. M. Fulljames was awarded the Military Cross; Lance-Corpls. T. Cummings and W. S. Smith and Pte. F. Lockey received the Military Medal. Losses amounted to 72, including 2nd Lieut. Britton and Capt. Jessop who were both wounded.

On August 16th the 41st Division were relieved, the Twentieth handing over their billets in Armentières to the Thirteenth. The Wearsiders entrained for the south a week later and then carried out battle training at Vaucourt Bussus. On September 6th the move to the Somme battle front commenced.

The Wearside battalion began to move away from the battle area on October 13th. Flanders was the destination of the division and the Twentieth arrived at Godewaersvelde by train on the 20th. After occupying huts at Ontario Camp, near Reninghelst, they took over trenches on October 24th in the sector near St. Eloi which was commanded by the enemy on the Wytschaete-Messines ridge. Here the winter was spent. The Twentieth found bad trenches and weak wire, but by working hard they effected great improvement. Patrols were so active that the enemy rarely ventured into " No Man's Land " and the efforts of the Durham snipers met with such success that German sniping virtually ceased. Many men of the battalion worked with the tunnellers who were busy with preparations underground for the offensive of the following June. On January 1st, 1917, the trench strength of the battalion was only 19 officers and 463 men.

With the New Year came colder weather and more opportunities for patrol work. The British artillery and machine-guns opened with great effect on several occasions when patrols located enemy parties working at night and then indicated the target. Several times during January the German guns and mortars bombarded the trenches of the Twentieth with great violence, but the losses of the battalion for this month were only 20.

Snow fell before February began and the hard

The Durham Forces in the Field

weather continued for several weeks; then a thaw reduced the trenches to filth and chaos. On the night of February 25th there was a patrol encounter in which the enemy fought stoutly and Sergt. Winter, M.M., was mortally wounded after bayonetting one German.

March was a fairly quiet month and the weather improved. There were few casualties, and drafts increased the strength of the battalion who greatly benefited by systematic training when out of the line, special attention being paid to musketry.

The Twenty-Second were on the move from July 3rd until the 8th Division came into the line at Cuinchy, just south of the la Bassée canal. By July 17th the Pioneers were assembled at Annequin, and put in nearly a fortnight's work with the 251st Tunnelling Company. British mining operations were a feature of the activity on this front, but the division harried the enemy in every way and provoked vigorous retaliation in kind. The Pioneers therefore worked under great difficulties. On the night of July 29th a German raiding party surprised a corporal and 3 men in a mine-shaft which they blew up with a mobile charge. Three of the Durhams were killed and one was captured.

On August 5th the battalion withdrew to Noyelles, but work continued on trenches and mine-shafts. On the 20th 3 men were buried by enemy shell fire, but were promptly dug out owing to the action of Lieut. B. B. White. Heavy rains now entailed elaborate draining operations and in September a party spent nearly a fortnight at Vermelles draining the listening galleries south of the Hulluch road. On the 23rd 80 good men joined from the 6th and 9th Durham Light Infantry.

In October the 8th Division were relieved by the 21st, and the Pioneers moved back on the 10th and entrained for the south after a few days' rest. They reached the Citadel camp on October 15th.

Three companies of the battalion reached the Citadel again on November 1st and A company arrived two days later. On the 7th the battalion marched to la

Trench Warfare, July, 1916—Mar., 1917

Briqueterie, near Montauban, a difficult journey over muddy roads congested with transport. The 8th Division were now going into the line before le Transloy, and the Twenty-Second started a period of strenuous work on the desolate battle grounds, across which communications had to be made good. Three companies worked on a new communication trench from Ginchy to the front line, while D company laid duckboards up to Flank Trench, so well known to the Eleventh. On the 10th the battalion lost 6 killed and 19 wounded by shell fire. A barrage of gas shells cut off the Pioneers from the forward end of their task next day, for the gas helmets of most of the men had become saturated with the wet and were of no use.

The division now went out to rest, but the services of the Pioneers were claimed by the Chief Engineer of the Corps and work was done on corduroy roads from Ginchy to Lesbœufs and Ginchy to Flers. The battalion also made fascines at Caftet Wood, near Carnoy, and filled in the pipe line from the remains of that village towards Maricourt. At last, on November 29th, the battalion left to join the 8th Division, doing most of the journey to Fornoy in buses. During the month casualties had totalled 46 killed and wounded.

Training was carried on during most of December and reinforcements of 226, not all fully trained, arrived. When the battalion moved up on December 26th, Major Davidson, Lieut. Cooke, C.-S.-M. Woods and C.-Q.-M.-S. Foles were left behind to form the staff of a new Works Battalion. The Twenty-Second reached camp at Bray, only to move on December 27th to another pioneer camp where accommodation was insufficient. The line taken over by the 8th Division was beyond Rancourt and faced the wood of St. Pierre Vaast. Work was commenced at once on communication trenches, but at the end of the month it was decided to do no new digging while the mud lasted. The front was to be held by "island" posts which could be connected when the ground was drier. The Pioneers soon had twenty of these posts under construction, though material was hard to obtain and progress suffered accordingly. On January 9th the

The Durham Forces in the Field

German gunners scored two direct hits on one "island," killing 3 men and wounding another, while one of the burying party was also killed. On the following day the Twenty-Second moved back to French billets at Chipilly, on the Somme. The camps here were so inaccessible by reason of the mud that the whole battalion had to work on moving some of the lines nearer the road, after draining the new ground. On January 22nd the Pioneers moved to Maurepas Ravine where shelters were fairly good. Work now commenced upon two main communication trenches, called Agile and Abode Avenues, going forward to the 8th Division line which ran roughly from north to south between Bouchavesnes and Moislains. Hard frost made progress slow and difficult and the trenches, owing to insufficient material, were not properly revetted and could not be expected to stand a thaw.

2nd Lieut. C. R. Burnett was wounded on February 6th. As the month went on the whole battalion gradually moved forward to Marrières Wood, about a mile behind Bouchavesnes. All work was in preparation for a projected attack but the thaw made matters difficult. Infantry carrying parties, bringing material for dug-outs, were delayed by the mud and by the traffic in the trenches and sometimes did not arrive.

The 8th Division were to attack the German positions east and north-east of Bouchavesnes, with the object of driving the enemy from the ground which gave observation of Bouchavesnes valley and the valley running north-west to Rancourt. A and C companies of the Twenty-Second were attached to the 24th Brigade on the left, and B and D companies to the 25th upon the right. As usual the task of the Pioneers was to dig communication trenches across "No Man's Land" when the infantry had entered the enemy line. The operations had been delayed first by the frost and then by the thaw; but now communications were fairly good, though Agile Avenue was only passable as far as the brigade headquarters at Aldershot and the dug-outs in the support line were unfinished.

At 5.15 A.M. on March 4th the infantry attacked. A company of the Twenty-Second were brought up and

Trench Warfare, July, 1916—Mar., 1917

started work by 8.10 a.m., the exact site of the trench having been decided on previously by Capt. G. P. Baines after personal reconnaissance. The hostile shell fire, feeble at first, grew in volume towards mid-day and at 2 p.m. was almost a barrage. But A company had now dug a sinuous trench about 210 yards long to a depth of 5 feet. This connected the junction of Pallas

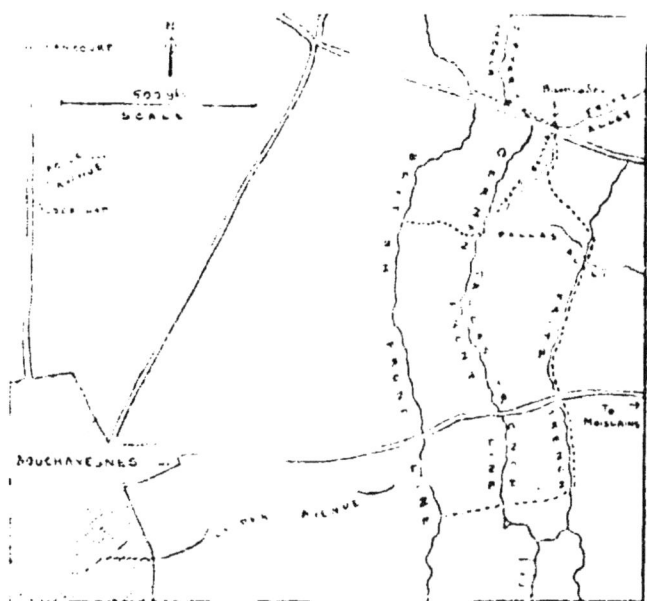

Trench and Pallas Alley with our old front line. The company withdrew soon after, but were engaged next day in assisting the 25th Brigade to consolidate the captured positions. A large quantity of wire and screw pickets were carried up, but work on Fritz Trench, which had been much damaged by the British shell fire, was impossible by day so all hands concentrated upon deepening Pallas Alley.

C company, under Capt. B. B. White, came forward

The Durham Forces in the Field

on the evening of the 5th, and met heavy shell fire before reaching the old British front line. 2nd Lieut. A. J. Allcock went forward and located the site of the task, though he was sniped at and his orderly was wounded in the leg. The company crawled out into the former "No Man's Land" under the German bombardment and reached a point on the extreme left flank of the attack. This was correctly gauged by means of a compass bearing; any deviation further left would have brought them to Jupiter Trench, still occupied by the enemy. The new communication trench, 150 yards in length, was dug 4 feet 6 inches deep but an attempt to wire it had to be abandoned as the night was not dark enough. On the two following nights the company dug a new trench, 150 yards long and 5 feet 6 inches deep with fire bays at short intervals, connecting Pallas Alley and Pallas Support. A part of the new front line which had been flattened by shell fire was re-dug and bombing barricades were erected in Fritz Alley and at the end of Jupiter Trench.

Capt. A. H. Robson, with Lance-Sergt. A. L. Stephenson and a runner, went forward early to tape out the communication trench on the right flank which was to be dug by B company. They accomplished this with great difficulty under the German barrage by crawling from point to point, taking advantage of every convenient shell-hole. There was considerable machine-gun fire and sniping from the right, so the company had to come forward in small parties and dig lying down. A small post was established 200 yards forward and about half that distance from the enemy line on the dangerous flank. At 6.30 p.m., when D company took over the task, the trench was 220 yards long, half of it 5 feet 6 inches deep and the rest 4 feet 5 inches deep. D company, under Capt. J. J. Everatt, worked steadily through the night, and got down to a uniform depth of six feet under occasional heavy shell fire which caused some casualties. On the next night the company went out again to wire the trench and put down trench boards, but the S.O.S. signal involved "standing to" and little work could be done.

The losses of the Twenty-Second were 14 killed and

Trench Warfare, July, 1916—Mar., 1917

28 wounded, including 2nd Lieuts. C. A. B. White and A. G. L. Mullen. Capt. A. F. Robson was awarded the Military Cross and Sergt. R. Carbutt, Lance-Sergt. A. L. Stephenson and Pte. R. Fopps received the Military Medal.

On the night of March 7th B company had 3 men wounded while digging and wiring the new front line of the 25th Brigade on the right; on the 9th the same company dug a new trench connecting Pallas and Fritz Trenches, D company putting out the wire. There were several casualties and 2nd Lieut. F. J. Summerscales was missing. By March 11th the continuous rain made the ground very difficult to work in and the troops were very tired. A and C companies withdrew to Maurepas Ravine for work behind the line, but C company came up again on the 12th to dig in place of D company who were exhausted. On the 13th 2nd Lieut. F. R. Richmond was killed.

The German retreat had now commenced and by March 19th Moislains was clear of the enemy. A newly dug grave there was found to contain the body of Lieut. Summerscales.

Three companies of the Twenty-Second, reinforced by two infantry battalions and the personnel of two trench mortar batteries, now fell to work on the repair of the roads. The Pioneers moved forward as the craters were filled in. On March 26th A and C companies were near Haut Allaines, and B and D in Vaux Wood, north of Moislains. All energies were now concentrated on the Haut Allaines-Aizecourt and the Moislains-Manancourt roads, but progress was slow as there was little transport available for bringing up material.

THE BATTLE OF ARRAS, 1917

THE opening of the Arras offensive meant, for the Tenth and Fifteenth, an attack upon the Hindenburg Line. The enemy had been working upon this elaborate system of field fortifications throughout the winter and his engineers had built into it the lessons learned upon the Somme. Yet the British guns blasted a way through the thick belts of wire and blew up the shelters and emplacements constructed of concrete and steel, so that on April 9th a wide extent of the Hindenburg Line was carried by the infantry without undue loss—as losses were reckoned in those days. Prominent among the successful battalions in this first advance was the premier Service Battalion of Durham.

The Tenth arrived at Dainville, a south-western suburb of Arras, on March 23rd and, after a plan of the German trenches had been carefully dug one foot deep, practice for the attack was carried out daily. Our aircraft were already engaged in their gallant and successful struggle for supremacy and the volume of our artillery fire steadily increased. On April 5th the battalion moved into the caves at Ronville, on the southern outskirts of the city. The front line had been pushed forward past Beaurains as the enemy retreated and assembly trenches were now dug beyond. These were occupied on the night before the attack, 2nd Lients. A. G. Bell, M.C., and P. Braidford going out to reconnoitre the enemy wire. The weather was wet and the ground very muddy.

At 7.34 A.M. on April 9th the Tenth advanced south of Telegraph Hill in four waves. "Moppers up," provided by the D.C.L.I., followed the leading line which went forward in perfect order and was obliged to halt before Nice Trench—the outer edge of the Hindenburg system—until the creeping barrage lifted. Here rifle and machine-gun fire caused some casualties,

The Battle of Arras, 1917

including 4 officers, but most of the Germans were in no condition to resist and the trench was soon taken. The enemy counter-barrage had been feeble and was now directed principally upon Telegraph Hill where several British tanks could be seen sitting upon the ruins of a German redoubt. Battalion headquarters reached Nice Trench about 8 A.M., but the commanding officer followed the advance which, without much lighting, had now reached the Ark on the eastern edge of the Hindenburg trench system. The defences were difficult to recognise from the map, for the British guns had played terrible havoc and most of the Germans encountered were thoroughly cowed by the bombardment and glad to surrender. The prisoners were turned into stretcher-bearers, while the victors helped themselves to the cigars and really excellent sausage found in the dug-outs which had escaped destruction. Machine-gun fire came from Telegraph Hill Trench further to the south, but when this had been dealt with the Tenth were able to reorganise in comparative quiet. Two companies held the front line and two were in support. Soon afterwards cavalry appeared, asked about the situation and sent out patrols; but they could make little headway against uncut wire and German machine-guns and, as they offered a splendid target to the enemy gunners, the Tenth were not sorry to see them withdraw.

About two hours after the Ark was taken another battalion came through to carry on the advance, but met with no success. Snow fell in the afternoon and a cold and wretched night was spent. On this day the Tenth captured four machine-guns, a sniper's rifle and telescope, and many Germans of the 162nd, 163rd and 31st Regts. Losses amounted to 5 officers and 112 men.

At half-past ten next morning came orders to attack the Wancourt Line at noon. The commanding officer managed to secure a concession of twenty-five minutes, which gave time for the Tenth to get close up to the barrage before it lifted. The Durhams started from their trenches at 11.50 A.M., the right of the battalion marching on Wancourt Tower, seen on the high ground

The Durham Forces in the Field

south of the Cojeul river. The advance was along the north slope of a broad valley and was enfiladed by enemy machine-guns, which may explain why the battalion on the right of the Tenth edged northward, so that the two units arrived intermingled before the wire which had been little damaged. As gaps were discovered groups of men forced their way in. The front trench was not held in strength but the support line, though much battered, contained many Germans. One party put up their hands in token of surrender and then shot a Durham sergeant who went towards them. This treachery was suitably punished and all resistance soon ceased.

The Tenth were now established in the Wancourt Line at a cost of over 100 casualties, including 2nd Lieut. Bell, V.C., mortally wounded while on the way to the rear with a message. He was a gallant youngster who had twice been recommended for the award of the Distinguished Service Order during his six months in France. 2nd Lieut. P. Braidford, who received the Military Cross, was among the wounded though he remained with the battalion until they left the line. Colonel Morant described these two young officers and Sergts. Cordon and Todd as " the heroes of the attack."

Further to the south the Germans were still holding the Wancourt Line, but in the evening the 41st Brigade came in and the Tenth withdrew in falling snow. At the old German trenches east of Beaurains another miserable night was spent; then the battalion were relieved by the 9th Durham Light Infantry and marched off through a blizzard on their way to recuperate at Sus St. Leger.

When, at the end of March, 1917, the 21st Division took over the front south of Boiry-Becquerelle, the British line was still pushing forward after the retreating enemy. On April 1st the Fifteenth moved up from Fendecourt through showers of snow and two days later came into the outpost line as centre battalion of the 64th Brigade between the northern outskirts of Croisilles and Henin-sur-Cojeul. In the offensive of

The Battle of Arras, 1917

April 9th the brigade were to form the extreme right where, although a great gain of ground was not vital, it was essential that the enemy be closely engaged. Opposite, on the high ground south-east of Martin-sur-Cojeul, ran the Hindenburg Line.

On April 5th the Fifteenth lost Lieut. V. A. V. Jessel, killed on patrol. Assembly trenches were commenced on the following day and all was ready by April 8th. The Durhams had the East Yorkshiremen on their right; on their left the 9th K.O.Y.L.I. had to advance from a sunken road further back and consequently it was not easy to keep in touch on this flank.

The battle of Arras opened in the early morning of April 9th, but the 64th Brigade did not attack until about four o'clock in the afternoon. C company on the right and D company on the left led the advance of the Fifteenth. One thousand yards away, near the top of a gentle slope, was the double belt of wire in front of the German line, but there were folds in the ground which in some places gave cover to the attackers from enemy fire and view. The feeble German barrage neither affected the perfect order and steadiness of the advance nor caused many casualties. B and A companies, who followed in support, halted in a sunken road where they waited till the red flares showed that the first German trench was taken. The leading companies had little difficulty in making themselves masters of this trench and C company at once joined hands with the East Yorkshires upon the right. But D company found Germans still on their left where machine-gun fire prevented the advance of the 9th K.O.Y.L.I. The company commander, 2nd Lieut. K. H. Saunders, promptly led a bombing attack and took 300 yards of the trench; but shortage of bombs then compelled a withdrawal, leaving the hostile machine-guns still active. This gallant officer, who had five wounds before he consented to relinquish his command, received the Military Cross.

B and C companies had now arrived, but in passing through the gaps in the German wire they had been caught by a very heavy barrage and some disorganisation was the result. Ordered to attack the German second line, these companies found the captured first trench wide and difficult to cross. While reorganising his men Capt. Cartman, M.C., learned that the 1st East Yorkshires on the right were not going on; moreover the battalion on the left had not yet succeeded in taking their first trench. A patrol, under 2nd Lieut. E. W. Williams, had gone out to reconnoitre the enemy second line; the officer was wounded, and the few men who got back reported three strong belts of wire uncut by our artillery and strong enfilade machine-gun fire from the left. Capt. Cartman accordingly reported to Colonel Falvey-Beyts that further advance was impossible without fresh artillery preparation.

The work of consolidating the captured trench went steadily on. Enemy bombers made a decided inroad upon the left flank and Capt. S. D. Thorpe, now in command of the front line, had a strong point constructed to meet this danger, the Fifteenth thus anticipating an order from the brigade.

Three platoons of the battalion in reserve were pushed up as reinforcements, but, as Capt. Thorpe now reported his line too thickly manned, some men were withdrawn to shell-holes in the enemy wire where they could provide support against a counter-attack. At the same time a communication trench, to connect the strong point with the sunken road, was put in hand. Thus passed the night.

At 5 A.M. next day came another bombing attack down the trench from the left. This was only repulsed after a fierce fight lasting for an hour and a half. In the afternoon an air report that the trench to the left was unoccupied was investigated by 2nd Lieut. Davies and a party of bombers, but they had not advanced 50 yards before they encountered the enemy in great strength and were forced to fall back. About a quarter of an hour later came another counter-attack from the left and after a struggle lasting twenty minutes the Germans were repulsed.

At 7.15 P.M. bombing was heard on the right and the East Yorkshires were seen retiring to the sunken road. Capt. Thorpe made an effort to resist this enemy

The Battle of Arras, 1917

attack, which threatened to overwhelm the isolated Fifteenth, but it was a hopeless task and the battalion had to give up the trench they had won.

The commanding officer was making preparations for another advance, sending forward all the men he could collect with supplies of bombs and ammunition, when the brigade cancelled further operations and directed the Fifteenth to withdraw to the second line of assembly trenches. They came back 211 strong, though others arrived later. The spirit of the men was as high as ever, but the troops in the battle front were about to be relieved and the Durhams moved back beyond the Arras-Bapaume road to Boisleux-St. Marc. Losses in the ranks amounted to 241. Of the officers 2nd Lieut. R. Weir was killed and 2nd Lieuts. A. H. Saunders, H. S. Vinycomb, D. B. Consar, I. Humphreys, V. G. Davies, R. N. Nicholson and E. W. Williams were wounded. Capt. Thorpe received the Military Cross and the following were recommended for the award of the Military Medal: Sergts. J. Blake (missing), J. Laydon and J. Robinson; Corpl. I. Waddle; Lance-Corpls. I. S. Bell, I. Blades, G. F. Dalton and Osborne; Ptes. I. Murray and I. Spencer. Pte. G. W. Croft, a very gallant man who was killed less than a month afterwards, received the Military Medal and the French *Croix de Guerre*.

Later in the month the Fourteenth were heavily engaged on the extreme left of the battle line, at the northern limit of the Canadian advance during the opening stages of the battle. They came under the orders of the 16th Brigade on April 18th and two days later went into the line south-east of Loos, occupying Netley Trench from the railway on the right to Novel Alley. On the following day the battalion were ordered to complete the capture of Novel Alley and take Nero Trench and the concrete strong point on the railway, where three attacks had already failed.

The British heavies pounded the German positions during the afternoon of April 21st, the advanced troops of the Fourteenth having been withdrawn to enable this to be done with safety. B and C companies were

137

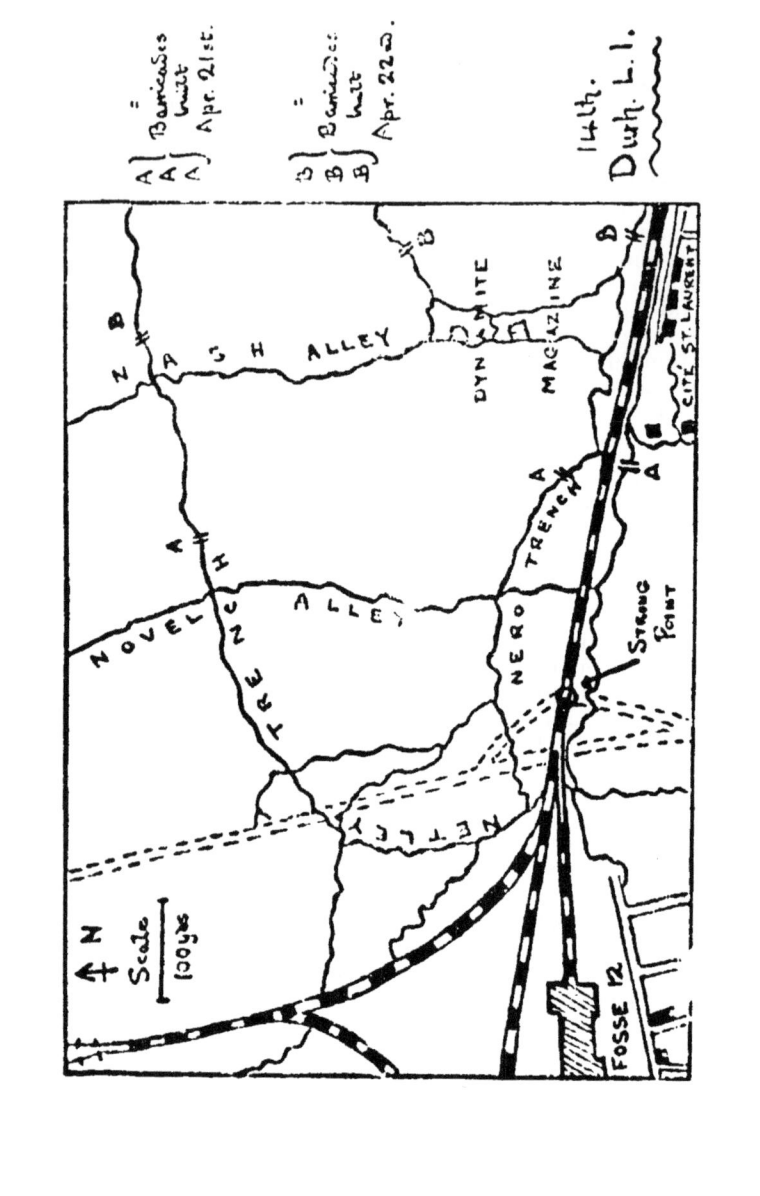

The Battle of Arras, 1917

detailed for the attack. At 5 p.m., supported by rifle-grenade and Lewis gun fire, a platoon under 2nd Lieut. L. W. Mansell advanced up Novel Alley and another, led by 2nd Lieut. W. Severs, attacked up Nero Trench. Meanwhile 2nd Lieut. C. R. Gold had crawled out with 18 men through the ruined houses to deal with the strong point. At zero hour the officer, accompanied by Sergt. W. Simpson, M.M., Corpl. S. Cable, Lance-Corpl. T. Pearson and Pte. H. Colwell, rushed it from the rear before the garrison could get their machine-guns into action. Twenty Germans were killed and 20 taken. 2nd Lieut. Gold then hurried along the railway embankment under heavy fire and called up reinforcements from Nero Trench. The whole attack succeeded, 33 prisoners were taken in all and numbers of wounded Germans were left in the hands of the Durhams. Casualties during the advance were few, but the Fourteenth suffered heavily from enemy shell fire both before and after the fight. Barricades were built in Netley Trench beyond Novel Alley and in Nero Trench and two bombing counter-attacks were repulsed with great loss to the Germans during the night.

At 8 a.m. on the morning of the 22nd, after our heavy artillery had done its best to smash the enemy positions, A and D companies advanced to take Nash Alley and the redoubt called the Dynamite Magazine. This was part of a bigger attack in which the troops on either flank joined. A company were on the right and D on the left, a squad of bombers from B company bombing up the trench south of the railway. Our shrapnel barrage was excellent and, although the enemy fought well, he was unable to get his machine-guns into action before the Fourteenth were upon him. All resistance was soon overcome and the objectives taken. A counter-attack which developed on the left about nine o'clock was repulsed without much difficulty and the Fourteenth proceeded with the task of consolidating the captured positions. The British artillery had laid most of the trenches flat and the Dynamite Magazine now consisted of one dug-out and a heap of earth, so there was little cover from the snipers and machine-guns firing from the houses of the

The Durham Forces in the Field

Cité St. Laurent. Two counter-attacks on the right were driven back and then at 3.45 P.M. the Germans put down a heavy barrage and attacked over the open on the left of the Fourteenth. The troops in this part of Nash Alley were driven out and half an hour later the German infantry assailed the left of the Durham line, while on the right they bombed the barricades. The Fourteenth, though very weak in numbers, maintained the struggle for some time, but had to give ground at last. Fighting hard they fell back slowly to Novel Alley, leaving only 3 badly wounded men in the hands of the enemy.

In the early morning of April 23rd the Fourteenth were relieved, and withdrew to les Brebis. Losses in the ranks amounted to 231 and among the killed was 2nd Lieut. L. W. Manseti. Capts. A. G. de Bunsen and A. E. Owles; Lients. S. Harvey-Smith and J. H. Stearn; 2nd Lieuts. A. Hickford, E. P. Barnett, C. Gillies, I. R. Welsh and C. E. Brogden were all wounded. Many honours fell to the battalion. Lieut. J. H. Stearn rushed a German machine-gun and, though wounded, remained in command of his company until the battalion withdrew; Capt. John Potts also took a machine-gun, which he turned on the enemy and when his company retreated from Nash Alley he covered the withdrawal in person, leaving not a man behind. Both these officers received the Distinguished Service Order, and the same honour was conferred upon 2nd Lieut. C. R. Gold. Pte. J. Collins who, though three times wounded, was among the foremost bombers throughout the two days, received the Distinguished Conduct Medal. Sergts. F. Burgess and G. Maw; Corpl. S. Cable and Lance-Corpl. J. Grayson; Ptes. H. Brook, J. Cawthorne, H. Colwell, J. W. Hall and W. Piper all received the Military Medal. Sergt. W. Simpson, M.M., was awarded a bar to his decoration.

The Fifteenth remained at Boisleux-St. Marc until April 14th and then moved further west to Blaireville, where a huge cave provided a novel bivouac. A draft of 75 arrived on the 17th and the Fifteenth then came

The Battle of Arras, 1917

forward by way of Mercatel and Boiry-Becquerelle to relieve a battalion of the 33rd Division in the captured Hindenburg Line near the scene of the previous fight. Trenches were taken over on April 25th. A quiet time was spent by most of the Fifteenth, but on the 28th four bombing squads were lent to one of the K.O.Y.L.I. battalions who were fighting their way down the Hindenburg Line south-eastwards towards Fontaine-lez-Croisilles. The struggle was very fierce and very little progress could be made against the Germans who fought stoutly behind formidable barricades, one of which was over twelve feet high. No prisoners were taken, though a dead man of the 55th Regt. was found. On the 29th the Germans attacked in their turn without success.

On May 3rd, when the British advance extended over sixteen miles of front, the Fifteenth were ordered to bomb down the Hindenburg system which was still held by the enemy west of Fontaine-lez-Croisilles. The front and support lines, both very wide and strongly defended, were too far apart to make communication and mutual support easy for the attacking troops. The men of the Fifteenth who held the foremost barricades were withdrawn on the evening of May 2nd while, for two hours, the German front positions were shelled by our heavy howitzers. The stormers went forward at 3.50 A.M. next day and encountered a German barrage which caused many casualties. The company attacking on the left down the support trench were held up by strong wire defences and machine-guns soon after four o'clock. The tank which was expected to assist did not arrive till nearly an hour later, when it reached the road running due east into Fontaine and began shooting down the trench. But the enemy concentrated the fire of his trench mortars and crippled it. At about a quarter to six Capt. Thorpe with 8 men stormed the German barricade, but on reaching the trench beyond 7 of the party were killed or wounded by a shell. The stranded tank was now the target for fire of all kinds, which reached our men coming forward behind it.

The company on the right could make little headway

The Durham Forces in the Field

down the front trench owing to heavy losses caused by the German barrage at the beginning of the assault and the stout resistance of the enemy. Colonel Falvey-Beyts now ordered Capt. Thorpe's company, reinforced by the company in support, to attack over the open between the two trenches; but this assault, delivered under heavy fire, failed before a cross trench where the wire defences were very strong. In the front line the fight still swayed to and fro. By mid-day we were holding our own in both trenches, but the long morning's struggle under a hot sun had left the troops very exhausted and in the afternoon the battalion were relieved. 2nd Lieut. C. W. Braildon and 10 others had been killed; Capt. W. Edmenson, Lieut. C. S. Herbert, 2nd Lieuts. E. Lyall, M. H. Grant, W. Bigg and W. I. Curnow and 68 men were wounded; 2nd Lieut. J. H. Baillie and 28 men were missing. May 4th was passed in divisional reserve and on the evening of the 5th, after a thunderstorm had rendered the heat a little less oppressive, the Fifteenth reoccupied their barricades in the Hindenburg trenches. 2nd Lieut. E. A. G. Macdonald was wounded on this day.

No further attack was to be made, but snipers and machine-gunners, both British and German, were active, the distance between our blocks and those of the enemy being about one hundred yards. On the morning of May 6th a movement was seen in a shell-hole not more than 40 yards from the Germans. It was a wounded man waving an empty water-bottle. To send out a stretcher-party while daylight lasted was, of course, impossible; but Pte. Michael Heaviside, stretcher-bearer and veteran of the South African war, a miner from Craghead, at once volunteered to take food and water to the sufferer.

Crawling forward steadily from shell-hole to shell-hole, pausing to rest when the ground offered a little protection, escaping as by a miracle sniper's bullet and machine-gun fire, Heaviside covered the distance unharmed. He found a badly wounded man, who had lain out for several days and nights suffering agonies from thirst, and rendered him such aid as he could. Then, when darkness fell, Heaviside made the return

PRIVATE M. HEAVISIDE, V.C.
15th Durham Light Infantry

The Battle of Arras, 1917

journey and with a stretcher-party went out again and brought the man in.

The cool unselfish courage which finds its expression in rescue or care of the wounded at great personal risk was a marked characteristic of the Durham soldier throughout the war. Pte. Heaviside's deed won for him the Victoria Cross.

During these days casualties were not heavy and on the 8th the Fifteenth were relieved, and went back to tents at Boyelles.

Before the end of April the Eighteenth came into the battle zone further to the north. On the 28th the battalion were attached to the 63rd Division, who had taken Gavrelle a few days previously, and at 11 P.M. that night A company were sent to occupy Hill 80, a commanding mound north of the Gavrelle-Bailleul road. There was heavy hostile shell fire, but casualties were few. In the evening of the following day the 93rd Brigade took over the line which ran round the eastern outskirts of Gavrelle and turned west and then northwards to Oppy and Oppy Wood, both still in German hands. A company rejoined next morning and the Eighteenth, as battalion in reserve, provided carrying parties for the rest of the brigade. The German gunners were still active and many casualties occurred.

On May 1st the Eighteenth withdrew to a position in the Hindenburg Line and at night were employed on preparations for the next attack, collecting ammunition, grenades, R.E. material, iron rations and water at two large forward dumps. Then, after a few days' rest, the Eighteenth came forward again, arriving in trenches west of Gavrelle at 1.30 A.M. on May 3rd. As they did so a hostile barrage came down and, though casualties were not heavy, B company lost some good men before the German fire slackened. The night was mild and there was a bright moon.

At 3.45 A.M. the three West Yorkshire battalions of the brigade went forward to the attack under a barrage. On the right, south of the ruined windmill, the advance was over fairly open ground and was expected to take

The Durham Forces in the Field

quicker progress than the attack further north. At first all went well, but soon after five o'clock the 16th West Yorkshires on the left asked the Eighteenth for reinforcements and B company were moved up. Then came bad news from brigade headquarters; the enemy had taken the mill, whence, if firmly established, he

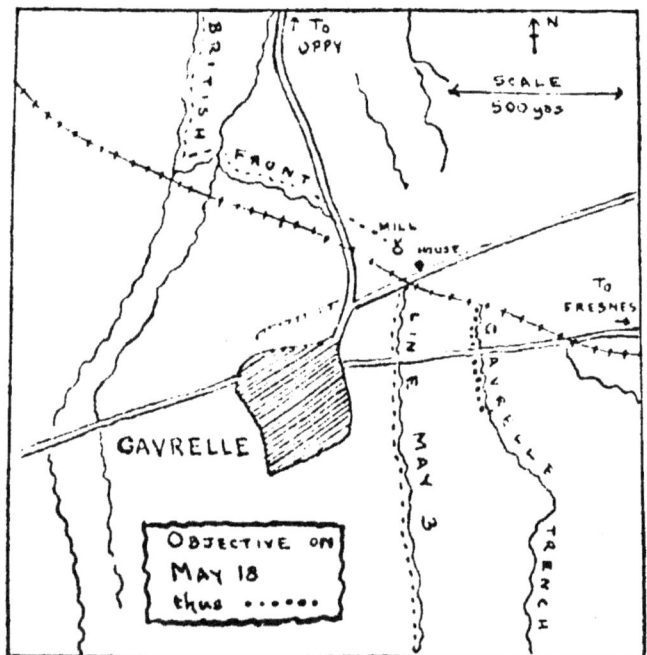

could enfilade the whole British advance. C company, under Capt. Hitchin, D.S.O., were detailed to counter-attack here at once.

Reports from the left were very disquieting. The 92nd Brigade attempt on Oppy Wood appeared to have failed and a German counter-attack was developing upon the left of the 93rd where the 16th West Yorkshires were holding on near the railway. B company

The Battle of Arras, 1917

were now drawn back to the north-west to meet any threat at the left rear of the brigade.

At half-past seven C company were seen approaching the windmill by short rushes, but their first attack appeared to be beaten back.

On the left the situation still caused much anxiety till at about nine o'clock 2nd Lieut. Findlay reported that B company were in position near the railway and that no Germans were visible. There were certainly none behind the line. Soon afterwards 2nd Lieut. Lean arrived, wounded, from C company and said that our own artillery fire prevented the occupation of the windmill. A message was accordingly sent back to the gunners.

Help was now needed by the battalion on the right of the line. Two counter-attacks had been dispersed by our artillery, but the enemy was now massing for a third. Soon after ten o'clock A and D companies moved up to strengthen the front here, though they were only able to get forward by degrees, heavy hostile shelling making movements of formed bodies of men almost impossible. An hour later Lance-Corpl. Taylor brought in a valuable report. Patrolling a trench running north towards Oppy he had located a barricade held by the enemy in force.

A message from Capt. Hitchin reporting that he had taken the windmill was received soon after 1 P.M. C company had started on their mission at half-past five in the morning. A short reconnaissance revealed no sign of the enemy at the windmill, so Capt. Hitchin decided upon a frontal attack in two waves, the house to the south of the mill marking the right flank. Sergt. Elliott, with No. 9 platoon, on the right and Sergt. Cross, with No. 10 platoon, on the left, formed the front wave. 2nd Lieut. Lean followed with No. 11 platoon and Sergt. Carnforth with No. 12 was in reserve. The attack was launched at 6.15 A.M., when a first rush gained the Oppy road. Although flares were sent up by the enemy and shrapnel burst overhead no one was hurt, but the next move drew a hail of machine-gun fire. The railway was reached, but the attackers had to withdraw to the road to reorganise.

115

The Durham Forces in the Field

They tried again and failed. Then Capt. Hitchin led another attempt which carried the advance to within 50 yards of the mill. Here a halt was necessary to prepare for the final assault. The Germans now began to retire and this movement was evidently seen by our artillery observers, for a bombardment by British howitzers followed and drove C company further and further back till they reached the road again, with half their number killed or wounded. Small fighting patrols were now sent in. These started at intervals of half an hour, creeping from shell-hole to shell-hole, till five posts were established, fan-wise, with Lewis guns upon the flanks. The mill was now abandoned by the enemy, but he still held the remains of the house, so Capt. Hitchin employed rifle bombs and before noon these Germans were driven out and the capture of the position was complete. Snipers of C company picked off many the Germans seen both to the north and to the south and later in the day the four Vickers guns and two Stokes mortars, with which the mill had been originally defended, were found and brought in. Communication was established by running a wire back and tapping in on the line of one of the Yorkshire battalions.

At 3 p.m. the troops on the left, including B company of the Eighteenth, began to push out northwards. Two hours later A and D companies were in position east and south-east of Gavrelle under orders of the right battalion.

There was no further attack or counter-attack and, after some vigorous hostile shelling on the morning of the 4th, a fairly quiet day followed. Relieved at night, the Eighteenth moved back to the northern suburbs of Arras. Losses in the ranks amounted to 40 killed, 84 wounded and 9 missing.

After one day's rest the battalion took over the line east of Gavrelle. The weather was wet, but the rain ceased about mid-day on the 8th. Our gunners certainly broke up any counter-attack if such were intended, but morning and evening the enemy shelled the village. Early on the 11th a West Yorkshire battalion relieved the Eighteenth who withdrew into

The Battle of Arras, 1917

reserve. A camp near Ecurie was reached later and here, until May 15th, training for a night attack was carried out.

The same trenches were taken over again on the wet, dark night of May 16th, but before this was accomplished 2nd Lieuts. Welford and Apperley were wounded. The Eighteenth were to capture Gavrelle Trench, an apparently deep and well traversed line which lay astride the Gavrelle-Fresnes road. With this trench in our hands there would be room for a support line in front of Gavrelle and our defence of the village would be made much easier. It was also important to give the enemy the impression that our operations on the Arras front were to be continued.

The fighting strength of the battalion was only 520 and the two strongest companies were chosen for the assault, with two extra platoons to act as carriers. Zero hour was 12.30 a.m. of May 18th and, although it was a night attack, there was no question of surprise. The enemy was very much on the alert and his continuous shower of Very lights revealed the attackers as soon as they left their trenches. There were some casualties in forming up, among them Capt. Dormand, commanding A company, but at the appointed time the troops advanced under a very good barrage. A company were on the right, south of the road, D company north of the road on the left, and each went forward in two waves with Lewis gunners between. The hostile barrage came down thirty yards behind them. A company, when just short of their objective, were greeted with showers of stick-bombs, while the bombing squad told off to enter the German trench on the right seems to have lost direction. But the company commander speedily organised another party who got into the trench and bombed the enemy out of several bays. They killed 12 Germans and sent back one wounded prisoner; but the position was untenable under the showers of enemy bombs and the company withdrew, pursued by machine-gun fire which checked a platoon coming up to reinforce.

Before D company reached the German trench 2nd Lieut. Richardson, the company commander, was

The Durham Forces in the Field

wounded and 2nd Lieut. E. Thompson killed. On the extreme left uncut wire foiled the attackers completely; on the right our artillery had so damaged the trench that the men overran it in the dark. Realising the mistake they came back and entered it, bombing northward and bringing Lewis guns into play overhead as occasion demanded. The Germans counter-attacked vigorously from both flanks and in front, and though fresh supplies of grenades were sent up—more men would have only crowded the trench—no further progress could be made. To hold what had been won was impossible in daylight, so all were withdrawn to the original line.

The result of this operation, which cost the Eighteenth 66 men in killed, wounded and missing, was a great disappointment, but the attack had been carried out at extremely short notice against an enemy in much greater strength than was suspected.

From daylight to dusk on the 18th the Germans shelled Gavrelle and the trenches before the village and our guns were busy in reply. Enemy aeroplanes flew overhead, and it was doubtful whether the enemy anticipated another attack or was preparing one in his turn. At night the Eighteenth handed over the line to a battalion of the 63rd Division and moved back north of Arras to camp in the old " No Man's Land " east of Roclincourt.

The Tenth came back into their part of the field on May 2nd, after spending ten days at Sus St. Leger. On May 3rd the battalion occupied trenches in the Wancourt line near the portion captured on the second day of the battle. Twice on this day the transport camp was shelled and had to be moved. It was not till May 8th that the Tenth moved into the front line, now well beyond Wancourt. On the 10th a man of the battalion crawled out 250 yards and brought in a wounded Rifleman who, for seven days, had kept himself alive by the food and water obtained from the dead around him. The enemy position, on the low ground south of the Cojeul river, was not well defined and patrol encounters were frequent, the Tenth making

The Battle of Arras, 1917

several prisoners. Lieut. Lodge was very active in reconnaissance and brought in many valuable reports.

The battalion moved back to support positions on May 12th and three days later to the vicinity of Beaurains, having lost 70 men killed and wounded, principally by shell fire. 2nd Lieut. J. E. Lucas was among the fallen. The remainder of the month was spent at work upon the improvement of communications, the activity in the air providing some relief from the monotony while on the 30th a violent thunderstorm washed the battalion out of their dug-outs and shelters.

TRENCH WARFARE

APRIL—JUNE, 1917

At the beginning of April the Eleventh were busy repairing the damage wrought by the Germans to the roads in the vicinity of Bus and Ytres. By April 4th all shell-holes and craters in the road between these villages had been filled in and wagons and guns were coming through. On April 15th a delayed action mine exploded and wrecked B company's headquarters at Ytres with a loss of 4 killed and 4 wounded.

The 20th Division had now begun to arrive before the Hindenburg Line which ran beyond Villers-Plouich. At the beginning of May the Pioneers finished their work on the roads and started a communication trench to the new front. The Eleventh were employed on tasks of this description until May 22nd, when they moved out to Bancourt, east of Bapaume, to rest. The 20th Division had given place to the 42nd, but only to relieve in turn the Australians further north. On May 24th the Eleventh relieved the Australian pioneers beyond the Cambrai road and settled down to work in the Noreuil sector. Laying sleepers for the Vaulx-Noreuil railway, making deep dug-outs for the gunners and keeping roads and communication trenches in repair were only some of the tasks of the battalion. On June 2nd Lieut. Wardle was wounded and next day a dump exploded at Vaulx, injuring 13 men of the Eleventh. At Vaulx-Vraucourt the Pioneers were located among the British batteries, but suffered few casualties in spite of the constant German shell fire. The good work performed by the battalion in this sector gained the acknowledgments of the divisional commander.

The Twelfth went to Merekeghem again for training on April 4th, but ten days later they returned to

Trench Warfare, April—June, 1917

Ypres and supplied workers to help the Australian tunnellers in preparing for the coming offensive. Thus only twelve platoons were available to take over the line beyond Zillebeke on April 19th. Although the enemy mortars were active, his artillery left the front line alone for the most part; life in Ypres was more uncomfortable.

When the Durhams were in the line again on April 29th a British aeroplane crashed in "No Man's Land" and the wounded pilot and observer were rescued under fire by a party of whom 2nd Lieut. W. L. Hughes was awarded the Military Cross, Pte. J. G. Gardner the Distinguished Conduct Medal and Pte. Olsen the Military Medal.

On the morning of May 1st the Twelfth arrived in the Steenvoorde to rest and refit, but the 23rd Division were about to occupy their battle front in the vicinity of Hill 60, so that the battalion soon came back again.

By dawn of May 11th the Twelfth were established in badly damaged trenches which only admitted of a line of posts in front, but work on these and on the wire had to be postponed as the whole battalion were required to dig assembly trenches. While the British guns were busy bombarding the enemy positions and cutting his wire the infantry had to toil ceaselessly on their preparations for the coming battle.

The Australians were obliged to blow a small camouflet near Hill 60 on May 17th to prevent the enemy firing a mine and 2nd Lieut. Tuffs and a small party of the Twelfth were held in readiness to occupy the new crater. First came a hurricane bombardment of the front and support lines of the battalion which necessitated a counter-barrage by the British guns; over an hour passed before the expected explosion. No crater was formed and 2nd Lieut. Tuffs led his men on till they encountered the Germans in the old craters further forward. There was a sharp fight with bombs as the Durhams withdrew slowly, but Lieut. Tuffs rallied his men when he reached the British posts and drove the enemy off. The battalion had 6 casualties in this affair and Pte. F. L. Dickinson, who

The Durham Forces in the Field

displayed great gallantry as a messenger, was awarded the Distinguished Conduct Medal.

After a tour which cost them 42 casualties from shell fire the Twelfth withdrew to Montreal Camp and provided large working parties for the R.E. About this time was announced the award of the French *Croix de Guerre* to Capt. E. W. Lafone, and of the Military Medal to Ptes. W. F. Showell, F. G. Smith and I. Dobbs.

From May 27th till the end of the month the battalion were attached to the 69th Brigade and practised the assault over a model of the German trenches in the Steenvoorde training area. On May 31st they came by train to Ypres, under considerable shell fire, and relieved the 9th Yorkshire Regt. in Railway Dug-outs and Zillebeke Bund. The German guns were now very busy, and on June 1st there were 20 casualties from shell fire, but the strife died down during the succeeding days, though gas shells proved annoying to the large working parties which were still required. Capt. T. Carr-Ellison was wounded on the 2nd. On June 4th the Twelfth withdrew to the ramparts at Ypres and the next move was to assembly positions for the battle.

At the beginning of April the Thirteenth went back to Millam for training and took over trenches again, south of the Menin road, on April 15th. The German shell fire was very violent for the remainder of the month. 2nd Lieut. Brady was wounded on the 22nd and when the battalion withdrew from Ypres on the last day of April they left in groups of three under a heavy bombardment.

About one week was spent in billets near Godewaersvelde, and then the Thirteenth went into the line near Hill 60. In the early morning of May 13th there was a fierce German bombardment followed by a raid on the right company of the Durhams, where trenches and wire had been very badly damaged. Major Downey anticipated trouble and had the battalion " standing to " half an hour earlier than usual. The enemy advanced at about 3.45 A.M. and, under

Trench Warfare, April—June, 1917

cover of the smoke and dust of the bombardment, got quite close before he was seen. On the left about 6 Germans got into the trench, but fled on being attacked; in the centre the raiders were seen and dispersed by Lewis gun and rifle fire before they reached the parapet. On the right the Lewis gun had been hit by several shells and was out of action, but the Durhams used their bombs and rifles with good effect and the Germans were driven off with many casualties. A second and stronger wave of the enemy was repulsed by the fire of the Thirteenth when half-way across "No Man's Land." The S.O.S. signal was not made, and the 27 casualties of the battalion— including 2nd Lieut. E. Parr, wounded— were all caused by the bombardment. Before and during the raid the Germans directed a fierce fire upon the left company, evidently to prevent them reinforcing the right.

2nd Lieut. H. C. Buckell, the company commander on the right, visited his whole line during the bombardment, and it was due to his dispositions that the raid was so easily repulsed. He and 2nd Lieut. E. Davis, who ably seconded him, were awarded the Military Cross. C.-S.-M.'s G. A. Woodruff and W. T. Bazeley and Sergt. N. Brough, N.N., showed great gallantry and resource and all received the Distinguished Conduct Medal, while the Military Medal was won by Lance-Sergt. N. Laurie; Corpls. R. McDonnell and J. Kirkus; Lance-Corpls. C. G. Armstrong and A. Harrison; and Ptes. H. Brankston, W. H. Bond and J. Umpleby.

The Thirteenth were relieved on May 14th and spent a few days at Zillebeke Bund, after which they supplied various working parties until they concentrated at Halifax Camp on May 21st. The award of the Distinguished Service Order to Major J. A. L. Downey and of the Military Cross to Capt. L. N. Greenwood appeared in the Birthday Honours.

On June 1st the battalion came into the line at Mount Sorrel. The British bombardment had now opened in earnest and the German reply was vigorous. On the night of June 2nd a party, under Lieut. Heselton and 2nd Lieut. Young, attempted a raid

The Durham Forces in the Field

but the enemy barraged the place of assembly, killing Lieut. Heselton and 11 men and wounding 2nd Lieuts. F. Hall and G. W. Wood and 19 others. There were 20 more casualties from shell fire by the time the battalion were relieved on June 4th. The 69th and 70th Brigades now took up their positions in the line ready for the attack and on the night of June 6th the Thirteenth moved into reserve, south of Zillebeke Lake.

The Fourteenth spent the early days of April working in the " Village " line, and went into the trenches again on the 5th. Three days later, when the 2nd Durham Light Infantry raided the enemy, his retaliation cost the Fourteenth some casualties. On leaving the front line the battalion put a raiding party in training at Mazingarbe, but soon came under the orders of the 16th Brigade and bore their part in the battle of Arras.

When the Fourteenth came back to the 18th Brigade they returned to Mazingarbe, which was reached on April 23rd. They were so weak in numbers that A and B became X company, and C and D W company, as a temporary measure. Thus organised the Durhams relieved the 1st West Yorkshires on April 26th in the trenches north-east of Loos, where the notorious Chalk Pit Wood marked the right of the line. The enemy was quiet during this tour.

At the end of the month a big reinforcement was received and the battalion extended their front southwards. After an interval of training at les Brebis, the Fourteenth took over trenches on the right of the sector and just north of the scene of the April fighting. Hostile shell fire was heavy and seemed to indicate a readjustment of the enemy line. Lieut. A. Rothfield investigated and, as a result of his reconnaissance, the battalion dug a new trench which joined with the 46th Division on the right and shortened the British line by 300 yards. Having lost 4 killed and 2nd Lieut. S. G. Highmoor and 14 wounded during this tour, the Fourteenth were relieved on May 16th and passed into divisional reserve. Before the end of the month they

Trench Warfare, April—June, 1917

came in on the left again under a gas bombardment. The Germans were now very aggressive here and employed aerial darts, gas, trench mortars, shrapnel and high explosive, so that the Fourteenth withdrew on June 3rd with 50 more casualties. Their strength was now less than 500.

The battalion, located at les Brebis, had to carry up trench mortar ammunition—a constant task in this sector—while D company were organised as a raiding company under Captain Moffitt.

The Fifteenth were not free of the Arras battle until they reached Boyelles on May 8th. Nearly all the rest of the month was spent at Bailleulval, near the Arras-Doullens road. Major H. W. Festing arrived on the 14th. The battalion moved up to bivouacs east of Boyelles on the last day of the month and took over front trenches on June 4th. These were situated in the Hindenburg Support Line almost on the scene of the strenuous April fighting.

Little remains to be told of the Eighteenth during this period. The battalion were at Roclincourt from May 22nd to the 27th working on the "Green" Line which ran along the spur behind Bailleul and reached the Arras-Gavrelle road at le Point du Jour. Then they moved west to Marœuil for training, returning on June 3rd to Roclincourt for work on roads.

The Nineteenth, repairing the ravages of the German retreat near Morchain, moved forward on April 3rd across the Somme canal to Quivières and Douvieux. A heavy fall of snow made their work heavier, but by April 8th the battalion were concentrated at Flez for training. The 35th Division now relieved the 61st in the line and the Nineteenth moved up, first to billets at Trefcon and then to trenches north-west of St. Quentin, north of the Omignon river. On April 10th the line was extended to the left, where it linked up with the 59th Division.

The enemy had retreated as far as he intended to go and was covering the re-establishment of his front

The Durham Forces in the Field

by violent shell fire; but when the Durhams commenced their second tour on April 18th the British line had pushed forward north-west of the village of Pontru. Quieter days followed, though 2nd Lieut. J. R. Ozzard was wounded, and the remainder of the month was spent in divisional and brigade reserve.

The Nineteenth took over front line posts with two companies on May 3rd. Two nights later Y and Z companies, under Capt. W. J. Oliver, were detailed to attack the new German line and Les Trois Sauvages Farm which was between Gricourt and the main St. Quentin-Cambrai road. W company were to push forward three posts on the left during the operation. There was no time available for proper reconnaissance. The attack was made in pouring rain and encountered heavy rifle fire, while the shrapnel barrage lagged and wounded some of the Durhams. Then a heavy hostile barrage fell upon the second and third waves of the advance and the German trench mortars opened. The Durhams pressed forward, but Y company, under Capt. C. E. S. Noakes, found the farm strongly held and apparently untouched by our artillery fire. They reached the uncut German wire and engaged the defenders with their rifles at close range. Meanwhile 2nd Lieut. F. Blenkinsop, who led Z company on the right, had fallen, but some of his men had reached the wire in front of the German trenches while others had conformed to the advance of Y company. Losses were heavy all along the line and there was now no hope of success, but the Durhams held on without thought of retreat. Capt. Oliver, coming up with his reserves through the German barrage, gave orders for the withdrawal and this was done slowly and in good order under the covering fire of the Lewis guns. All the wounded who could be found in the darkness were brought in and Sergt. Carver made repeated journeys under fire, rescuing four men single handed.

W company got forward and established their three posts, although that on the right was covered by the German barrage, 2nd Lieut. G. E. Haddon and Corpl. Dibb doing gallant work. Losses in the ranks amounted

Trench Warfare, April—June, 1917

to 58, 2nd Lieut. G. F. Golightly died of his wounds and 2nd Lieut. Gray was severely wounded.

The relief of the battalion came on May 8th, just after W company's posts had been driven in, though not without heavy casualties to the Germans. At Trefcon the Nineteenth carried out training and worked on the roads till the 35th Division moved northwards in the line. The Durhams had marched to Peronne and eventually went into billets at Villers-Guislain behind the new front, which ran across the high ground east of the village into the ravines south-east of Gonnelieu. After a quiet tour in trenches opposite Hennecourt, the battalion withdrew on June 2nd to divisional reserve at Aizecourt-le-Bas, where a bomb accident wounded Capt. C. E. S. Noakes and 2nd Lieut. J. Robertson.

The Twentieth were in the trenches near Hill 60 at the beginning of April. 2nd Lieut. J. A. Ballantyne was wounded during the tour, but casualties were small in spite of the incessant shell fire. On coming out of the line the Wearsiders went back to Eperlecques to practise the attack and consolidation. By April 25th they reached camp near Reninghelst and thenceforward worked hard on preparations for the offensive. Hostile shell fire was a serious embarrassment and at 8.55 p.m. on May 7th every gun in the Second Army began five minutes' intense fire on the German communications. This was repeated at 11 p.m. and thenceforward the enemy was much less aggressive.

On May 12th the Twentieth were back in the old trenches, their last tour before the battle. There were several patrol encounters, and a valuable identification was secured, though the Germans were very watchful and displayed no desire to come to grips. 2nd Lieuts. Carroll and Fletcher distinguished themselves in these affairs.

Capt. A. Pumphrey was awarded the Distinguished Service Order in the Birthday Honours, and Lieut. F. Wayman received the Military Cross. The French Médaille Militaire was conferred on Sergt. E. Priestley, M.M., who was always prominent on patrol. The first

The Durham Forces in the Field

few days of June were spent at Woodcote Camp, near Reninghelst mainly in recreation, for all preparations for the offensive were now complete. On the night of June 5th the Wearsiders began to move up.

The Twenty-Second worked their way forward, repairing the roads as they went. At the beginning of April they were in the vicinity of Moislains; at the end of the month they had reached Heudicourt, Gouzeaucourt and Villers-Guislain. All this was not done without frequent casualties from shell fire, but the work was never delayed on that account. On the night of May 3rd a shell pitched in the midst of 2nd Lieut. C. Fosbrooke's platoon and the survivors were complimented by Colonel Morgan on the courage and coolness they displayed.

A week was spent on new communication trenches before the division left this part of the line. The Pioneers then rested at Vaux Wood, north of Moislains, till May 26th, when they entrained at Peronne for the Ypres front. Bivouacs near Dickebusch were eventually occupied, in the midst of the British batteries. The battalion were now employed in constructing water-troughs in preparation for a pipe line; laying a light railway; and making a corduroy road from Kruisstraat to the Zillebeke road. Hostile shell fire was very heavy on the roads and on the night of May 29th the doctor and stretcher-bearers of the Twenty-Second were busy tending the wounded of an ammunition column. One company was devoted to the making of gun emplacements for the Corps heavies at the beginning of June. On the 3rd gas shells interrupted work on the corduroy road. Three days later the Twenty-Second withdrew to rest at Strazeele.

THE BATTLE OF MESSINES, 1917

THE battle which thrust the Germans from the Messines ridge is unique by reason of the British attack from underground. For nearly two years mining and counter-mining had been in progress on the front of the Second Army, and to assist in this work the skilled labour which the County battalions could provide was much in demand. So many a Durham man had played his part in the preparations for June 7th, when the explosion of no less than nineteen mines killed and wounded large numbers of Germans and destroyed their front trench system.

In the British battle line, stretching from Ploegsteert Wood to Mount Sorrel, the 41st Division occupied a sector between St. Eloi and the Ypres-Comines canal. The 123rd Brigade were on the left, the Twentieth being in support to the other three battalions who were each allotted a platoon of Wearsiders for "mopping up." The task of the Twentieth was to go forward and consolidate the first and second line German trenches, as soon as they had been captured, while the advance continued as far as the Damm Strasse, a road which ran between high banks across most of the front but became a causeway where it traversed the lower ground upon the right.

A trying time was spent by the Twentieth on the night previous to the attack. Another brigade, which was to follow the 123rd, started so early that they blocked the communication trenches and this congestion combined with heavy hostile shelling to delay the battalion and cause many casualties. Eventually the Twentieth moved over the open to the assembly positions already taped out by 2nd Lieut. Shepherdson. The night was fine and not very dark.

At 3.10 A.M. on June 7th the great mine under the craters at St. Eloi exploded with a deafening roar and

The Durham Forces in the Field

ere the shock had passed away the Twentieth pressed forward to the shattered German trenches, escaping by the swiftness of their advance the worst of the hostile barrage which fell behind them. The enemy support line had been almost flattened by the British artillery fire and dead and wounded Germans lay there in great numbers. A few dug-outs were bombed, but there was little opposition to overcome. The prisoners were sent back bearing the British wounded with them and the Durhams were soon digging new trenches and getting out wire. Two platoons who were in reserve received orders to go on and assist in the taking of the Datum Strasse, but news came that a portion of A company, having thrust forward with great zeal into the forefront of the battle, were already there.

An hour after zero the Datum Strasse was captured along the whole brigade front and all the ground gained was soon cleared, while the work of consolidation went on apace. Later in the day the Twentieth sent four Lewis gun teams to assist the troops on the right.

By their bold and skilful leadership in the advance and their good work in directing the consolidation of the captured positions, 2nd Lieuts. W. C. Brown, W. R. Brooke and B. Wilkinson all won the Military Cross. Sergt. W. McPherson, Corpl. W. H. Hare and Ptes. E. Best, J. J. Betteridge, B. Fenwick, J. Harris, L. Kingston, T. H. S. Mathieson, J. Parkin and M. Quinn were awarded the Military Medal. The Twentieth captured a complete searchlight installation, a rocket apparatus, a trench mortar and a quantity of arms and equipment, besides two machine-guns which were used against their late owners with good effect.

The enemy shell fire was, as usual, heavy upon his lost trenches, but did not do much damage to the new lines dug by the Twentieth. Losses at the end of the day amounted to 2nd Lieuts. R. M. Upton and Penrice killed, 2nd Lieut. Kipps wounded, and 102 others killed and wounded.

Consolidation, including the construction of strong points and the putting out of wire, continued on June 8th. The traverses of the new trenches were

The Battle of Messines, 1917

made about 14 feet thick, as the German batteries further north were able to take the position in enfilade.

But it was not till the evening that the hostile shelling became really heavy. Then one of our aeroplanes signalled a German counter-attack and the positions in which the Twentieth were now strongly established received a bombardment from guns of all calibres. Our artillery was very active for an hour and a half and spasmodic bursts of fire continued throughout the night, while our machine-guns swept the German line continually. Losses in the Twentieth during this and the following day only amounted to 8 killed and 13 wounded.

June 10th brought cooler weather and there was mist in the early morning when Lewis guns repelled two inquisitive German aeroplanes. At 10.30 p.m. the S.O.S. signal from the British front line caused an hour of furious bombardment by both sides, in which machine-guns played their part. Although the trenches of the Twentieth were damaged in places, only 3 men were wounded. Next evening A and B companies were relieved and twenty-four hours later the whole battalion assembled at Bois Confluent behind the old British front line south-west of St. Eloi.

The 23rd Division formed the extreme left of the British attack. At Hill 60 the 69th Brigade had to advance on both sides of the Ypres-Comines railway and the Twelfth were to take Impartial Trench, the left portion of the final objective of the brigade. The Durhams were in position, lying in the open near Larch Wood, by 1 a.m. on June 7th. At three o'clock there was a lull in the British bombardment and ten minutes later came the explosion of the mines. For a moment Hill 60 and the Caterpillar were seen as one great fiery furnace; then the British guns opened and the leading waves of infantry went forward to the assault, while the machine-gun barrage added a new clamour to the familiar din of battle. The Twelfth had yet to wait and nearly two hours had passed before they followed in the wake of the advance over the remains of the German trenches, where the Yorkshire men of the 69th

161

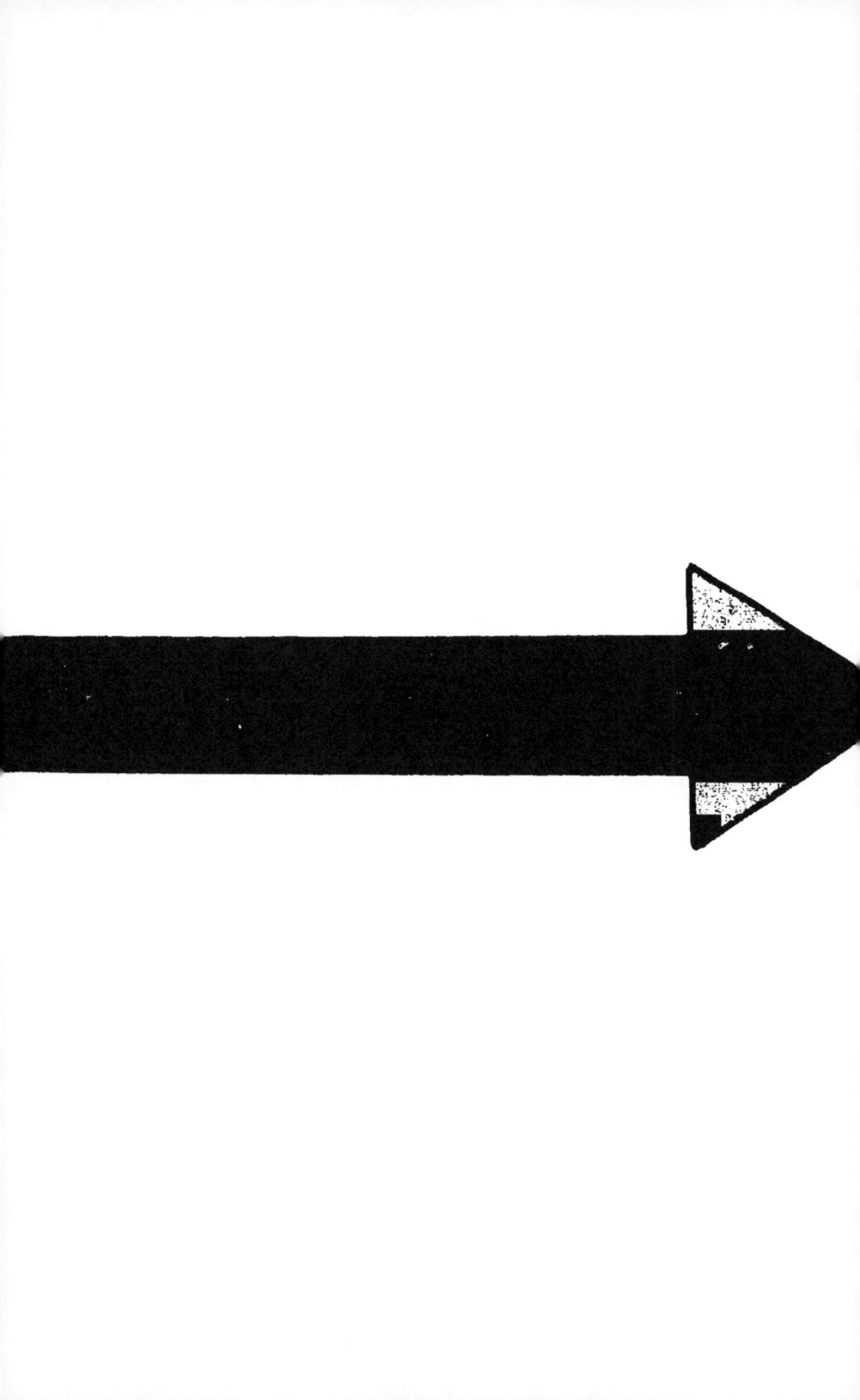

MICROCOPY RESOLUTION TEST CHART

ANSI and ISO TEST CHART No. 2

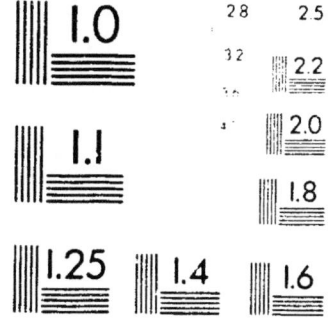

APPLIED IMAGE

The Durham Forces in the Field

Brigade were consolidating. At 6.50 A.M. the battalion passed through the second objective and attacked Imparti̇al Trench which was taken with a loss of only 15 killed and wounded. On the left Capt. E. W. Lafone pushed on still further and reached the houses of

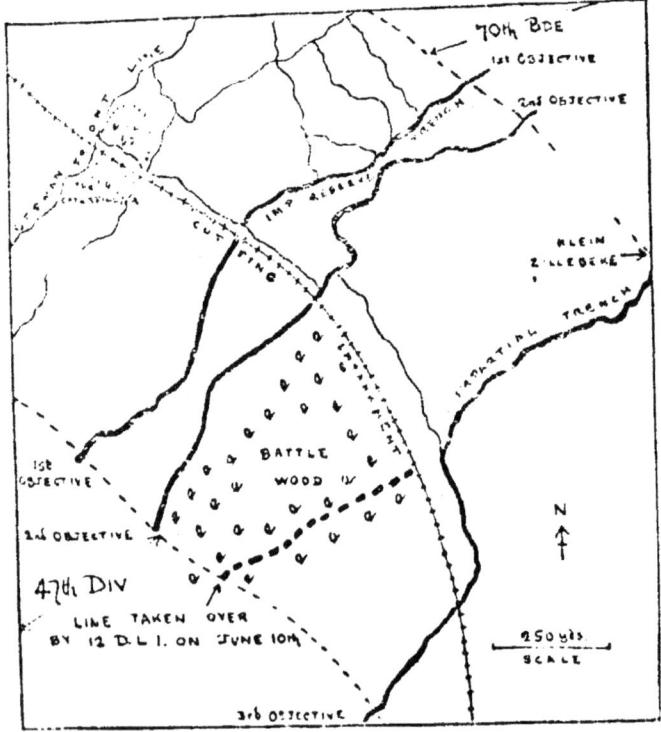

Klein Zillebeke, where the British shells were falling. 2nd Lieut. W. R. Hill with his Lewis gunners captured 4 German officers in the village, but our own barrage made it necessary to withdraw to the line now being consolidated forward of Impartial Trench. This work went on during the heat of the day. About noon enemy aeroplanes located the position, with the result

The Battle of Messines, 1917

that heavy shell fire took the trench in enfilade from the north and caused heavy losses. By 6 p.m. over 200 men had been killed and wounded and, in view of the danger of a counter-attack, the Thirteenth were called upon to take over the line. This was accomplished before dawn of June 8th and on the following day the Twelfth reached Montreal Camp to bathe and rest there. But on the evening of the 10th the battalion came up and relieved the 10th Duke of Wellington's Regt. in Battle Wood on the right of the line, so that the whole brigade front was occupied by Durham men who held it until the 23rd Division were withdrawn.

The Twelfth found that the line was about 150 yards short of the desired objective, owing to the troops on the immediate right having been held up by a machine-gun post on the canal which bent to the south-east in front of Battle Wood. The first task was to improve the trenches on the line already won and a good defensive position was made in spite of the machine-guns of low-flying German aeroplanes and the hostile shell fire which never ceased. On the morning of the 13th Lieut. N. C. V. Hall was killed and two other officers wounded.

Every night patrols visited the German dug-outs situated near the final objective. Before relief on the night of June 13th by a unit of the 17th Brigade this line was successfully occupied by the platoon of Lieut. C. Vaux, who, without artillery support, pushed forward in the darkness and accomplished a very smart piece of work in the face of the enemy. The in-coming battalion were forbidden to hold these advanced posts and contented themselves with the front and support lines, now consisting of good continuous trenches. In the early morning of the 14th the Twelfth went down the railway track through a barrage of gas-shells to Vlamertinghe and entrained for the Berthen area.

Capt. E. W. Lafone, Lieut. C. Vaux and 2nd Lieut. W. R. Hill were awarded the Military Cross. 2nd Lieut. Thos. Brandon, who captured 20 Germans with the help of one man on June 7th, and 2nd Lieut. N. B. Hill, a gallant and zealous trench mortar officer,

The Durham Forces in the Field

received the same decoration. Sergts. E. Matkin, F. Taylor and F. Walker; Lance-Corpls. H. Woodhall, H. G. Leach, J. F. Watson and J. Belcher; Ptes. J. Tait, T. McNeal, R. W. McMahon, A. Mitchell, J. I. Sykes, R. Campbell and T. Hay all won the Military Medal. Sergt. J. A. Speed, M.M., and Pte. J. W. Harness, M.M., were each awarded a bar to the decoration.

The Thirteenth, under Major J. A. L. Downey, were in reserve south of Zillebeke lake at the opening of the battle. A and B companies moved forward to Battersea Farm, on the south-eastern side of Zillebeke, at 9.15 A.M. and at ten o'clock at night were ordered to relieve the Twelfth in Impartial Trench. This was done by 5 A.M. next morning at the cost of only 6 casualties, but shell fire afterwards killed 2nd Lieut. J. Young and 3 others and wounded 2nd Lieut. J. Brady and 25 more. C and D companies moved up in the early hours of the 9th, casualties on this day amounting to 20. In the evening Major Downey took over command of the whole 69th Brigade area north of the railway. At night C company and a company of pioneers got to work on a support line behind Impartial Trench. This new trench, called Durham Lane, was occupied by C company, while A and D occupied the front line. B company remained in Imp Reserve Trench.

By the night of the 11th the heavy enemy fire had killed 2nd Lieut. A. L. Hamilton and wounded 2nd Lieut. T. Murgatroyd and there were 56 more casualties in the ranks. At 12.15 A.M. on June 12th D company's posts in the dug-outs along the railway were driven in. Following a bombardment by a Stokes mortar, Lieut. T. G. Saint counter-attacked with a bombing party and regained his lost positions at the second attempt, after being wounded and losing several of his men.

In the early morning of the 13th the battalion vacated the trenches on relief by a battalion of the 24th Division, marched back to Vlamertinghe and left by train for Godewaersvelde.

The Battle of Messines, 1917

The honours awarded after this action included the Military Cross to Lieut. C. I. W. Sauerbeck, who had repeatedly braved the intense enemy shelling in his capacity of intelligence officer and, though wounded, held on till the battalion were relieved. Capt. E. Gray, for his fearless and skilful direction of the consolidation of the forward objective and his initiative in pushing out patrols, also won the Cross and C.-S.-M. G. Thompson, who was particularly prominent during consolidation under the heavy shell fire, received the Distinguished Conduct Medal.

On June 14th the Twentieth were in support to the 122nd Brigade, who attacked successfully and did not need any assistance. The Wearsiders took over the line, now on the forward slope which overlooked Hollebeke, in the evening of the 19th. Wet weather had turned the trenches into filthy ditches and at dawn of the 20th the German batteries were very active. Battalion headquarters were soon shelled out of the White Château and, by order of the brigade, moved further back.

A new support line with thick traverses was dug by the battalion, but men in the front trench were nearly waist deep in water and a portion of the parados fell upon Colonel North when he was making his rounds. He was dug out, fortunately little the worse. The West Kents relieved the battalion on the night of the 23rd, all three front line companies coming out at the same time, thanks to the efforts of the sappers who had bridged the ornamental water at White Château. In spite of the German shell fire the Twentieth had had less than 30 casualties, including Major G. McNicholl, D.S.O., wounded.

The battalion, now in support, occupied the old German front line and provided working and carrying parties until June 27th. While here losses amounted to 15 killed and wounded.

Another tour in front followed. Bombing posts and Lewis guns held the line by day and much work was done at night, but the rain persisted and the trenches grew worse and worse. On the last day of

The Durham Forces in the Field

the month a unit of the 47th Division took over the line and the Twentieth floundered back through the mud, in which many of the heavily laden men stuck fast. During this last tour 12 men had been killed and 33 wounded and 2nd Lieut. P. F. Large had died of his wounds.

NOTE.—69th Brigade Orders show in detail everything carried by the infantryman in the attack at the battle of Messines. This equipment, which varied little in the subsequent actions, is worthy of record. It consisted of the following, in addition to rifle and bayonet:

Steel helmet	2 Grenades (1 in each top pocket)
Haversack (on back)	120 rounds S.A.A.
Water-bottle (filled)	2 Flares (1 in each bottom pocket)
Entrenching tool	
Waterproof sheet	1 Iron ration
Tube gas helmet	1 Day's preserved meat and biscuits
Box respirator	
2 Sandbags	Field dressing

Every other man carried a large tool on his back (in the proportion of 5 shovels to 2 picks). Lewis gunners, signallers, &c., carried their own weapons and equipment. Wire-cutters, Very pistols and cartridges, and S.O.S. rockets had also to be taken forward.

TRENCH WARFARE

JUNE AND JULY, 1917

On June 3rd the Tenth went into trenches again, taking over a portion of the line between Chérisy—still in German hands—and the Cojeul river. Capt. Salmon and 4 men were wounded on this day. At 2 o'clock next morning a patrol of 7 Germans entered the line, but fled on being attacked. One man, mortally wounded, was left in the hands of the Tenth. June 6th was the worst day of shell fire which, coming from the Chérisy direction, took the trenches partly in enfilade. An aeroplane spotted for the German gunners until it was driven off by British machines.

After this tour the Tenth moved back by degrees until they arrived at Bus-les-Artois for training and recreation. On July 12th they entrained for Bailleul and marched to Mont Vidaigne, on the Belgian frontier, where training continued.

The Eleventh, still working in the Noreuil sector, had accomplished a great deal by the middle of June. Railways had been repaired and a new communication trench was cut through a railway embankment and camouflaged. On June 26th the work on the second line of defence was finished and the Pioneers reached Domart at the end of the month. Training, sports and recreation filled the days until the move of the division to Ypres. The Eleventh entrained at Doullens and, on arrival in Flanders on July 21st, occupied a camp at Proven, C company starting work on railway construction at once.

After the Messines battle the Twelfth spent a week training assiduously in the Berthen area before moving by lorry on June 21st to camp at Dickebusch. Here

The Durham Forces in the Field

the battalion were shelled every night and large parties were employed in burying cable. Five days later the Twelfth went back to Flêtre, but on the last day of the month the whole of the brigade marched up in pouring rain towards the line.

On July 4th the battalion paraded to see the King pass along the la Clytte-Reninghelst road. They went into the trenches again on July 10th near Klein Zillebeke, where German concrete shelters afforded better protection than had ever been available before. A raid was done during this tour, Lieut. Weightman and 2nd Lieut. E. G. Freeman with 40 men rushing a German " pill-box," around which a box barrage had been placed. Both officers were wounded and there was some sharp fighting, but 5 men of the 8th Jägers were brought back. 2nd Lieut. Freeman—who personally captured one of them, helped back a badly wounded raider and afterwards went out to search for 3 men reported missing- received the Military Cross.

The Twelfth were relieved on July 13th and spent the weeks that followed training for the attack at various places behind the line. On July 30th the battalion arrived at St. Omer by train and marched to billets at Esquerdes.

The Thirteenth were located at Mont des Cats after the Messines offensive. They also saw the King near Reninghelst and on July 6th they took over trenches near Klein Zillebeke.

At 12.15 A.M. on the 7th, 2nd Lieut. Frederick Youens and 3 men left the right of the battalion front to get into touch with the troops on that flank. A strong party of Germans endeavoured to surround and capture this small patrol, but after a fight, in which 2nd Lieut. Youens and one man were wounded, the Durhams regained their own lines. Soon a fierce bombardment fell upon the trenches of the Thirteenth and about 2.30 A.M. some 50 Germans attempted to raid the right company. A shell-burst scattered one Lewis gun team, but 2nd Lieut. Youens, who was receiving medical aid in a dug-out, rushed forth without shirt or jacket and rallied the men. A bomb was

The late SECOND-LIEUT. F. YOUENS, V.C.
13th Durham Light Infantry

Trench Warfare, June and July, 1917

thrown amongst them, but he hurled it out of the trench. Another came and this also he seized; but it exploded in his hands, wounding him so seriously that he died. The German raid failed and this gallant young officer was awarded the Victoria Cross.

The Thirteenth were relieved by the Twelfth on July 10th and eventually withdrew to Mont des Cats again. On July 30th they moved to billets at Wizernes.

When the Fourteenth came into the line in the Loos sector on June 9th they left their raiding party behind. It had been arranged that the German trenches should be entered by daylight on the 12th and the artillery now cut gaps in the enemy wire, trench mortars and machine-guns preventing the Germans from repairing the damage. The raid had to be postponed as a patrol—consisting of 2nd Lieut. C. S. Cope and 2 men—was missing, but the officer returned alone on June 14th, having spent two days and nights behind the German line.

The morning of June 15th was misty. Parties of Germans were working on their parapet and putting out wire in front. These were not disturbed, but at 6.30 a.m. a terrible commotion was heard further down the line, where the 16th Brigade were carrying out a "dummy" raid. Then the protective barrage came down and the Durhams advanced, 2nd Lieut. W. R. Bruce leading the centre party and 2nd Lieut. A. Rothfield the men on the left. Ninety seconds later 2nd Lieut. A. Y. Lascelles led forward the party on the right.

All entered the German trenches without trouble. On the right the junction of Nash Alley with the front line was captured and Sergt. W. Simpson led a rush which captured a barricade and accounted for all the defenders. A block was established about 100 yards up Nash Alley and nine dug-outs were either burned or bombed. A feeble counter-attack was easily repulsed, 11 Germans of the 153rd Regt. being killed and 5 taken. The raiders in the centre and on the left met and worked to the right together, killing

The Durham Forces in the Field

9 of the enemy and coaxing others from their dug-outs. About 20 Germans ran away over the top, but came under the fire of rifle grenadiers and snipers left on the parapet for this purpose.

The raiders, half of whom had only joined the Fourteenth a month before, returned after spending fifteen minutes in the German trenches which were found to be wide and rather shallow. Casualties were only 2 killed and 6 wounded. Capt. J. P. Moffitt, who organised the affair, and 2nd Lieut. A. Rothfield were awarded the Military Cross; Sergt. Simpson and Pte. T. Thompson received the Distinguished Conduct Medal; and the Military Medal was won by Lance-Corpl. W. Moore.

The German gunners now opened a vengeful bombardment and by the time the Fourteenth withdrew to divisional reserve on June 19th, 2nd Lieuts. E. A. Cash and P. L. Thompson and 11 others had been killed and 2nd Lieut. W. R. Bruce and 47 men wounded.

Early in July when the Fourteenth were in the line again they raided the Germans at the same place. At 6 A.M. on the 9th the 16th Brigade obliged with a smoke screen and "dummy" bombardment while three parties of 10 men went over. The few Germans who were seen fled at once and after several dug-outs had been bombed the raiders withdrew. They reached their own trenches safely, but the German bombardment came down and caused 8 casualties before they could get under cover. On this occasion 2nd Lieut. E. C. Wylie won the Military Cross and Sergt. J. C. Adamson and Corpl. C. Harding the Military Medal.

The Fourteenth were relieved the same night and did much work on the trenches until they departed by bus for Caucourt—west of the old Roman road to Arras—on July 14th.

After an uneventful tour in the line at the beginning of June, the Fifteenth moved to bivouacs on the Fenin-Croisilles road for a week's work on the trenches. They then moved by easy stages to Bienvillers-au-Bois. Nine days were spent here and on June 30th the

170

Trench Warfare, June and July, 1917

battalion took over, in wet weather, the old Hindenburg Line which ran south from the Sensée river, Hindenharg Support being still in the hands of the Germans. 2nd Lieut. C. F. Kemp was wounded during this tour which passed without special incident. A week at Moyenneville, with A and B companies occupying posts further forward, was followed by a tour in the line north of the Sensée before returning to Moyenneville again.

The Eighteenth took over reserve trenches north of Arras on June 9th and provided working parties till they moved into the front line at Cavrelle six days later. This front was now much more peaceful and the only incident of note occurred on the evening of the 28th, when the battalion put out dummy barrages and sent up flares to distract attention from the attack carried out by the 94th Brigade north of the windmill. German retaliation only caused 6 Durham casualties.

Relieved on July 3rd, the Eighteenth went back to Roclincourt to work on the railway. Then the 31st Division commenced to relieve the Canadians in the Vimy sector and on the 14th the Durhams moved to Mont St. Eloy for a week of training and recreation. On coming forward to Thélus they found that the old caves and quarries, if cold and damp, afforded good cover from the German shell fire. Working parties were now supplied nightly till the battalion took over the front line on the low ground in front of Mericourt. This was on the evening of July 29th.

The Nineteenth moved up to brigade reserve positions in the Cauche Wood sector on June 10th and occupied the front line later. On the night of June 23rd they assisted to dig and wire a trench in advance of the left of the line south-east of Connelieu. This was accomplished without enemy interference. The end of the month was spent at Feudicourt and then the battalion moved back to Longavesnes. On July 6th they relieved cavalry in support positions north-east of Fargicourt, where the nights were spent

171

The Durham Forces in the Field

digging and wiring the front line. These trenches were occupied by the Nineteenth a week later.

After dark on July 19th the enemy opened a heavy mortar and artillery fire with smoke and then attempted to rush a post held by the battalion. A sunken road offered the Germans a good line of approach and a brisk fight ensued before they were driven off, leaving behind them many rifles, bayonets and bombs, a Bangalore torpedo and 2 of their number who had been killed. The Nineteenth had 26 casualties—mostly from the bombardment—and Pte. G. B. Bell won the Military Medal for his gallantry.

The battalion was relieved on July 23rd and withdrew to Aizecourt-le-Bas.

The Twenty-Second remained at Strazeele till June 11th and then moved forward again. A and B companies arrived at Ypres on June 15th and commenced to dig two new communication trenches in the Zillebeke sector. This was night work, as the German observation balloons overlooked the scene.

On June 20th enemy shell fire caught two platoons filling sand-bags in the open and caused many casualties and by the end of the month the Twenty-Second had lost Capt. J. P. L. Grindell, 2nd Lieut. C. Jarah and 2nd Lieut. R. V. Hodgson killed and nearly 50 others killed and wounded. A and C companies were now located west of the Ypres-Comines canal at Swan Château, a dangerous locality. Nine casualties occurred here on July 2nd.

The efforts of the Pioneers were chiefly concentrated upon the repair of communications which suffered constant damage from the German fire; but C company were employed upon a new light railway which was to run south of Hell Fire Corner, on the Menin Road, forward to the line. On July 7th Capt. G. P. Baines was wounded and there were 10 other casualties. About this time came a welcome reinforcement of 30 men, most of whom had served with the 1/7th Durham Light Infantry. On July 13th C company withdrew to a camp about eight miles north-west of Poperinghe for a course of light railway construction. Two days

Trench Warfare, June and July, 1917

later a barrage of mustard gas shells stopped all the work of the battalion and little could be done on the two following days, though casualties were few. 2nd Lieuts. W. Sherriff and C. Fosbrooke were killed on July 19th. There was a very violent bombardment of gas and high explosive on July 22nd, during which B company pushed the light railway forward 150 yards over difficult ground. They had 19 gassed cases, including 2nd Lieut. Ruscoe, and 10 other men were incapacitated for a day.

On July 25th the Twenty-Second concentrated at Winnipeg Camp for a much-needed rest, though a platoon had to go up every night to keep trenches and light railway in repair.

THE THIRD BATTLE OF YPRES

CHAPTER I

The third battle of Ypres begins with the tale of the Twentieth, the 41st Division being on the right of the British line when the attack opened on July 31st, 1917. Colonel North's battalion had spent the first three weeks of the month at Mont des Cats, where over 250 men were absorbed from drafts. Training for the attack continued after moving to Xenora Camp, near Westoutre, and the Wearsiders came into the line on July 25th with their left on the Zwarteleen-Klein Zillebeke road. This position was a little forward of the ground won by the Twelfth at the battle of Messines.

As no preparations had been made here it was as well that the offensive was postponed, for it gave time for the Durhams to dig their assembly trenches and to form dumps of battle stores. C company occupied forward posts on the slopes of Fusilier Wood, with D company in support not far behind. July 26th was a fairly quiet day and cost the battalion only 8 casualties. On the morrow came news of a further postponement till July 31st, so inter-company reliefs were carried out and Capt. A. Pumphrey, D.S.O., was put in command of the battalion front. During the night 14 casualties were sustained and next day came a steady bombardment of Fusilier Wood. A company lost 2nd Lieut. A. R. Willis and 5 men killed and 33 wounded or gassed before they could be withdrawn, leaving Lewis gun posts to hold the line. July 29th was spent by Capt. Pumphrey and 2nd Lieuts. Shepherdson and Walton in reconnoitring the assembly area for the coming battle. At night, while laying out string to mark the positions for the tape-layers,

171

The Third Battle of Ypres

they exchanged shots with an enemy patrol. The German fire of high explosive and gas shell never slackened during these days and before the zero hour casualties in the Twentieth had risen to about 100 killed, wounded and gassed. When D company began to move up to the assembly position from the rear two shells pitched right into the leading platoon as they passed battalion headquarters at Hill 60 and 16 men were killed and wounded.

At 3.50 A.M. on July 31st the buglers of the Twentieth sounded the charge and the Wearsiders went forward to the attack. C and D companies led the way and, in the face of considerable shell and machine-gun fire, the first German position was taken. The Durhams passed on down hill and arrived on the line of the next objective. On each flank there ran from front to rear a line of concrete "pill-boxes," in which snipers, bombers and machine-gunners offered a stubborn resistance. Near the road on the left the Germans were soon routed out, all being either killed or captured. On the right, where the Twentieth had had heavier losses, the "mopping up" operations were not so successful and many of the enemy still held on. The Wearsiders started to dig in and soon afterwards the adjutant, Capt. F. Wayman, M.C., was killed by a shell which slightly wounded the commanding officer. Germans now poured out of a group of "pill-boxes" between the front and support lines on the right. This interrupted the digging but they were repulsed, partly by the fire of a Vickers gun operated by Colonel North in person.

A further attempt to "mop up" the remaining concrete strongholds was organised, but owing to shortage of men and bombs proved only partially successful. Messages had to be sent to the rear by pigeons, as few runners survived the heavy German barrage, and one bird bore a request for reinforcements.

It began to rain as the afternoon wore on. About four o'clock the Germans massed for a big counter-attack and 2nd Lieut. Shepherdson was sent to hurry up the two companies asked for to strengthen the line. The enemy infantry came on and were checked by

The Durham Forces in the Field

the Twentieth whose rapid fire inflicted heavy losses; but on the right of the Wearsiders the attack was more successful and reached the Germans who still held the " pill-boxes " there. The Twentieth formed a defensive flank to meet this danger. Only battalion headquarters, 15 men of B company and a few machine-guns were available, but the German advance was stayed. Colonel North was now so badly wounded by a shell that he had to leave the line and Capt. Fulljames, M.C., who had just come up, assumed command. This officer had been incapacitated by concussion from a shell-burst early in the morning, but hurried to the front as soon as he was sufficiently recovered to do so.

Capt. Pumphrey, with two companies of Rifles, soon afterwards arrived upon the scene and the British guns opened in response to the messages of the Twentieth. Every available man joined in an advance which restored the line completely. After some sharp fighting all the " pill-boxes " were cleared and a junction effected with the battalion on the right. The whole ground was still searched by hostile shell and machine-gun fire, while the Twentieth continued to consolidate their positions. The weather grew worse during the night and at dusk on August 1st the enemy launched another counter-attack. It was smashed completely by the rapid fire of the Wearsiders, promptly supported by the British artillery.

The battalion were relieved that night and spent the next day resting in the tunnels at the Bluff. Then, through drenching rain, they moved to bivouacs near Elzenwalle Château, beyond the Ypres-Kemmel road.

Losses in the ranks amounted to 431. Capt. M. Hand, who had pushed beyond the objective with some of his company and had sent back most valuable reports, was killed, and Lieuts. W. K. Walton and T. M. Fletcher, M.C., and 2nd Lieuts. E. W. Britton and J. A. Ballantyne were also among the fallen.

Colonel North, by reason of his resolute leadership, acquired a bar to his Distinguished Service Order. Lieut. T. M. Fletcher was wounded before the zero hour, but returned with a bandaged head to lead his company until he was killed; 2nd Lieut. J. G. R. Pacey

The Third Battle of Ypres

replaced his fallen company commander, bombed out German snipers from their lairs and did good work both in consolidation and in resisting counter-attacks; 2nd Lieut. Edwin Smith performed similar service and himself slew many Germans; 2nd Lieut. L. W. Shepherdson not only did valuable reconnaissance work before the battle, but guided the reinforcing troops forward through a heavy barrage. These four officers received the Military Cross and the same decoration was won by Capt. H. P. Wilson, R.A.M.C., who displayed the utmost contempt of danger as he dressed the wounded under heavy fire. Sergt. A. Houston of Sunderland received the Distinguished Conduct Medal for bombing out a nest of snipers after being the sole survivor of two attempts to do so. Next day he was prominent in organising the defence of the captured ground. The gallantry of Sergt. B. Scott; Lance-Corpls. T. Hannah and J. Ramsden; Ptes. E. Bell, W. Burke, N. Darrell, R. Dixon, R. Ellison, E. Howard, J. Kirkup, W. Mears, J. E. Thompson and T. Yeomans; and Bugler R. Mordey was rewarded with the Military Medal.

The Twentieth spent some days at Elzenwalle Château, where Major R. C. Smith of the 1st Durham Light Infantry assumed command on August 4th. The battalion, now the weakest in the division, were reorganised in two companies, each of three platoons. Heavy fighting on the divisional front brought them into reserve positions south-west of the Caterpillar on August 6th, but on the 12th the Wearsiders left by lorry for the Meteren area and took over tents at Fontaine Houck. Here drafts were received and training was varied by inspections, sports and football.

The Tenth were the next to enter the battle. They arrived at Zillebeke Bund on August 20th and on the following day the officers reconnoitred the brigade line which lay astride the Menin road, west of Inverness Copse. At 2 A.M. on August 22nd the battalion came forward through a bombardment of gas shells to occupy support positions for the attack. By the time a hostile barrage in Sanctuary Wood was passed casualties

The Durham Forces in the Field

already amounted to 60. At 5 a.m. A company were in the open on Stirling Castle ridge, south of the Menin road; B company in support trenches in Sanctuary Wood; and C and D companies in the tunnels under the road. When the attacking battalions advanced two hours later, the Tenth occupied the old British front line. But one company had to follow the Somersets on the right, and form a defensive flank facing south,

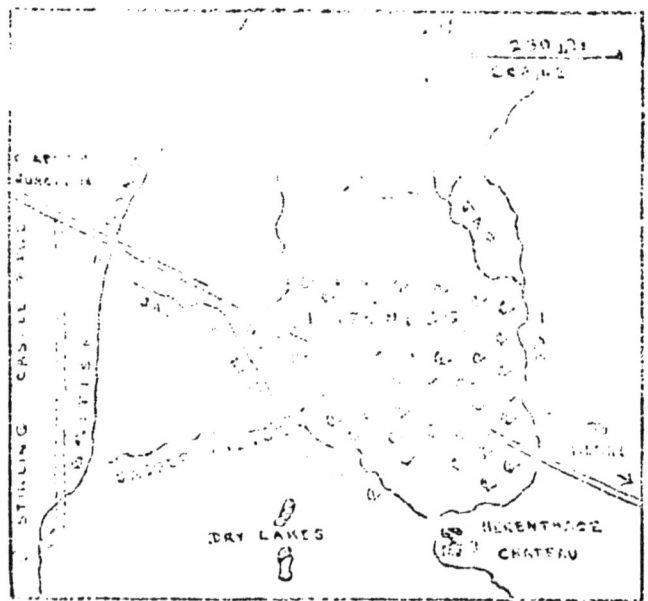

besides sending a bombing section and some rifle-grenadiers up Jasper Lane to meet and escort a tank. The monster did not keep the appointment, but this party pushed on and captured a German machine-gun and its detachment as well.

Meanwhile the rest of the company had pushed forward on the right and established themselves in the vicinity of Dry Lakes. Here the company commander was killed after organising a successful attack upon a

The Third Battle of Ypres

machine-gun, which was taken, together with 5 Germans. The leading platoon managed to reach Herenthage Château and the platoon commander and his surviving men accepted the surrender of the garrison. There were 50 prisoners to bring back, but few, if any, of the party survived the terrific shell fire encountered on the way. What remained of this company of the Tenth withdrew during the morning to a position in Jasper Avenue.

The Somerset L.I., who led the brigade attack upon the right, had passed through Inverness Copse and would have taken Jap Trench if the left battalion had not been held up at their first objective. To conform to the line on their left the Somersets now had to fall back to a position in the copse, astride the Menin Road. At 8.50 A.M. they asked for reinforcements. Two platoons from one of the reserve companies of the Tenth went forward and dug a post north of the copse, where they were in touch with the Cornwalls who were lying in a chain of shell-holes in front of the trench they had taken. At eleven o'clock more reinforcements were required and a company of the Tenth were sent forward to the western edge of Inverness Copse. In response to later appeals more of the Tenth were put in, till, by evening, the whole battalion had gone into the copse to reinforce the line.

The night was comparatively quiet, but at 4.30 on the morning of August 23rd British tanks arrived upon the scene and at once became a target for the German guns. One tank, which had evidently lost its bearings, travelled along the northern outskirts of the copse and fired upon the post there, wounding 2 men. Afterwards it was put out of action, being hit twice by German shells. No ground was gained on this day and at night the hostile shell fire was much heavier, while our own gunners put down a heavy barrage. In the small hours of the next morning, when the German bombardment was worse than ever, the Cornishmen on the left sent up the S.O.S. signal and reported that the enemy had broken through. All at Clapham Junction, the headquarters of the Tenth, turned out and 2nd Lieut. Lodge was killed by a machine-gun bullet as he

The Durham Forces in the Field

led his men forward to the north-west corner of the copse. The Germans came forward in groups all along the line with parties bearing flame throwers and light machine-guns. That the attack was not delivered with greater weight is to the credit of the British artillery. Even so the line north of the copse had to be withdrawn, the post occupied by the Tenth since the morning of the 22nd being the last to retire. Pte. Warden was captured here and was kept in a shell-hole close to the British line. There were about 20 Germans present and the prisoner was given water and cigarettes. During the day one German asked to be taken over to the British as a prisoner and another, who overheard, asked if he might come. Thus there rejoined the Tenth at dusk Pte. Warden, in German equipment, carrying a German rifle and accompanied by 2 stalwart Bavarians, one of whom wore the Iron Cross.

The other men from this post had joined their company which held on inside the copse north of the road. Here Capt. Jerwood put up a stout defence, despite withdrawals upon the flanks, repulsing the German attacks by rifle-grenade, Lewis gun and rifle fire. At 3.30 p.m. he had to withdraw to the extreme north-west corner owing to heavy casualties from our own guns.

2nd Lieut. Dennison, leading his own platoon and some stragglers collected on the west edge of the copse, had held a defensive flank on Capt. Jerwood's left and retired in conjunction with that officer after 24 of his 30 men had been killed by our own artillery. Some Riflemen who had reinforced him suffered to an equal extent.

The right of the line held fast in the neighbourhood of the Dry Lakes. Two platoons drove off an attack from the south and afterwards helped to re-establish the centre of the line. 2nd Lieut. Harold Storey, who was the leader here, continued in command and after being wounded and sent back valuable reports.

In the early morning of the 24th a bombing attack was directed upon our defensive flank near the junction with the British original front line on the right. Sergt. W. Rolland, found in a shell-hole with a Lewis gun which had jammed, was made prisoner. The Germans

The Third Battle of Ypres

also collected an officer of the Machine Gun Corps and a private of the Tenth, but were driven off by a Vickers gun firing from Stirling Castle and the prisoners escaped.

Losses, especially in officers, had been very heavy, and by nightfall the whole line was withdrawn to Jasper Avenue and Jasper Lane, the only part of Inverness Copse which remained in British hands being the north-west corner. The fierce artillery barrage rendered it impossible for the Germans to advance and occupy the copse, which the defenders would never have relinquished had they not been shelled out by our own guns.

Early on August 25th the Tenth were relieved and moved back to Zillebeke Bund, departing by bus for Devonshire Camp, near Ouderdom, the same day. Losses amounted to 14 officers and 355 others out of a battalion strength of 20 and 608 at the beginning of the battle. Capt. J. F. Jerwood and 2nd Lieuts. J. S. A. Dennison and F. Storey each received the Military Cross, which was also conferred upon Capt. P. Grant and 2nd Lieut. R. Green, who removed his respirator and reorganised his company in the midst of the gas shelling on the way up to the line. Though gassed he did excellent work throughout the action. Another recipient of this decoration was Capt. F. F. Davies, described by his colonel as "one of our best officers." When his company reinforced the line he found the platoons were widely scattered, but under heavy fire he visited and encouraged them all. He was badly wounded on the evening of the 24th and was never seen again.

C.-S.-M. Donnelly, D.C.M., that irrepressible warrior from Benwell, also bore a prominent part in the fight, showing his usual fine example and ability as a leader of men. He received a bar to his medal. The awards of the Military Medal included Sergts. W. Bolland and J. McNay; Corpls. B. Roberts and J. W. Huie; Lance-Corpl. J. Coxon; Ptes. Burlinson, J. Caffrey, E. Carick, L. Dick, T. Hepworth, F. Hewitt, C. Kirby, A. Murray, A. Robson, Waggett, T. N. Walton and D. Wilson; Pte. J. J. Bloomfield (attached

The Durham Forces in the Field

to 43rd Machine Gun Co.) and Pte. E. A. Cerdes (attached to Signal Co., R.E.).

The Twentieth continued battle training at Esquerdes after August 24th and on September 14th began to march back to the battle line. Five days later the Wearsiders arrived and next morning the other brigades of the 41st Division delivered an attack upon the German positions south of the Menin Road, east of Bodmin Copse and Clonmel Copse. This formed part of the third great advance and resulted in heavy fighting along more than eight miles of front. Zero hour was at 5.40 A.M. on September 20th, but it was not till nearly ten o'clock in the morning that the Twentieth were moved into the old British front line near Bodmin Copse. Just before noon D company were detached to link up on the right with the 39th Division who had not yet succeeded in taking the second objective, known as the " Blue " Line. At mid-day Colonel Smith was instructed to find out the situation in his immediate front, where all was not going well. The Wearsiders were eventually told to strengthen and consolidate the " Blue " Line and about 3 P.M. they crossed the Basseville Beek. On reaching the " Blue " Line they began to dig, although the troops on the right did not appear to be east of the stream. The " Green " Line, final objective of the division, was on the other side of the Tower Hamlets ridge, which now confronted the battalion. An attack was ordered for the evening but there was no time to make the necessary preparations, the different units being much scattered. At 6 P.M. D company, having completed their mission, rejoined the battalion. Fighting patrols were sent out at dusk to link up the 122nd Brigade on the left with the Middlesex, who were supposed to have reached the " Green " Line on the right. This advance did not clear up the situation, but resulted in the capture of 2 German officers and 6 men.

The hostile shelling, very heavy during the day, slackened somewhat at night, but on the right flank of the battalion German snipers were busy. The Twen-

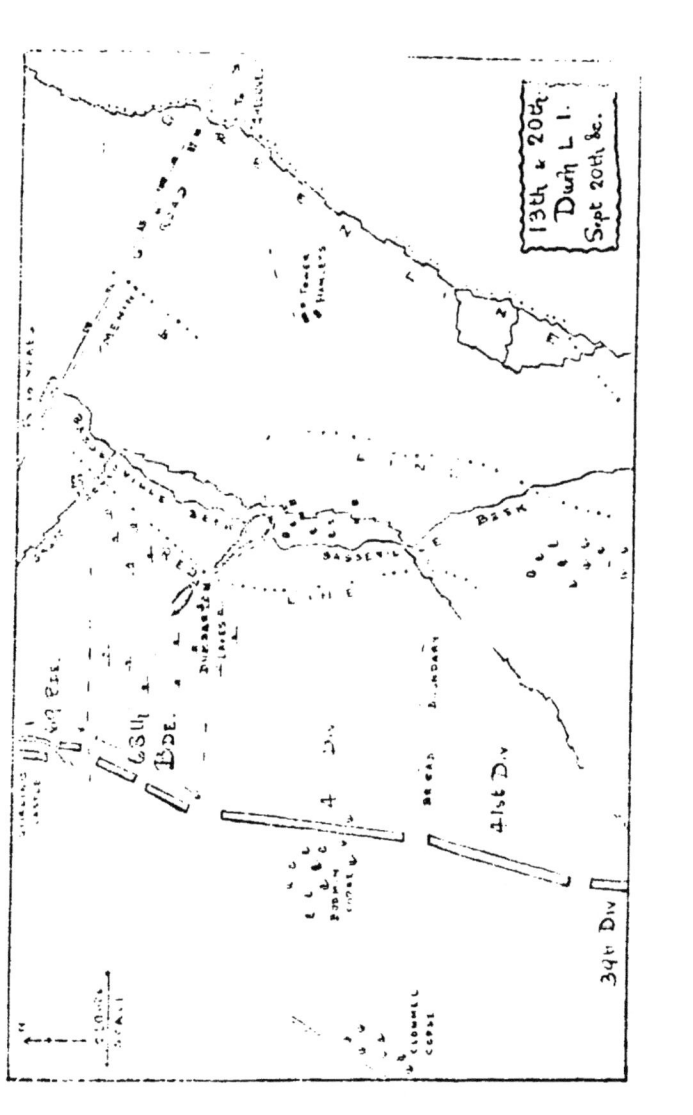

The Durham Forces in the Field

tieth had already lost many officers. 2nd Lieut. A. T. Charlton was killed; 2nd Lieuts. J. Corbet, C. S. Cunningham, A. H. Carner and A. C. Roden were wounded; and 2nd Lieut. E. Russell had been sent back sick.

At seven on the morning of the 21st came orders for an attack on the centre of the " Green " Line, the Twentieth to be the left battalion. When, at 9.8 A.M., the Wearsiders went forward the barrage proved a failure and the German machine-guns and snipers were practically untouched. The attack was pushed for about 200 yards at a heavy cost of killed and wounded; then the Twentieth dug in. Capt. Arnold Pumphrey, D.S.O., had been shot through the head as he led a rush upon a German machine-gun and the death of this gallant officer was a great loss to the battalion. 2nd Lieut. N. H. W. Cartwright was also killed on this day and 2nd Lieut. T. C. Bamborough mortally wounded. Among the wounded were Capts. F. Southwell and E. Smith, M.C., 2nd Lieuts. E. P. Smith, W. S. Prudhoe, P. L. Dobinson, F. W. Hampton and A. S. Davison.

About 3 P.M. the Germans advanced over the Tower Hamlets ridge, but were driven back by Lewis gun and rifle fire which inflicted heavy losses upon them. This enemy counter-attack was attempted without artillery support. An hour later a hostile barrage came down on the forward slope of the ridge behind Basseville Beek and then a box barrage was put on the line held by the Twentieth. Under cover of this came another counter-attack at about 7.40 P.M., but it was repulsed by artillery, Lewis gun and rifle fire.

September 22nd was a quieter day, the enemy contenting himself with putting down a barrage west of the stream in the afternoon. At night the Wearsiders were relieved and reached Micmac Camp by eight on the morning of the 23rd. The total losses in the ranks, which amounted to 303, were much the heaviest in the brigade.

Besides Capt. Pumphrey, another Twentieth officer of great distinction fell during this action in the person of Major Graham McNicholl, D.S.O. He was killed

THE 13TH DURHAM LIGHT INFANTRY BEFORE THEIR ADVANCE ON SEPTEMBER 20TH, 1917

The Third Battle of Ypres

while commanding the 26th Royal Fusiliers of the 124th Brigade.

On September 20th the 23rd Division attacked immediately north of the 41st. The 68th Brigade, on the right, had first to advance through the swamps round Dumbarton Lakes and take the "Red" Line about 100 yards west of and roughly parallel to Basseville Beek; then to go on across the stream to the "Blue" Line, 750 yards ahead on higher ground; and, finally, to capture the "Green" Line situated on the forward slope of the plateau astride the Menin road. The two nearer objectives were allotted to the Fusilier battalions and the Thirteenth were to go through and take the "Green" Line. Under the command of Capt. D. F. Clarke, M.C., they assembled at the tunnels at Observatory Ridge in rain and darkness on the night of the 19th. Everyone was wet through, but there were few casualties and before the zero hour the rain ceased and the sky cleared. A ground mist then served to conceal the movement of the troops.

At 5.40 A.M. the leading battalion of Fusiliers advanced to the attack under an excellent barrage, pushing on quickly so that the enemy shell fire fell behind the support and carrying parties. It was half-past seven when the Thirteenth moved forward to the "Blue" Line. Patrols had reported that the ground near the lakes and Basseville Beck consisted of shell-holes filled with water and almost impassable swamps, so half the battalion went round over the higher ground to the north and half, with a company of the Twelfth attached, used the 41st Division area to the south. The Thirteenth reached the "Blue" Line at half-past eight and at the appointed hour advanced steadily and in perfect order upon the "Green" Line. The British artillery served them well. There were German machine-gunners still in action in the cellars of some of the houses on the Menin road, but many concrete dug-outs were found full of German dead. Those of the enemy who continued to resist were all killed or captured after some fierce fighting; those who fled as

The Durham Forces in the Field

the men of the Thirteenth approached they had to run the gauntlet of Lewis gun, rifle and shell fire. Their own machine-guns were also turned upon them.

So, although disaster befell the tanks in this portion of the field, the Thirteenth took the "Green" Line soon after 11 A.M. and, under cover of the protective barrage, the work of consolidation commenced. The battalion were in touch with the Duke of Wellington's Regt. on the left, but an officer's patrol could not discover any troops of the 41st Division on the "Green" Line to the south. On this flank a company of the 11th N.F. helped to make the line secure, all digging in with a will under the fire of some rather troublesome German snipers. At 3 P.M. came the first counter-attack, about 100 Germans advancing in small parties upon the left company. They were dispersed by Lewis gun and rifle fire. By evening the Thirteenth had a strong continuous trench. Carrying parties had brought up ammunition, bombs and wire, while captured machine-guns and others salved from a derelict tank were added to the defence. The battalion had lost a good officer in Capt. H. C. Buckell, M.C., killed in the advance. Lieut. H. J. L. Parker and 2nd Lieuts. R. W. Gill, H. R. Wheatley and G. L. Orchard were wounded on this day and losses in the ranks amounted to 237.

The British artillery put down a barrage in the early morning of the 21st and at 8 A.M. came another and stronger counter-attack against the left of the line. The Germans were repulsed by rifle and Lewis gun, leaving one officer and 5 men in the hands of the Thirteenth. Two more attempts were soon made by the enemy, one of which, delivered up the Menin road, was severely punished by a platoon pushed out north of the road to take the attackers in enfilade.

After an hour's bombardment the enemy advanced up the valley from the direction of Gheluvelt at 3 P.M., only to be dispersed by the rifles and Lewis guns of the company on the right. At four o'clock a heavy enemy bombardment began and continued for two hours. Germans were then seen concentrating south of the Menin road near Gheluvelt, but the rockets of

The Third Battle of Ypres

the Thirteenth brought a timely response from the guns. The British barrage came down and dispersed the enemy before he was well on the move. There were no counter-attacks during the night. The Thirteenth, who had sustained 52 more casualties, were kept busy repairing the damage done to their trenches.

Early next morning troops of the 70th Brigade began to take over the line, but battalion headquarters and two platoons of B company were not relieved till dusk of the 22nd. The night was spent in the Torr Top dug-outs on Observatory Ridge and the Thirteenth withdrew to camp at Dickebusch next day.

Capt. E. Gray, M.C., had led many attacks upon strong points during the advance. He killed many Germans and was responsible for the consolidation and defence of the "Green" Line against the counter-attacks of the enemy, so his Distinguished Service Order was well earned. 2nd Lieut. W. J. Arris commanded his platoon with great skill and courage during the German counter-attacks; 2nd Lieut. G. C. Wright brought up two platoons under heavy fire and formed the defensive flank to the south, afterwards remaining in command, though wounded, during a counter-attack; 2nd Lieut. F. E. C. Douglas Smith had led the platoon which enfiladed the German counter-attack on the Menin road; Lieut. R. S. F. Mitchell carried out his duties as intelligence officer under continuous and heavy fire and afterwards replaced the company commander who fell in the advance; Lieut. J. P. Carroll was in charge of brigade signals and kept the line in repair under heavy shell fire, although he was blown up on one occasion; 2nd Lieut. W. I. Caldwell was also prominent for skilful and gallant leadership. All these officers were awarded the Military Cross. Three sergeants were awarded the Distinguished Conduct Medal: Sergt. R. Mineards for good work upon the exposed flank, both in consolidating and repulsing counter-attacks; Sergt. R. Cowell for similar service, though wounded; and Lance-Sergt. G. W. Jackson, who commanded an advanced post during several counter-attacks and captured a German officer. Many

The Durham Forces in the Field

Military Medals were won, and Corpl. I. Bellerby, M.M., received a bar to his decoration.

Major E. Borrow, former adjutant of the battalion, served with the 10th Duke of Wellington's Regt. on September 20th. He was twice wounded, but led the advance to the "Green" Line on the left of the Thirteenth and was awarded the Distinguished Service Order.

After the battle the following letter was received by the commanding officer of the Thirteenth from the O.C. 156th Brigade R.F.A. (33rd Division), whose guns had been in action behind the Durhams:

"We of the 33rd Divisional Artillery cannot let you go without wishing you the best of luck and giving you our heartiest congratulations. All our F.O.O.'s,* B.C.† and all, are full of the 13th D.L.I., and we all look upon you as our own infantry. We all hope we may again have the honour of supporting you and doing still more for you. We have had the best of good hunting together. I hope you will go off think all so much of the 33rd D.A. as they do of you."

The Twelfth were reserve battalion in the attack, but they supplied carrying parties to the other units. A and B companies reached Torr Top on the night of the 18th and carried up stores and ammunition to the forward dumps on the following day.

When the 11th N.F. moved forward to the attack at zero on the 20th, D company of the Twelfth followed closely and became involved in the fighting in Dumbarton Wood, where Germans in "pill-boxes" offered a fierce resistance. One such place was overlooked by the attackers and Sergt. B. Cruddas of Darlington left the carrying party of which he was in charge and went on alone to reconnoitre. He then took 3 men and attacked it, accounting for all the garrison after a brief struggle. For this exploit the sergeant was awarded the Distinguished Conduct Medal. D company formed a big ammunition dump in the neighbourhood of the big lake, well forward of the enemy barrage. After digging in near this spot

* Forward Observing Officers. † Battery Commander.

The Third Battle of Ypres

they were moved forward to the "Red" Line and later to the "Blue" Line, where they were on the right of B company of the 10th N.F. At 1 a.m. next morning D company were withdrawn, but on the night of the 22nd they provided carrying parties until relieved on the afternoon of September 24th.

A and B companies followed the 10th N.F. in the attack on the "Blue" Line and entrenched a little forward of Jasper Trench at 8 a.m., supporting the Fusiliers. On the evening of the 21st these companies were to have been withdrawn, but owing to the German counter-attacks A company were sent forward to reinforce the troops in the neighbourhood of the "Blue" Line about 7.30 p.m. Two hours later this company returned to Jasper Trench and both moved back to Torr Top next morning. On the two following days A and B companies worked as carriers until relieved at 7 p.m. on September 24th.

C company, without their Lewis guns, followed the Thirteenth on the 20th and dumped their loads at the "Green" Line soon after the objective was captured. Three journeys from the Green Line to the forward dumps and back again were made that day and two more on September 21st, after which the company returned to Torr Top. Their Lewis guns had been sent for at 10 a.m. on the day of the attack and came forward to support the Thirteenth. At night the guns were put in to strengthen the front and right flank of the "Green" Line and one was knocked out by a shell. At 9 p.m. the detachments returned to Torr Top. The whole of C company occupied reserve positions during September 22nd, 23rd and 24th, till troops of the incoming division took over the line.

By carrying forward material and ammunition under heavy fire the Twelfth had rendered great assistance in holding the captured ground and opportunity for the display of gallantry and initiative had not been wanting. 2nd Lieut. Wm. Dodd, commanding C company, directed the carrying to the front line and was with his Lewis guns when they assisted to repel a counter-attack; 2nd Lieut. J. Noble had done good work with the carrying parties; 2nd Lieut. W. F.

The Durham Forces in the Field

Farris had taken his company forward under a heavy barrage when a counter-attack threatened and, though wounded, remained with his men till the danger was past. These officers received the Military Cross and C.-S.-M. C. Miller of Spennymore, who dug out single-handed several men hurled in a dug-out by a shell, received the Distinguished Conduct Medal. The Military Medal was won by Sergts. J. Clasper, J. Parmley, J. Pearson and J. Watson; Corpls. R. Defty and W. Littlewood; Lance-Corpls. J. Carter and S. H. King; and Ptes. F. E. Burgess, T. Fletcher, P. Gray, A. Crouch, F. G. Farrison, E. Jones, W. Lewins, J. Moore, G. Nelson, J. Newlands, R. Nixon, R. Outhwaite, W. Stokoe, F. Stott, C. Wilson and J. Yates.

The losses in the ranks of the Twelfth amounted to 110, besides Lieut. A. T. Hunt and 2nd Lieuts. J. Maitland, C. E. S. Phillips, G. B. Chester, A. Boyd-Smith, W. F. Farris, J. R. Etherington, G. Dalziel and W. R. Fill, M.C., who were all wounded.

The next great attack was carried out on October 4th, when the 21st Division were in the line east of Polygon Wood. The Fifteenth, one of the battalions of the 64th Brigade selected for the assault, drew their battle stores at Ridge Wood on October 2nd. When the brigade took over the line that night the Durhams were led astray by their guides, but managed to dig in by 1.30 A.M. on October 3rd, south-east of Glencorse Wood. The German heavies systematically searched the whole area from the front line back to Hooge and the Fifteenth suffered so severely during the day that they were replaced in the attack by a battalion of the K.O.Y.L.I. So many men had been killed and wounded that the survivors were reorganised in two companies.

The brigade attacked in wind and rain at 6 A.M. on October 4th, with their right on the Hooge-Reutel road. Three hundred yards ahead was Joist Farm and then the Polygonbeke stream had to be crossed before Reutel was reached. Joist Farm was only carried after fierce fighting and the stream was

The Third Battle of Ypres

enfiladed from the right, and therefore not easy to cross. But this was done and the three Yorkshire battalions then tackled the "pill-boxes" on the rising ground beyond. To the south the 5th Division had found it more difficult to get forward and 2nd Lieut. J. Sedgwick, with A B company of the Fifteenth, sent up under heavy fire to dig in on the Joist Farm line, altered his dispositions. The company established themselves south of Joist Farm, facing south and south-east along the north edge of Cameron Covert. This was accomplished by 2 p.m. and the East Yorkshires prolonged the line forward.

The British guns had already broken up one counter-attack and a more serious advance now threatened from the south-east. The Germans, coming on with great determination, established machine-guns in Polderhoek Château, and entered Cameron Covert in large numbers. But John Sedgwick's men used their rifles and Lewis guns with great effect and held the enemy at bay. At nine in the evening touch was obtained on the right with troops of the 5th Division and soon afterwards Colonel Falvey-Beyts came forward with the rest of the Fifteenth and joined A B company. Early on the morning of October 5th the commanding officer organised an attack upon a "pill-box," containing three machine-guns, in Cameron Covert, but the Germans surrendered to the attacking party under Lieut. C. S. Herbert. Hostile shell fire was heavy all day, and the Germans advanced again in the evening. In another counter-attack at 11 p.m. Colonel Falvey-Beyts was killed and the adjutant Capt. N. R. Pease, was wounded. Lieut. Sedgwick assumed command of the battalion and Lieut. C. S. Herbert took up the adjutant's duties. Both these officers received the Military Cross and Colonel Falvey-Beyts the Distinguished Service Order.

On the morning of the attack 2nd Lieut. W. Tweddell, with 20 men of the Fifteenth, had been sent up with ammunition to the furthest limit of the advance. They got there after negotiating a heavy barrage and stayed near the western outskirts of Reutel until the brigade were relieved, proving of great

The Durham Forces in the Field

assistance to the East Yorkshiremen in repelling counter-attacks. 2nd Lieut. Tweddell was given the Military Cross, which was also received by 2nd Lieut. J. G. Raine and by Capt. J. W. Watthews, R.A.M.C., for his devoted work among the wounded. Sergt. E. J. Lloyd was awarded a bar to his Military Medal, a decoration conferred for their gallantry on Sergts. J. T. Booth, J. Pope and A. G. Robson; Corpl. T. Fall; Lance-Corpls. W. Moreland and W. Northey; Ptes. W. Baines and J. Spoors.

The Fifteenth were relieved when the line was readjusted during the night and reached dug-outs at Zillebeke on the morning of the 6th, after sustaining 5 casualties on the way. The total losses of the battalion amounted to 20 officers and 410 men, which includes the third commanding officer of the Fifteenth killed or mortally wounded in action.

CHAPTER II

To hold the line while each fresh attack was in preparation or waited upon the weather—proved hardly less of an ordeal than to advance; so that the experiences of the battalions while thus maintaining the captured ground also belong to the story of the battle.

On October 10th the Tenth moved up in fighting order from Redford House, which was near the Ypres-St. Eloi road. Their way led over a duckboard track to a reserve position in Sanctuary Wood. Here they lived in shell-holes, bits of trench and wretched shelters, providing carrying and working parties. Sanctuary Wood and the forward route were shelled day and night. On the 13th the Tenth took over a portion of the front, going up in file along the duckboard track. A company, in the rear, had 18 casualties from shell fire before Stirling Castle ridge was passed; otherwise the relief was accomplished without much trouble.

The Third Battle of Ypres

The line faced south-east between the streams called Reutelbeke and Polygonbeke and the right was on open ground. The left passed through Cameron Covert.

One company were in reserve in Cameron House on the right of the line, and 200 yards further west was battalion headquarters, established in a "pillbox." Here there were petrol tins to sit on, but all slept on the floor which was often covered in water and was never really dry. The enemy shelled the positions steadily, though there was generally a quieter spell from dawn till eight o'clock in the morning. Polderhoek Château, opposite the brigade on the right of the battalion, afforded the enemy a view of the whole of the sector held by the Tenth. The front line and support trenches were more or less continuous, but the two companies on the right in the open were isolated from the rest of the battalion during the day. There were, of course, no communication trenches. Orders had been given to push posts forward on the right and left, but the ground was a morass and little could be done. However, two new posts were established, which served to link up the battalion line and provide touch with the troops on the left across the Polygonbeke.

Relieved on the 18th, the Tenth got out safely by the Glencorse Wood track and the Menin road and marched back to camp at Ridge Wood. The last seven days had cost the battalion 26 killed, 2 officers and 75 others wounded and 7 missing. Besides these, 43 men, including 9 gassed and 5 with trench foot, were evacuated sick. The weather had been fair for the most part.

A few days were now devoted to rest and cleaning up, but a visit was received from enemy bombing planes. On October 21st came another move forward, the Tenth being one of the two battalions left by the Brigade to work on tracks and light railways in the vicinity of Birr Cross Roads and Sanctuary Wood. With the weather very cold and wet, life at Kruisstraethoek, in a waterlogged bivouac camp which was shelled now and then, proved the reverse of pleasant. The

The Durham Forces in the Field

enemy planes were persistent in night bombing and all ranks were very glad when the battalion left by bus on October 30th for the rest area around Berthen. Here, and at billets near St. Omer, a full month was spent.

The Twelfth spent three days at a camp near Westoutre on coming out of the Menin Road action. The battalion moved up on September 28th to Ridge Wood camp as a reserve to the other brigades of the division still holding the line. Working and carrying parties of 200 men per day were supplied till October 1st, when the Twelfth departed by bus to Meteren. Tents at Thieushock were reached on the 3rd and training was carried on in the rain; but two days later the battalion moved to Dickebusch, where they lived in the mud with little protection from the weather. Working parties had to be supplied for burying cable. The battalion took over the line east of Polygon Wood on the night of October 13th and found themselves just beyond the scene of the fighting in which the Fifteenth had been engaged at the beginning of the month. The mud and the hostile shelling made the relief difficult and there was no respite during the three days the battalion held the line. The German aeroplanes were very active and on one occasion a group of nineteen, flying low, machine-gunned the trenches of the Twelfth. On the evening of the 16th the Durhams were relieved and withdrew to rest and reorganise. Losses during the tour amounted to 90, of whom a third were killed, and Capt. C. Powel-Smith and 2nd Lieut. W. R. Chapman were among the wounded. On the evening of the 19th the Twelfth came up again. Shelling interfered with the relief, but on the following day, when a patrol found an enemy machine-gun and brought it in, the German gunners paid most attention to the back areas. German aeroplanes flew low every night, firing Very lights which revealed every movement on our forward tracks. On the evening of October 21st guides were sent to Hooge Crater and conducted the Fifteenth to the front line. Relieved before dawn, the Twelfth, with casualties much

The Third Battle of Ypres

tighter than those of the previous tour, withdrew to Zillebeke Bund.

The experiences of the Thirteenth were similar to those of the Twelfth. On September 27th Major Longden had left the battalion, and Capt. D. H. Clarke, D.S.O., M.C., again assumed command. In taking over the line near Reutel on the evening of October 10th, 2nd Lieut. A. G. Sebborn and 33 others were wounded and 3 men were missing. The relief was not complete till eight o'clock the next morning and the battalion were shelled throughout the day and the next night. By the time the Thirteenth were relieved on the 13th and withdrawn to the bund at Zillebeke, casualties were increased by 2nd Lieut. C. Fands and 5 others killed and 2nd Lieut. J. C. Witherspoon and 44 wounded. B and D companies had been left behind in a support position. The rest of the battalion moved back to Dickebusch next day. On the 16th there was a great presentation by the divisional commander of honours won during the Flanders fighting. Pte. A. Constantine had been awarded a bar to his Military Medal, while the ribbon of that decoration was given to Sergts. F. Burns, W. Powell, J. Robson, F. Saltmarsh, W. Sledge and E. Wilkinson; Corpls. J. Anderson, T. Cassinelli, C. W. Jefferson, T. F. Patterson, W. Thompson and N. Walton; Lance-Corpls. J. Bowman, J. O. Dean, J. McKenna and J. Roy; Ptes. F. Byrne, T. Cornthwaite, J. Donnan, J. J. Fenderson, E. Hodges, J. L. Holt, W. Howe, T. W. Howlett, G. Kempster, A. Lucas, D. Patterson, C. S. Rowell, H. Shaw, J. Sim, E. C. Smith, W. Webster and J. T. Woodruff. The battalion reunited at Railway Dug-outs on October 17th.

The Thirteenth took over the front line again near Reutel on the evening of the 18th. The usual three days of ceaseless shelling followed. At dawn and dusk the Lewis guns engaged the enemy aeroplanes flying low over the trenches and snipers on both sides were active. On the afternoon of October 21st a party of the enemy was seen near Judge's Copse and dispersed by Lewis gun and rifle fire. The same evening the

The Durham Forces in the Field

Thirteenth handed over trenches to a battalion of the 21st Division and came back to Zillebeke Bund. The tour had cost the battalion 66 in killed and wounded, besides 2nd Lieut. J. P. Carroll, M.C., wounded and gassed.

The Fifteenth had had little respite since the fighting at the beginning of October. After two days at Ebblinghem the battalion reached Ypres by bus on October 11th. Then came five days' work, principally on railways, followed by a whole day's rest. On the 20th the Fifteenth arrived at Zillebeke Bund, moving forward to take over the front line. This was accomplished, as has been related, the battalion relieving the Twelfth by the dawn of the 22nd.

The weather had been wet for several days, but now came a fine morning followed by showers in the afternoon. The line ran roughly north-east from the site of Reutel cemetery and Germans were rarely seen during the day-time. Their exact positions were difficult to locate, as they pushed posts forward at night.

Shelling of the tracks to the front line and of our battery positions hardly ever ceased. The rains had converted most of the country into a morass and a man had to keep to the duckboards unless he were very lightly equipped. The activity of the German planes at night was always a great annoyance.

Relieved during heavy hostile shelling in the early morning of the 23rd, the Fifteenth went back to a support position near Joist Farm and Clapham Junction and a few days later got some rest in divisional reserve near Kruisstraethoek. But on the 30th the battalion were at Zillebeke Bund again and took over the line on the extreme left of the divisional front next evening. All tracks on the way up were shelled with mustard gas, mixed with salvoes of high explosive, and the Fifteenth lost 50 men.

The weather improved during the first days of November. On the 2nd German trench mortars opened and the enemy gunners and airmen were particularly active on the following day. At about

The Third Battle of Ypres

10 P.M. two German patrols approached posts of the Fifteenth. The enemy was allowed to come quite close; then Lewis guns and rifles opened and he dispersed. It was difficult to get out across the mud, but the corpse of a sergeant-major of the 5th Reserve Infantry Regt. was brought in.

On November 4th three companies returned to Zillebeke Bund and B company remained in reserve to the relieving battalion. On the 6th the Fifteenth withdrew to Scottish Wood. The last tour in the line had cost over 60 casualties, including one officer hit in an attempt to rescue a wounded man lying in a shell-hole. Pte. A. Broadwell of Bradford, who went out at once and brought in the officer under the fire of several German snipers, was awarded the Distinguished Conduct Medal.

On October 17th the 35th Division took the extreme left of the British front, next to the French. The Nineteenth arrived at Proven by train on the 16th and came into the line where it crossed the high ground north-east of Koekuit on the night of October 18th. The weather was vile and forward of battalion headquarters no duckboards provided a way across the mud. Artillery was active on both sides and there was much gas shelling to be endured till the 21st, when the Nineteenth were relieved and withdrew to camp at Elverdinghe.

There was a combined attack by the French, the 35th Division and a brigade of the 34th on October 22nd, when some ground was gained on the southern edge of Houthulst forest. The Nineteenth were not involved, but took over the left of the divisional line on the night of the 23rd. Many men were killed and wounded during the relief and there was a heavy hostile bombardment next morning when the enemy was seen massing for a counter-attack opposite the junction of the Nineteenth and the French. At 6 A.M. the German infantry sent up red lights and then advanced under a barrage. But the Nineteenth were ready with Lewis gun and rifle and lost less than 20 men, while the Germans could make no headway

The Durham Forces in the Field

and withdrew, leaving 60 or 70 dead upon the ground. On the night of October 27th the Nineteenth were relieved and came by train from Boesinghe to Proven. Casualties amounted to 230, of whom half were sick. After cleaning up and refitting, the battalion moved to huts at Dykes Camp on the 30th, and Lieut.-Col. W. B. Greenwell, who had been gassed on the 20th, became too ill to continue in command any longer. He handed over to Major S. Huffam on the last day of the month.

On November 2nd the Nineteenth moved up to a support position, W and X companies being at Kockuit and the rest of the battalion back at Wijendrift. 2nd Lieut. G. N. Allen was wounded on this day. At night a heavy gas shell bombardment took heavy toll of the battalion. The commanding officer, Capts. J. W. Ryall, C. B. Pearson and H. G. Rice, R.A.M.C.; and 2nd Lieuts. R. C. J. Allan, C. E. Brown, R. A. Edgar, C. Pugh and N. Wharton were all gassed. The shelling was repeated on the following night when the adjutant, Capt. R. M. Middleton, with Capt. W. T. Oliver and 2nd Lieut. G. K. Prior, was added to the list of victims. When the battalion were relieved on November 4th there had been 125 casualties in the ranks, chiefly from the same cause. The Nineteenth withdrew to Proven, whence three more subalterns were sent to hospital. The loss of 16 officers including commanding officer, adjutant and 4 company commanders all within a few days when the battalion were not fighting, or even holding the line, is probably unique.

Major V. E. Gooderson from the 18th H.L.I. took command on November 8th. All energies were now directed to improving the camp, protective mud walls being built round the tents. On the 14th came another move to the line and four days later the Nineteenth took over the left portion of the front between the stream called Lekkerboterbeek and the Poelcappelle-Westroosebeke road. The time was held by posts in " pill-boxes " or the ruins of farm buildings.

At 5.15 a.m. on the morning of the 19th a strong German patrol, led by an officer, approached the " pill-

The Third Battle of Ypres

box" on the right of the battalion front. The sentry, Pte. Pinkney, challenged and then exchanged shots with the enemy. One German fell dead and the rest withdrew under a brisk fire, but a little later the same patrol came again, approaching the "pill-box" from the rear. Pinkney challenged again and the German officer replied in English: "Oh, it's all right!" but he was now near enough for his cap to betray him. The man of Durham shot the officer dead and the rest of the garrison easily dispersed the enemy. Later in the day this adventurous patrol came to an untimely end on the left of the line, where 12 of them were killed and 6 captured. They proved to be men of the 166th Regt.

Later on the same morning Z company, in the centre, dispersed a patrol of 30 Germans by rifle and Lewis gun fire. They all fell, but some were presumably unhurt, though the intervening ground was a swamp and our men could not reach them. In the afternoon W company captured 3 prisoners, largely through the action of Corpl. Coyle who also secured another man he had mortally wounded.

Hostile shelling was heavy on the following day when the battalion were relieved, but the casualties during this tour only amounted to 10.

No troops contributed more than the Pioneers to the hard-won successes in Flanders during the summer and autumn of 1917. Their work in preparation for the offensive had been strenuous and had cost many casualties; but, as the advance progressed and the weather got worse, it was only by unceasing labour on roads and tracks that the awful ground could be made passable for stretcher-bearers, pack animals, carrying parties, fighting troops, limbers and guns.

The Twenty-Second were engaged on the opening day of battle. While the 8th Division took Bellewaarde ridge on July 31st and pushed on to the outskirts of Westhoek, the battalion followed, carrying forward roads and tracks on the very heels of the advance. C company had been attached to the 7th Canadian Railway Construction Company and were working on

The Durham Forces in the Field

a light railway running forward to a point north of Zillebeke Lake. On the night of July 30th the rest of the Pioneers came up to Swan Château, south of Ypres and west of the Ypres-Comines canal. A company's task was to push forward a track from the Zillebeke road towards Westhoek, while B company worked on a parallel track 500 yards further south. D company had to make and repair a road, which was to run from Château Wood to Zonnebeke, via Westhoek, as the advance progressed.

Having given the infantry time to clear the enemy from his forward positions, A company, under Capt. W. H. Perkins, moved off at 7.15 A.M. on July 31st and commenced work at 8.40 A.M., sappers marking out the track a little way ahead. Slow but steady progress was made all the morning over difficult ground. For the first two hours high explosive shells burst in the vicinity, but not near enough to interrupt the work and very few men were hit. In the afternoon the chief trouble was machine-gun fire which grazed the ridge north of Bellewaarde Lake. The track now approached Idiot Reserve Trench, where the ground was very bad, but by 6 P.M. the way was made for field guns up to but not over Jacob Trench, near the crest of Bellewaarde ridge. After spending an hour on improvements the company rested at Idiot Support Trench, where rain began to fall. By midnight everyone was wet through. The Pioneers assembled in the rain at six o'clock the next morning and began to work forward towards Ziel House, making such general improvements as were possible. The track was now a perfect quagmire owing to heavy pedestrian and mule traffic all through the night and early morning. It was half-past ten when the long and weary march back to Pioneer Camp, near Dickebusch, was commenced. In his report on the work carried out the company commander remarks that there was "much scope for patience and coolness," and 2nd Lieut. Bruce, C.-S.-M. White and Corpl. Leeming are particularly commended.

At 8.30 A.M. Capt. A. H. Robson, M.C., arrived with B company at a point in the old British front trench just north of Zouave Wood and work was

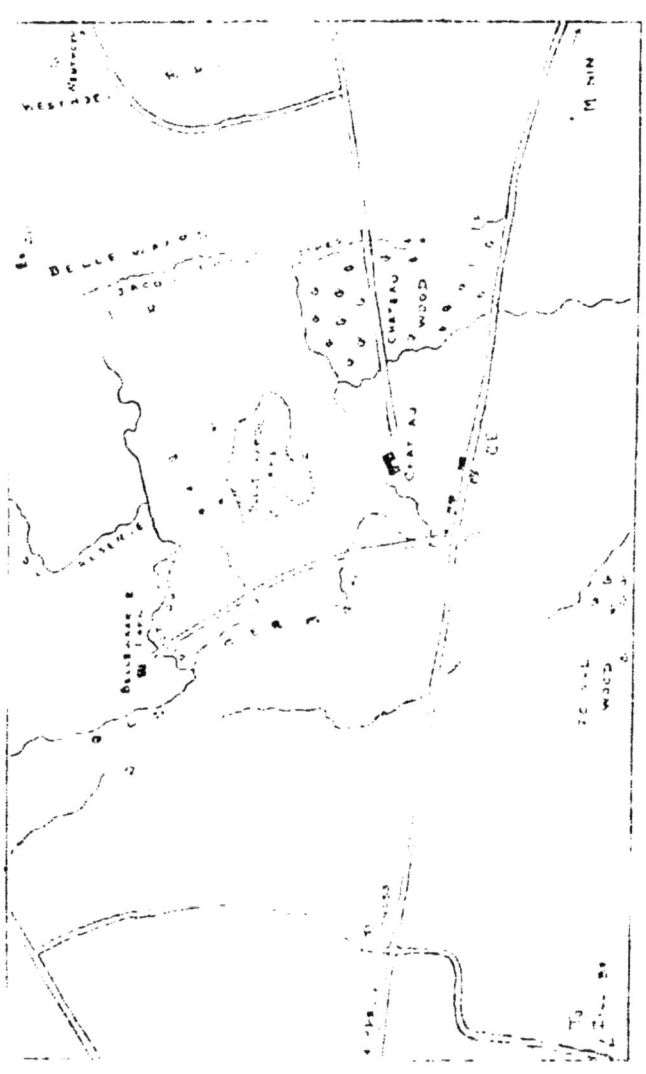

The Durham Forces in the Field

commenced on a track across "No Man's Land." Heavy hostile shelling made the work difficult from the start and C... Robson was hit in the left wrist by a shell splinter. When he left the company, 2nd Lieut. L. S. Wood assumed command till 2nd Lieut. L. W. Andrews arrived. Rain came on at half-past four and when the company sheltered for the night in the old German trenches, 2nd Lieut. Wood and 12 men had been wounded. Three others, not so badly hit, remained on duty. At 4.15 a.m. on August 1st work was resumed in rain which never ceased and the track slowly lengthened round the south of Château Wood and then onwards to the edge of the Westhoek road. There was not so much shelling and the allotted task was done in three hours, B company arriving in Pioneer Camp before mid-day.

The adventures of D company were the most exciting. Major T. G. Davidson's men were confronted with a heavy barrage astride the Menin road west of Hooge and an effort was therefore made to get round on the left. At 11 a.m. the company arrived on the west edge of Bellewaarde Lake. From Château Wood came machine-gun and rifle fire, showing that small posts of Germans still held out there, but work commenced on the road. At 2 p.m. the German fire from the front wounded several men, so a Lewis gun section came into action. Soon afterwards Major Davidson and an officer of the sappers reconnoitred towards Westhoek ridge and saw Germans advancing. No other British troops were in the vicinity, so the company withdrew to James Trench. In the words of the company commander: "We could not carry the work any further till the ridge was definitely occupied by our forces." In these circumstances D company returned, picked up rations and water at the Birr Cross Roads dhoup and eventually reached Swan Château at 7.15 p.m.

On August 2nd the three companies moved to Halifax Camp on the Vlamertinghe-Ouderdom road. Here the men were issued with new clothing which was badly needed and the Corps commander paid the Pioneers a visit. Congratulations on the work done

The Third Battle of Ypres

were received from the Commander-in-Chief. A move was made to Dominion Camp on the 5th.

The following awards of the Military Medal for gallantry during June and July were now gazetted: Sergts. J. H. Howells and B. Veasey; Corpl. A. P. Hodgson; Lance-Corpl. J. A. Brown; and Pte. A. Robinson.

The 8th Division had moved out of the line, but there was still plenty of work for the Pioneers. On August 7th a detachment of 2 officers and 30 men were sent to Lock 9 on the Comines canal, with orders to clear up the ground forward to the old British line. On this day D company started to enlarge the accommodation at Swan Château, while company commanders reconnoitred the ground on which work was to be done when the 8th Division came back for the next advance.

Enemy bombing planes had become very attentive to the camps along the Ouderdom road, but no casualties were suffered by the Twenty-Second. On August 13th the battalion moved to bivouacs at Belgian Château, on the road to Kruisstraat, and at night A company went to work on a double duckboard track south of Bellewaarde Lake and up over Bellewaarde ridge. B company improved the pack track towards Ziel House and D company's energies were directed upon another double duckboard track still further to the north. 2nd Lieut. O'Dell commanded a detachment, with three Lewis guns, which was established on Zillebeke ridge for anti-aircraft work.

On the 16th the 8th Division attacked with their left on the railway and their right on Westhoek, the advance being north-east towards Zonnebeke. The communications on which the Pioneers were now working at night were thus of the utmost importance, more particularly as the weather was so bad. But there was yet another task for the Twenty-Second. On the day before the attack 40 men from A company, under 2nd Lieut. Adamson, and the same number from B company, under 2nd Lieut. Howen, went to the dump at Birr Cross Roads where each man equipped himself with a light portable bridge. At 4.45 next morn-

The Durham Forces in the Field

ing, when the advance began, these men of the Twenty-Second went forward too as far as the Hannebeek stream, and in the face of heavy fire the bridges were placed in position for the attacking infantry to cross. On their way back the bridging parties assisted the wounded and escorted prisoners, their own losses amounting to one man killed, 15 wounded and 7 missing. General Grogan, commanding the 23rd Brigade, afterwards wrote to Colonel Morgan as follows:

"I should like to thank all ranks of your battalion who co-operated with the 23rd Brigade on August 16 in crossing the Hannebeek. The bridging parties who went over with the leading wave did their work in a most efficient and soldierly manner, with the utmost coolness and disregard of fire. The bridges very materially contributed to our success, and valuable information in regard to the situation was brought back by bridging parties on completion of their task."

All three companies were busy on the night of the 16th pushing on with the track passing south of Bellewaarde Lake and then going northwards along the west side of the ridge on its way to the new front line. The boards were carried up and then fixed in position on trestles and this work continued until the 21st. It was possible to work during daylight in small parties under the cover afforded by Westhoek ridge and few casualties were sustained.

A move was made to rest in the vicinity of Caestre on August 22nd, after C company had rejoined the battalion.

The work of the Eleventh during the early days of the Ypres battle was somewhat similar to that of the Twenty-Second. C company began work in the Ypres area on July 21st, when a start was made on railway construction. On July 31st the remainder of the battalion came up by light railway to the Yser canal at a point about a mile north of Ypres. They were to push forward roads towards the battle front, which, as a result of the day's advance, was now well beyond the Pilckem ridge and within 1,000 yards of Langemarck. Very heavy rain delayed the work and the

THE 105th DURHAM LIGHT INFANTRY MOVING UP ON JULY 31st, 1917

The Third Battle of Ypres

three companies stayed out all night, having received rations and water in the evening. The east side of Pilcken ridge was searched continuously by the German gunners, but not till 2 P.M. on August 1st did B and D companies return to camp. A company followed in the evening, everyone being very wet and tired out. C company had just completed 100 yards of light railway track—heavy work under persistent shell fire.

The work continued till August 4th, when A, B and D companies had a day's rest; they needed it, for they had been marching fourteen miles daily to and from their tasks, at which they spent six hours. C company persevered with the light railway. The 20th Division took over the front of the 6th and two companies of the Eleventh were able to go into dug-outs in the canal bank vacated by the Welsh pioneers, work being continued on the roads, tracks and railways which were needed before the next attack upon the 16th. Losses were not heavy during these days, Lieut. Hopkinson and a few men being wounded.

At 4.45 A.M. on August 16th the 20th Division took part in the new advance and captured Langemarck. A, B and D companies remained at the canal bank until 9 o'clock, when they went forward to make a route for wheeled traffic across the Pilcken ridge. During this and the following day of strenuous work under heavy fire the Eleventh had Capt. J. Taylor wounded and 31 other casualties. On August 18th the Welsh pioneers came in again and B and D companies moved to Leipzig Farm on the road to Elverdinghe. This camp was shelled and 2nd Lieut. Gardner wounded. C company were left behind to continue work on the railway, but the rest of the battalion left Elverdinghe by train on August 19th and went back to the vicinity of Proven. For nearly a week the three companies did not touch spade or pick. Drill was the order of the day, though a large anti-aircraft detachment of Lewis guns had to be furnished. The end of the month saw all the men available doing platoon training, while the instruction of specialists was also carried on. C company were

The Durham Forces in the Field

still at work on the railway with very occasional days of rest.

During the first week in September parties were provided for work on the Pilckem road, for the R.E. dumps and for burying cables.

The Eleventh took over from the Welsh pioneers again at the dug-outs on the canal bank on September 9th, 2nd Lieut. F. Atlay with six Lewis guns going forward at once for anti-aircraft work. The 20th Division were now relieving the 38th and the three companies devoted a day to improving their own accommodation. On September 12th C company moved back to rest after their work on the railway. Next day nearly all the men available were busy carrying material to the forward dumps in preparation for the next attack. This work, together with the wiring of a trench in the forward area near Schreiboom, went forward until the day of the advance, September 20th.

On the eve of the attack the weather, which had been fair since the beginning of the month, turned to rain. The Eleventh supplied a detachment of 50 men and six Lewis guns, under 2nd Lieut. Atlay, to take over all anti-aircraft work forward of the old front line when the division had captured their objectives. In the evening A company came up to the new front and, by working all night, completed four strong points south-east of the Staden railway, thereby making the left flank secure. D company were led astray by their guides and only arrived in time to complete one strong point. More night work followed, all the companies being engaged upon the repair of the roads leading forward to Langemarck. Here the tanks detailed to clear a trench still held by the enemy became bogged and all efforts to dig them out failed. The whole area was heavily shelled day and night and the ground forward of the Pilckem ridge was waterlogged. Under these difficulties the Pioneers persevered until, at 2 A.M. on September 24th, a storm of gas-shells made work impossible. On the following night the Eleventh were wanted for digging and wiring in the front line and this continued till relief of the division on Septem-

The Third Battle of Ypres

ber 28th. A duckboard track from Langemarck to the line was also completed, in spite of the fierce hostile fire.

The end of the month brought to a close the tour of the Eleventh in this part of the front. During September casualties in the ranks amounted to 60 and would have been considerably heavier if the working parties had not been handled with such skill and judgment. Capt. W. G. L. Sear, who so successfully directed A company in the construction of the strung points on September 20th and in their subsequent nightly tasks, was awarded the Military Cross. Officers wounded during the month included 2nd Lieuts. V. E. Towlson, E. Fleming, J. R. Branch and R. Morton.

TRENCH WARFARE

AUGUST TO NOVEMBER, 1917

The Tenth were at Mont Vidaigne till August 6th. Then they marched in bad weather to billets near Caestre, where "mopping up" practice was a feature of the training. Eventually the battalion reached Dickebusch and moved up to Zillebeke Bund on August 20th on their way to battle.

Coming down from the line the Tenth spent a few days at Devonshire Camp, where drafts were received before the departure of the battalion to the Berthen training area at the end of August. The weather was very wet. A new brigadier paid a great compliment to the Tenth at this time. He said they "showed a marked superiority over the remainder of the brigade group as regards marching, march discipline generally and equipment."
The battalion spent most of September training at various places near Bailleul. On the 20th they went into trenches on the low ground east of Messines, near Gapaard, where hostile shell fire never ceased and the enemy aircraft were very bold. On September 29th the Durhams withdrew to Kortepyp, south of Neuve Eglise, having sustained 20 casualties including 2nd Lieut. P. Braidford, M.C., killed. Training and working parties kept them busy until October 6th. Then, after a few days near Westoutre and la Clytte, the Tenth returned to the battlefield of Ypres.

The Twelfth moved to Serques on August 7th and found that training facilities were not so good there. Rehearsals for the attack continued till August 25th, when the battalion came up to Cornwall Camp, near Ouderdom. On August 29th the O.C., 3rd Canadian

Trench Warfare, Aug.—Nov., 1917

Casualty Clearing Station, sent the following message: "I wish to bring to your attention the gallant conduct of Pte. C. Woodward in giving blood to a patient in this hospital on July 12, 1917."

Now the battalion moved up to huts near Dickebusch, whence the battle line was reconnoitred and a visit was paid to model trenches. But on September 5th the Twelfth were back at Noordpeene, west of Cassel. Training here comprised an attack on a strong point, lining up on tapes and gas drill. The move towards the line commenced on September 14th and on the night of the 18th A and B companies arrived in the vicinity of Observatory Ridge, east of Zillebeke.

On October 21st the Twelfth said good-bye to the battleground of Ypres. Next day buses took the battalion westward to St. Martin-au-Laert, beyond St. Omer, where they prepared for the journey to Italy. New clothing was fitted, drafts of young soldiers were absorbed, and many inspections culminated in a visit from the Commander-in-Chief, who saw the 68th Brigade on October 31st. About this time the award of the Military Medal to Lance-Corpl. H. Wilson and Ptes. R. Daglish, A. J. Edwards and J. Snowball was announced. Route marches, musketry and other training kept the Durhams busy and all men unfit for hard campaigning were sent away. On November 5th Major J. M. Longden succeeded Lieut.-Col. Tyndall in the command of the battalion.

The Thirteenth, who moved from Wizernes to Moulle early in August, continued training until they came forward to camp at Reninghelst on the 25th. After a few days in a muddy camp at Dickebusch they went back to Noordpeene. On September 11th, Capt. C. T. W. Sauerbeck, M.C., serving on the staff, was killed by a shell. The battalion, now commanded by Capt. D. H. Clarke, M.C., reached Dickebusch again on the 16th and three days later advanced to Railway Dug-outs. At night they occupied assembly positions for the attack on the morrow.

209

The Durham Forces in the Field

When the Twelfth moved back to St. Martin-au-Laert, the Thirteenth took up their quarters in the adjacent village of Tatinghem and also prepared for the journey to "an unknown destination."

The Fourteenth trained at Caucourt until August 22nd, relieving Canadian troops in support in the Loos sector on the following evening. About a week before the Colonials had taken historic Hill 70 and the Durhams soon found themselves in the new front line which consisted of a chain of shell-holes exposed to a continuous bombardment. Losses during this tour amounted to 2nd Lieut. H. F. Waud and 14 killed and 43 wounded. Work on the defences and a week of training in divisional reserve at Nocux-les-Mines intervened before the Fourteenth came up again. The British line was now in better shape and, though the Germans were as aggressive as ever, the Durhams had only 7 casualties.

On the night of September 21st a new front was taken over, west of the Lens-la Bassée road. Here two unsuccessful enemy attempts were made to rush an advanced post, known as the Brickstacks, which was held by C company.

Although there was no rest by day or night from shell, trench mortar and machine-gun fire, the Fourteenth wired the whole front during this tour. Losses amounted to 3 killed and 10 wounded and Capt. J. Potts, D.S.O., was gassed. The battalion took over trenches again on October 1st and two nights later B company repulsed another raid by rifle, bombs and Lewis gun fire. On the following day a heavy barrage came down along the whole battalion front and three parties of Germans advanced. A post of the left company was completely demolished by a heavy mortar shell, everyone there being killed or wounded. Germans rushed in and secured a prisoner, retreating before they could be engaged. Casualties during this tour were 4 killed and 31 wounded. Two days in support followed and on October 7th the Fourteenth withdrew to reserve, where training in preparation for further attacks on Lens was interrupted by bad weather. On the evening

Trench Warfare, Aug.—Nov., 1917

of October 19th, when the Durhams were in the line again, a heavy barrage of mortar shells, aerial darts, shrapnel and high explosive caused many casualties and preceded an enemy attack upon a post. The Germans were beaten off by Lewis gun and rifle fire and by the promptness of the gunners in responding to the S.O.S. signal. One company escaped heavy loss by going forward from their trenches to shell-holes in front, but, even so, Lieut. L. Codwin and 2nd Lieut. J. W. Young were wounded and 3 men killed and 42 wounded before relief on October 20th.

The battalion had now seen the last of the Lens trenches. Reaching billets at Noeux-les-Mines on October 21st, they went northwards by rail to Fontes. Training was done here and afterwards at Amplaines, where attack practice with tanks over a flagged course and the training of pack transport still left time for football and cross-country runs. On November 15th the Fourteenth marched to Frevent and entrained for Peronne. Billets were at Haut Allaines, where the transport rejoined the battalion, and a further move was made at once to Equancourt which was not reached till 4 A.M. on November 17th owing to the roads being so congested with the traffic of troops, tanks and guns now moving in darkness and secrecy to deliver the blow upon the Cambrai front. At 5.30 P.M. on the 17th the Fourteenth left for Fins and went into tents at Bois Dessart, north-east of the village.

When the Fifteenth came into trenches again on August 1st the line had been readjusted and the battalion now held the trenches south of the Sensée river on the extreme left of the divisional front. The weather was wet. About half an hour before "stand to" on the morning of August 3rd the enemy put down a barrage and blew up a concrete blockhouse, destroying the Lewis gun there and driving out the garrison. About 100 Germans made for the evacuated trench but were driven off by Lewis gun and rifle fire from the right, whilst 2nd Lieut. B. S. Smyth-Pigott— who was afterwards awarded the Military Cross— rushed up a party of bombers and reoccupied the

The Durham Forces in the Field

strong point. At 2 p.m. on the same day 2nd Lieut. T. Lowery and 3 others went out and began to cut the German wire. They were fired on and the officer and a sergeant were wounded, the former afterwards being killed by a bomb. The next tour of the Fifteenth was on the extreme right of the divisional line, north-west of Bullecourt, and then the battalion withdrew to the rest area, reaching Simencourt behind the Arras-Doullens road on August 28th.

Now came a move northwards to participate in the struggle at Ypres. On September 16th the battalion entrained at Aubigny for Cassel and eventually reached billets at St. Sylvestre-Cappel. Here and at Thieushouck, near Caestre, practice for the attack was carried out in dry, hot weather. On September 28th the Fifteenth marched in lighting order to a camp on the Reninghelst-la Clytte road, and spent the last two days of the month in studying a relief model of the objectives to be taken in the coming operations. On October 1st the Fifteenth moved to Ridge Wood.

Arrived in Scottish Wood on November 6th the Fifteenth soon moved to Dominion Camp at Onderdom and six days later started on the march southwards. On November 22nd Bray, near Mont St. Eloy, was reached, but after a week's training here the journey was continued by rail from Aubigny. Rumours of a move to Italy had proved unfounded.

In trenches near Méricourt at the beginning of August the Eighteenth had a quiet enemy opposite them, so much necessary work could be done. Patrols were active among the long grass and shell-holes of " No Man's Land," as a German withdrawal was anticipated.

After ten days at Winnipeg Camp, Mont St. Eloy, the Eighteenth made acquaintance with the Acheville portion of the front. On August 20th 150 men were supplied to assist in the installation of the projectors for a great discharge of gas on the Germans in Fresnoy and Acheville. Retaliation, apart from " a rather good display of fireworks," was feeble. The Durhams next

Trench Warfare, Aug.—Nov., 1917

crossed over and occupied the trenches further north at Mericourt again. On August 30th, when the enemy attempted to raid the West Yorkshires, the Eighteenth lost 2nd Lieut. Keith, killed, and 3 men wounded.

On September 4th a German aeroplane was brought down just behind the British line. The occupants were killed and C.-S.-M. Currey was wounded while in charge of the burying party. At midnight the enemy deluged the Vimy area with high explosive, shrapnel and mustard gas. The usual precautions protected the Eighteenth from heavy casualties, though a direct hit upon a Lewis gun post afterwards compelled the evacuation of 8 men suffering from gas poisoning, the effects of which were not felt till the following afternoon. A company of the 4th Canadian Mounted Rifles, whose dug-outs had no proper protection, were practically all casualties. The shelling continued intermittently all day on September 5th and in the evening the 4th C.M.R. relieved the Eighteenth who passed into divisional reserve at Bray. A comprehensive training scheme was carried out and after an R.A.F. lecture several officers and men were taken for a flight, which is recorded as being "very interesting, useful and enjoyable."

The Eighteenth relieved the 13th East Yorks in support in the Arleux sector on September 19th. The month ended with a tour in the front line and during these days the German trench mortars and low-flying aeroplanes caused much annoyance. Relieved on October 1st the Eighteenth withdrew to Ecurie, behind Roclincourt, large working parties being in demand for the elaborate defensive works in process of creation. When in support again in the Arleux sector near Willerval, there came a hurricane bombardment of gas and high explosive on the early morning of October 16th, but losses were light. After another tour in the front line during which artillery activity continued, the Eighteenth were relieved on October 25th and went by train to Ecoivres, near Mont St. Eloy. The weather was very bad, but much useful training was done here.

On November 9th the Eighteenth took over a

portion of the "Red" Line near Arleux. This was the support position and large parties were busy on the defences. The division had now taken over the whole Corps front and when the front line was occupied the battalion had to spread out and hold a line of posts, the intervening trenches being filled with wire and left to the survey of patrols by night. After a turn in support the Eighteenth came up again before the end of the month. The return of the divisional pioneers, who for nearly six months had been detained for railway work near Ypres, now relieved the infantry of some of the arduous work which had fallen upon them.

On August 1st the Nineteenth moved to cellars and tents at Lempire and Ronssoy, reserve positions in the Birdcage sector south-west of Épehy. Here the divisional line, 8,000 yards in length, faced the Hindenburg Line but the enemy held various forward positions on commanding ground which covered his main defensive system. One of these was on the spur containing the ruins of Gillemont Farm, the British and German lines being close together on the flat top of the hill.

The Nineteenth had an uneventful tour on the left of the line and came into the trenches here after the 18th H.L.I. had captured the ruins of the farm. Certain shell fire was heavy but the tour passed without incident of importance, the H.L.I. taking over on August 24th. Leaving W company to hold Cat Post, further to the south, the Nineteenth retired to cellars in Lempire. Next morning came the news that the Germans had counter-attacked in the small hours, recaptured the farm and secured a footing in the British front line at the salient called Blunt Nose.

Two howitzer batteries bombarded the lost positions all day and in the evening the Nineteenth advanced to turn the enemy out. The three companies—all weak in numbers—went straight across country and formed up for the assault in the communication trenches, where a Stokes shell fell by accident among X company. Everyone got clear before it exploded. The

Trench Warfare, Aug.—Nov., 1917

artillery barrage was so good that when the attack was launched the Durhams were upon the Germans before the latter had emerged from cover. Rifle fire from the west side of the ruins caused some casualties to Y company and some of the Jägers fought desperately at Blunt Nose where 6 of them were killed; but in ten minutes the British line was established. The Nineteenth had 50 casualties, including Capt. G. R. Forster—an excellent officer who had been with the battalion since its formation. 2nd Lieut. G. W. Berry was also among the fallen. One heavy machine-gun was captured and two Lewis guns, three Stokes guns and a quantity of ammunition were recovered from the enemy.

The Germans now put down a barrage and attacked soon afterwards with bombs from their trenches on each flank. They were repulsed and when, at 8.30 p.m., they approached over the ground from the south-east fire was opened and they dispersed. The Nineteenth remained in the trenches all night with the H.L.I. and were relieved next morning.

Before the end of the month the Durhams did another tour in the line and the total losses during August amounted to 100, including 2nd Lieut. C. E. Brown, wounded on the 27th. September proved uneventful. A week was spent in divisional reserve and the battalion did two tours in the Birdcage sector, where the Germans on the crest of the ridge commanded a small British work on the reverse slope. Drafts received included 120 good men from the Twenty-Second. Early in October the 35th Division handed over the line preparatory to going northward into the Ypres battle.

The Nineteenth left Peronne by train for Arras on October 6th and spent a week at Montenescourt. Here a draft of 240 men arrived from the Eleventh. On October 14th the battalion entrained at Aubigny for Esquelbecq and reached Proven two days later.

On coming out of battle on September 23rd the Twentieth were destined for many new experiences. They moved in buses to Teteghem, near Dunkerque,

The Durham Forces in the Field

on the 16th, and next day relieved the 2/7th Lancashire Fusiliers in the vicinity of Zuydcoote. The 41st Division were now relieving the 42nd in the Nieuport Bains sector of the Belgian Front and the Wearsiders were introduced to sand dunes, sea bathing and battalion drill on the sea shore. The weather was wet when the battalion went into the line on October 6th for a tour during which hostile shell fire was continuous but casualties were few. Later in the month came training at Bray Dunes and on November 4th the Twentieth returned to the Teteghem area. Preparations now commenced for a long journey to another front.

The award of the Distinguished Conduct Medal to Sergt. T. Robinson should now be recorded. As transport sergeant he had done excellent service in bringing up rations under heavy fire during the fighting east of Ypres. On many occasions his cool judgment had saved casualties to his men and animals.

On August 26th the Twenty-Second moved up to Nieppe, and three days later A and C companies commenced repairing two communication trenches leading to the front line south of Warneton and west of river Lys. This work was taken over from the New Zealand pioneers. There had been two advances in this sector since June 6th and although little ground had been gained there was much work to do. D company were employed on tramways forward of Ploegsteert wood, and B company repaired roads. In dry weather, and with little interference by the enemy, great progress was made although drainage operations had to await the arrival of thigh gum boots. 2nd Lieut. H. S. Bruce was wounded on September 19th and on the following day four German aeroplanes dropped bombs on Nieppe and caused many casualties to both troops and civilians. 2nd Lieuts. J. Williams and P. T. Marston were wounded, the latter dying the same evening. A draft of 210 men from the R.E. was received on September 21st and brought the battalion strength up to over 1,200, but the Twenty-Second had to supply reinforcements to the infantry: a draft of

Trench Warfare, Aug.—Nov., 1917

120 men was dispatched to the Nineteenth and 90 went to join the Fourteenth.

Every effort was now made to get the forward communication trenches finished before the winter set in, infantry parties lending their assistance. Six Lewis guns were placed in position by the Twenty-Second to cope with the enemy aircraft, now a source of great annoyance. Rain came on October 9th and unfinished trenches suffered accordingly. Later in the month, although the enemy artillery became much more active, a duckboard track was completed from the Ploegsteert-Messines road along the valley of the Douve river and other such tracks were put in hand. Advantage was taken of the November early morning mists to work on the support line. On November 13th the Twenty-Second handed over to the pioneers of the 3rd Australian Division, and went back to rest in the Bailleul area. Four days later the battalion commenced to move towards Ypres, arriving there on November 19th. Headquarters and two companies inhabited cellars under the station, while two companies went further forward to sandbagged shelters at St. Jean. Till the end of the month half the battalion worked on two double duckboard tracks, about 200 yards apart, running north-east towards Passchendaele; another company was employed on a corduroy road running forward by Gravenstafel from Kansas Cross Roads which lay about a mile east of Fortuin. In spite of heavy shell fire and the awful condition of the ground good progress was made and the Lewis guns did effective work in keeping the German aeroplanes at a distance.

217

THE BATTLE OF CAMBRAI, 1917

Following the third battle of Ypres came the fighting before Cambrai which commenced with a successful surprise attack on November 20th. In this triumph of the tanks the Eleventh and the Fourteenth each played a part and each battalion were involved in the subsequent German counter-attack and the bitter fighting by which a serious disaster was eventually averted. On the opening day of battle the 20th were on the immediate right of the 6th Division and the experiences of the Eleventh will therefore be recorded first.

The 20th Division came south from Ypres by train to Bapaume at the beginning of October, and on arrival the Eleventh marched south-eastward to Barastre. On the 6th of the month they took over the pioneer camp of the 40th Division who were relieved in the line by the 20th south-east of Villers-Plouich. There was plenty of work to do on tramways and communication trenches, but the Eleventh now had to send 200 good men to the infantry, the ranks being replenished by others of lower medical category who were yet deemed fit for the arduous work of a pioneer battalion.

November was devoted to repair of the roads forward from Couzeaucourt in preparation for the attack. Sixty tanks were allotted to the division and it was essential that there should be good going for these monsters when the advance began. One company spent several days in the construction of a model of the country over which the division were to move and this model played an important part in the preliminary training of the infantry. On November 19th all preparations entrusted to the Eleventh were complete. Three days prior to the offensive Lewis guns of the battalion had been placed in position at Fins,

218

The Battle of Cambrai, 1917

Heudicourt and other places behind the line to assist in preventing the approach of enemy aeroplanes.

A and B companies were called upon before the zero hour on November 20th. The road from Villers-Plouich to Marcoing crossed the complete Hindenburg defensive system and, although the leading tanks carried faggots of brushwood to bridge the trenches, there was great need for pioneer assistance to make the ground possible for cavalry and guns. These two companies were at work as soon as the tanks and infantry were through the main Hindenburg Line. At 6.40 A.M. the rest of the battalion came up, C and D companies commencing communication trenches forward to the hamlet of la Vacquerie, now in the hands of the division. 2nd Lieut. D. Ellwood, with eight Lewis guns, did anti-aircraft duty at various points in the captured Hindenburg Line. It was a day of hard work and few casualties, but Lieut. W. W. Inglis was killed and 2nd Lieut. D. Macgregor wounded.

The 20th Division had made an advance of over four miles, and the amount of pioneer work to be done in the captured area was naturally very large. The Eleventh were fully employed up to the fateful morning of November 30th, when B and D companies were located in the Hindenburg support line about one mile south of Ribécourt. A company were in shelters in a railway cutting at Villers-Plouich and the headquarters of the battalion, with C company, remained at Couzeaucourt.

On the night of November 29th B company, under Capt. Jee, went out to work on a new strong point. While they were returning westwards along the low ground south of Marcoing in the early morning of the 30th a heavy hostile barrage of smoke and high explosive came down. The position in the Hindenburg support line was reached without hindrance, but at 6.15 A.M. came reports of British infantry in retreat. Capt. Jee prepared to resist any enemy advance from the direction of Marcoing and, though his dispositions were somewhat modified by the nearest brigadier, B company remained in this vicinity all day. Fire was opened on advancing German infantry several times

The Durham Forces in the Field

and low-flying enemy aeroplanes were engaged. At 5.30 p.m., having lost 10 killed and wounded, including one officer, Capt. Jee moved further to the right and joined D company in a trench on Welsh Ridge. D company, under Capt. Pemberton, had been here in the morning during the German bombardment until stragglers reported that the enemy had broken through.

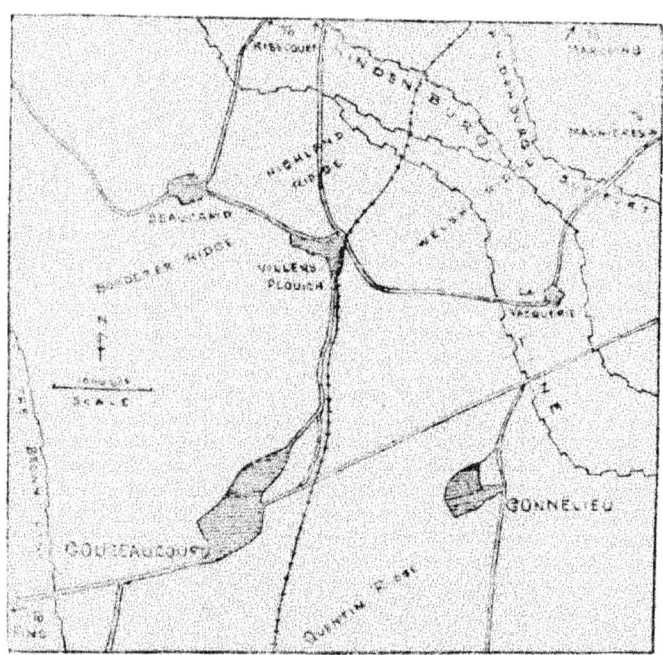

A little later came a call for reinforcements and D company moved forward till touch was obtained on the right with a battalion of the Rifle Brigade. When, in the afternoon, the troops on the left took over more ground D company returned to their original positions. Capt. Sear, M.C., had A company working on the Villers-Plouich-Marcoing road when the German attack came. On returning to Villers-Plouich the division

The Battle of Cambrai, 1917

ordered the company to Borderer Ridge in case the Germans approached northward from Gouzeaucourt. Trenches were dug on the ridge under some shell and machine-gun fire but only 2 men were hit.

The outlying companies thus responded to the demands of the situation in their own vicinity but without becoming deeply involved. The headquarters of the battalion and C company in Gouzeaucourt were put a severer test and played a part in one of the most exciting episodes of the whole battle. Gouzeaucourt was well behind the line and filled with the transport of various units; it was the headquarters of the 29th Division and some 9-inch howitzers were established in the village.

In the early morning a few bullets fell but they were thought to be from an enemy aeroplane. A report that the Germans had broken the line was not believed and a few shells came over without causing undue alarm. But about nine o'clock the truth was known. Gunners and transport men began to get their horses and wagons away in hot haste and all the troops turned out. Colonel Hayes, the commanding officer of the Eleventh, went with Major Lloyd to a knoll south of the Fins road. They saw large bodies of infantry in field grey on Quentin Ridge, south-west of Connelieu and barely a mile away; to the north and south British troops were retiring and the German machine-gun fire increased. Major Lloyd then noticed the tops of steel helmets in the valley, but these proved to be German for the enemy was now across the railway and closing in upon Gouzeaucourt. To defend the village was impossible and the howitzers had to be abandoned; but a defensive position was occupied, first along a bank behind a road running southward and then at the " Brown " Line 400 yards further back. This was a part of the British trench system and, though not properly wired, was capable of defence if the various units could be organized. While this was being done Lieut. Freeman was killed and Major Lloyd sprained his ankle. Sergt.-Major McEvoy was prominent in covering the withdrawal which was accomplished by the time the enemy entered Gouzeaucourt. The

The Durham Forces in the Field

German infantry advanced very steadily in perfect order and as soon as the village was theirs they opened fire from the houses. Hostile shelling ceased but machine-guns harassed the defenders, particularly from the right flank. In the "Brown" Line, where men from five different divisions had gathered, order was evolved out of chaos. South of the Fins road sappers held the trench and Major Lloyd, with C company of the Eleventh under Lieut. Bushell, was just north of the road, Colonel Hayes having gone further to the left to reconnoitre. There was little ammunition and machine-guns were badly needed, but Capt. Tollit, adjutant of the Eleventh, providentially discovered a staff car in the Fins road. He motored back and returned later with guns and ammunition borrowed from the tanks.

The Germans showed caution in approaching the "Brown" Line. Their scouts fell back when fired on and the shooting of the grey-clad infantry was wild. At this time Major Lloyd saw an artillery ammunition column coming, all unsuspecting, up the road from Fins. His warning shouts sent them back in galloping retreat.

As the morning wore on the British line grew stronger. On the right of the sappers the 20th Hussars appeared and the foremost troopers, who were reckless enough to jump the trench, fell from their saddles under a hail of German machine-gun bullets. But dismounted, and with their Hotchkiss guns, the hussars were a welcome reinforcement.

It was about an hour after mid-day that the Guards came through to restore the situation. They had no artillery to help them but swept forward, disdainful of machine-gun fire, and turned the Germans out of Gouzeaucourt. The troops to the south of the Fins road joined in the advance, urged forward by an enthusiastic brigadier who had come upon the scene, but the Eleventh remained in the "Brown" Line for the rest of the day and night. Losses amounted to 40 killed and wounded.

December 1st was a day of heavy shelling, principally from British guns now in German hands. The

The Battle of Cambrai, 1917

enemy was still attacking and at night A company were moved into the support line in front of la Vacquerie. C company had gone forward in the morning to a position near Villers-Pouich and when darkness fell were employed in converting a communication trench of the Hindenburg system into a fire trench. B and D companies carried rations to the front line at night. The German bombardment continued all next day. A company had no British troops in front of them and 2nd Lieut. H. S. Parkin and his bombers drove the Germans out of 40 yards of trench. The bomb supply was then exhausted but the trench was held until the line was re-adjusted and rendered secure. B company were also put in to close a gap in the front line but on the morning of the 3rd the Eleventh concentrated at the "Brown" Line and marched to billets at Fins the same night. Casualties during these last three days had amounted to 4 killed and 42 wounded.

The Fourteenth had moved to a camp near Fins on November 17th and occupied their assembly position on the evening of the following day. The 18th Brigade were in reserve until the remainder of the 6th Division had completely broken the Hindenburg Line north of Beaucamp and Villers-Plouich. Then the 18th Brigade had to pass through the other troops and establish a defensive flank along the ridge from Premy Chapel westward towards Flesquiéres, the general direction of the advance being north-east in order to make good the crossing over the Scheldt Canal at Marcoing. B company of the Fourteenth were to lead the battalion and push on to Marcoing in order to strengthen the British hold on the bridgeheads there until such time as the 29th Division came up to push the advance beyond the canal. The task of C company was to dig in on the track leading from Premy Chapel to Marcoing, while the other two companies were held in reserve to meet any counter-attack from the direction of Nine Wood.

The advance began at 6.20 a.m. on November 20th when along a front of about 6 miles the British infantry

The Durham Forces in the Field

followed the tanks forward as the barrage of high explosive, shrapnel and smoke came down. Good progress was reported from the outset, though no definite news was received by the Fourteenth for some time. At 8.15 a.m. the 18th Brigade moved up in artillery formation with the West Yorkshire men in the van. In their left rear came the 2nd Durham Light Infantry;

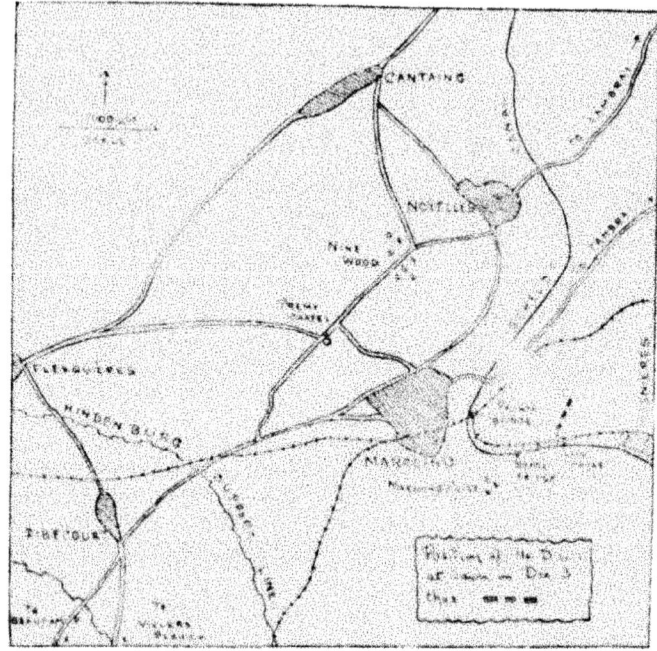

the Fourteenth were in a similar position on the right, with their left on the Beaucamp-Ribécourt road.

Seventy-two tanks were attached to the 6th Division and before ten o'clock some of them could be seen crawling up Premy Chapel ridge; everyone then pushed forward as quickly as possible. It was a wonderful experience for the infantry to gain ground so rapidly and at so small a price. By mid-day all

The Battle of Cambrai, 1917

companies of the Fourteenth had reached their allotted positions and that with a total loss of 7 men wounded. Soon B company reported that troops of the 29th Division were beginning to pass through Marcoing and by 3 p.m. the whole battalion were consolidating the Premy Chapel position. On the left the 51st Division were still fighting for Flesquiéres.

Early next morning the Highlanders entered Flesquiéres, but at 11.30 a.m. they had not reached Cantaing which was still held by the Germans, though at least one tank had been in and out again. Some patrols of the Queen's Bays were held up in front of the village. The officer commanding the Fourteenth, who had been called upon to fill a gap in the line in this direction, sent on B and C companies, following himself with A company. In the face of hostile machine-gun fire Cantaing was carried by the Durhams soon after one o'clock in the afternoon and many Germans were taken. For this exploit Lieut.-Col. J. B. Rosher was awarded the Distinguished Service Order.

Almost at once Gordons of the 51st Division arrived and the Fourteenth were withdrawn to the Premy Chapel line. The boldness and promptness with which the companies had been launched at the village was well justified, casualties hardly amounting to double figures, but a very gallant and valuable officer was killed in the person of Capt. C. R. Gold, D.S.O.

Until November 26th the Fourteenth worked on their portion of the Premy Chapel line, putting out wire and creating a thoroughly strong defensive position. Losses during this period were again very slight though the ridge was shelled at frequent intervals.

The battalion then moved to cellars in the village of Ribécourt. The 18th Brigade had relieved the Guards in the new front line beyond Cantaing and the Fourteenth were now employed every night in carrying up material for the sappers. Cantaing was heavily shelled, but a belt of wire 8 feet wide was put out along the whole brigade front in two nights. On the night of November 29th parties of the Fourteenth were employed in strengthening this.

The Durham Forces in the Field

When on November 30th the enemy dealt his counter-blow the line in front of the Fourteenth held firm. During the morning the Durhams were sent to occupy a position in the Hindenburg Line on Highland Ridge, just north of Villers-Plouich. Patrols were sent out and touch was obtained with the troops on the right and in front. In the evening Colonel Rosher was given two battalions of Sherwood Foresters and two companies of sappers to assist in holding the position. It was the transport of the battalion which was in action on this day; from Gouzeaucourt a retirement had to be made to Fins, with the loss of 2 men wounded. For the whole month of November the casualties of the Fourteenth only amounted to 25.

The battalion remained on Highland Ridge with patrols out day and night until December 2nd when, under orders of the 16th Brigade, a unit of the 29th Division had to be relieved in the trenches east of the canal at Marcoing. The Fourteenth moved up in the darkness and had taken over the line before dawn of December 3rd. The right flank of the battalion was thrown back along the canal in touch with troops of the 29th Division to the south; the left joined with the 1st King's Shropshire Light Infantry.

There were three companies in the line and, though the two on the left found themselves in fairly good trenches, A company's trench on the right was only 2 or 3 feet deep in places and very badly sited. A new one was commenced at once, but slow progress was made in the chalky soil. There was no wire at all in front.

Soon after ten o'clock on the morning of the 3rd a fierce hostile barrage came down on the whole line and German infantry attacked the troops south of the canal and also A company of the Fourteenth. Artillery support was asked for by telephone and obtained but the wretched trench of A company could not withstand the German assault, though rifle grenadiers, directed by Lance-Sergt. A. Wilson, of Boldon Colliery, took heavy toll of the assailants. The company commander, Capt. A. M. Lascelles, V.C., had been wounded during the bombardment but he

The Battle of Cambrai, 1917

and Sergt. Wilson hastily collected 11 men and delivered a counter-attack. The gallant band was outnumbered by five to one, but many Germans were killed or wounded and the remainder driven from the trench.

The signal wires had been cut by the bombardment and from now onward there was no communication with the rear. At half-past eleven another heavy barrage came down and again the grey infantry streamed forward to the attack. On the left the line held but there was disaster upon the right. A company were driven back, Capt. Lascelles was captured and the enemy established a machine-gun in the house by the lock. The reserve company were thrown in to counter-attack and drove the Germans from the trench once more, in spite of deadly fire from the lock house. The indomitable Capt. Lascelles took advantage of the confusion to escape and rejoin his company.

Soon after midday came another fierce assault. This failed before the companies on the left where many Germans died; on the right the front trench was lost again and now a barricade was erected to protect this flank, but there were no bombs with which to defend it. The enemy still came on and the weight of numbers began to tell. The Shropshires on the left and the left company of the Durhams had to give ground, while from the direction of Masnières fresh columns of German infantry could be seen advancing. Step by step the companies fought their way back until the survivors of the Fourteenth united in the reserve trench and turned to do battle anew. It was clear that the position beyond the canal could be held no longer, but for the moment the enemy was in no condition to press his advantage and so the Durhams were able to withdraw unmolested across the railway bridge.

In a sunken road west of the canal Colonel Rosher reorganised his men and moved round to lend support to the troops of the 29th Division on the right. A line was occupied on a ridge south-west of Marcoing Copse, but in this quarter a successful counter-attack

The Durham Forces in the Field

had prevented the enemy moving down the north side of the canal towards the Marcoing crossings.

At four o'clock in the afternoon, supported by a company of Bedfords, the Fourteenth advanced to the attack once more. The canal had been bridged on this side by means of a barge and here the Durhams crossed. There was fierce fighting on the railway beyond but the old reserve trench was retaken, together with 4 prisoners, and many Germans were killed. Another company of Bedfords arrived and with this help the Fourteenth were able to push on and cover both barge bridge and railway bridge. The old front trenches were now full of Germans who attempted to bomb into the new position near the canal on the right. There were no bombs with which to reply but somehow the line was held till at 10.15 p.m. came the order to withdraw again. This was done and both bridges were blown up by the sappers. Before morning the survivors of the Fourteenth reached a position in the Hindenburg support line, north-east of Ribécourt.

The battalion were about 450 strong when taking over trenches on the night of December 2nd. Two-thirds of these were killed and wounded and among the fallen were Capt. J. P. Moffitt, M.C., Lieut. J. H. Stearn, D.S.O., 2nd Lieuts. D. I. Smith, C. H. Mathieson and R. M. Malcolm. Capt. C. F. B. Simpson died of his wounds; 2nd Lieut. C. E. Brogden was wounded and missing; 2nd Lieut. H. Forbes was missing and is presumed to have been killed. Capt. C. A. V. Newsome, M.C., Capt. A. M. Lascelles, M.C., Lieut. A. Rothfield, M.C., 2nd Lieuts. J. Foster and A. G. Brewer were all wounded.

Lieut.-Col. J. B. Rosher, M.C., added a bar to his newly-won Distinguished Service Order. Lieut. A. Rothfield, M.C., also gained a bar to his decoration. He had walked along the parapet during the enemy bombardment to reorganise his company and, though badly wounded, remained with them until he collapsed. Lieut. W. H. Davies, who led a counter-attack after being buried by shell fire on three occasions, and 2nd Lieut. E. G. Wylie, who led another successful counter-

The late CAPTAIN A. M. LASCELLES, V.C., M.C.
Durham Light Infantry

The Battle of Cambrai, 1917

attack and fought his way out with his men after being surrounded, both received the Military Cross. C.-S.-M. J. Nicholson, M.M., of Bishop Auckland, helped to bring in a wounded man lying 50 yards beyond the parapet and worked a Lewis gun during a counter-attack after the whole team had been killed. He and Sergt. Wilson received the Distinguished Conduct Medal. Lance-Corpl. J. Wharton, M.M., received a bar to his decoration, and the Military Medal was won by Sergt. C. Barrell, Corpl. G. McKane, Lance-Corpl. I. Tallentive, and Ptes. E. Stephens, J. Walker and J. W. Turner.

Capt. Arthur Moore Lascelles, M.C., commanded at the weakest part of the line in a trench he could not hope to hold. Three times wounded and then captured, he escaped and was still the inspiration of the defence. It was fitting that he should receive the highest honour of all—the Victoria Cross.

The divisional commander issued a special "order of the day," congratulating many units on their prowess during the battle. The Fourteenth are mentioned for their exploit at Cantaing, but their defence of the canal crossings at Marcoing on December 3rd is recorded as the finest achievement of all.

ITALY

NOVEMBER, 1917—FEBRUARY, 1918

The Caporetto disaster in the autumn of 1917 threatened the complete overthrow of the Italian Armies and, as soon as possible, several French and five British divisions were dispatched from the Western Front to restore the battle line in Italy. In this force the 23rd and 41st Divisions were included, to the general satisfaction of the Twelfth, Thirteenth and Twentieth. Men who had endured the misery and horror of the fighting beyond Ypres could not but welcome the news of a move to a different theatre of war.

The 23rd Division moved first, the Twelfth and Thirteenth both entraining at Arques on November 8th. Each battalion were accommodated in two trains and ten days' rations were carried. The route lay through Abbeville and Amiens to Paris and thence south by Dijon and Arles to Marseilles—a tedious, uncomfortable journey under gloomy skies. On railways so overburdened with traffic there were many delays, but impromptu games of football sometimes provided relief from the cramped confinement of the trucks.

After leaving Marseilles came a different experience for those fortunate enough to be in the trains that passed along the Riviera in the golden sunshine of Sunday, November 11th. The scenes are described by an officer of the Twelfth as follows: " A short halt was made at all the more important stations—Nice, Monaco, Monte Carlo, Mentone and San Remo. At each place the station platforms were crowded with people who had turned out to see the British troops pass through. Cigarettes, apples, grapes, flowers, picture postcards and chocolate were showered on officers and men alike and the departure of the train from each station was the signal for enthusiastic clapping, cheering and waving of flags. Indeed it was not only in the stations that the troops received a welcome; all along the line the people cheered, waved and threw bunches of flowers into the carriages and trucks."

On reaching Ventimiglia, the first stopping place in Italy, the Twelfth detrained and marched through the town with their band playing, to the manifest delight of the inhabitants who gave the battalion a rousing farewell when the journey was resumed.

The route lay along the Italian coast until Genoa was reached. Then, turning northward, the sunshine was left behind and the journey continued through flat, wet plains covered with vineyards, while train-loads of refugees from the invaded areas were encountered upon the way. Sometimes the Alpine snows could be seen and once to the south-east appeared the peaks of the Apennines.

One half of the Twelfth detrained and spent a day at Asola where the men were billeted in the theatre and received by the townspeople as honoured guests; but in the course of November 13th, 14th and 15th both Durham battalions concentrated at Cabbiana, a village about ten miles from the ancient city of Mantua. The journey by rail was now over and there followed several days of route marching and general preparation for the move forward of the 23rd Division across the Venetian plain.

This march commenced on November 18th, the troops starting every morning before sunrise, when the roads were covered with a film of ice, and halting by the way for dinner if billets could not be reached early in the afternoon. The highways, tree-lined, and often bordered by streams, were excellent though dusty and crowded with motor transport. Now the remnants of the retreating Italian 2nd Army were met and still more refugees. The way led eastward and then northward from Montagnana, leaving the Euganean hills upon the right. At Montegalda the Twelfth were fortunate enough to be billeted in the beautiful castle of Count Grimani of Venice. It had been expected that the British would have to entrench in this vicinity and occupy the line of the Bacchiglione river, for it

The Durham Forces in the Field

was doubtful if the Italians could hold the enemy at the Piave unless the long desired floods came quickly to help the defence. But the Piave was held and the march of the 23rd Division continued.

The Twelfth halted for three days at Lobia and reached the village of Brugoporco, near the old fortified town of Castelfranco, on November 29th. After a rest at S. Ciorgio-i-Busco the Thirteenth arrived at Piombino on the same date. Now came an interval of training and recreation, for the 68th Brigade were in reserve to the rest of the 23rd Division who took over the line. On December 2nd both battalions marched through Montebelluna to Biadene, under the south-western side of the Montello plateau. Here Italian troops were relieved and two whole days spent in cleaning billets.

On issuing from the mountains the Piave river flows round the Montello on its right before continuing its course south-eastward to the sea. The plateau rises to a height of about 600 feet, and its length from east to west is about eight miles. The twenty-one parallel roads which run from north to south across the hill provided convenient lines of approach to the front from the reserve positions.

Both Durham battalions soon settled to work. Ranges and bombing pits had to be constructed and many men were required to work with the tunnellers, while training was carried on systematically. As protection from hostile shell fire slit trenches had to be dug outside the billets. The rifle range constructed north-west of Biadene was in full view of the enemy; but he was very far away across the river and by camouflaging both targets and firing points it was "hoped that the troops would not be fired at."

On December 16th there was a fall of snow which turned to rain and mist before Christmas. The festival was kept by both Twelfth and Thirteenth at Biadene, though the 68th Brigade had relieved the 70th on the 19th and the two N.F. battalions now held the line. There were 8 casualties from shell fire in the Thirteenth on December 23rd, and Boxing Day was memorable for the visit of no less than thirty-three Austrian aero-

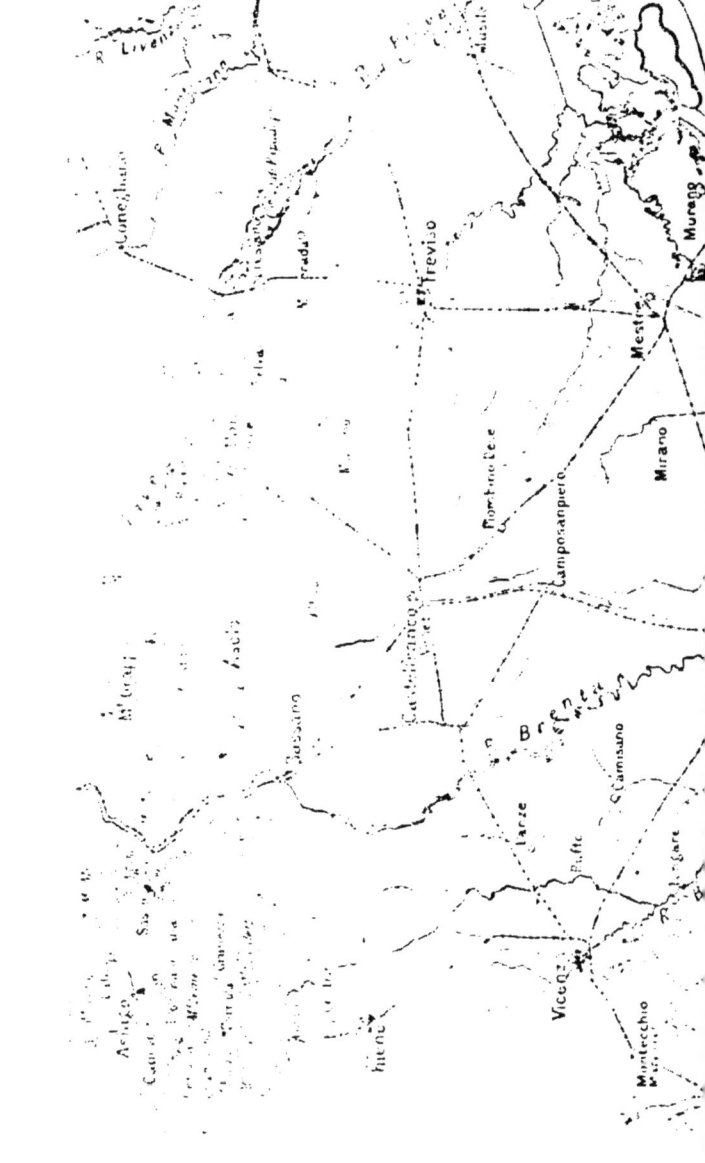

The Durham Forces in the Field

planes which flew recklessly low and dropped bombs indiscriminately. Nine of these were brought down on the Corps front, one falling to the Lewis gunners of the Twelfth who buried the bodies of the three occupants. This raid was reported to be in revenge for our effective bombing of an Austrian leave train in Conegliano station some few days before Christmas.

On the evening of the 27th the Durhams relieved the Fusiliers in the front line, the Thirteenth taking over the right next to the 70th Brigade and the Twelfth going in on the left next to the Italians. There was a heavy fall of snow that night. The line, which extended from Chino to Rivasecca, ran along the river bank. The enemy opposite were inactive, apart from some desultory shell fire, and all hands concentrated upon the improvement of the defences. These consisted of front and support trenches, with machine-gun posts along the edge of the river bed; a second line of defence along the top of the Montello; an intermediate machine-gun line; and a reserve line. Life in the trenches here was quite a new experience. Company headquarters were all in houses, the support companies were also in houses or farms and the reserves lived in billets. Strict orders were issued that men were not to show themselves in the front trenches; neither were they to dry washing on the wire. In the words of one private, "It was a picnic to Passchendaele."

The river was still rising and though fords existed they changed with the course of the stream which ran in many channels and presented a difficult problem to patrols. At night several powerful searchlights, provided by the Italians, came into action and frequent reconnaissances were made by each Durham battalion. On December 30th the Austrian gunners scored a direct hit on the headquarters of the Thirteenth, causing 4 casualties. A patrol of the Thirteenth crossed seven streams on the last night of the year and found no sign of the enemy on the further bank. The Twelfth patrols had similar experiences.

The Durhams were relieved on January 4th and the Thirteenth withdrew to Pederiva, west of Biadene, as reserve battalion. The Twelfth were in

Italy, Nov., 1917—Feb., 1918

support and had to supply large working parties for the front line. On the 7th came another heavy fall of snow.

Major D. H. Clarke, M.C., of the Thirteenth, was now awarded the Distinguished Service Order for his services during the third battle of Ypres and the long and efficient service of Capt. Snow, the quartermaster of the battalion, earned him the Military Cross.

The Durhams went into the line again on January 12th, the right sector of the brigade front being occupied by the Twelfth who had several patrol encounters during this tour. On the night of the 18th 2nd Lieut. Morrison took out a patrol, supported by a Stokes gun detachment. They crossed four streams, were challenged by the enemy, were fired on and forced to retire in the face of greatly superior numbers. The Stokes gun fired one round.

On January 18th the two battalions withdrew into reserve at Biadene, Pederiva and the vicinity, where training was carried on until the end of the month although working parties were still in great demand. By this time there was accommodation in tunnels or concrete dug-outs for all the men in the line, so that, in spite of the Austrian reply to the increased activities of the British gunners, life in the trenches was preferable to that in billets which were frequently bombed at night by Austrian aeroplanes.

The 68th Brigade took over the right sector of the divisional front on February 3rd, the Thirteenth going into the support position and the Twelfth remaining in reserve at Vennegazu, south of the Montello. On the 10th the N.F. battalions were relieved in the front line, the Thirteenth being then on the right. Both of the Durham battalions had patrols across the Piave during this tour, the moonlight being of some assistance. A patrol of the Thirteenth went out from the right of the line on the evening of the 15th and reached the enemy wire. The Austrians then opened rapid fire which was replied to before withdrawing with one man slightly wounded.

This sector was taken over by the 41st Division on February 17th and the Durhams withdrew to

The Durham Forces in the Field

Biadene, leaving next day for Altivole, about four miles south-west of Montebelluna. Two days training in hill warfare was now carried out, the battalion as proceeding for this purpose by lorry to Asolo. Here among the foothills of the Alps, within sight of Mount Grappa, officers and men became more or less accustomed to the extra strain demanded of leg and lung when fighting in mountainous country.

On February 24th the Thirteenth returned to Pederiva and relieved the Twentieth there. The Twelfth replaced the 11th Queen's in the support position of the left sector of the old divisional front, were relieved here by the Thirteenth four days later and returned to billets at Biadene.

During this month was announced the award of the Belgian *Croix de Guerre* to Ptes. T. Armstrong and F. G. Miller, of the Thirteenth.

The Twentieth entrained at Loon Plage for Italy on November 14th and crossed the Italian frontier in the early morning of the 18th. They also received a rapturous welcome, in which flowers, fruit and cigarettes played a prominent part. At Genoa the second half of the battalion were accorded a public reception by the Mayor. At Isola della Scala, north of Mantua, and at Cerea, which is east of that city, the Twentieth detrained on November 19th and 20th. The 41st Division now concentrated north of the 23rd and commenced their forward move. By way of Barbarano and Camposanpiero the Twentieth reached Ghivera on November 29th, a journey of 105 miles. After spending the night here the Durhams relieved a part of the Umbrian Brigade, 1st Italian Division, in the trenches along the right bank of the Piave river above Nervesa. On the right of the line the main stream was close in and there was a precipitous slope from the plateau to the river bed; on the left there was a more gentle slope, with some cultivated ground and shingle beds between the hill and the river.

The Twentieth found very little trench or dug-out accommodation, but the steep hollows in the sides of the hill were made sung with the Italian shelters avail-

Italy, Nov., 1917—Fch., 1918

able. Day was the time of rest and the work of improving the trenches went forward at night. Observation posts were established along the river bank, but the main line of resistance ran further back on higher ground. This needed much work on it.

Soon after the battalion had taken over the trenches Lieut.-Col. R. C. Smith was severely wounded while reconnoitring the front line. He died on December 1st and was succeeded in the command by Major A. V. A. Thayer, D.S.O., from the 23rd Middlesex Regt.

The 23rd Division came into the line on the left of the 41st at the beginning of December.

Patrols of the Twentieth made repeated attempts to cross the Piave, though the water was icy cold and the current swift. 2nd Lieut. P. L. Davies, who persevered in these endeavours until quite incapacitated, was awarded the Military Cross. The battalion were relieved on December 6th and withdrew to billets at Selva, on the south side of the Montello. Training, including musketry, was done here until they moved into a support position on the left sector of the divisional front. The Twentieth relieved the 23rd Middlesex in the line on the 26th and stayed there till the end of the year. Casualties in the ranks during December only amounted to 4 killed and 5 wounded and there were no other losses while the battalion were in Italy.

On January 2nd the Twentieth withdrew to Giavera and only had one more tour in the front trenches before moving on the 18th by way of Giavera and Musano to the vicinity of Castelfranco. In this area the whole of the 41st Division assembled for training, but before the end of the month the Twentieth were sent to Possagno for work on a reserve line which was to run from La Rocca to Costalunga. On February 7th the Durhams marched to Altivole where training was continued for a week. Then the 123rd Brigade relieved the 69th Brigade of the 23rd Division, the Twentieth taking over reserve billets from the West Yorkshires in Biadene. Relieved in turn on February 24th by the Thirteenth, the Wearsiders marched to Montebelluna and thence to Camposanpiero where they arrived on the 26th.

The Durham Forces in the Field

There was now great need of more troops in France, and the 41st were one of the British divisions selected for withdrawal from Italy. The Twentieth entrained at Camposanpiero on March 3rd and the first half of the battalion reached Doullens on the 7th. Two days later the Wearsiders concentrated at Ivergny and carried out training in the forest of Lucheux until March 16th. The 41st Division now reorganised on the new basis of three battalions per brigade and the Twentieth were transferred to the 124th Brigade. They marched to Warluzel on the 17th and were played into camp by the bands of their new comrades, the 10th Queen's and the 26th Royal Fusiliers.

AEROPLANE PHOTOGRAPH SHOWING POELCAPPELLE — WESTROOSEBEKE ROAD: VICINITY OF GOUDBERG SECTOR

TRENCH WARFARE
DECEMBER, 1917—MARCH, 1918

On December 3rd the Tenth went by train from Wizernes to St. Jean, and took over a camp near Wieltje. It was very cold and enemy bombing aeroplanes were active. Six days later the Durhams struggled up over duckboards, broken and slippery with frost, to the front line on the Passchendaele spur. For the last 2,000 yards the ground was a swamp and many of the men who fell into the mud had to remain there till they could be dug out in daylight. The relief cost the battalion 15 casualties.

The line faced due north, about half a mile beyond the remains of the hamlet of Goudberg, and consisted of shell holes and odd lengths of trench. It was the opportunity of the sniper and the machine-gun. Fortunately the Germans respected the Red Cross, and thus the wounded could be carried back by day; the ground was too bad to allow of this being done in the darkness.

The Tenth were relieved on December 13th and withdrew to dug-outs and shelters near St. Julien. Losses during the tour amounted to 29, besides 7 men sick and one officer and 34 others suffering from trench foot. On the 15th there were 9 casualties from shell fire. The next sojourn in the line cost 40 in killed, wounded and sick, besides 2nd Lieut. Herries, who died of his wounds, Lieut. R. M. Leveson killed by a sniper, and Colonel Morant and Capt. Berisford both slightly wounded.

On December 20th the Tenth left by light railway for a camp near Vlamertinghe to rest and clean up. The next move came on Boxing Day when Wizernes was reached by rail, the Tenth then marching north-westward to billets at Zudausques. Here Major E. B.

The Durham Forces in the Field

Ward assumed command when Colonel Morant went on leave.

On January 2nd the Durhams entrained at St. Omer for the south and eventually occupied billets at Morcourt, on the river Somme. Training continued in frost and snow.

The 14th Division were now in the Fifth Army, whose task it was to relieve the French as far south as the river Oise. Leaving Morcourt on the 22nd and going by way of Harbonnières, Mesnil-St. Nicaise and Guiscard, the Tenth took over billets from our Allies at Mondescourt on the 25th. Next day Colonel Morant, who had been appointed to the command of the 3rd Brigade, came to say farewell to his old battalion. He thanked all ranks for their never-failing support and obedience to orders, their cheerfulness and their discipline. Referring to the coming disbandment, he reminded them that orders must be obeyed and that " we can rest content that the battalion will have completed its task in the Great War with a reputation second to none."

On the same evening the Tenth relieved part of the 414th French Regt. in the line near Vendeuil. The trenches were muddy and needed repair, but the only sign of the enemy was the chatter of machine-guns through the fog.

In this part of France the existence of the Tenth came to an end about six weeks before the German torrent rolled forward and swept the Fifth Army to ruin. No drafts had been received by the battalion since the fighting at Inverness Copse, but, apart from numbers, they had never been in finer fettle than when the authorities at home selected them for disbandment as one of the junior battalions of the division. " One of my finest battalions," was the opinion of Sir Victor Couper, the divisional commander.

On February 3rd the Tenth paraded in detachments which departed to join the 2nd Durham Light Infantry, the Fifteenth and various Territorial Battalions of the Regiment. The band—formed at the end of 1915 as the result of a generous money gift for the purchase of instruments—went complete to the Regular Battalion.

Trench Warfare, Dec., 1917—Mar., 1918

Major Ward wrote to General Morant: " I enjoyed every moment of my six weeks' command; there was such a wonderful spirit in the battalion and the men were splendid. I loved the little ditty they used to sing on the march.

The " little ditty," well-known throughout the Regiment—drafts sang it to enliven the long march up to Etaples- is just this:

> We are the lads from Durham, we are.
> We have just arrived in town.
> We make a show wherever we go,
> We're in the front line, we're in the know,
> We know all the pretty girls from Ypres (Shields, etc.)
> Up to Durham, to Durham,
> So wake up and shake up the dear old town—
> We are the lads from Durham.

For the Twelfth, in Italy, Colonel Longden procured the band parts which were the work of a man who served in the Eighteenth.

The Eleventh left the scene of the Cambrai battle early in December, 1917, after putting in a few more days' work on the trenches. The move was northwards to Ypres again and the battalion reached Wardrecques some miles south-east of St. Omer, on December 11th.

After a few days spent in training there the Pioneers moved to a camp near Dickebusch and were employed, until January 5th, in wiring the Corps line of defence, suffering some casualties from shell fire during this period. On December 30th 50 men had been sent to the Fourteenth and 50 to the 2nd Durham Light Infantry.

Early in January, 1918, the 20th Division relieved the 30th in the sector astride the Menin road west of Gheluvelt. The Eleventh moved into quarters at Zillebeke Bund and settled down to five weeks' work in the worst weather imaginable. Snow was followed by rain and then came sleet and more snow as the Pioneers strove to keep in tolerable shape the tracks which ran forward to the line through the swamps at Dumbarton Lakes and over Basseville Beek. On February 8th the division extended their line northward

241

The Durham Forces in the Field

to Polygonbeke and a welcome reinforcement of 118 men from the Fourteenth reached the Eleventh the same day.

The 37th Division took over the front on the 17th and the Eleventh, who had had few casualties during weather which rendered fighting all but impossible, secured a few days' rest at Racquinghem before they entrained for the south on February 21st.

Nesle was reached next day, and the Pioneers marched to Muille-Villette and Golancourt, south of Ham. The 20th Division, now in the Fifth Army, were kept in reserve and the Eleventh devoted some days to training and the necessary reorganisation consequent upon the reduction of pioneer battalions to a three-company establishment. C company were abolished and the men distributed among the other companies.

On February 27th all hands began work on the Ham-Noyon railway, and this continued during March, a little essential instruction being introduced where possible. On March 14th A company moved to Voyennes on the Somme canal.

On December 4th the Fourteenth moved back to the catacombs at Ribécourt and rejoined the 18th Brigade. Wiring and carrying parties were supplied for the front line on Premy Chapel ridge, after which the battalion—now formed into two weak companies—did little until they arrived at Heudicourt by bus on December 11th. Here drafts were received and training began on the usual four-company basis. Five days later the Durhams departed for a support position beyond Mory, in the Bullecourt salient, headquarters being established at Noreuil. Four frosty days were spent here, working and wiring parties being supplied at night. The battalion arrived at Heudicourt again on December 21st and training continued both before and after they moved to Bienvillers. The Fourteenth reached Achiet-le-Petit on January 10th and a week later moved, by way of Courcelles-le-Comte and Bapaume, to the Fremicourt area. Arriving here on January 19th, twelve Lewis guns were at once mounted for anti-aircraft work and next evening the Fourteenth relieved the

Trench Warfare, Dec., 1917—Mar., 1918

7th Gordons in trenches north of Louveral which is on the Cambrai road. Eight days were spent in the line and misty weather enabled much necessary work to be done on the trenches which were in an appalling state after the thaw. A mining platoon were employed upon the dug-outs. The last few days of the month were spent in brigade reserve, big working parties going up to the line every night.

When the disbandment of the Fourteenth commenced at the beginning of February the battalion strength was 43 officers and 839 other ranks. The reorganisation of the infantry in France appears to have been a policy settled in detail at home so there was no chance for even such a fine fighting unit as the Fourteenth to escape disbandment. Our only consolation is that officers and men departed to be a source of strength to many other battalions of Durham soon to be involved in one of the bloodiest struggles of the whole war.

On December 1st the Fifteenth arrived at Tincourt by train and, marching forward through Guyencourt, relieved the Liverpool Irish in a line of posts north-east of Epéhy the same night. The tour was uneventful and on the 5th came a turn in support in dug-outs on the railway. Here Major F. A. Wilson arrived and assumed command of the battalion. The 21st Division now took over ground to the north as far as Chapel Crossing—where the railway cut the Villers-Guislain road—and on December 7th the Fifteenth went in on the left of the line opposite Villers-Guislain. On this evening, as a result of a patrol encounter, a German of the 185th Regt. was brought in. Relieved by the 1st Lincolns after two days, the Fifteenth then spent a week at Heudicourt where some drafts were received. Then they took over trenches near Vaucelette Farm. There was snow on the ground when at 5.30 A.M. on the 22nd 2nd Lieut. A. Shearer and two men, all dressed in white, went out on patrol. They appeared to have lost their way on the return journey; at all events, they suddenly encountered an enemy post where three Germans were seen. 2nd Lieut. Shearer shot one and pursued the others, who fled, but many Germans

The Durham Forces in the Field

appeared from dug-outs in the vicinity. Although the two Durhams killed three of the enemy they had to crawl back under heavy machine-gun and rifle fire. The officer was never seen again.

The Fifteenth were relieved on Boxing Day and remained at Liéramont till January 4th. The next tour was in the trenches in front of Épéhy, and here 2nd Lieut. A. W. N. Hooper was killed on January 7th. On the following day the battalion withdrew to Saulcourt and after another tour in bad weather and dirty trenches spent the rest of the month at Épéhy and Liéramont. Casualties in the ranks during January amounted to 7.

On February 3rd 4 officers and 116 men arrived from the Tenth. The disbandment of the 10th K.O.Y.L.I., which began a few days later, reduced the 64th Brigade to the new establishment of three battalions.

On February 7th the Fifteenth relieved the 6th Leicesters in the line beyond Épéhy, and during this tour 2nd Lieut. C. W. Bodman was wounded. After a week in the trenches came a fortnight's training at Haut-Allaines where, on the 24th, Lieut-Col. H. W. Festing took command. Four days later the Fifteenth moved to Liéramont again and continued there for three weeks, providing working parties for the rear lines of defence.

The award was now announced of the Belgian *Croix de Guerre* to Corpl. J. W. Westgarth and Pte. C. Waugh (attached 64th T.M.B.).

The Eighteenth were in the line at Arleux at the beginning of December when artillery and machine-guns had to co-operate in retaliation for the German bombardment of communications. Relieved on the 7th the battalion spent a fortnight training at Ecoivres in wintry weather. Musketry was done on the range at Bray. The Durhams spent Christmas in brigade reserve at Ecurie camp, and on the 28th they relieved the 18th West Yorkshire in front line posts near Willerval under a bright moon. This was probably observed by the enemy who opened with his 5.9's almost

Trench Warfare, Dec., 1917—Mar., 1918

at once, but a quiet tour followed. The frost-bound earth made work on the line very difficult and slow.

On December 30th Major T. C. Gibson, from the 15th West Yorkshires, replaced Major Twist in command of the battalion who were relieved on January 3rd and returned to Ecoivres again for twelve days. Then came the thaw with heavy rain and the Eighteenth, in support at Arleux, toiled hard on the trenches which were in a terrible condition. On January 19th they relieved the front line over the top. Major Gibson had been succeeded in the command on the previous day by Major Anderson, of the 12th East Yorkshires.

The rain continued. A patrol of the Durhams found a tangled mass of wire about 3 feet high in front of the German trench which was shallow and dilapidated and unoccupied for a distance of 200 yards. After four days in the line the battalion withdrew to Ecurie, where Major D. E. Ince became commanding officer.

After another turn at Ecoivres the Eighteenth came up in support at Arleux on February 5th. The 93rd Brigade and the 31st Division were now undergoing reorganisation. Both the 16th and 18th West Yorkshires were disbanded, and the three-battalion strength of the brigade was made up by bringing in the 13th York and Lancaster Regt. The 4th Guards Brigade replaced the 94th Brigade in the division. On February 7th 7 officers and 143 men joined the Eighteenth from the Fourteenth and a new draft of 44 arrived on the following day.

During the next tour in the line a daring German patrol reached the British parapet and nearly captured a party carrying a container of hot food to one of the posts. But the alarm was given, the enemy repulsed at the cost of 2 casualties and the hot meal was delivered. The 4th Grenadier Guards took over on February 17th and the battalion carried out training and provided working parties till the last day of the month. Then a long and muddy march brought the Eighteenth by Aubigny and Bethonsart to Magnicourt-en-Comte on the river Lawe. Next day Lieut.-Col. R. E. Cheyne took a final leave of his men before going

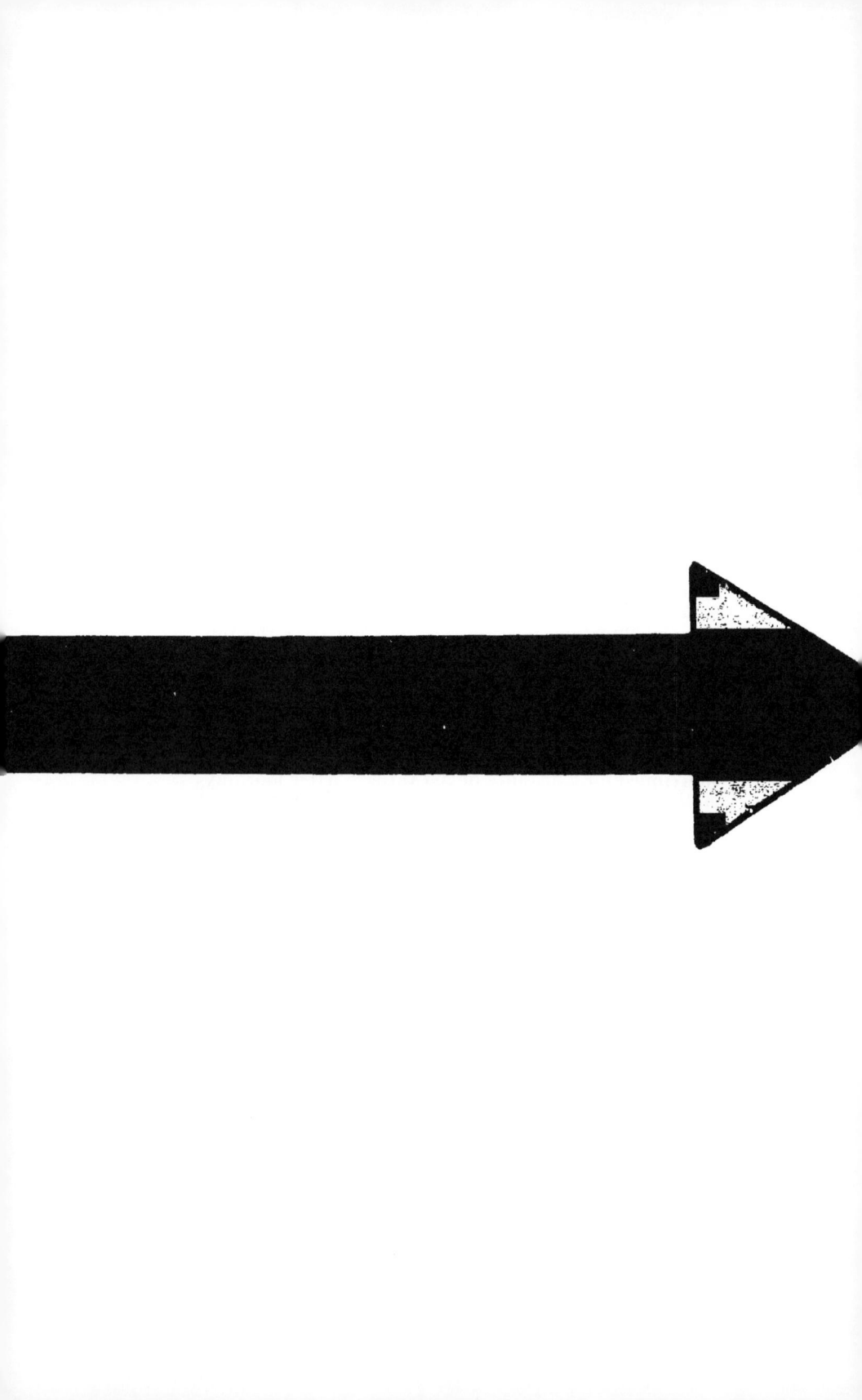

MICROCOPY RESOLUTION TEST CHART

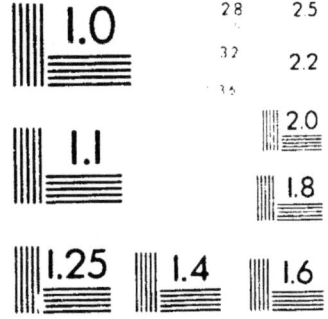

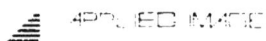

The Durham Forces in the Field

home for six months' duty. During his tenure of the command he had proved himself a fine soldier and all ranks viewed his departure with regret. Major Ince replaced him until the arrival of Lieut.-Col. H. F. G. Carter, M.C., K.O.Y.L.I.

On March 11th the Eighteenth moved to Bajus and Frévillers, exchanging billets with the 13th York and Lancaster Regt.

The Nineteenth withdrew for a week of rest and training when relieved in the line by the 18th Lancashire Fusiliers on November 20th. They afterwards came up to the bank of the Yser canal and supplied working parties, but moved back to Road Camp, not far from Proven, on December 11th. Colonel Greenwell had rejoined ere this.

Now came a month of training during which a large draft was absorbed. The weather was very wet but changed to frost and sunshine by January 8th, when the Durhams came by rail to Boesinghe and began work with the tunnellers and with the sappers and pioneers of the division who now came into the line again. Snow and rain were followed by a real improvement in the weather. On January 21st the battalion relieved the 12th Royal Sussex south-west of Westroosebeke where two companies occupied the front posts. The enemy was very quiet. Before the end of the month came a tour in the left sector nearer Poelcappelle where the open ground was beginning to dry, although there were still swamps in the valleys of the streams.

Early in February the Nineteenth were transferred to the 104th Brigade which now consisted of the Durhams and the 17th and 18th Lancashire Fusiliers. The battalion took over a chain of front line posts in the Langemarck sector on February 10th and then changed over for a tour in the line on the right. The last week of the month was spent in reserve where 10 officers and 200 men joined from the Fourteenth. Casualties during February only amounted to 12.

On March 1st the Nineteenth went in on the extreme left of the Langemarck sector. Snow fell next day and in the evening Z company took one prisoner. On the

Trench Warfare, Dec., 1917 - Mar., 1918

early morning of the 5th the battalion raided the huts east of Colombo House, on the Houthulst road. In mud and darkness the raiders penetrated the enemy wire without much difficulty but found that the Germans had fled to their main line. There were 9 casualties from machine-gun fire during the return journey, including 2nd Lieut. G. L. Hounam mortally wounded. Sergt. W. Dixon and Pte. J. Pearson were awarded the Military Medal for their gallantry on this occasion.

Relieved on March 5th, the Nineteenth remained in and around Langemarck as support battalion for four days and then withdrew to Elverdinghe, where training, rest, and recreation were interrupted by the constant call for working parties. There was a practice manning of the Army Battle Zone in the pouring rain of March 19th. Three days later came orders to entrain.

The Twenty-Second were still at work behind the Passchendaele front when, on the night of December 1st, the 25th Brigade co-operated with the 32nd Division in a surprise attack by moonlight north of the Passchendaele village. B company of the Pioneers provided two platoons to escort prisoners and guides; C and D companies were distributed in small groups with dumps of material along the forward roads and tracks to repair the damage caused by the constant hostile shell fire; A company were available for any other work required. Casualties only amounted to 6 wounded on this occasion.

The 8th Division were then relieved, but the Pioneers, still employed on tracks and roads in the forward area, only sent back to rest one company at a time. A new camp was erected near the Dixmude Gate at Ypres and then the work of draining and metalling the Frezenberg-Zonnebeke road was taken in hand. The plank road in the vicinity of Gravenstafel was shelled continuously at this time and on December 10th Capt. B. B. White was wounded and working parties had to withdraw. Dumps of material were established along the route so that rapid repairs could be made and all three companies worked at the task of pushing this road forward. There were three shifts, and at no

The Durham Forces in the Field

time did the work cease, but the hard frost combined with the enemy shell fire to make progress very slow. Soon another task fell to the Twenty-Second who were required to clean out and repair the German "pillboxes" so that they might be occupied by our infantry.

Among the New Year's Honours were the names of Capts. B. B. White and G. P. Baines, awarded the Military Cross, and Sergt. H. C. Welsh received the Meritorious Service Medal.

The Twenty-Second now sent away 48 men to the Nineteenth and 50 to the Eighteenth, these being replaced by 100 "B1" men from the Base. On January 16th came heavy rain; part of the Gravenstafel mule track was soon under water, a portion of the road beside the Pavebeck was washed away and other tracks were also submerged in places.

On February 7th a reinforcement of 7 officers and 150 men arrived from the Fourteenth. Early in the month, too, C.-Q.-M.-S. Thomas Danby was awarded the Belgian *Croix de Guerre*.

The Chief Engineer of the 8th Corps thought so highly of the work accomplished by the Twenty-Second at this period that he specially commended them to the Corps Commander. This spontaneous tribute to Durham's youngest battalion was in the following terms:

I wish to bring to notice of the Corps Commander the excellent work carried out by the undermentioned unit during the past 24 days in the Army Battle Zone and forward roads and the exceptionally good services rendered by the officers and men of this unit specified hereunder:

22nd Durham Light Infantry (Pioneers), 8th Div., Commander Lieut.-Col. C. B. Morgan, D.S.O.

During the greater part of the above period three companies of the battalion have been employed on—

(a) Construction of new double plank road forward from Devil's Crossing.
(b) Construction of bridge east of Frezenberg.
(c) Generally supervising the labour allotted to various sections of forward roads for maintenance work and to the construction of the diversion near Kansas Cross.*

* Where the Zonnebeke-Langemarck road crossed the Ypres-Mosselmarkt road.

Trench Warfare, Dec., 1917—Mar., 1918

For the last few days one to two companies have been employed on the Army Battle Zone, chiefly on wiring. The results produced by this battalion have exceeded all expectations, and have been due not only to sound, steady, solid work, which has been carried out by all ranks with such consistent energy and unfailing good spirit, but also to the careful and conscientious supervision which has invariably been exercised by the officers and N.C.O.'s of the battalion. I would particularly bring to notice the energetic manner in which Major J. D. Mitchell has personally superintended the work throughout, and the keen interest he has shown in getting the double plank road at Devil's Crossing pushed forward. I would also like to specially mention the good services rendered by Capt. A. W. H. Cooke and 2nd Lieut. W. H. Gibson in the work of general supervision and the construction of the bridge on the Frezenberg road respectively. On the occasions I have visited forward roads I have been much impressed by this battalion's capacity for work and the cheerfulness and good spirit with which it has met all demands made upon it.

Work on the western slopes of Passchendaele ridge and the lower ground by Gravenstafel continued throughout the month of February. The unpunctuality of the trains on the light railway was a great annoyance and hindrance; in some cases parties waited and then had to march to work. The frost also proved a great handicap. Another task accomplished was the construction of three dams across the Ravebeek—a stream which flowed south-west from the high ground west of Passchendaele—as part of the defensive system. The 8th Division had come into the line again, and early in March again withdrew, but the Twenty-Second were still employed under the Corps. On March 7th D company were broken up and the men distributed among the other companies to conform to the new establishment for pioneer battalions. Companies now took turns in going out to rest, but it was not till March 21st—the first day of the German offensive—that the Twenty-Second concentrated and moved by train to Poperinghe on their way to rejoin the 8th Division, who had already gone southward.

ITALY

MARCH TO SEPTEMBER, 1918

On March 4th the Twelfth and Thirteenth took over the left brigade front from the Fusiliers and found that the river was rising rapidly, forming new channels as it did so. The activities of patrols were consequently limited, while a great deal of drainage work had to be undertaken. After eight days in the line the Durham battalions were relieved by Italian troops as the 23rd Division were about to move into the mountains. The return to France of two British divisions meant little rest for those who remained in Italy.

The Twelfth left their billets at Pederiva and the vicinity on March 13th for Castelfranco. Next day they arrived at a small village near Vicenza called Lanze, where they rested while the officers reconnoitred the new line. Having moved in similar fashion the Thirteenth were now at Ruffo. Colonel Lindsay rejoined and assumed command of the battalion on March 16th.

Training, sports, football, and a horse show filled the days until the 68th Brigade moved to Thiene on March 25th. This was the first stage of the journey into the mountains. On the morrow the Durhams and Fusiliers were crowded into F.I.A.T. motor-lorries and soon left the genial spring weather of the plains for the snow and mist of the Alps. It was a unique experience for all, moving upward, to and fro, by precipitous mountain roads while a vast extent of the Venetian plain appeared below. Soon after midday the troops arrived in the snow-covered valley of Carriola. The mist cleared sufficiently to disclose Mount Magnaboschi and the broad valley of the Asiago away to the north—a dull and cheerless prospect to the men who had to settle down in damp and dirty huts.

The Durhams now made acquaintance with many

Italy, March to September, 1918

kinds of strange gear—fur boots, snow goggles, alpenstocks, and ice grips. The heavy transport had been left in the plains below but the light vehicles came thus far, and the number of pack animals, who were to be the chief means of supply, was augmented.

On the evening of the 27th the Twelfth relieved Italian troops in the line which was reached by way of elaborately camouflaged roads. The position on the left is described by one of the officers of the battalion as follows :

" The western half of the front taken over lay along the southern side of the narrow gorge of the Ghelpac, a stream draining the Asiago valley to the east. Here trenches had been blasted out of the living rock at varying altitudes on the cliff side with winding rock staircases connecting the different sections. In some places, where the face of the cliff was almost vertical, tunnels had been driven through the heart of the rock, emerging in the form of trenches further on. From these tunnels galleries and caves opened out, providing safe and fairly comfortable accommodation for a large number of men."

In the centre and on the right, where the valley broadened, trenches were of much the usual type and the Austrian lines were nearly a mile away, so that patrols had a great field for their activities. But the mountains in rear presented peculiar problems for the defence, chiefly as regards communications. The high winds made it impossible to hear over the telephone and visual signalling came into general use.

The 68th Brigade occupied the western end of the new British front line with the Twelfth on the extreme left. It was a three battalion front and the Thirteenth remained in reserve at Boscon. Everyone suffered from the cold. Austrians were seen digging on a hillside opposite the centre of the Twelfth but the Durham patrols did not get contact with the enemy, although their reconnaissance of the ground in front was useful.

The 7th Division came in before the end of March and the Twelfth reached rest billets at Magnaboschi on April 1st. Next day the two Durham battalions were both at Granezza where they stayed for nine days,

The Durham Forces in the Field

practising hill and wood fighting in rain and snow. Colonel Longden now left the Twelfth and was succeeded by Major J. H. E. Holford, D.S.O., of the Sherwood Rangers Yeomanry.

The Durhams relieved units of the 70th Brigade in the line on April 11th. This was nearer Asiago, on new ground, where the British line ran round the northern slopes of Mount Kaberlaba. Here in the wide stretch of " No Man's Land," where the Ghelpac river bed lay before the Austrian positions, patrols became very active. An outpost line was taken up in " No Man's Land " every night and replaced by snipers at dawn.

On the night of April 13th a party of the Twelfth crossed the river bed and advanced as far as the hamlet of Morar where there were Austrian advanced posts in front of their main trench. The patrol withdrew, apparently unobserved, but a strong party of the enemy threatened to cut them off as they retired. Austrian rifles, machine-guns and trench mortars opened, and the Durhams did well to get in with only one man missing.

A patrol of the Thirteenth explored the hamlet of Roncalto on the same night and discovered several Austrian sentries on the further side, but they could not be approached owing to trip wire and other obstacles. Two nights later a patrol reached Coda, on the river bank, and had to withdraw fighting, 2nd Lieut. E. Davies, M.C., and 4 men being wounded. During this period the British guns maintained a steady fire on the Austrian positions.

On April 15th Colonel Lindsay left the Thirteenth for the Machine Gun Corps, and Major D. H. Clarke, D.S.O., M.C., was confirmed in the command of the battalion.

The Fusiliers took over the line on April 17th and the Durhams withdrew to support positions where working parties had to be provided. On April 22nd commenced the relief of the 23rd Division, who were due to depart for the training area. The Twelfth arrived at billets in the vicinity of Longare on April 29th, after taking two days' rest upon the way. Hill tracks had to be negotiated in file, drag ropes were

Italy, March to September, 1918

necessary for the vehicles and one Lewis gun detachment marched ready to come into action against enemy aircraft. The Thirteenth had a shorter journey and reached Costo on April 25th.

All ranks were now practised in patrolling and climbing over hilly country until the journey back to the line commenced in the middle of May. Both Durham battalions arrived at Granezza again on the 18th and on the morrow took over the Asiago line.

The Twelfth had an uneventful tour, during which 2 men were wounded on patrol. The Thirteenth also found a quiet enemy, but there was a patrol skirmish on May 23rd when the Durhams were outnumbered and withdrew. A dead Austrian was discovered next day. Two nights later, Ave, a small hamlet near the Austrian line on the road running north to Asiago, was explored and found deserted. The Fusiliers came in on May 26th and the Twelfth went into support positions. The Thirteenth, now in reserve, had to supply parties to carry up artillery ammunition.

At this time preparations were practically completed for an offensive on the Asiago front, but this was indefinitely postponed.

On June 3rd the 68th Brigade passed into divisional reserve for a week and the Thirteenth moved down to Mare in the foothills to escape a kind of mountain fever which resembled influenza. But on the morning of June 10th the brigade replaced the 69th in the left portion of the Asiago sector with the Twelfth on the left and the Thirteenth on the right. On June 12th the line of the 68th Brigade was thickened by putting in the 11th N.F. on the left.

The 14th was an exceptionally quiet day, but at 3 o'clock next morning a very heavy Austrian bombardment commenced and all outposts were withdrawn. A large proportion of gas shells were used by the enemy whose fire was extremely accurate on communications and gun positions, though few of his batteries appeared to have carried out any previous registration. The bombardment quickened at 4 A.M., slackened rather more than an hour later, quickened again at 5.45 A.M. and continued so until the Austrian assault was launched.

The Durham Forces in the Field

Durham patrols had reported the enemy assembling for the attack in " No Man's Land " and at about 6.45 A.M. the Austrians came on, headed by " storm troops " with detachments of bombers, machine-gunners and men with flame-throwers. The S.O.S. signal went up all along the British line; but it was a misty morning and some of our guns had already been put out of action by the enemy artillery, so that the protective barrage was not so effective as it might have been. The Austrian advance was checked by the rapid fire of rifles and machine-guns which inflicted heavy losses. Ten of the enemy reached the trenches of the Fusiliers upon the left but were killed at once; in front of the Durham battalions no Austrian penetrated the wire. S. Sisto ridge, further to the right, was taken, but the 70th Brigade counter-attacked and soon restored the situation. On the left of the 68th Brigade the enemy had some success, securing a footing in the trenches of the 48th Division, and the Fusiliers became hard pressed on their threatened flank.

The Thirteenth on the right saw the Austrians forming up on the line Poslen-Malga Gheller at about 8.30 A.M. and they took heavy toll of them as they advanced. Soon after nine o'clock the enemy appeared to be digging in from Guardinalti to Poslen, Partut and Tescia, but he made repeated attempts to get forward. Three of the foremost Austrians were killed on the wire of the Thirteenth and their identifications were secured. Reinforcements appeared in the rear and came under the fire of the British artillery, but at about half-past eleven more enemy troops concentrated beyond the Ghelpac river in the vicinity of Morar. All the afternoon the Austrians strove to make headway and at 4 P.M. the front trenches of the Thirteenth were under heavy shell fire. Soon afterwards Lewis guns of the battalion opened on a party of Austrians in Roncalto, but by this time it could be seen that the attack had definitely failed. At about 5.45 P.M. A company sent out patrols who returned with 7 prisoners, described as " very poor specimens of humanity." Austrians were still wandering about " No Man's Land " as the evening advanced and the snipers of the Thirteenth found many

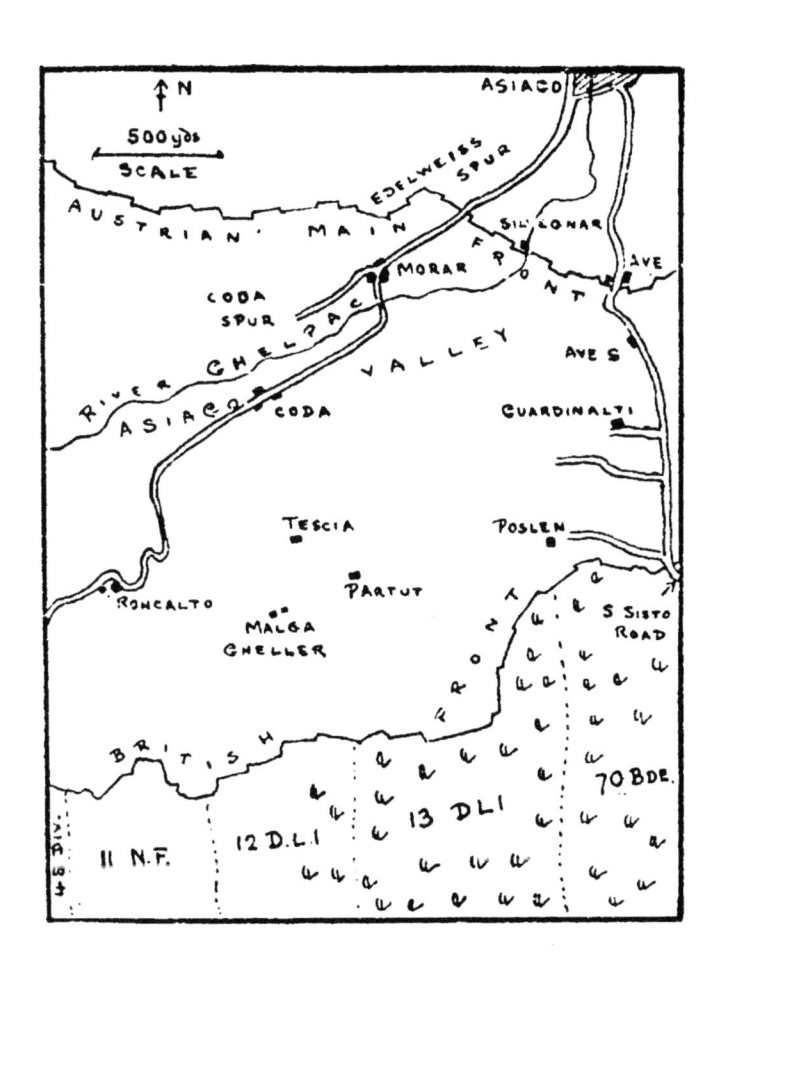

The Durham Forces in the Field

targets. Casualties on this day amounted to 2 killed, and 2nd Lieut. P. G. Smith and 23 wounded. Sixteen of the enemy were taken.

The Twelfth had a defensive patrol out in front when the Austrian bombardment began. These men, under 2nd Lieut. J. E. Rasche, helped to repel the first attack and then withdrew, bringing in all their wounded. About noon Colonel Holford suggested that the Twelfth should sally forth and capture or kill those of the enemy who lay in folds of the ground near the wire, but the project was not approved by the brigadier. At dusk a body of 200 Austrians was observed in retreat and the rifles and Lewis guns of the battalion accounted for nearly all of them. On this day the Twelfth lost a good officer in Major E. W. Lafone, M.C., but only 4 others were killed. 2nd Lieut. J. E. Rasche and 31 men were wounded; and Capt. W. L. Hughes, M.C., and 4 men were also hit, but remained at duty. The wounded Austrians brought in numbered 21, including 2 officers, and 7 unwounded prisoners were taken.

The night was quiet and patrols scouring " No Man's Land " found none but dead and wounded Austrians there. By 6 P.M. on June 16th the captures of the Thirteenth amounted to 3 officers, 45 men, and three machine-guns. The Twelfth had collected a number of trophies, including four machine-guns, five field telephones, seven trench mortars of different calibres and ammunition of various kinds.

At night a patrol of the 8th York and Lancasters left the line of the Thirteenth to occupy the Austrian trenches at Edelweis Spur, beyond Norar. They encountered the enemy at Coda Spur and had to withdraw, after which the Austrian artillery shelled the trenches of the Thirteenth who had 4 casualties. The British guns were also busy before dawn.

The afternoon and evening of the 17th were very wet. A few more wounded Austrians were brought in and patrols were busy clearing the battlefield until June 20th, when the Durham battalions withdrew to support positions.

In this action both Twelfth and Thirteenth won

Italy, March to September, 1918

many honours. Capt. C. Gibbens, M.C., of the Twelfth, was awarded a bar to his Cross for able handling of his company; Lieut. J. E. Rasche received the Military Cross for his work in command of the patrol and for continuing at duty when wounded; C.-S.-M. T. Martin, D.C.M., of Scotswood, won a bar to his medal for organising a party which bombed out some enemy snipers established close to the wire; and the Distinguished Conduct Medal was awarded to Sergt. J. A. Speed, M.M., of Blackhill, for directing the repair of signal wires under the violent Austrian bombardment. Among the recipients of the Military Medal were Sergt. J. O'Hara and Lance-Corpl. F. Cooper; Ptes. T. R. Kirby, C. Woodward, F. Macdonald, J. Saltmarsh, R. Fedley, J. Cook; and Bugler C. Harrison. Lance-Sergt. E. V. Teague was awarded the *Croce di Guerra*.

In the Thirteenth Capt. I. Bewley displayed great initiative as a company commander, sending in valuable reports and following up the enemy with patrols when he retired. Next morning he made a reconnaissance in person and killed 2 Austrians. He won the Military Cross, as did 2nd Lieuts. N. F. Willis and C. F. Bishop for similar good work. The Distinguished Conduct Medal went to C.-S.-M. W. Donaldson, of Pelton, for his gallant example during the bombardment and his energy in following up the retreating Austrians and bringing in prisoners. Sergt. J. Anderson, M.M., of Wingate, was also awarded this medal. He handled his Lewis guns with great skill and personally accounted for the whole of the team of an enemy machine-gun. Lance-Sergt. R. Morrell, Lance-Corpls. W. Hall and G. Hewitt, and Ptes. T. Armstrong, F. Parnaby, G. Neale and J. D. Gault were awarded the Military Medal. Corpl. W. Clair, M.M., received a bar to his decoration.

On June 26th the 68th Brigade were withdrawn to divisional reserve, but replaced the 70th in the line again on July 4th. The Thirteenth were now on the left and the Twelfth in reserve. There was much raiding activity and retaliation by the Austrian batteries followed. An enemy bombardment persisted all day on the 7th and the Thirteenth took up battle positions in

The Durham Forces in the Field

the afternoon after a Lewis gun team had been killed by a direct hit and several others wounded. The rest of the tour was quiet and on July 10th the Twelfth and Thirteenth changed places. Two days later the divisional artillery supported a raid of the French troops further east and the trenches of the Twelfth were shelled, one man being killed and 4 wounded. Patrols of the Twelfth were active in the vicinity of Morar and one Austrian was killed.

The 48th Division relieved the 23rd on July 20th and both Durham battalions marched down the mountains to Arzignano—west of Vicenza—which was reached four days later. Here, in hot weather, training was carried out and the troops felt the benefit of their newly issued tropical clothing—khaki drill and sun-helmets.

On August 15th came a move forward to the line again by way of Marisano and thence by mule track till, on the 19th, the Twelfth arrived at Mount Cavaletto and the Thirteenth at a camp near Mount Brusabo. The 68th Brigade were now in reserve preparatory to taking over the left of the British line with which they had made acquaintance on the first move to the mountains in March.

Musketry, hill training and reconnaissance of the forward area were done by the Durhams before the Thirteenth relieved the 9th Yorkshires in trenches on August 27th. The Twelfth moved into support at the same time and provided working parties and patrols. There was some hostile shell fire, but it was difficult to gain contact with the enemy whose infantry were not desirous of an encounter.

The Twelfth relieved the 11th N.F. on the right of the brigade front on September 4th when the other Fusilier battalion replaced the Thirteenth, who withdrew to support positions about Mount Lemerle. While here they provided patrols who worked with an Italian searchlight but found little sign of the enemy. There was some expectation of an Austrian retirement and all troops were held in readiness to advance if such should occur.

But the Thirteenth were now for France again. On

Italy, March to September, 1918

reduction to a three-battalion strength every British brigade in Italy contributed one battalion to the reconstituted 25th Division for service in France. On September 11th the Thirteenth were relieved by the 8th K.O.Y.L.I. and marched to Centrale that same night. Here two days were spent in preparation for the journey and on September 14th the battalion entrained near Thiene for France.

The Twelfth were relieved in the front trenches on September 10th and, after spending six days in reserve to the 69th Brigade, they withdrew to divisional reserve at Mount Magnaboschi. When they moved up to a support position on the left, four days later, patrols were provided as usual and, following a raid by Italian troops further west, the Ghelpac gorge was explored for wounded. This brought to an end the stay of the Durhams in the mountains, for on September 26th they were relieved by the Italians and proceeded by march route and lorry, with some intervals for rest and training on the way, till on October 5th they reached Montecchio Maggiore.

THE GERMAN OFFENSIVE, 1918

CHAPTER I

On March 21st, when in the fog of the early morning the German hosts attacked the whole wide front held by the British Fifth and Third Armies, no Service Battalion of Durham was actually in the line; but the 21st Division occupied the sector about Epéhy and the Fifteenth, in reserve at Liéramont since the beginning of the month, were soon thrown into the fight.

At 5.25 a.m. they moved forward to a position of readiness south of Heudicourt and at noon were ordered to occupy the " Brown " Line in front of that village. To do so they had to pass through a cloud of gas and the new position was soon shelled fiercely. Serious news came during the afternoon. The enemy had broken the left of the divisional front and the " Yellow " Line from a point south of Chapel Hill— a commanding spur, over which ran the road from Heudicourt to Villers-Guislain—to some distance south of the Heudicourt-Peizière railway, was in his hands.

The Fifteenth, ordered to counter-attack and recover the " Yellow " Line south of the Heudicourt-Vaucelette Farm road, assembled for this purpose about the cross-roads at Railton—half a mile east of Heudicourt - before 7.15 p.m. Thirty minutes later the assault was delivered in the face of heavy rifle and machine-gun fire. The Durhams persevered in spite of considerable losses. They reached the trenches and drove out the grey infantry from both the front and support lines. First in was C. Q.-M.-S. G. Potts, of Sunderland, who commanded a platoon. Though wounded he remained on duty, and was afterwards awarded the Distinguished Conduct Medal for his gallant work. One officer and 60 other Germans were

The German Offensive, 1918

taken and heavy losses were inflicted on the enemy; but Lieut.-Col. H. W. Festing, D.S.O., who had led his men with great gallantry, was killed in the advance. Capt. S. D. Thorpe, M.C., now assumed command.

The Fifteenth joined hands on the south with the 2nd Lincolns, but the enemy still held the trench to the left. Though fiercely shelled all the night through the Durhams made an effort at 3 o'clock next morning to bomb their way northwards towards Chapel Hill, which was still in British hands. Some progress was made, but the Germans had established machine-guns in the dug-outs along the road which crossed the trench and it was impossible to push past this point, where a barricade was established and held. These operations were under the direction of 2nd Lieut. S. Walton, who had assumed adjutant's duties and who for this and his subsequent good work received the Military Cross.

At 8 a.m. the enemy bombardment increased in volume and an infantry attack followed. This was repulsed by Lewis gun and rifle fire. Later in the morning the Germans came on again, but the line of the Fifteenth still held firm. The hostile shell fire never slackened and at noon German infantry were observed massing for a fresh attempt. The Durhams now received orders to withdraw, a difficult task with the enemy threatening both flanks, but the battalion retired steadily in good order, thanks largely to Capt. A. Roberts, who commanded in the front line. He also won the Military Cross.

The Fifteenth crossed the "Brown" Line and marched back to Liéramont which was now a target for the German gunners. The battalion moved out to the Nurlu road, and at 6.30 p.m. withdrew to a position in the "Green" Line on the high ground north-west of Templeux-la-Fosse. This retirement was rendered necessary by the advance of the enemy from the south and south-east which had turned the right flank of the division. Here the other battalions of the 64th Brigade were struggling desperately and, during the night of March 22nd, the 1st East Yorkshires and

The Durham Forces in the Field

9th K.O.Y.L.I. fought their way through to the "Green" Line. The Fifteenth were now in touch with the 110th Brigade on the left, but the 14th Gloucesters had come in between the Durhams and the Yorkshiremen. Rations and ammunition were available and were very welcome.

At 8 o'clock on the morning of the 23rd the situation to the south was so bad that the 64th Brigade were ordered to continue the retreat. The Yorkshiremen on the right were attacked in the fog before they could move, but the Fifteenth had to retire in order to conform to the line on the left. The German infantry were now advancing upon the whole front and the Durhams withdrew steadily, fighting all the way, through a wood on the southern slope of the high ground. At midday the battalion were in position behind and to the north of the little village of Aizecourt-le-Haut. The Gloucesters had disappeared and there were no British troops on the right, but on the other flank the Fifteenth were now in touch with the 62nd Brigade. The fog still hung in the air and through it came the Germans, still pressing their attack. On the left of the Fifteenth the line began to retire and the battalion followed suit. They went back through Haut Allaines and across the little Tortille river and the canal, till, at the cross-roads at Feuillacourt, the brigadier began to collect his scattered command. A line was formed east of the Peronne-Bouchavesnes road by the exhausted infantry of the 64th Brigade—there were barely 1,200 left—with the right on the cross-roads. Here two field guns were in action, replying valiantly to the accurate fire of the German batteries now established at Aizecourt-le-Haut, while the road to Cléry was blocked by all kinds of transport in retreat. But the two British guns were soon silenced and at about two o'clock in the afternoon the enemy to the south occupied the spur at Mont St. Quentin which commanded the brigade line. A retirement commenced at once, straight across country under enfilade fire from the right, and the survivors of the Fifteenth came to a stand east of Cléry, with the right on the river Somme. On the Cléry road a great quantity of trans-

The German Offensive, 1918

port fell into German hands. Fighting continued in the moonlight and the enemy made further progress, so that the right of the Durhams drew back to the eastern edge of Cléry where there were some of the Machine Gun Corps.

At 8 A.M. on March 24th a furious German bombardment was followed by an infantry attack in great force half an hour later. Cléry could not be held and the line went back again to a position north-east of Hem and, eventually, another 500 yards to the west. The 35th Division were now beginning to arrive and in the afternoon a counter-attack carried the line forward again; but at five o'clock came another German thrust and the ground thus gained had to be relinquished. As darkness fell the right of the Fifteenth rested on the Somme at Curlu. Here the 35th Division took over the line and the survivors of the battalion withdrew to billets at Suzanne.

A move back to Bray was made on March 25th and here the 64th Brigade formed a Composite Battalion. The Fifteenth provided one weak company under Capt. C. S. Herbert, M.C., and in this way the division got together a brigade 1,500 strong which, under General Headlam, was available as a reserve. Capt. Herbert's men, after various movements, found themselves in position the same evening in trenches north and north-east of Bray.

Another composite company was formed by the Fifteenth at Chipilly on March 26th. This detachment, which numbered 70, was placed under the command of Lieut. W. Good and joined a second Composite Battalion. Meanwhile the stragglers who came in were collected at the transport lines at Beaucourt and later at Bonnay. On March 30th the Fifteenth were located at Allonville where, on the last day of the month, Capt. Herbert and Lieut. Good rejoined with their men, having been in reserve the whole time. Major C. E. R. Holroyd-Smyth, M.C., 3rd Dragoon Guards, now arrived to take command of the battalion.

In the heavy fighting of the four days commencing on March 21st the Fifteenth had lost 486 in killed,

The Durham Forces in the Field

wounded and missing, besides 16 officers. Among the killed, mortally wounded and missing were Lieut.-Col. H. W. Festing, D.S.O.; Capts. T. A. L. Welch and C. W. T. Barker, M.C.; 2nd Lieut. W. H. Wilson, H. J. Hale, A. W. L. Husband, W. Park, W. Gardner, L. Wilson, and H. S. Turner. Capt. J. Sedgwick, M.C.; Lieuts. C. H. Saunders, M.C., M. S. O. O'Brien and J. Key; and 2nd Lieuts. J. C. Tregea and C. Stephenson were wounded.

  Soon after the Fifteenth entered the battle the Eleventh began to assist in covering the British retreat south of the Somme. The 20th Division were in reserve behind the right of the Fifth Army and the Pioneers, located principally at Golancourt and Voyennes, received orders to "man battle stations" at 6.20 A.M. on March 21st. Early in the afternoon the companies concentrated in heavy marching order at Colancourt and left for Villers St. Christophe, north of the Somme canal. Here Capt. Jee, with 6 officers and 133 men, was detached to report to the Divisional Reinforcement Battalion at Matigny and later in the evening D company, under Lieut. M. Cooper, were sent to the 61st Brigade.
  The next morning brought no news, but heavy firing was heard away to the north-east in the direction of Holnon Wood and St. Quentin. Colonel Hayes arranged to support the 59th Brigade and in the afternoon the two companies moved to Germaine accordingly. But orders then came from the division. The Eleventh were required to fill a gap between the 61st and 60th Brigades on the line Tugny-Lavesne. Coming southward at once, the commanding officer found a support company of the 12th King's (61st Brigade) and his own D company dug in astride the Tugny-Dury road. By 8 P.M., when A and B companies arrived, the King's had had to evacuate Tugny and the support line thus became the front line. A and B companies, from right to left, filled the gap between D company and the Shropshires of the 60th Brigade in position further north. Before 9 P.M. Capt. Endean reported that D company and the King's had retired,

The German Offensive, 1918

leaving the right flank of A company exposed. A thick fog had gathered and the enemy in Tugny could now be heard shouting in English and making a lot of noise. Colonel Hayes would not retire without orders while there were still troops on his left, so posts were dug to cover the right flank. Patrols soon found, however, that the enemy were already through the line. Soon after midnight B company were rushed from the right rear and there was confused fighting, with Durhams, Shropshires and Germans all mixed together in the fog. On the right Capt. Endean and A company fought stoutly, but in withdrawing one party came under machine-gun fire at close range and were all killed or wounded.

About 70 men of the Eleventh, with 30 of the Shropshires and some of the Machine Gun Corps, were collected south-west of Aubigny and withdrew down the Ham road, leaving a rearguard under 2nd Lieut. English to support two Vickers guns which were still in action. On the way to Ham Colonel Hayes received orders to hasten to Offoy and hold the bridgehead there.

Meanwhile Capt. Endean, with 2nd Lieuts. Galley and Craig and about 40 men of A company, had fought a way out in the fog through Dury to Ham. C.-S.-M. I. J. Craggs, of Bishop Auckland, had done the same with a party of B company and some men of the Rifle Brigade. For his gallantry in the retreat this warrant officer was afterwards awarded the Distinguished Conduct Medal.

In the early morning of March 23rd Colonel Hayes reached Offoy and organised the men who were with him into one company under the command of Lieut. Bushell. 2nd Lieuts. Martin, Naylor and English were also available, and so was C.-S.-M. Craggs, who had managed to rejoin. By this time the 12th K.R.R.C. had arrived and taken over the defence of the canal at Offoy. The Eleventh, with a few of the Shropshires, prolonged this line to the right where another battalion of pioneers had been digging before retiring at daylight. The position reached as far as the outskirts of Canizy and touch was obtained with the 30th

The Durham Forces in the Field

Entrenching Battalion, holding the line of the canal and that village. There was telephonic communication with the 60th Brigade at Hombleux and the day passed quietly. At dusk the German snipers were active and after dark came bursts of machine-gun and trench-mortar fire.

At about 4 o'clock on the morning of March 24th Capt. Eudean, 2nd Lieut. Galley and over 30 men of A company rejoined. The movements of the troops on the right were very uncertain, so Colonel Moore, commanding the Rifles, obtained the assistance of two platoons of the 2/7th Warwicks to secure the right flank. They were instructed to dig in south-east of Canizy and to keep a standing patrol at the broken footbridge. At 6 A.M. German artillery and mortars concentrated on Canizy and assistance from the British artillery was asked for but brought no reply. When daylight came there was a thick fog. No reports had been received from the Warwicks at Canizy and a patrol sent out did not return. A whole company of the 2/7th Warwicks now arrived and were pushed out towards the right flank. At about 8 A.M. rifle and machine-gun fire was opened on the railway from Canizy and B company retired. As the fog lifted the Germans were seen advancing from the village, but fire was opened on them and they retreated, B company regaining their trench. A German aeroplane flew low over the position and Capt. Eudeau reported that the enemy were coming down the Ham-Nesle road. Other retiring troops of many units now helped to form a defensive flank on the right and a counter-attack kept the enemy in check. But Colonel Hayes, with Lieut. Cooke and 2nd Lieut. Ellwood, reconnoitred to the south and found a great gap in the line extending as far as Estrery Hallon. Colonel Moore, with some of his own regiment and some of B company of the Eleventh under C.-S.-M. Craggs, were still holding on by the railway, but parties of British troops were now retreating down the road towards Nesle and also through Hombleux. Early in the afternoon the Germans were on the ridge overlooking the Hombleux road and B company and the Rifles just managed to

The German Offensive, 1918

get away in time through Hombleux to the canal at Breuil. Their retreat was covered by the fire of some Canadian motor machine-guns.

All the men of the 20th Division who could be collected were placed in position west of the canal between Buverchy and Breuil. The night was quiet, except for bursts of rifle and machine-gun fire from the French troops who assisted to hold the canal bank. On March 23th Colonel Hayes and Lieut. Cooke were sent to assist in restoring the situation at Languevoisin, where the line threatened to give way. In the evening the troops near Breuil found their flanks had been driven in and a fighting retreat was made through Cressy to Roye, where there came a breathing space. Colonel Hayes, who had been affected by gas shells during the day, now collapsed and went for a few days to Rouen. He was succeeded by Capt. Scar. M.C.

Capt. Jee's party rejoined at Roye next day. On the evening of March 22nd they had dug a rearguard position north of the Matigny-Douilly road, facing northeast, and had retired from this line to Voyennes at midnight. Next morning they covered the withdrawal of the 2nd Scottish Rifles across the canal bridge there and marched back at 9 A.M. over the Noyon canal to dig a line facing north-east near Languevoisin. Until midday 2nd Lieut. King and 20 men held a front post on the left flank of the Rifles. In the afternoon came orders to support the 59th Brigade and a position was accordingly taken up at 5 P.M., facing north, about a mile north of Rouy-le-Petit. At dawn of the 24th came another German onslaught and by nine in the morning the Durhams were holding a part of the front. An hour later they gave supporting fire to an unsuccessful counter-attack of the 61st Division from Mesnil-St. Nicaise towards Bethencourt. In the early afternoon the enemy took Rouy in the rear and a defensive flank was dug on the hillside overlooking the village. Here 2nd Lieut. Dodds was wounded. Eventually a line was established to cover Nesle, north of the Nesle-Ham road, but an intense fire beat upon the trenches next morning. Troops on the left were

The Durham Forces in the Field

forced to retire, involving Capt. Jee's withdrawal astride the main road from Nesle to Roye. French troops were now arriving and, in conjunction with them, an outpost line was taken up 200 yards south-west of the Herly-Billancourt road. When at 5 P.M. the Germans attacked again the Durhams covered the withdrawal of the French, retiring on the latter when they were established in Réthonvillers. In the early hours of the 26th came orders to rejoin the battalion at Roye.

On the afternoon of March 26th the Eleventh were detailed to dig defences in the neighbourhood of le Quesnel, and at 7.30 P.M. they marched off down the Amiens road to Arvillers. Near this village the night was spent in digging and improving trenches and Capt. Jee performed a valuable reconnaissance as far as Erches and Bouchoir. The remains of D company now joined the battalion.

When discovered by the commanding officer in trenches before Tugny on the evening of March 22nd, D company were at the disposal of the 12th King's. They were suddenly ordered south of the Somme Canal and bivouacked for the night on the Ollezy-Sommette-Eaucourt road in support to a company of the King's on the canal bank. The Germans crossed the canal at Ollezy before morning and D company then dug and held two posts in the path of the threatened advance. Lieut. Cooper, with three platoons, was located about three-quarters of a mile west of Annois and 2nd Lieut. Duckett, with the other platoon, was a mile further west. At two in the afternoon of March 23rd a company of the 12th King's retired and Lieut. Cooper covered them with his fire; but the enemy was in no great strength, and the King's advanced again into Annois Wood. 2nd Lieut. Duckett also advanced to support another company of the King's in front of Cugny. He and his platoon were no more seen. At 6 P.M. a company of the King's retired again and about 20 men of the Somerset Light Infantry, with 2 officers, withdrew across the railway on the left. They reported that there were no British on that flank and this was confirmed by a patrol. Before 7 P.M. it

The German Offensive, 1918

appeared that the troops on the right had retired to Cugny and D company then retreated in that direction. Lieut. Cooper came upon a company of an Irish regiment, but he decided to continue his withdrawal in the direction of Guiscard. The village of Cugny was deserted and the Durham men led on in the darkness, 2nd Lieut. Banks being left to assist the Irish officer to get his men back. They did not follow and were not seen again. At Villeselve were found the headquarters of the 61st Brigade and D company procured three boxes of ammunition, biscuits, and some tinned meat—all very badly needed. At 6 A.M. on the morning of March 24th D company moved forward in the fog from Villeselve but found no unit of the 61st Brigade, so dug in facing north on a road about a mile out, in company with some Irish troops, Machine Gun Corps and others. At noon the mist cleared and the position was shelled from the south and the east. The troops on the left retired at 3 P.M. and half an hour later the company followed as far as a sunken road just outside Villeselve. Here were found the 7th D.C.L.I. At four o'clock cavalry and French *mitrailleuse* came back through the position and reported the enemy advancing steadily. His machineguns were soon able to sweep the top of the road and a German aeroplane flew low over the position. At 6 P.M. field guns opened from barely a mile away; then high explosive shrapnel burst overhead and the line could hold no longer. The only way of retreat lay through Villeselve and for the first 200 yards was swept by machine-gun fire. Before eight o'clock D company reached Guiscard, to find the place crowded with men and horses in retreat amidst clouds of gas. In the darkness and confusion the Durhams became scattered and Lieut. Cooper reached Muirancourt two hours later with only 4 men. He pushed on south-westwards to Bussy, where, in the middle of the night, he found 2 other officers and collected 25 stragglers of the 61st Brigade. At 3 o'clock on the morning of March 25th some cavalry came through and reported that there were only mounted men in front and that they were retiring. Lieut. Cooper then set out for Roye, which

The Durham Forces in the Field

he reached in the afternoon, and next day he rejoined the battalion.

On the morning of March 27th troops of the 36th Division on the right of the Eleventh began to retire. This exposed the flank of the Pioneers; but the German advance seemed to be towards the left of the line and patrols sent out at dusk found no signs of attack upon the battalion front. The French were to take over early on March 28th and had already begun to do so when a short, fierce bombardment was followed by a German advance.

An advanced post of the Eleventh received several direct hits which damaged the Lewis guns and forced the men to withdraw. German infantry were now seen passing in the woods on the right and the battalion threw back a defensive flank. A counter-attack was organised, but it was obvious that the enemy were too strong; still the position was maintained till later in the day, when orders were received to retire on Fresnoy. By the evening the Eleventh, now in reserve, had reached a wood behind Mezières, where the night was spent in the rain. Capt. R. L. S. Pemberton, M.C., rejoined the battalion here and took command.

Next morning the Germans attacked along the Amiens road and entered Mezières. At 3.15 p.m. the Eleventh were called upon to recapture the village, though they had only 130 men left. At four o'clock the little force emerged from the wood and went forward with great spirit. Crossing the open ground, a trench mortar barrage was encountered and enfilade machine-gun fire smote them. Only here and there could small groups of men get through the barrier of bursting shells and Capt. Pemberton had about 20 Durhams with him when he entered the village. He pushed on until only 2 survived, and then withdrew. On the left 2nd Lieut B. H. King had also reached Mezières, but all his party were killed and wounded and after working a Lewis gun with great effect he returned alone. Both officers were awarded the Military Cross.

The Eleventh were now withdrawn to a position between Thennes and Hourges, and passed the night in peace. On the morning of March 30th a retirement

The German Offensive, 1918

was observed on the left and the French troops on the right were also seen to be in retreat. The Germans were now in Moreuil wood and the battalion formed a defensive flank in this direction. Later in the day cavalry restored the line here.

Next morning the enemy attacked again. Capt. Pemberton took his men up the hill south-east of Thennes and joined the cavalry in line less than half a mile from the enemy in the woods. At 4 p.m. came a determined advance, but rifle and Lewis gun fire stopped the grey infantry who retreated, leaving many dead and wounded behind them. Capt. Endean was wounded during this action. There was some shelling after this, but the evening and night passed without further incident and no fresh attack developed on April 1st. In the evening came relief. Marching to the Amiens road, the battalion—now the strength of a strong platoon—journeyed by bus to Quevavillers, some twelve miles south-west of the city.

Losses in the ranks during these ten days totalled 455, and there were 19 casualties to officers. Among the killed or missing were 2nd Lieuts. W. G. Craig, R. R. Galley, H. Rutherford, W. T. Alexander, W. Banks, V. G. Duckett, F. Arnott, D. E. Ellwood, I. W. Applegarth and C. A. Morris, and Lieut. R. Bushell. 2nd Lieuts. P. Naylor, E. W. English, N. F. Gibson, J. H. Dodds, A. E. Wilkinson and H. J. Whitfield, and Capts. W. G. L. Sear, M.C., and W. J. Endean were all wounded.

Sergt. W. Bayfield, of South Shields, had greatly distinguished himself in handling his Lewis guns, carrying on despite his several wounds. He was awarded the Distinguished Conduct Medal. Corpl. B. Harrison, who had done gallant and devoted service both during the retreat and in the Flanders fighting of 1917 while in command of the divisional observers, received the same reward.

The narrative of the Twenty-Second, who fought on the immediate left of the 20th Division, now concludes the story of the retreat south of the Somme.

As soon as the storm broke the 8th Division were

The Durham Forces in the Field

hurried forward and March 23rd saw the Twenty-Second billeted in Rosières after coming south from Ypres. The battalion were in reserve, but next day the 8th took over part of the front of the sorely harassed 50th (Northumbrian) Division and at 4 A.M. the Pioneers began their march forward through Chaulnes, Fresnes, and Marchelpot. They rested awhile at Omiecourt, then moved to Pertain. In the afternoon A company took up a position west of Morchain, but fell back in the evening to a line 500 yards west of Potte Wood where, with B Company, new trenches were dug and occupied. The battalion were under orders of the 25th Brigade and bridged a gap between the 8th and the 20th Division on the right. C company remained in reserve at Pertain.

During the night 2nd Lieut. W. I. O'Dell, M.M., made a successful reconnaissance to Mesnil-St. Nicaise and Potte Wood, bringing in valuable information. At 9 A.M. on March 25th came an attack by masses of German infantry who had ample artillery support, but the Twenty-Second held on till they were in danger of being surrounded. Fighting all the way, the Durhams then retreated. They reached Omiecourt by noon and held on there till ordered to retire to the ridge north-east of Chaulnes. This line was reached in the evening. Heavy losses were sustained this day and many gallant deeds were done. Capt. A. I. Robson, M.C., led his company very gallantly and extricated his men with great skill from a critical position when half had been killed or wounded. 2nd Lieut. A. J. Hossack, M.M., went forward under heavy rifle and machine-gun fire and got in touch with the troops on the left of the battalion. Lieut. Chas. Gillott led his men until he had been wounded three times, and was afterwards awarded the Military Cross. Lieut. T. W. Fowey and Corpl. Joseph Green blocked a communication trench down which the enemy were advancing to turn the flank of their company and, in spite of machine-gun fire and snipers, they got a Lewis gun in action to sweep this trench. Corpl. Green was awarded the Military Medal. Corpl. E. Dodds, who won the same decoration, remained with his men,

The German Offensive, 1918

though wounded, and by his example helped to save a critical situation. Pte. William Walson collected a party of stragglers and reinforced the line, taking command where all the N.C.O.s had fallen. Pte. Robert Coltman, a company runner, was wounded early in the attack but continued his duties under heavy fire until very badly hit. Corpl. Thomas Stonehouse was in charge of two Lewis guns and when all the team of one gun were hit he served the gun himself till all the ammunition was gone. Then he brought it back under deadly fire. Pte. Walter Ransome continued to serve his Lewis gun till all had retired and then brought it out of action. All these gallant men received the Military Medal.

At dawn on March 26th the battalion withdrew to Lihons and at 7 A.M. were in position east of the village astride the Lihons-Chaulnes road. In the afternoon they went back beyond Rosières, being now in divisional reserve with the 25th Brigade.

Before noon next day the enemy had pressed his advance along the southern bank of the Somme to the left of the 8th Division and the situation near Proyart was critical. At 1.30 P.M. the Twenty-Second started for Harbonnières to counter-attack in company with the 2nd Devons. Deploying north-east of the village with B company on the right of the regular battalion, the counter-attack was launched with great determination. The Germans were driven back across the main Amiens road and retreated towards Proyart, leaving many prisoners in the hands of the Devons and Durhams. A thousand yards beyond the road a trench was seized and held. Though losses were light, considering what had been accomplished, Lieut.-Col. C. B. Morgan, D.S.O.—who had taken the Twenty-Second to France in 1916 and continued in command ever since—was so badly wounded that he died two days later. The command devolved upon Major J. D. Mitchell. Capt. A. H. Robson, M.C., was again prominent in action, as were 2nd Lieut. Hossack, M.M., and 2nd Lieut. G. V. Eastwood. Sergt. (acting C.-S.-M.) Robert C. Wherley and Sergt. F. Benson won the Military Medal for their work as platoon com-

The Durham Forces in the Field

manders. Lance-Sergt. James Wigham, who killed many Germans, was given the same decoration and another very gallant man was Lance-Corpl. Ernest Lambert who took charge of his platoon when both subaltern and sergeant were killed or wounded.

The position thus won could not be held for long, as by the morning of March 28th the whole line of the 8th Division was in danger of being enveloped from the north and south. A and C companies of the Twenty-Second withdrew to Caix and then to Morisel. This was not done without difficulty, but Lieut. George C. Reay handled his Lewis guns boldly and well, inflicting heavy losses on the enemy and checking his advance. B company came back later to Caix and then moved to Jumel, upon the river Noye, where on the evening of March 29th the whole battalion concentrated.

The next day the Twenty-Second moved north to Guyencourt, and then to Cottenchy, but in the evening they took up a position north-west of the Moreuil-Demuin road with their right flank on the edge of Moreuil Wood. B and C companies held the front with A company in reserve.

The morning of March 31st passed quietly. At noon a furious bombardment opened and fifteen minutes later the German infantry came on in great numbers. Heavy toll was taken of them by the rifles and Lewis guns of the Twenty-Second, but they entered the wood on the right and the British line had to give ground. Capt. A. H. Robson, who won a bar to his Military Cross, was badly wounded as he moved about among his men during the bombardment and Major J. D. Mitchell, awarded the Distinguished Service Order, was also hit. But now, in conjunction with the cavalry on the right where the survivors of the Eleventh were still fighting, an advance of 500 yards was made and the position consolidated under heavy fire.

There was artillery and air activity on April 1st, but no infantry attack. On the following day the French took over the line and the Twenty-Second marched back to refit. No less than 23 officers and 469 others were by this time killed, wounded or miss-

The German Offensive, 1918

ing. Among the fallen were Capts. A. W. F. Cooke and R. Thwaites, Lieuts. H. G. Legge and J. Stirland, and 2nd Lieut. John Scott. The 8th Division had engaged units of eighteen different German divisions.

Capt. R. W. Pearson, R.A.M.C., the medical officer of the Twenty-Second, was awarded the Military Cross for his devoted care of the wounded. He was ably seconded by his orderlies, Lance-Corpl. Fred Armstrong and Pte. Fred Sykes. The gallantry of the stretcher-bearers, notably Ptes. A. Chapman, J. W. Gibbons and B. Sharp, had prevented many wounded falling into the hands of the Germans. Among others who should be remembered for their deeds of valour were Lieuts. J. A. Crutchley and A. Elliff, 2nd Lieut. Hossack, Sergt. Robert Blackett, Pte. (Acting Sergt.) J. L. Mackie, and Pte. Harry Pearl, a company runner.

The Nineteenth came south from the Ypres front on March 23rd and may be said to have entered the battle just north of the Somme river as the survivors of the Fifteenth withdrew. The 104th Brigade were the last of the 35th Division to arrive and they concentrated round Maricourt, in reserve, on March 24th. The Nineteenth detrained at Corbie that morning and marched to Sailly-le-Sec, where buses took them forward. In the afternoon they occupied a line 600 yards east of Maricourt and here an uneventful night was passed.

The 35th Division now held the line from Curlu, on the Somme river, to Trones Wood and before 8 A.M. on March 25th came a determined attack along the whole front. At noon the Nineteenth were moved up to support the 106th Brigade on the left, who were involved in desperate and confused fighting. At 3 P.M. the line about Favières Wood, on the slope north-east of Maricourt, began to give way and the Nineteenth were called upon to restore it. Two companies were sent forward in succession under fierce shell fire and after advancing 1,000 yards a halt was made and a strong assaulting line built up. The other companies followed in support and reserve and the Durhams then went on and forced their way into the lost trenches.

The Durham Forces in the Field

Lewis gun fire wrought havoc among the retreating Germans, whose resistance for the time was broken, and the Nineteenth occupied for the night a position about 200 yards in front of the old line. Capt. Kingsley Smith, who was in command of the two leading companies, won his Military Cross in this successful affair. Casualties included 2nd Lieut. E. Walton, killed, and Lieut. W. G. Legat and 2nd Lieuts. R. E. N. Coke-Harvey and H. J. Worack wounded. Lieut. E. A. Parke, acting adjutant, and 2nd Lieut. H. R. Cunliffe were also wounded but remained at duty. The latter, who led his platoon with great resolution during the counter-attack and inflicted heavy losses on the enemy, was awarded the Military Cross.

During the night burning dumps and aerodromes pointed to another retirement and orders reached the Nineteenth at 1 A.M. on March 26th. The reserve company acted as rearguard to the 106th Brigade and did not move till nearly 5 A.M. Half this company moved back straight across country and marched down the main road to Carnoy, the other half reaching that place by moving down the valley. The battalion went on to Bray and rejoined the 104th Brigade there, taking up a position along the Albert road. The bearing of the whole battalion was splendid, but Capt. H. Heaton, M.C., 2nd Lieuts. W. G. Dyer and H. R. Cunliffe, Corpl. A. Burt, Lance-Corpl. Marsden, and Ptes. J. H. Bowditch, A. Riddle and J. Scott had been specially prominent for gallantry and coolness.

Orders for retirement across the Ancre were now issued, though for the moment the front was clear of the enemy. But rations and water, which were alleged to have been dumped further up the Albert road, were hard to find and ammunition could not be replenished as all transport was withdrawing behind the river. There were no means of getting the wounded away and the troops were footsore and weary. At 9.30 A.M. the first German shell came over; then mounted scouts, followed by infantry, were seen on the ridge to the east. No guns supported the defence and at 2.30 P.M. the outpost line was withdrawn as the enemy located the British positions and came forward more con-

The German Offensive, 1918

fidently. Very steadily, under heavy machine-gun and artillery fire, the retirement began. The village of Morlancourt was choked with civilian carts, guns, tanks and tired infantry making for the Ancre crossings, but at 8 p.m. the Nineteenth reached their new position at Buire, in the centre of the 104th Brigade line. Here the cookers were found and a hot meal put new life into the men. Two companies held the road running west from the village, while W and X companies were thrown forward to hold the railway line. The night was quiet.

At 10 a.m. next day X company crossed the river again and occupied Treux, with one platoon on the high ground to the south-east of the village and one platoon on its eastern outskirts. The Germans attacked further north, but beyond heavy shell fire the Nineteenth were left alone. 2nd Lieut. T. W. Harris was reported missing on this day.

At dawn on March 28th the Germans tried a surprise attack on Treux, attempting to establish themselves in the woods to the south of the village. Z company came forward and Y company followed as reserve, and the position was maintained under heavy shell fire, though there was little artillery support and the enemy infantry delivered three attacks. 2nd Lieut. W. G. Broad was mortally wounded.

After dark came a relief, the Nineteenth handing over to the 15th Sherwood Foresters and withdrawing to a support position in a quarry outside Buire. Heavy rain fell all night, but the next day passed without incident until the evening when the battalion relieved the 17th Royal Scots along the railway embankment between Buire and Dernancourt, the centre of the brigade line. This position was held all next day, with posts thrown forward to the line of the river. There was much shell fire, but it did little harm, though one of our batteries was identified as shooting short. At night the Australians arrived to take over and the Nineteenth marched back to la Hussoye on the main Amiens-Albert road, where March 31st was spent resting in billets. Casualties in the ranks during these operations reached a total of 160.

The Durham Forces in the Field

But newly arrived from Italy, the Twentieth had had time for some training, and were in excellent fettle when called upon to bear their part in stemming the German tide. They arrived at Albert by train on the night of March 21st and the journey was continued under long range artillery fire to Achiet-le-Grand. This village was reached at 2 next morning and a three hours' march brought the Twentieth to Favreuil. The 124th Brigade occupied at once a portion of the "Army" line north-east of Beugnatre preparatory to relieving a brigade of the 6th Division, who were fighting doggedly as they retreated from the Cambrai front. The afternoon was spent by the Wearsiders on work upon the trenches which were none too good, though the wire was of satisfactory strength. Sounds of the struggle in progress at Vaulx-Vraucourt, barely a mile away, could be plainly heard and, as the afternoon wore on, the weary infantry of the 6th Division came slowly back. By the evening the 124th Brigade had no British troops in front of them. Patrols of the Twentieth were active during the night and the Queen's came up on the right of the Durham battalion who had sustained 16 casualties.

At 8 a.m. on March 23rd a fierce bombardment opened on the trenches of the Twentieth and masses of German infantry advanced. They were received by the Wearsiders with deadly rifle and Lewis gun fire and those who survived were forced to withdraw. Again and again the attack was renewed with unfailing courage and resolution, while the German gunners redoubled their exertions and German cavalry advanced in rear to take advantage of any success which might be gained. But the result was always the same. After six enemy attempts the Twentieth still held their line intact and the foremost Germans lay dead upon the wire. For this day's work Lieut.-Col. A. V. A. Gayer, D.S.O., was given a bar to his decoration; Lieut. H. Goodley, who organised communications under the bombardment, received the Military Cross; Lance-Corpl. E. Foreman, of Bearish, an intrepid Lewis gunner who took toll of the advancing enemy from an exposed advance position, won the Distin-

The German Offensive, 1918

guished Conduct Medal. B company were astride the road from Vaulx-Vraucourt where the fight was fiercest; their commander, Capt. J. H. Iveson, was killed. 2nd Lieut. R. R. Kay also fell, 2nd Lieut. N. W. Turnbull was slightly wounded and losses in the ranks amounted to 83.

The night was quiet and patrols of the Twentieth were again active. In the morning heavy fighting was heard in progress away on the right where British infantry could be seen in retreat. To the north the view was limited, but enfilade shell fire seemed to indicate that there also the line had given ground. Communication to the rear had practically ceased and the Twentieth held on under a heavy and increasing bombardment. At 5 p.m. came orders to go and B company went first in order to cover the retirement of the remainder of the battalion. The withdrawal was over strange ground, but was accomplished in splendid order, though belts of wire—good wire with no trenches behind it—were encountered on the way. German aeroplanes did their best to harass the movement with their machine-guns, but the grey infantry made no attempt to press on. The new front of the brigade ran west of Favreuil and the Twentieth held the left of the line.

Losses on March 24th included 2nd Lieut. A. Brown, wounded, and 50 others killed, wounded, or missing. The 124th Brigade had not been so heavily engaged on this day as the other troops of the division who, on the right, felt the effects of the vigorous enemy thrust towards Bapaume.

It was this pressure to the south that caused a further withdrawal in the very early hours on March 25th. The Twentieth arrived south of Sapignies and began to dig in at once. But the Germans soon reached and occupied the village and by 9 A.M. the Wearsiders once more retired fighting, first to a position along the Bihucourt-Sapignies road. The enemy occupied Bihucourt early in the afternoon and the left flank of the battalion was also threatened, so the retreat continued to a line on the reverse slope of a ridge in front of Achiet-le-Grand. Most of the division had already

The Durham Forces in the Field

reached positions in this vicinity and now the 42nd Division took over the front. The Wearsiders moved to Logeast Wood in the afternoon, but at 7 p.m. the line withdrew again and the tired Twentieth marched to Gommecourt where the night was spent.

Capt. B. Wilkinson, M.C., and 2nd Lieut. I. S. Duddy, D.C.M., were wounded on this day, Lieut. H. D. Munro was missing, and there were 80 casualties in the ranks.

Early on the morning of the 26th the battalion occupied a part of the old German front line as it existed before the battle of the Somme in 1916. A report received about 11 a.m. said that the Germans were in Hébuterne, but this proved to be a false alarm. There was some hostile shelling and casualties comprised 2nd Lieut. A. D. Parsons, died of wounds, 2nd Lieut. J. Carmichael, mortally wounded, and 30 others.

Throughout the fighting Capt. A. S. Davison had led his company with exceptional courage and skill, as had 2nd Lieut. H. Waters, D.C.M., who replaced a fallen company commander. 2nd Lieut. I. S. Duddy, D.C.M., another capable leader, carried out a valuable reconnaissance under heavy fire. These officers received the Military Cross and Lance-Sergt. W. Fowler, of Chester-le-Street, was awarded the Distinguished Conduct Medal for able handling of his platoon.

On March 27th the Twentieth went back to Bienvillers to rest, reorganise and, so far as possible, reequip. At 7.30 a.m. on the 28th the Wearsiders were warned that they would have to move up again and in the afternoon they came forward and occupied a support position east of Gommecourt. Patrols were sent out at night to get in touch with the troops in front and to explore Rossignol Wood upon the right flank. All was quiet, and casualties were few. On the night of March 29th the battalion moved into the front line again, occupying high ground in front of Bucquoy. At this point the German attack had now spent itself, but there were many casualties from shell fire during the last two days of the month, including Lieuts. C. F. Rutlle and J. Black, both wounded. The German gunners were less active on April 1st and at night the

The German Offensive, 1918

Twentieth were relieved by the 17th Lancashire Fusiliers and withdrew to Bienvillers. Their task in this part of the field was now ended. General Clemson, their new brigadier, said, in a letter to Colonel Leather, "They were simply splendid . . . and no praise I could write would be enough to half describe my own feelings about them." The 93rd (Army) Brigade, R.F.A., also expressed its admiration of the conduct of the battalion whose total losses amounted to 11 officers and about 320 men.

The Eighteenth, in billets at Bajus and Frévillers, attended a ceremonial parade on March 21st to take leave of their divisional commander. In the evening came orders to move and the battalion marched out at 7.15 next morning. Buses took them through St. Pol to Doullens and thence up the Arras road—a long, hot and dusty journey. Orders to billet at Poirier were cancelled in view of the bad news from the line and the procession turned off at Beaumetz-lès-Loges for Blairville. Here the Eighteenth were deposited at about 9 P.M., but after getting into fighting order the buses were boarded again. The 31st Division were replacing the 34th Division in the battle front between Nory and Croisilles and the Eighteenth alighted at the "Army" line of defence near Boyelles. All was quiet here and the battalion occupied a support position astride the railway in front of the village.

There was some hostile shelling on March 23rd, but the Eighteenth only lost 2 men wounded. In the evening the whole of the 93rd Brigade moved to the right, the Durhams replacing the 2nd Irish Guards of the 4th Guards Brigade astride the Arras-Bapaume road. Later the whole battalion moved east of the road and just west of the village of St. Léger. A further readjustment of the line early next day brought the Eighteenth still further south to a position in front of Hamelincourt astride the Bapaume road.

March 24th was a critical day. On the front of the 93rd Brigade the Germans attacked at 7 A.M. after a heavy bombardment of the front line. They were repulsed with heavy losses by artillery, rifles and

The Durham Forces in the Field

machine-guns. This was repeated at about 11 A.M. with the same result. Then came a few hours' respite, but soon after three in the afternoon the enemy came on again in great strength only to be driven off once more. Communications to the forward battalions were under the fire of hostile machine-guns established west of St. Leger, and it was impossible to get the wounded away before dusk. After dark the situation on the right became serious. The Germans entered Ervillers from the south-east at about 10 P.M. and began firing on the trenches of the 4th Guards Brigade—the right brigade of the division—from the rear. Ervillers was retaken during the night, but the enemy had reached Gomiecourt now and a withdrawal of the whole line was necessary to avert disaster. The Eighteenth were therefore ordered to move back on March 25th to take up a position east of Courcelles along the railway in touch with the 92nd Brigade upon the right. The Durhams moved south of Hamelincourt, dug the new line, established outposts and settled down for the night. D company captured an enemy patrol, but a German officer, from whom valuable information might have been gained, was unfortunately killed. On this day the splendid shooting of the British artillery smashed every concentration of German troops in front of the 93rd and the 4th Guards Brigade.

At 8.30 A.M. on March 26th came belated orders for another withdrawal. This was rendered necessary by the German advance to the south, though the Eighteenth were not being pressed. The retirement was intended to take place before dawn but now had to be carried out in broad daylight under heavy hostile shell fire. All went well, however, and soon after 10 A.M. the Eighteenth arrived in a support position behind the 13th York and Lancasters, who held Joyenneville. In front, on the right, the 15th West Yorkshires were in touch with the left of the 92nd Brigade. The 4th Guards Brigade were now in divisional reserve.

The Germans were evidently reorganising before resuming their advance, but their gunners were active while the Durhams dug in on their new line. Colonel Carter and Capt. G. B. Stafford were wounded and

The German Offensive, 1918

Capt. L. A. Dick took command. Soon afterwards orders arrived for a general retirement to the Adinfer-Ficheux line. The Eighteenth commenced to withdraw in conjunction with the York and Lancasters on the left, two platoons of C company covering the movement. Nothing was seen of the West Yorkshiremen. The two battalions passed the right flank of the Guards Division and then, when within three-quarters of a mile of Adinfer, fresh orders were received. The retirement appears to have been an error of the brigade-major, who was suffering from shell shock, and an attempt had now to be made to regain the Moyenneville position. This was a very difficult operation as the Germans were now in Moyenneville and commanded all approaches to the village from the west. By dusk the Guards' line was prolonged to the right and when darkness fell the Eighteenth and the York and Lancasters moved forward in order to entrench as near Moyenneville as possible. Few tools were available and daylight came before a defensive line could be established, so both battalions were forced to withdraw again. But B company of the Eighteenth, under Lieut. A. A. McConnell and 2nd Lieut. R. R. Turnbull, turned to good account some existing trenches 600 yards west of Moyenneville and held on there.

They found themselves on the left rear of the 15th West Yorkshire Regt., who occupied a ridge south-west of the village. The Yorkshiremen had received no orders to retire and, though unsupported, had held their own all the previous day and night against tremendous odds. Perhaps the full story of their heroic resistance will some day be written. It was the privilege of B company of the Eighteenth to take their share of the unequal struggle during the daylight hours of March 27th, when, in the face of repeated attacks and the fierce fire of the enemy, retirement was impossible. At dusk the survivors fought their way back. Few of the Yorkshiremen were left and B company of the Eighteenth had lost over 100 killed and wounded. The two officers survived and each received the Military Cross.

Meanwhile Capt. Dick had been absorbed by the brigade staff and Capt. F. G. Stone succeeded to the

The Durham Forces in the Field

command of the battalion till Major W. D. Lowe, M.C., arrived later in the day. The other three companies of the Eighteenth had not been in action and losses from shell fire were not heavy. At night the brigade front was held by the York and Lancasters with A company of the Eighteenth in close support, the line running north-east of Ayette village. The remainder of the Durham men dug and occupied a support position astride the Bony-St. Rictrude-Ayette road.

The night of March 27th was quiet and by next morning the Ayette ridge position consisted of a line of good trenches. Two attacks were delivered on the front held by the Guards and York and Lancaster Regt., and although the line was entered at one point the enemy was immediately ejected by D company of the Eighteenth. C company afterwards came in on the left of the Guards to strengthen the fighting front, C and A companies thus holding the line between the Irish Guards and the York and Lancaster Regt. B and D companies, reinforced by a company of an East Yorkshire battalion, dug cover for themselves in the dry bed of the Cojeul river near the Douchy road. The enemy shell fire continued and there were many casualties.

On the morning of the 29th the Eighteenth sidestepped to the left and took over part of the York and Lancaster line, but early on the 30th the relief of the brigade was effected. The harassing fire of the enemy had died down before this and the Eighteenth reached billets at Lienvillers without trouble, though the outskirts of the village were shelled next day. On April 1st the battalion marched to Ivergny, north of the forest of Lucheux. Losses during the March fighting amounted to 320 killed, wounded and missing.

CHAPTER II

During April nearly all the Service Battalions of the County then in France were engaged in the fighting which brought to a standstill the German offensive on the British front. The operations extended over a large

The German Offensive, 1918

portion of the line, and it will be most convenient in this case to tell the story of each battalion in order of seniority.

Of the Eleventh there is not much to record. Lieut.-Col. G. Hayes and several other officers rejoined the battalion at Quevavillers, where a large reinforcement was received on April 4th. After training at various places the Eleventh reached Frévillers, near the Lens mining district, on April 18th. On the previous day Colonel Hayes had vacated the command owing to ill-health and was succeeded by Lieut.-Col. R. E. Boulton, K.O.Y.L.I. By this time drafts amounting to 14 officers and 578 other ranks had brought the battalion almost up to strength, though 80 unfit men had been sent down to the Base. Training and inspections occupied the rest of the month.

The 21st Division went to Flanders at the beginning of April, the Fifteenth entraining at Amiens on the 1st of the month. They arrived at Houpoutre next morning and travelled by bus to huts at Locre. Here drafts amounting to 468 men were received and on April 4th the battalion relieved the Australians in the line. Two companies of the Fifteenth and two of the 9th K.O.Y.L.I. held the front, which was south of Holleheke on the low ground beyond the Messines ridge. After a quiet tour the Fifteenth returned to Locre on the 7th.

It was on April 9th that the enemy advanced and overwhelmed the Portuguese at Bois Grenier, but east of Ypres the British positions were as yet unchanged. The 64th Brigade relieved the brigade in reserve behind the Polderhoek line on the 10th and the Fifteenth moved up to Glencorse Wood. But the Germans launched their attack upon the Messines ridge on this day and the Fifteenth were brought back to Lankhof Camp, about a mile and a half south of Ypres, on April 11th; the enemy had won a footing on the ridge and the 64th Brigade were now in support to the 9th Division. The Fifteenth, after moving back to Ridge Wood, came into the line on April 13th, the left of the battalion front of two companies joining the 26th

The Durham Forces in the Field

Brigade at about the south-west end of the Dan Strasse. On the right were the 1st East Yorkshire Regt.

Nothing of moment happened till April 16th which was an anxious day. At 5 a.m. a furious hostile bombardment preceded a fierce attack which carried the village of Wytschaete, standing on higher ground to the south of the Durhams. A defensive flank was formed facing south across the slope between the Vierstraat and St. Eloi roads. Here the support company of the Fifteenth came into the line with two platoons of the reserve company in rear. Shortly after midday the S.O.S. signal was sent up by the 26th Brigade holding the Dan Strasse. German infantry were seen in the woods in front and later the line of the Fifteenth was threatened, but no attack developed though a terrific bombardment visited the British line and caused many casualties. At night Colonel Holroyd-Smyth was informed that the defensive flank must be held at all costs.

Intense shelling had again to be endured on the morning of April 17th. It lasted for over two hours and then, at 7.30 a.m., came a general advance of the grey infantry. The British gunners ably supported the fire of the men in the trenches and the German losses were terrible, but weight of numbers told in the end and the break in the line at Wytschaete was widened. Somer Farm, on the extreme left of the defensive flank, was taken, but the Fifteenth still held North House—due north of Wytschaete. Then came a gap in the line, but touch was obtained with the South Africans of the 9th Division on the other side of the Vierstraat road. This position was held all day in spite of two more attacks about four in the afternoon, both of which were repulsed by artillery, machine-gun and rifle fire with further heavy loss to the enemy.

At half-past five on the morning of the 18th A company attacked Somer Farm and a trench in front of it. The trench was won, but the farm buildings were too full of machine-guns to be rushed. At night reinforcements reached the trench and the line was firmly established and joined up. During this fighting 2nd Lieut. D. Tyrie was killed and 2nd Lieut. J. D. W. Mills

The German Offensive, 1918

wounded. The next day, which was fine and cold with occasional showers of snow, saw no further attack though persistent shell fire had to be endured. There was an alarm on the evening of the 20th when the S.O.S. signal was sent up to the right of the Fifteenth and both the British and the German batteries opened in response.

The Durhams remained in their trenches under a steady bombardment till the night of the 24th, when, on relief by the 5th West Yorkshire Regt., the battalion withdrew to camp near Dickebusch. Lieut. W. Gow and 2nd Lieuts. C. W. Licence, G. Foy, and E. L. Waight had all been wounded.

At 2.30 a.m. the enemy drenched the back areas with gas shell and the Fifteenth had to leave camp and occupy shell holes further in rear. At dawn came the great German thrust which took Kemmel Hill and drove the few who survived to hold the 64th Brigade line back beyond Vierstraat. The Fifteenth were sent for hurriedly and occupied trenches behind Cheapside Road, north of Kemmel village, one company going forward to hold a gap in the front. The adjutant, Capt. J. R. Pease, was wounded on this day.

The next day there was a gallant counter-attack by the 9th K.O.Y.L.I. who, on the right, reached the Kemmel-Vierstraat road. The Durhams moved up in support, but although prisoners were captured the ground gained could not be held, exposed as it was to enfilade machine-gun fire from both flanks. At midnight on April 26th, all that was left of the two battalions —about 160 men of each—were back in the Cheapside trenches where some of the Tank Corps strengthened the line.

On the morrow the 4th York and Lancaster Regt. relieved the Fifteenth who marched back to Busseboom, near Ouderdom. A day of rest followed. Then on the night of the 28th came an alarm and the battalion turned out, but were not required to move.

The enemy attack on April 29th brought the Fifteenth up to Ouderdom, but the German advance was now held. The battalion reached Steenvoorde the same night and marched to camp in the Volcknickhove

The Durham Forces in the Field

area on April 30th. Casualties in the ranks during these operations amounted to 290, with 9 officers killed or wounded. The other battalions in the brigade suffered more, but the Fifteenth had been the weakest in numbers at the beginning of the battle.

During this month the medical officer, Capt. J. W. Watthews, M.C., was awarded a bar to his decoration; Lance-Corpl. I. B. Waistrell, M.M., received a bar to his medal; and the Military Medal was given to Corpl. R. Simpson, Pte. G. Burton, and Pte. W. H. Mudd. These rewards were for gallantry during the March retreat.

The Eighteenth left Ivergny on April 2nd for their old billets at Frévillers, where a draft was received and training was carried on. Suddenly on April 10th came orders for Flanders and the battalion moved off in buses an hour and a half later. Alighting at Vieux Berquin the Eighteenth marched on to Outtersteene, where A company provided an outpost line to the east and south-east of the village. This line was strengthened on the afternoon of April 11th as the Germans were reported to be in strength at la Becque.

It was the German threat to Hazebrouck which had brought the 31st Division so hurriedly into this portion of the line. The 93rd Brigade received orders to attack south-eastward and recapture le Verrier, Farm du Bois, la Rose Farm, la Becque and the line of the Steenwercke road beyond. The 13th York and Lancasters were on the right of the Eighteenth, who assembled along the road in front of the stream called the Rau du Leet on the evening of the 11th. C and D companies were in front with A and B companies in support from right to left. A machine-gun barrage had been arranged, but the hour of the attack was altered from 7 P.M. to 7.30 P.M. in order to permit the artillery to co-operate. However, the York and Lancasters advanced at seven o'clock and the Eighteenth followed suit in perfect order. There was machine-gun fire from houses and farms, but the attack went in splendid fashion. C company, on fairly open ground, halted at one point for nearly fifteen minutes to wait for the rest of the advance. Sergt.

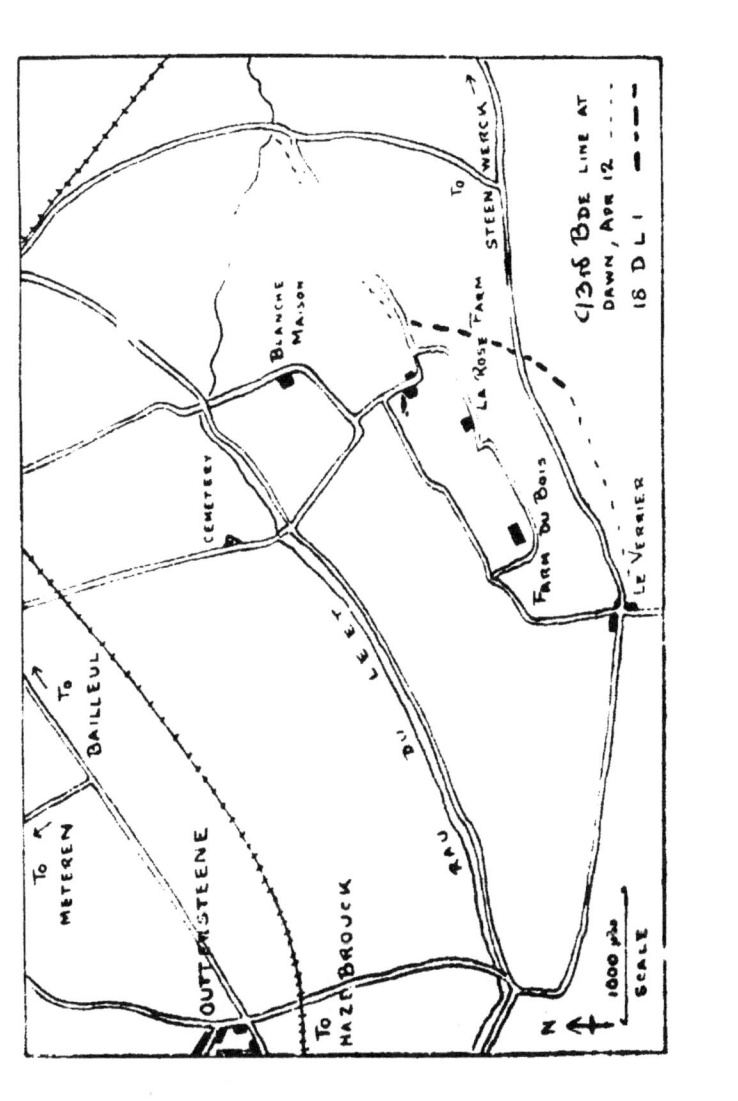

The Durham Forces in the Field

Gillespie took the lead in rushing la Rose Farm, and 2nd Lieut. Long and 2nd Lieut. A. M. Freer—who won the Military Cross took la Becque. Each place held a garrison of Germans, and these were all killed or captured. Two light machine-guns were taken by C company, who crossed the Steenwercke road and dug in beyond, A company prolonging the line to the left.

D company, moving over enclosed country, came more slowly but none the less surely. Near la Becque Lieut. Seymour found an abandoned machine-gun which he turned on the enemy. Touch on the left was obtained with the 74th Brigade, but these troops retired soon afterwards and the Eighteenth extended and did their best to cover the gap. Pte. H. Mitchell won the Distinguished Conduct Medal during the advance by rushing a troublesome machine-gun and bayonetting three of the team. The losses of the battalion were not heavy and by dawn of the 12th the line was well dug in and patrols were active in front. The 15th West Yorkshires had now come up on the left.

Soon after daylight on April 12th the enemy could be seen concentrating for a general attack and, though the British artillery opened on him with great effect, by 8 A.M. all three battalions were hard pressed. The right of the brigade line was in the air and fell back first and then the Eighteenth gave ground slowly, inflicting heavy losses. D company on the left were the last to go. The line of the farms captured on the previous evening was the next position to hold and this was only possible for a short time. The battalion had now lost 270 men and it was not long before the whole brigade were back on the line of the stream, where they came under the fire of the British guns. Enfilade machine-gun fire from the right soon caused a further retirement, but a strong point at the cemetery was stoutly held.

The German skirmishers were now coming on in swarms, supported by light mortars and machine-guns and skilfully employed artillery fire. On the roads cavalry and cyclists could be seen and enemy balloons were close enough behind to see every movement of the defence. It was difficult to get orders to the scattered

The German Offensive, 1918

groups still fighting desperately. The commander of D company with 15 men held on to the Rau du Leet line north-west of Maison Blanche; B company commander with a few of his own men and some West Yorkshires made a stand near the cemetery and succeeded in holding up the enemy advance for a time after the Rau du Leet line had been vacated. The railway south-east of Outtersteene was the next position of defence, but it proved to be little more than a death trap. There was dead ground in front and no cover for the firing line, while from the west came accurate enfilade machine-gun fire. Here the Eighteenth found themselves on the left, but units were mixed and the whole brigade were only about 400 strong.

The 15th West Yorkshires, now on the right, retired first. Then Colonel Lowe held on with the right half of the battalion, while the adjutant withdrew the left through close country and thick hedges until he found another place where a stand could be made. In this way the Bailleul-Outtersteene road was crossed. There was no communication with brigade headquarters and the remnants of the three battalions—the West Yorkshires were lost and found again—fell back until, midway between Bailleul and Meteren, they came upon the 18th Middlesex Regt. The Eighteenth, with the 15th West Yorkshires on the right, now filled a gap in the line here, facing south and east between the Middlesex men and another battalion covering the southern approaches to Meteren. There were only rifle posts to occupy, but no time was lost in converting them into continuous trenches.

Very prominent in the retreat had been Acting R.-S.-M. E. Oldridge, of Darlington. Twice he was one of the last group to withdraw and he handled his men with great skill and courage. C.-S.-M. W. Benneworth, of Sunderland, conducted a very gallant reconnaissance and did good work in helping to cover the retirement. Pte. J. Atkinson, of Newcastle, had volunteered to take a message to the front line under deadly fire and did so, though wounded twice on the way. All these were afterwards awarded the Distinguished Conduct Medal.

At 10 o'clock on the morning of the 13th came an

The Durham Forces in the Field

hour's fierce bombardment and in the afternoon three hours of heavy shell fire had to be endured. D company did excellent patrol work at night, searching a wood in front and establishing touch along the whole line.

April 14th was a day of fierce shelling and repeated infantry attacks, which were always repulsed by Lewis gun and rifle fire aided by the field batteries which came into action in the early morning. Lieut.-Col. C. W. Tilly, who had recently left the Eighteenth to take command of the 15th West Yorkshire Regt., was killed by a shell splinter on this day.

But the relief of the remnants of the 93rd Brigade was now possible. On the early morning of April 15th Colonel Lowe took them back to Borre, the 5th Battalion of the Tank Corps replacing the brigade in the line. At Borre the details of the brigade were found. They had dug and held a line west of Merris on April 12th and 13th and had been under heavy shell fire till relieved by the Australians on the following day.

A Composite Battalion about 475 strong was formed from the survivors of the Eighteenth and West Yorkshires and Colonel Lowe assumed command. Borre was heavily shelled on the 17th when this battalion moved back to l'Hoffand in reserve to the rest of the division who manned a portion of the Hazebrouck defences. On the following day a move was made round Hazebrouck to le Grand Hasard on the Aire road. Reinforcements arrived here and the Eighteenth were organised as a battalion again. Two days later they came under the orders of the 92nd Brigade and took over a portion of the front south of the Hazebrouck-Strazeele railway. D company, with a detachment of the Tank Corps, filled a gap between the 6th Australians and the 11th East Yorkshires; the remainder of the battalion were responsible for the series of posts which formed the support line. Much work was done on the defences during the following days under a heavy fire of gas and high explosive shell. At night German aeroplanes came over and opened fire with their machine-guns.

At 4.15 A.M. on April 26th an officer and 20 men went out to try and rush a house reported occupied by

The German Offensive, 1918

a machine-gun. The British barrage fell too far back and in the face of three machine-guns and growing daylight the enterprise had to be abandoned. Early on the morning of the 27th a successful raid by the East Yorkshiremen brought retaliation, battalion headquarters and the aid post of the Eighteenth being shelled out by 5.9's.

The 1st Border Regt. came up in the evening to relieve the battalion who were able to get away by the early morning of the 28th. It was a weary march to tents near Sercus and here there was little rest, for 300 men had to be supplied daily to work on defensive positions and training was also carried out.

The German attacks south of the Somme were still causing anxiety at the beginning of the month and on April 4th the Nineteenth moved up to Bonnay to support the Australians holding the line of the river from Aubigny to Vaire. On the following day 2nd Lieut. C. Mosley was gassed, 2 men were wounded and 6 were gassed as a result of enemy shell fire. Fighting in this quarter now died down. On April 8th the battalion moved back to la Hussoye, next day to Querrieu, thence by bus to Acheux and on to billets at Hédauville. On the 9th the Germans shelled la Hussoye with a high-velocity gun and caused casualties to the transport of the brigade moving through the village.

On April 19th the Nineteenth came into the line south of Martinsart and spent six days there. Before relief on the night of the 17th the German field guns and 4.2 howitzers shelled the trenches persistently but few casualties resulted. The following day was spent at Hédauville in the rain and under the accurate harassing fire of a German high-velocity gun. The battalion marched down to Warloy on the 19th, casualties from shell fire including 2nd Lieut. B. Fish wounded, 4 men killed and 5 wounded. After two days' training in the attack the Nineteenth took over a portion of the line which ran across the valley south of Martinsart Wood. An attack was planned for 7.30 p.m. on April 22nd, but a quarter of an hour before zero the enemy opened with shrapnel on the support

The Durham Forces in the Field

trenches, while his heavies pounded Martinsart Wood. Fortunately this only lasted five minutes. Three minutes before the advance was timed to start our trench mortar barrage came down on Aveluy Wood which our aircraft visited with bombs and machine-gun fire. At 7.30 p.m. the Irish bombardment began, but the Nineteenth were required to wait for several minutes in order to conform to the barrage. When the battalion went forward on a two-company frontage they were met by the fire of the German machine-guns. W company on the right gained 250 yards, but were enfiladed from both flanks and suffered heavily. The company commander was wounded and no further progress could be made. The company on the left went forward nearly 400 yards and were then brought to a halt by the British barrage. At 9 p.m. it appeared that W company on the right were in touch with the 14th Royal Welch Fusiliers and that a gap existed between W and Y companies. X company sent forward a platoon to join the line and Z company did likewise to reinforce W company, now very weak in numbers. On the left of the battalion the 15th Cheshire Regt. had not been able to make progress and orders were issued later for troops to dig in as they lay. But Y company were in a position untenable by daylight, so at 4 a.m. on April 23rd they withdrew to the original front line. Capt. H. Heaton, M.C., with W and Z companies, held the forward posts on the right until relieved at dusk. The Nineteenth then moved into reserve at Bouzincourt for a few days and on April 26th returned to the familiar valley near Hédauville. Casualties in this action amounted to 117 killed, wounded and gassed, besides Capt. G. W. Howes and 2nd Lieuts. J. Bell and A. C. Paterson, killed; 2nd Lieuts. W. G. Hayman, R. Hall, and C. Grummitt, wounded; and 2nd Lieut. R. Richardson, gassed.

Reinforcements of one officer and 126 men joined before the battalion went into the line again near Aveluy Wood on April 29th.

The Twentieth were wanted at Ypres early in the month. Leaving Bienvillers on April 2nd the Wear-

The German Offensive, 1918

siders travelled by bus and train and march route to a camp in the Steenvoorde area. Here two days were spent in absorbing a draft of 448 young soldiers. On April 7th the Twentieth moved up to Vlamertinghe and, the following day, arrived in a reserve position at St. Jean. The German pressure now forced an abandonment of the ground so painfully won during the summer and autumn of 1917. On the night of April 12th the battalion were suddenly moved up and set to making new strong points behind the front line which crossed the Hannebeek stream north of the Ypres-Zonnebeke road. These posts were mostly centred on old German "pill-boxes," trenches being dug round or near them in order to accommodate a garrison of any number up to a whole company. At nightfall on April 14th a composite detachment drawn from A and C companies were left on this line and the rest of the battalion moved back to begin a new defence system. Digging and wiring occupied the day and night of the 15th, the men working in four-hour shifts. Reliefs were then arranged, which left all C company holding the new outpost line.

In the early morning of the 16th the troops in front withdrew, according to orders, and C company were now nearest the enemy who followed up during the afternoon but did not come within half a mile. Work continued on the rear defences under some shell fire during the next few days. On the 17th strong enemy patrols came out in daylight with the obvious intention of occupying Hill 35 on which the Twentieth had a post. The Germans were dispersed by artillery, machine-gun and rifle fire.

At 5.45 A.M. on April 19th about 50 Germans rushed Hill 35. Capt. Wild organised a counter-attack, which was delivered with spirit by two platoons after a six minutes' bombardment, and before 11 A.M. Hill 35 was once more in the hands of the Twentieth, but there was ground on the right front where the enemy could assemble unperceived. Some hostile shelling followed and the machine-gun fire from the "pill-box" called Gallipoli was heavy and accurate. Small parties went forward in rushes to deal with this menace, but 40 of the enemy suddenly appeared on the right and took the

The Durham Forces in the Field

movement in the flank. Falling snow made it difficult to direct the fight and 2nd Lieut. Oliver and some of the Twentieth were surrounded. Heavy machine-gun fire from Gallipoli and the Somme "pill-box" swept the crest of the hill which had to be yielded to the enemy. 2nd Lieut. G. R. Oliver was missing and 2nd Lieut. H. N. Ridley was left behind wounded, although two men were hit in an attempt to get him away under heavy fire. Eighteen men returned wounded and 13 others who were missing were probably killed or badly hurt.

It was not until the night of the 28th that the battalion were relieved and withdrew to trenches about Potijze, which were to form the new front line. There was much work to do here while the German shell fire grew in volume and extended even to railhead at Proven.

The Twenty-Second, by way of Sains-en-Amienois and Ailly, arrived at Fourdrinoy on April 2nd. After a rest Condé was reached upon the 4th and here a draft of 150 men was received. They looked to be of poor physique, but the battalion soon had cause to be proud of them. On April 5th Lieut.-Col. B. C. James, D.S.O., from the 2nd Devonshire Regt., assumed command of the Twenty-Second and a comprehensive training programme was at once put in hand. On April 12th the Twenty-Second came under the orders of the 25th Brigade and moved to Bussy-les-Daours, where training was continued until the 20th. Then, in battle order, the battalion marched to Blangy-Tronville and B company relieved a company of Australians in the reserve line at Aubigny. The 8th Division now barred the way to Amiens, being astride the main road that runs due east towards St. Quentin. The companies of the Twenty-Second were made up to a strength of 200 and the rest of the men worked for the tunnellers on the following day. The Aubigny line was improved until April 24th, when the whole battalion took up battle stations there in the midst of a heavy bombardment of gas shells.

It was on this morning that the Germans, by the

The German Offensive, 1918

use of smoke, gas, flame-throwers and tanks, took Villers-Bretonneux; but they could not debouch from the village in face of the British fire.

Two brigades of Australians were the only fresh troops available and to them was entrusted the task of retaking the village that night. The Twenty-Second were to "mop up," entering Villers-Bretonneux from the north-west between the railway and the Aubigny road, while the 2nd Northamptons did similar work from the south side. It was a bright moonlight night and the way of the Twenty-Second lay up a bare slope still swept by German machine-guns. The first attempt failed, but small parties were able to get forward up the railway line and in this way some of C company accounted for two German machine-guns. At 4 A.M. on the morning of the 25th the 2nd Royal Berkshire Regt. came up on the left and together the two battalions entered Villers-Bretonneux and began to rout out the defenders. It was slow and difficult work, and the Berkshire men were recalled at ten o'clock, but the Twenty-Second stuck to it until only a few Germans were holding out in the south-eastern corner of the village. The battalion were then withdrawn to their former position north-west of Villers-Bretonneux. Of the 400 prisoners captured in the village 6 officers and 80 men were taken by the Twenty-Second, as well as very many machine-guns. 2nd Lieut. A. C. Rowley was killed and Capt. R. W. Pearson and Lieut. S. G. Highmoor slightly wounded. These two officers remained at duty.

In the early hours of the 26th the Pioneers were moved round to a support position at the south-east corner of Villers-Bretonneux. A and B companies took up this line behind the Australians who faced south-east astride the railway. C company remained in reserve.

Twenty men were called upon to reinforce the machine-gun post of another unit just south-east of Villers-Bretonneux and these were taken up under heavy fire by Major C. C. F. Fall who, for his handling of the situation, received the Distinguished Service Order. Lieut. S. G. Highmoor was of great assistance

The Durham Forces in the Field

and went for ammunition under close-range rifle fire, thereby winning the Military Cross. On this day 2nd Lieut. A. J. Hossack, M.M., was mortally wounded and 2nd Lieuts. V. Vincent and L. Hickman were gassed.

Relieved by the Australians on the next evening, the Twenty-Second returned to Blangy-Tronville and moved to Daours on April 28th. The last thrust of the Germans for Amiens had been parried at a cost to the battalion of 260 casualties. Other honours won by the Twenty-Second on this occasion comprised the Military Cross, awarded to 2nd Lieuts. C. S. Willmer and L. Hickman; a bar to the Military Medal given to Corpl. E. Dodds, M.M., and Pte. A. Robinson, M.M.; and the Military Medal received by Lance-Sergts. W. T. Carroll, F. Harper and J. Wright, Ptes. A. W. Stobbs, F. Edwards, F. G. Harrison, F. Dinning and J. Sullivan.

CHAPTER III

AMONG the battle-weary troops selected for a quiet tour of duty on the French front between Rheims and Soissons, Durham was well represented. The Fifteenth and the Twenty-Second went south, in addition to the County battalions of the 50th (Northumbrian) Division.

The 21st Division had fought as hard and often as any, both on the Somme and in Flanders, and orders for the move were welcomed in Colonel Holroyd-Smyth's battalion. Large drafts of young soldiers were received at Volkerinckhove and on May 4th the battalion entrained at St. Omer. Bouleuse was reached soon after mid-day on the 6th and the Fifteenth marched southward to billets in the region of Olizy et Violaine. In this well-wooded country of hills and streams the Durhams received a warm welcome from our Allies, both military and civilian. Training was proceeded with apace, for the French were anxious to relieve their own troops as early as possible and the battalion

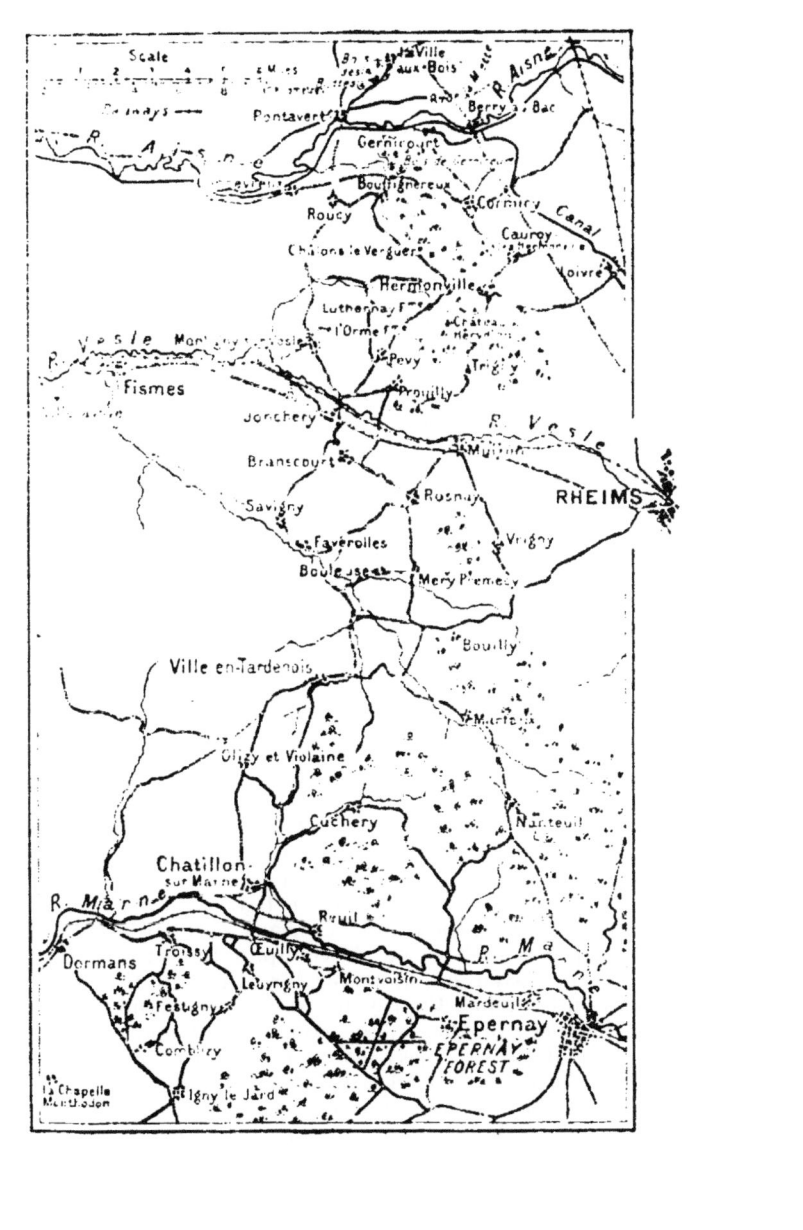

The Durham Forces in the Field

consisted largely of young soldiers with no experience of warfare.

The 21st Division were to form the right of the British Corps and the front to be taken over extended from a point about one mile north of Loivre, on the Aisne and Marne canal, to Berry-au-Bac, the junction with the 8th Division. On May 12th, in beautiful weather, the Fifteenth went by light railway to Savigny and marched across the river Vesle to the little village of Pévy. Next morning they reached Hermonville and at night relieved the 6th battalion of the 299th (Bayard) French Regt. in the line. There was plenty of good wire, but a perfect maze of disused trenches proved rather an embarrassment; the enemy showed little signs of activity and, in the words of the French, the whole front was *très calme*. In their shirt-sleeves the Durhams went about their trench duties and basked in the sun. On May 19th a patrol entered the German line, but the enemy ran away. Two days later the Fifteenth were relieved and withdrew to a support position near the main road to Rheims (Route 44). On the following day they went into reserve at a camp at Chalons-le-Verguer. Training was done here and a church parade was held on the morning of May 26th. Warning of the expected attack was received the same evening and when, at 1 A.M. on May 27th, the battalion turned out a heavy bombardment of mustard gas shell came down upon the camp. The Fifteenth moved off in respirators through the dense fumes and reached Cauroy by way of woodland tracks. The defences of the village consisted of many strong points and its weakness lay in the number of disused trenches which ran back from Route 44.

At 10 A.M. C company were sent forward to reinforce the 9th K.O.Y.L.I., but the Yorkshiremen had had to give ground and the German infantry were already on the main road. This company accordingly reinforced some of the 14th Northumberland Fusiliers holding the Avancée de Cauroy, while B company pushed out on the left to hold the Boyau de la Sorne. This protected the left of the line and it was hoped to get in touch with the Leicesters of the 110th Brigade, reported

The German Offensive, 1918

to be at the redoubt called Centre Vrublin. D company occupied the strong points Bon de la Cuve, Bon de la Lavoir, Redout Nord and Redout Central.

The Germans came on in determined fashion, supported by a fierce bombardment, and pushed B company back to Avancée de Cauroy. The Durhams counter-attacked with bombs and a bloody struggle was waged in these trenches on the outskirts of the

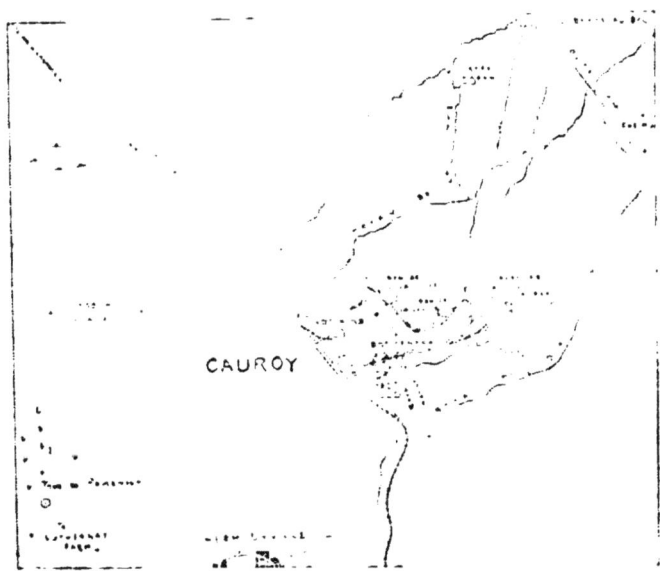

village until the German numbers prevailed. During the afternoon the enemy occupied part of the Boyau de Beau Sejour and bombed his way into Avancée de Cauroy, so that, in spite of their desperate resistance, B and C companies were forced back to the sunken road east of Redout Sud. At 5.30 P.M. the 97th Field Company, R.E., arrived from Hermonville and reinforced the left flank on the light railway west of the village. Two hours later came another onslaught in overwhelming strength and the British line was

The Durham Forces in the Field

obliged to draw back to the road behind the village; but the Germans tried in vain to debouch from Cauroy and desisted in their attempts as darkness fell. On the right the Fifteenth still held some advanced posts, but soon after midnight came orders to withdraw. This was done in the darkness without hurry or confusion, for the Germans did not seem to be aware of the retirement.

Reassembling at Tour de Rougemont, the Fifteenth made their way to a camp near Luthernay Farm which was reached at about 4.30 A.M. on May 28th. They were now in brigade reserve; but the Germans made rapid progress on the left flank and three hours later the Durhams were under machine-gun fire. A position was hurriedly taken up on the eastern end of the ridge which runs from the Château Hervelon westward to Montigny; but before this was accomplished Colonel Holroyd-Smyth was wounded. Major S. D. Thorpe, M.C., succeeded him. The Germans were attacking in front and advancing rapidly round the left flank of the battalion, but the fight was stoutly maintained. At length the line withdrew 500 yards, but stood fast there until it became necessary to retreat in order to escape annihilation. The next position in rear was already occupied by mixed units of the 64th Brigade and others, in conjunction with the French. It was on a ridge extending from before Trigny on the right to a point south-east of Prouilly. Not all the survivors of the Fifteenth arrived here. Sergt. S. Garnett, a Cheshire man from Daresbury, was last seen with a small party, all fighting desperately though surrounded. Others of the battalion came in during the afternoon.

The trenches, situated on a forward slope, were very shallow, but the wire was good. In front woods concealed the movements of the enemy, but on the high ground beyond large bodies of German infantry appeared to threaten attack. A prisoner of the 7th Reserve Division brought in by the Fifteenth said that the advance would be renewed next morning. The tired troops were assailed with heavy shell fire and German patrols were active, but no fresh infantry attack developed that day. In the evening the brigade

The German Offensive, 1918

were divided into two detachments, the 6 officers and 40 men of the Fifteenth who now remained being included in that commanded by Lieut.-Col. W. N. S. Alexander, D.S.O., of the East Yorkshire Regt.

The Germans were known to be in Jonchery and before dawn of May 29th the line was brought back to the river Vesle. The Durhams first held the south bank west of Muizon, and were then moved to a support position. A fierce enemy bombardment continued, till at 2.30 p.m. the Fifteenth were relieved by French troops and moved back to Rosnay, resting for the night south of the village. Marinux was reached next day by way of Méry Premercy and the march continued to bivouacs south of the river Marne in the forest of Epernay. On the last day of the month a move was made to a camp at Chaltrait.

In the heavy fighting of May 27th and 28th the Fifteenth had lost 456 men in killed, wounded and missing, the heaviest casualties in the brigade. Among the officers Capt. C. S. Herbert, M.C., and 2nd Lieuts. F. Burgess, J. Carter, V. G. Davies, J. Dawson, A. E. Foster, R. C. Gutteridge and E. Joicy were killed or missing. Lieut.-Col. C. E. R. Holroyd-Smyth, M.C.; Capts. A. Roberts, M.C., and A. N. Clark, D.S.O.; and 2nd Lieuts. J. Davidson, W. Husband, J. Sinclair and R. Whillis had been wounded.

Major S. D. Thorpe, M.C., and Capt. C. P. Grant, M.C., were each awarded a bar to his decoration and 2nd Lieut. G. R. Abbott was given the Military Cross. It was largely owing to the efforts of these officers that the Fifteenth succeeded in checking the German advance at Cauroy and had fought such a splendid rearguard action on the following day. Sergt. Garnett was awarded the Distinguished Conduct Medal.

The survivors of the Fifteenth who could still handle a rifle were called upon again. With the help of first reinforcements and details a company was organised to join the fifth Brigade Composite Battalion, the Fifteenth providing both commanding officer and adjutant in the persons of Major F. H. Bousfield, M.C., D.C.M., and Capt. C. P. Grant, M.C. By the evening of June 2nd this battalion were in the line south of the

The Durham Forces in the Field

river Marne at Troissy, where they remained for twelve days under shell fire, eventually rejoining on June 19th.

The Twenty-Second left Saleux for the south on the night of May 4th and training was resumed when they arrived at Villesavoye, south of the river Vesle. The 8th Division took over the line in the Roucy sector— from Berry-au-Bac to a point about a mile and a half north-east of la Ville-aux-Bois—and the Pioneers then moved to Camp de l'Orme, north of Montigny-sur-Vesle.

The Twenty-Second eventually had one company at Gernicourt, one at a position near Bois des Buttes and the rest of the battalion at Bouffignereux. There was plenty of work, but the weather was fine and the line quiet until the evening of May 26th when the Corps sent a warning message regarding the German attack expected early next morning. The company of Pioneers near Bois des Buttes remained in position there; the rest of the battalion moved at once to Gernicourt where Colonel James assumed command of the defences.

The company near Bois des Buttes was on the forward edge of the battle zone, in rear of the 1st Worcesters. At about 5 A.M. on May 27th this battalion and the 2nd Northamptons were attacked and offered a stout resistance. Then the Germans crossed the river Miette and assailed them on the right flank and in rear. The British fought to the end. "Few of these battalions were seen again," reported the divisional commander. Their fate was also the fate of the company of the Twenty-Second who supported them.

The remainder of the battalion, with whom were some French Territorials, had suffered a heavy bombardment of gas and high explosive which swept the Gernicourt defences at one o'clock in the morning. The remnants of the 23rd Brigade from the left of the line afterwards fell back across the Aisne and Pontavert was in the hands of the enemy before the fog dispersed. He then crossed the river a little to the east and entered the Bois de Gernicourt. The

The German Offensive, 1918

divisional commander says: "Details of the fighting on the Gernicourt position are difficult to obtain, but apparently this position was turned from the south-west, for the enemy got into the Bois de Cernicourt and then east through Bois Popeux,* and got round the defenders. The garrison . . . fought well, but were surrounded and overpowered." But many of the Durhams fought their way out and stayed in support behind the right of the line when, early in the afternoon, the 75th Brigade from the 25th Division had absorbed other fragments of the 8th and were holding a line through Bouffignereux, Rouey and Concevreux. Some of the Pioneers, with men of the 1st Sherwood Foresters and Machine Gun Corps, were still reported to be fighting in Gernicourt at this time.

The retreat was continued towards the Vesle, going south and rather west to keep in touch with the 50th Division on the left. But no stand could be made on the river line and by the evening of May 28th the survivors of the Twenty-Second appear to have been in position south-west of Branscourt, in support to fragments of the 23rd Brigade, with French troops on either side. Twenty-four hours later the Durham men held the line south-west of Faverolles, between two battalions of the 58th Brigade. The transport got away safely in the retreat, crossing the Marne at Dormans.

On June 1st the headquarters of the Twenty-Second was at Joslins, and some men were contributed to the Composite Battalion formed by the 8th Division and sent up by bus on the night of the 2nd to help to hold the line. Casualties in this last battle, or series of battles, mounted to 19 officers and no less than 194 other ranks. Among the fallen were Major C. C. H. Hall and 2nd Lieut. V. Vincent. Lieut. C. R. V. Grimshawe was included in those who were missing.

Although the fighting strength of the Twenty-Second was 23 officers and 174 men on June 29th, the Pioneers received no more drafts. They had arrived at Friancourt, on the French coast, a few miles from le Tréport, on the 23rd. The shattered units of the 50th

* Adjoining Bois de Gernicourt.

The Durham Forces in the Field

(Northumbrian) Division were recuperating in the vicinity and early in July the Twenty-Second were absorbed by the 1/7th Durham Light Infantry (Pioneers).

Thus the existence of the youngest Service Battalion of Durham came to an end. The County may well be proud of the—best of pioneers and best of infantry, as the occasion demanded. One may regret that there were no Twenty-Second to participate in the final triumph of the British arms; but if they had to lose their identity it was good that they should merge with the Territorial Pioneer Battalion of Durham.

HOLDING THE LINE

MAY TO AUGUST, 1918

On May 2nd the Eleventh left Frévillers, marching to the Château de la Haie, west of Ablain-St. Nazaire. The 20th Division were now relieving the Canadians in their positions round Lens and A and B companies of the Pioneers moved up to Liévin. The rest of the battalion were located at Carency. There was much work to do on communication trenches, strong points and new defensive works in l'Hirondelle Wood on the high ground north-east of Givenchy.

A great deal of gas was liberated during May. The biggest operation of this nature took place on the 23rd, when nearly the whole of the Eleventh were engaged in pushing up to the front line 75 trucks, each containing 21 gas cylinders. The Pioneers worked in parties of 20 and two tramway lines were used. In the front trench the gas was discharged without removing the cylinders from the trucks which, as soon as the operation was over, were pushed back again.

Retaliation followed a few days later and was only too effective. On May 26th and 27th Liévin was drenched with mustard gas and all work had to be suspended. The Eleventh lost Capts. P. V. Kemp and A. Philip; 2nd Lieuts. T. A. Atlay, R. Conacher, G. F. Wood, E. R. Harbron, G. Cain, G. H. Ault and J. C. Ratcliffe; and 122 men all gassed. Capt. Kemp died later and there were 14 other casualties during May.

June was a month of hard and monotonous work. On July 3rd the German gas shells claimed 19 more victims among the Eleventh who had a certain satisfaction ten days later in pushing up the trucks for another large gas attack. Lieut.-Col. T. H. Carlisle, D.S.O., M.C., who came from the R.E., succeeded Colonel Boulton in command of the battalion on August

The Durham Forces in the Field

14th. At this time the division moved further south, the new line extending from just north of Fresnoy to Avion. In spite of the many calls upon them the Eleventh were giving intensive training to three platoons daily before the end of the month.

Till June 3rd the headquarters of the Fifteenth remained at Chaltrait, where some stragglers rejoined. A draft was sent to join the Composite Battalion before moving to Congy and on to les Essarts, where no British troops had stayed before. A further reinforcement was dispatched to the Composite Battalion on June 6th.

On the 14th the battalion headquarters went by bus and train to Moyenneville and the journey was soon continued to Villers Campsart, where the company from the Composite Battalion rejoined, and large drafts amounting to 6 officers and 432 men arrived from the Base. Busy days spent in reorganisation and training were interrupted by another move before the end of the month and early in July one more train journey brought the Fifteenth to Puchevillers, north of Amiens once more.

On July 17th the Durhams, now fit for the field again, boarded buses which took them to Acheux, on the Doullens-Albert road. In the evening they went into the line, relieving the Drake Battalion (63rd Division) in trenches west of the river Ancre and near the ruins of Hamel. There was little activity here and casualties only amounted to 10 during the tour. Before the end of the month came news of the award of the French *Croix de Guerre, avec palme,* to Major Bousfield and Private J. Rice.

The Fifteenth came out of the trenches on **August 1st** and spent a week in reserve. During their next tour more line was taken over on the left. On **August 14th** the Germans evacuated their trenches north of the Ancre, New Zealand troops reached the site of the village of Serre, and Beaucourt was found to be free of the enemy. On the 16th the Fifteenth were relieved in the new advanced line which they had been holding and went back to bivouacs in Acheux Wood,

Holding the Line, May to August, 1918

on their way to billets at Raincheval. Four days later they came up again and moved to a position east of Mailly-Maillet on the following morning.

The tide of battle had already turned. Early in the month the success before Amiens was the prelude to the final victorious advance in which the Fifteenth were now to bear their part.

The Eighteenth were at Sercus until May 9th. Arrangements had been made for breaking up the 31st Division, but these were cancelled to the great relief of everyone concerned. The next move, made partly by bus, brought the Durhams into support positions north-west of Meteren, between Australians and French troops. The trenches were poor and most of the sector was overlooked by the Germans in the remains of Meteren and on the higher ground north of the village. After a tour in reserve the Eighteenth went into the front line, where patrols were active in the thick mists of the early mornings. Relieved on May 24th, the battalion moved back to Campagne, about ten miles south-west of St. Omer, where training and recreation were somewhat interrupted by an epidemic of influenza. Sergt. W. Siddle, of Sunderland, who, as transport sergeant, had done good work in March near the Ayette ridge, further distinguished himself during May, when the limbers bringing up rations had to run the gauntlet of persistent gas shelling. He was awarded the Distinguished Conduct Medal.

The Eighteenth moved forward again on June 15th. After a few days' work on a defensive line east of Morbecque they relieved the 1st Lancashire Fusiliers of the 29th Division in the reserve line at Grand Sec Bois, near Vieux Berquin. On June 22nd the front line, which faced the stream called Plate Becque, was taken over. Patrolling was difficult under the bright moon and in the face of an alert enemy, but on the evening of the 25th No. 9 platoon established and wired two forward posts on the right, at a cost of 5 casualties.

On the next night C and D companies got out of their trenches and lay up behind the parados while

309

The Durham Forces in the Field

nine platoons of the 13th York and Lancasters came through to attack Ankle Farm. There was no preliminary bombardment, but the advance, protected by an excellent barrage, carried the farm and a new forward line was established along the Plate Becque. Meanwhile No. 9 platoon, under 2nd Lieut. W. Allbeury, with a double Lewis gun section, had followed the second wave of attackers and occupied the posts dug on the previous evening. Work then commenced on others to link up the new forward line with the old front trenches to the south. German machine-guns opened at close range, but were tackled by parties of Durhams led by Capt. H. E. Hitchin, D.S.O., M.C., M.M., and 2nd Lieut. W. Allbeury. The Germans threw bombs, but declined a hand-to-hand fight, leaving one gun and 3 prisoners in the hands of the Eighteenth. Shortly afterwards Capt. Hitchin was wounded, but before 1 a.m. the defensive flank was completely established. Losses in the ranks only amounted to 10 and 2nd Lieut. Allbeury received the Military Cross for his cool and skilful leadership.

Late on the evening of the 27th 2nd Lieut. A. Everatt, with part of A company, took over the new defensive flank while B company and two platoons of D relieved the York and Lancasters in Ankle Farm and along the line of the stream. Early next morning the 15th West Yorkshires had to advance to the line of the Plate Becque farther south and 2nd Lieut. Everatt's people were to swing forward to the line of the stream and thus complete the new front. As the enemy posts west of the Becque were too near to be dealt with by artillery, Colonel Lowe arranged to barrage them with rifle grenades and machine-gun fire from the factory building just north of the Vieux Berquin road.

At 6 a.m. on June 28th the advance began. 2nd Lieut. Everatt's men went forward in small columns, meeting with little opposition. One post which showed fight was soon dealt with and small groups of Germans, evidently taken by surprise, fled southwards. Others were shot or bayonetted in the shell holes they occupied. The Durham men were on the line of the stream in a few minutes and started to dig in, while Sergt. H.

Holding the Line, May to August, 1918

Goldsborough, of Bishop Auckland, and Pte. A. A. Taylor, of Birmingham, crossed the Becque with a Lewis gun team and stalked a party of German machine-gunners in the standing corn beyond. These were killed and their gun was captured. On the left two more machine-guns fell into the hands of the Eighteenth, who had only sustained 2 casualties in the advance. The prisoners taken numbered 30.

2nd Lieut. Everatt was awarded the Military Cross and Sergt. Goldsborough and Pte. Taylor each received the Distinguished Conduct Medal. C.-S.-M. B. Dolan, of Thornaby-on-Tees, won the same decoration for supervising the distribution of rations under fire before the advance began and guiding ammunition parties to the new front line through a heavy German barrage.

On the night of June 29th the Eighteenth relieved the 15th West Yorkshires on the right—a difficult operation carried out under a storm of gas and high explosive. The new position extended southwards from la Becque and was subjected to heavy shell fire until the Durhams were relieved on July 4th.

The 4th Guards Brigade now left the 31st Division, and were replaced by the troops—mostly dismounted Yeomanry—from Palestine who formed the reconstituted 94th Brigade.

After a week's training near Morbecque the Eighteenth took over the line immediately south of their previous position. While here a lost machine-gun team of the 132nd German Regt. walked into the arms of an A company post on the right and on the evening of July 13th a corporal and 2 men accounted for a troublesome German machine-gun which they brought in after killing one of the team.

Relieved on July 14th, the battalion moved to reserve positions in the forest of Nieppe, where A and B companies—including many newly-joined men—trained for another enterprise, using a model of the enemy positions. On July 18th the line south of la Becque was taken over and an operation designed to bring the whole brigade front up to the Plate Becque was fixed for the following morning. There was no time for reconnaissance, but the outgoing troops reported

The Durham Forces in the Field

the German line weakly held so a barrage was deemed unnecessary. South of the farm building known as la Becque A and B companies of the Eighteenth were to advance with the West Yorkshires on their right. At 7 A.M. on July 19th the attack was launched, small columns with scouts in front creeping through the corn. B company, on the extreme left, were soon met with machine-gun fire. North of the road was a ruined building enclosed by hedges and a Lewis gun team advancing along the north hedge were all killed or wounded. 2nd Lieut. Turnbull attempted to rush the place with a section of riflemen, but all his men were hit. This officer made another attempt from the rear, but accurate machine-gun fire rendered the enterprise impossible. Lance-Corpl. Adams had tried to co-operate from the west side. He got his Lewis gunners through the hedge and engaged the machine-gun firing on Lieut. Turnbull's party, but a platoon of Germans at once left the building and bombed this section out. 2nd Lieut. Langley reached the south-west corner of the enclosure and shot a German machine-gunner, but every attempt to get further forward failed.

The men on the extreme right of B company had got beyond the enclosure along the road to the south. Taken in rear by machine-gun fire, they were then compelled to withdraw into line with the rest of the company, now digging in about 40 yards west of this enclosure with the idea of trying again at dusk. Snipers in the trees were now active and bursts of machine-gun fire visited every movement.

2nd Lieut. W. L. Henderson, on the left of A company, went forward until the stream was visible only 80 yards away, when his platoon suffered heavily from the German machine-guns and snipers. The officer, with Sergt. W. Barker, of Darlington, occupied a shell hole into which they had drawn several wounded men. Suddenly about 16 Germans rushed up and Lieut. Henderson got 2 with his revolver. The remainder fell back and threw bombs, but Sergt. Barker threw one bomb back before it exploded and killed 2 more of the enemy who then fled. This platoon was isolated, but hung on until ordered to retire later in

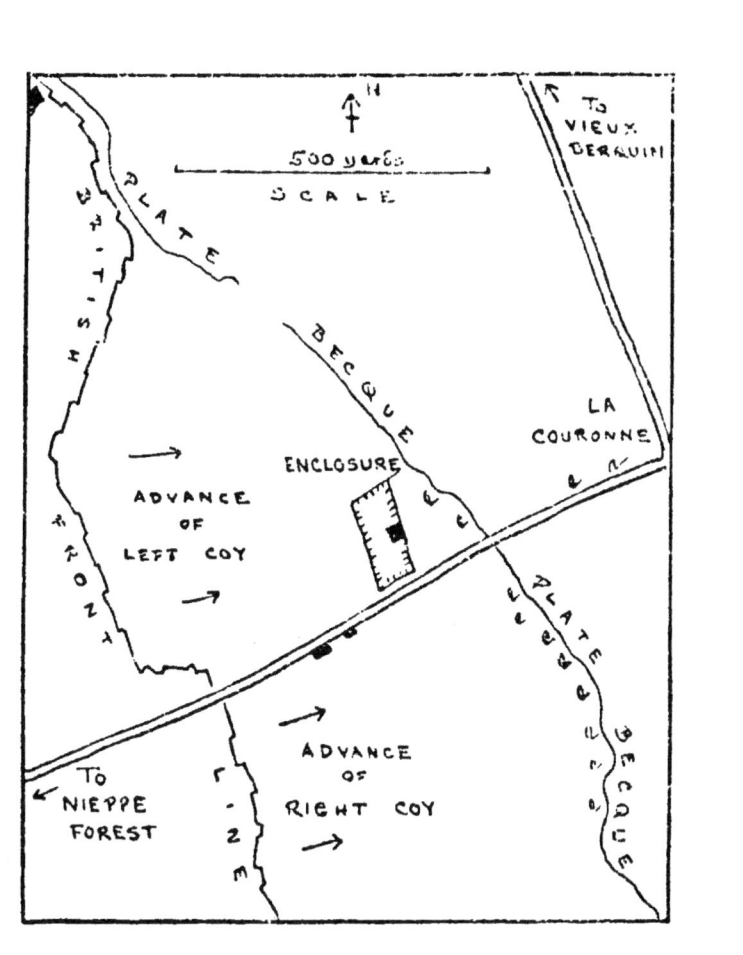

The Durham Forces in the Field

the morning. The platoon following 2nd Lieut. Henderson's men were checked further back by enfilade fire, though some on the right managed to get forward. 2nd Lieut. W. Brown, who led the right of the Eighteenth, made good progress at first, but eventually his platoon suffered heavy casualties. In attempting to deal single-handed with an enemy post this officer fell badly wounded and was not seen again. Sergt. Whitfield led up the rear platoon with great resolution to thicken the line here, but he was afterwards killed. Many other gallant deeds were done in this confused fighting on the right, where the German machine-guns maintained a deadly fire from the willows along the stream. Pte. W. Harper, of Spennymoor, and Pte. R. Cowling, of Doncaster, stalked successfully two enemy posts, getting 7 hits, including a German officer; Corpl. C. Lloyd, of Houghton-le-Spring, went forward alone, shot 2 Germans and silenced a machine-gun, though he was wounded in so doing. Sergt. Barker and these three men received the Distinguished Conduct Medal; Lieut. Henderson was awarded the Military Cross.

The troops on the right of the Eighteenth had returned to their trenches after suffering heavy loss and the position of A company, who were on that flank, became critical. It was difficult to convey orders for a withdrawal and in some cases small groups of men elected to remain to protect the wounded. The only way to retire was by creeping backward carefully through the corn and some of the Eighteenth did not get in till ten o'clock at night when C and D companies took over the line. Lieut. C. L. Welford and 2nd Lieut. R. W. Langley were wounded and losses in the ranks amounted to 100 killed, wounded and missing. Tracer bullets and bullets turned by the standing crops inflicted nasty wounds.

War dogs were used as messengers during this operation, but with indifferent success. One man and his dog were killed together; another man was killed and his dog returned at once to brigade headquarters; only one animal brought in a message. It was unfortunate that an enemy relief had brought into the line the 187th

Holding the Line, May to August, 1918

German Regt. who were not only of much better fighting spirit than their predecessors, but also held the stream and posts in front of it in such strength that an advance without artillery preparation was doomed to failure.

No further fighting developed before the Eighteenth were relieved on July 22nd. After spending a week near Morbecque the battalion came into the reserve line by Grand Sec Bois, where working parties were in demand. During July they lost 3 officers and 194 men in killed, wounded, missing and sick, but these losses were more than replaced by drafts and by men who rejoined from hospital.

On August 1st the Eighteenth came into the trenches again opposite Vieux Berquin, but took over the old line two nights later under incessant hostile shell fire. On the 6th 600 drums projected gas into the enemy lines, C and D companies being withdrawn to enable this to be done.

Rumours of an enemy withdrawal were now rife. On the afternoon of the 7th two snipers reported to C company that the enclosure of evil fame had been evacuated. 2nd Lieut J. G. Perry, with Corpl. F. Wright, took out a small party to investigate. Near the western hedge they came upon some Germans who made signs to the Durhams to surrender. But the latter had come to take prisoners, not to yield themselves as such, and eventually returned under fire without a casualty, bringing in no less than 14 Germans and a light machine-gun. By this exploit 2nd Lieut. Perry won the Military Cross and Corpl. Wright the Distinguished Conduct Medal.

That night the front line companies advanced their line 200 yards and this new position was dug and wired without much enemy interference; but patrols found the enclosure re-occupied and drew machine-gun fire from the direction of the stream. The battalion were relieved on August 10th and returned to Morbecque once again, the 31st Division handing over to the 40th before replacing the 9th Division in the Meteren sector further north. On the 22nd the Eighteenth passed through Hazebrouck and after a long, exhausting

The Durham Forces in the Field

march went into trenches north-east of Meteren which was now in British hands again.

The Nineteenth came out of the line near Aveluy Wood on the evening of May 1st, withdrawing to Hédauville and then to Toutencourt for training and recreation. Some work was done on the defences running through Engelbelmer and Bouzincourt, known as the "Purple" Line. The battalion went into the trenches again on May 29th, having lost Capt. G. Johnson, the quartermaster, and 2nd Lieut. T. Y. Corkin, wounded by shell fire in the valley at Hédauville two days before when there were also 7 casualties in the ranks.

The brigade held the north-western portion of Aveluy Wood, the line running thence south-west to Martinsart. In the early morning of June 1st the 17th and 18th Lancashire Fusiliers made a valiant attempt to clear Aveluy Wood of the enemy, but were too much hampered by the thick undergrowth and hostile machine-gun fire. The Nineteenth, in reserve, had no casualties in this action, but withdrew to the "Purple" Line in the evening and were shelled out, with a loss of 6 killed and 2nd Lieut. F. R. Cunliffe and 51 others wounded, at dawn on June 2nd.

On the 17th, when the last tour of the battalion in this part of the line was drawing to an end, a raid was made upon the enemy. Two parties entered his trenches, but found them empty and on the return journey 8 casualties were sustained from machine-gun and trench-mortar fire. The division were now about to move north, but the Nineteenth stayed for nearly a fortnight at Beauquesne, where Colonel Greenwell relinquished the command and was succeeded by Major H. R. McCullagh.

On July 1st the battalion marched to Doullens and entrained for St. Omer whence they moved to billets at Tilques. Three days later they took over reserve billets from the French at Boeschepe, in the Locre sector, now a quiet part of the line. The first tour in front commenced on July 12th and early next morning the Germans attempted to raid a post. They

Holding the Line, May to August, 1918

were driven off without much trouble, 2 of the Durhams being wounded.

On the night of July 27th a raiding party of 28 men from X company, under Capt. Smith, M.C., and 32 from Z company, led by 2nd Lieuts. W. C. Dyer, M.C., and Jordan, accomplished a very successful enterprise under the direction of Capt. F. Featon, M.C. Heavy artillery, field guns, Stokes mortars and machine-guns all contributed to a perfect barrage on and around the German trenches opposite Locre Hospice. A Bangalore torpedo was placed in the German wire before the zero hour and just after 11.30 p.m. the enemy line was entered at two points. Either the Germans were forming up for an attack or a relief was in progress, for the trenches were found full of men. In the fierce hand-to-hand struggle which followed quite 20 of the enemy were killed. On the left Capt. J. W. Ryall led a rush upon a machine-gun post and, though seriously wounded, saw the team killed, after which he brought in the gun with the assistance of his servant. Prisoners were hard to get, for the Germans would not surrender and although four were hauled out of the trench only two reached the British lines. No one of the Nineteenth was killed. 2nd Lieuts. F. W. Jordan and W. C. Dyer were slightly wounded and there were 21 other casualties, few of them serious. Capt. Ryall and 2nd Lieut. Jordan were given the Military Cross.

After another turn in reserve the Nineteenth went back to Terdeghem, about two miles east of Cassel, to refit, but came up in lorries to Boeschepe again on August 3rd and next evening took over the front trenches. The enemy was suspected to be retiring to the hill of Kemmel and a patrol penetrated his line to a depth of 80 yards on the night of the 8th, finding no sign of him. Next day the Nineteenth returned to Terdeghem where musketry was made a feature of the training.

The Twentieth were still holding a sector of the Ypres defences on May 1st. East of the city the British line now ran through Hell Fire Corner, where the

The Durham Forces in the Field

Roulers railway crossed the Menin road. In the evening the battalion were withdrawn to Vlamertinghe, in reserve, and worked on the line of defence there. On May 11th came another tour in the front line north of Zillebeke Lake. The weather was fine and the Menin road was actively patrolled, a wounded German of the 458th Regt. being brought in. When not in the trenches there was much work to be done, for there were successive lines of defence in preparation west of Vlamertinghe, through Brandhoek and through Poperinghe.

The last three days of the month were spent in training—particularly musketry—near Vlamertinghe. During May 41 men had been evacuated sick but there were no killed or wounded.

Most of June was spent in the Second Army training area, a move forward commencing on the 28th. On the evening of the last day of the month a French battalion were relieved in the Scherpenberg sector, about due west of Kemmel village. Water in the forward area was suspected to be contaminated, so that all supplies had to be brought up from the rear, and there was much work to do on the trenches. The Twentieth were relieved on the night of July 5th and came into the line again two days later. There were many young sodiers in the ranks and while in support and reserve positions training was carried on in places free from enemy observation. The German artillery fire was considerable during the month and the battalion lost Capt. J. T. Saunders and 2nd Lieut. A. Graham wounded and 3 men killed, 40 wounded and 61 evacuated sick. The last six days of July were spent in reserve near Reninghelst.

On August 2nd the Twentieth were organised with the 1/108th Americans into two composite battalions, A Battalion consisting of the two A and B companies and B Batfalion of the C and D companies. In the evening the A Battalion relieved Americans in the front line and B Battalion the 26th Royal Fusiliers in support. During the following days and nights the Americans learnt much of trench duties and patrolling, while the German guns continued their activity. On

Holding the Line, May to August, 1918

August 7th the Twentieth became one battalion again and after a tour in the support line went back to Reninghelst where work was done on the Scherpenberg-Dickebusch Lake line. On August 29th the Wearsiders were again in support. Casualties during the month amounted to 70, including Lieut. F. S. Mackinlay, wounded, but more than half were through sickness.

On June 19th at Brookwood, Surrey, the training cadre of the 2/7th Duke of Wellington's Regt., which had returned from France, were used to form the nucleus of a new battalion called the 29th Durham Light Infantry. They were to form, with the 33rd London Regt. and the 18th York and Lancasters, the 41st Brigade of the reconstituted 14th Division. Lieut.-Col. F. S. Thackeray, D.S.O., M.C., 2nd H.L.I., assumed command and to join his 9 officers and 50 men came a draft of 103 of the West Ridings, followed before midnight by 800 men—West Yorkshires, East Yorkshires, Northumberland Fusiliers, K.O.Y.L.I., York and Lancasters, Duke of Wellington's, Durham Light Infantry and Cyclist Corps. None of these answered to more than the " garrison duty abroad " standard of fitness. The next day, which was dull and wet, saw the organisation of the battalion and the fitting of equipment. Training was hurried on during the rest of the month and the men improved rapidly, their musketry being particularly good. Over 300 men were found to be unfit, but a draft of 100 from the 27th Durham Light Infantry were received.

On the night of July 2nd the Twenty-Ninth entrained for Folkestone and embarked at 8 A.M. on the 3rd. The battalion left Boulogne next day and spent the rest of the month in training, first at Fiennes, then at Moulle. On the 17th a draft of 167 was received from the 28th Durham Light Infantry. At the end of the month—with Major B. W. Ridley, M.C., now in command, as Colonel Thackeray was acting brigadier—came a move to the St. Sylvestre Cappel area, but on August 12th the Twenty-Ninth entrained at Steenvoorde and moved back to St. Momelin, north of St.

The Durham Forces in the Field

Over, and stayed at Nieurlet and Zudrove until August 20th.

Then came another train journey, this time to Proven, and on the 27th the battalion relieved the 1/4th Cheshire Regt. in brigade reserve at Brielen. Major Ridley was now confirmed in the command of the Twenty-Ninth, Lieut.-Col. Thackeray returning to his own regiment. The battalion moved into Ypres on the 28th and provided working parties while the officers reconnoitred the front line.

The late LIEUT.-COL. G. E. R. HOLROYD-SMYTH, D.S.O., M.C.
15th Durham Light Infantry

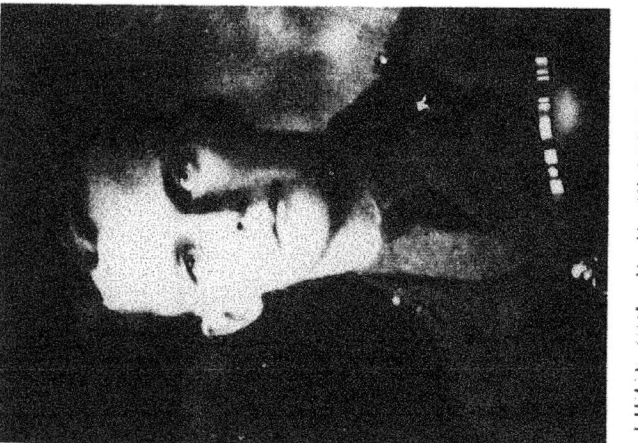

LIEUT.-COL. D. H. CLARKE, D.S.O., M.C.
15th Durham Light Infantry

THE LAST CAMPAIGN, 1918

CHAPTER I

THE battle in front of Amiens and subsequent successful operations had made possible the great advance of the Allied armies which began on August 23rd, 1918, and ended in victory. Most of our Service Battalions fought in Flanders during this period, but the Fifteenth bore their full share in the series of battles which rolled the enemy back towards Maubeuge.

They moved at noon on August 21st through a storm of gas and high explosive to a position east of Beaumont Hamel and on the evening of the following day replaced some Yorkshire Territorials in a ravine north of the ruins of Beaucourt. Between Beaucourt and St. Pierre Division the 64th Brigade, having already bridged the Ancre, passed some troops across the river, but the Germans were still on Thiepval ridge.

Now the brigade were given the task of seizing the high ground south of Miraumont. Few tools were to be carried, as existing trenches and shell-holes could be adapted for defence when the objective was won and it was essential that the troops should be lightly equipped for the difficult advance. The Fifteenth crossed the Ancre by foot-bridges at 11 P.M. on August 23rd and formed up on the south side under considerable fire. An hour later the brigade advanced in artillery formation with the Durhams on the right. It was difficult to keep direction and touch in the darkness, for the ground was pitted with shell craters, seamed with old trenches and intersected by deep gullies. The British barrage was ineffective, but the enemy appeared to have little idea of what was happening. Some Germans fought obstinately in Battery Valley, west of Grandcourt, but the Yorkshires and Durhams drove ahead until the K.O.Y.L.I.

The Durham Forces in the Field

overran Grandcourt and the attack reached the Grandcourt-Courcelette road. Here the line was reorganised, the reserve company of each battalion forming a defensive flank to the right. It was 3.36 A.M. when the advance was resumed—only an hour to daylight and a mile and a half to go. The men scrambled upward and onward. The ground on the left was easier, so that the K.O.Y.L.I. arrived first on the final objective, but the Fifteenth were barely ten minutes behind them: most of the East Yorkshires had lost touch and remained on the western edge of Boom Ravine which, over half a mile in rear, ran down to the river bed.

Day was breaking as the battalions reached their goal. The German machine-gun fire was heavy but high while the line was established facing north-east, with the left thrown back to confront Miraumont on the north and the right also drawn in as a defensive flank.

General H. A. McCulloch had been wounded during the advance and Colonel Holroyd-Smyth, M.C., assumed command of the brigade who were now in a very precarious position, almost entirely surrounded by the enemy. Germans came out of Boom Ravine in the rear and signalled to the British to surrender, but they were soon dispersed by rifle fire. At 8 A.M. an attack was launched from Miraumont across the river, but failed before the Lewis guns and rifles of the Fifteenth and the K.O.Y.L.I. Another attempt from Boom Ravine was dealt with in similar fashion, but the enemy machine-guns, snipers, and mortars maintained a heavy fire which caused many casualties.

Later a British aeroplane flew over Boom Ravine, but came no further. Pigeons liberated by the brigade in the early morning only reached divisional headquarters in the afternoon and reports sent back by the 1st East Yorkshire Regt., west of Boom Ravine, gave the impression that the advance had halted there. Preparations were put in hand to attack the ravine and the ground beyond, but the wounded brigadier, who had started back at 8.30 A.M., eventually made matters clear. The brigade-major also returned with a report and the 110th Brigade then advanced to secure the right flank.

The Last Campaign, 1918

As the morning wore on and the British troops further south also made progress the enemy fire slackened, so that the Fifteenth and the 9th K.O.Y.L.I. were able to move about more freely and do something towards strengthening their position. To the north Miraumont fell to the 42nd Division and the crisis passed, though it was nearly midnight when the Fifteenth withdrew to Boom Ravine, now clear of the enemy.

Colonel Holroyd-Smyth, M.C., was awarded the Distinguished Service Order and the divisional commander, in a congratulatory order, described the exploit of the 64th Brigade as " one of the finest deeds performed by any brigade in the war." Lieut. W. Tweddell, M.C., who had led his men with great skill and courage until he was wounded, was granted a bar to his decoration and 2nd Lieut. W. Jackson, also among the wounded, won the Military Cross for his good and gallant work.

Next morning the other brigades of the 21st Division continued the action and the Fifteenth rested on the scene of their achievement. They moved forward to a position south of Pys in the evening, Colonel Holroyd-Smyth returning to the command. The British advance continued to be pressed with great energy and on the morning of August 26th the 64th Brigade assembled on the spur west of le Sars to drive the Germans from the sunken road running south from Ligny-Thilloy to Luisenhof Farm.

The Fifteenth were on the right and the way led past the ruins of le Sars, south of the Butte de Warlencourt and then up over the high ground. The distance was long and machine-gun fire lashed the Durhams when at last they descended the slope towards the sunken road. Only a few men reached it, for the advance had not been able to keep up with the barrage and Ligny-Thilloy was still in German hands. During the evening a counter-attack was repulsed by the Fifteenth and at 9 A.M. on August 27th two platoons pushed forward and managed to establish posts in the road north of the farm.

The battalion were relieved that night, having lost 14 officers and 268 men since August 21st. Among the

The Durham Forces in the Field

fallen were Lieuts. J. Brady and W. G. Charlton, and 2nd Lieuts. C. W. Bodman and W. Jackson, M.C.

During the operations Lieut. F. V. P. Perrott had performed many daring reconnaissances and acquired much valuable information and on August 26th 2nd Lieut. A. Rae had distinguished himself in the attack. Both these officers received the Military Cross.

After two days' rest the Fifteenth moved up south of Le Barque to bury dead and clear the battlefield, while the advance pressed on. Beaulencourt fell to the 110th Brigade on September 1st, but the Durhams were in Corps reserve and did not enter the battle again till later. They moved up east of Manancourt on September 7th and assembled next evening for an attack on Chapel Hill, just north of the scene of their successful counter-attack at the beginning of the March retreat.

East and slightly north of the village of Heudicourt were two copses about 300 yards apart called Genin Well Copse No. 1 and No. 2. The attack was to be launched from the eastern edge of the latter, "if clear of the enemy," but as the leading companies approached the western side in the early morning of September 9th they came under machine-gun fire. The only thing to do was to halt and form up where they stood.

Chapel Hill was defended by a redoubt and Cavalry Support Trench—still known by its old British name— ran south-east from it across the railway. Roughly parallel to this line and from 200 to 300 yards beyond it was the old Cavalry Trench. C and D companies of the Fifteenth led the advance up the exposed slope and forced their way into the first line despite the stout resistance of the Germans. Heavy machine-gun fire made further progress impossible for a time, but the Durhams were ready for another attempt at half-past five in the evening. Then, after a short but bloody struggle, Cavalry Trench was won and a counter-attack which followed from Chapel Crossing, north-east of Chapel Hill, was flung back. But the Germans came again in the darkness and the Fifteenth were forced to withdraw to Cavalry Support. At 7 A.M. next day about 30 of the enemy suddenly bombed their way in,

The Last Campaign, 1918

but Lance-Corpl. T. Eardley headed an attack which took them in flank and drove them off. He was awarded the Distinguished Conduct Medal.

The Fifteenth were relieved that night and withdrew to bivouac at Elson Copse, east of Manancourt. Casualties amounted to 7 officers and 270 men and included 2nd Lieut. E. J. Brinkworth, died of wounds. Six days were now spent in reorganisation and training and on September 18th the battalion moved at 12.30 a.m. to a position for an attack upon the trenches defending Villers-Guislain. C company were to follow the 62nd Brigade and the rest of the battalion moved in rear of the K.O.Y.L.I. and East Yorkshires, coming up between them as the advance progressed. The attack was launched at 5.10 a.m., and soon afterwards Lieut.-Col. C. E. R. Holroyd-Smyth, D.S.O., M.C., fell, severely wounded. Capt. C. P. Grant, M.C., assumed command of the battalion. A company, on the left of the East Yorkshires, carried the beet factory on the Peizière road and soon after nine o'clock the line was reorganised, B company coming into position astride this road between the two Yorkshire battalions. A company were withdrawn soon afterwards. At noon B company sent patrols into Villers-Guislain and discovered that the Germans were holding the north-eastern side of the village in some strength. Four hours later, after an enemy concentration had been broken up by the British guns, D company moved up on the right of the East Yorkshires where, in the trenches and sunken roads, they fought the enemy with bombs. The company commander, Lieut. C. Stephenson, led his bombers in person and did well to maintain the position, as there were no British troops on his right. He was awarded the Military Cross.

A and C companies were now in support positions, but early on the 19th A company were brought forward and took over Munier Trench, due south of the village. On the right a raiding party from D company attempted, but failed, to rush Derby Post in the sunken road leading south-east from Villers-Guislain. During the morning Lance-Corpl. R. Mitchell, of Felling-on-Tyne, won the Distinguished Conduct Medal by an act

The Durham Forces in the Field

of audacious bravery. He was looking for w...ed between the lines when he noticed a German m...ne-gun post. Quietly collecting some bombs which... re lying about he rushed in single-handed, killed 6 Germans and brought the gun in, although he was severely wounded in the legs.

About 9.30 P.M. the Fifteenth were relieved and returned once more to Elson Copse. September 18th and 19th had cost 76 men killed, wounded and missing, and losses would have been heavier if the troops had not had an excellent barrage and kept close to it during the first advance. Unfortunately, Colonel Holroyd-Smyth succumbed to his wounds; a very gallant officer and a fine soldier, he was a great loss to the Fifteenth.

Several days were spent at Elson Copse and Lesbœufs where a draft of 300 men joined the battalion and Lieut.-Col. H. H. Neeves, D.S.O., M.C., became commanding officer. The British advance continued, but the Fifteenth remained in reserve until October 5th when the 64th Brigade moved forward once more. The Durhams crossed the St. Quentin canal south of Bantonzelle, passed through troops of the 110th Brigade in the Hindenburg system and in the evening occupied the le Catelet-Nauroy line in readiness to attack.

The Beaurevoir defensive system, well wired and strong in concrete machine-gun emplacements and shelters, was held in great strength by the Germans who also occupied Montecouvez Farm and other advanced positions. The assault was delivered without artillery support at 6 A.M. on October 6th, with the Fifteenth on the right and the East Yorkshires on the left. In spite of machine-gun fire the Durhams pushed on with great resolution and by 11.30 A.M. one company had carried Montecouvez Farm, while two companies, after hard fighting, were established in the road running south-east towards the Beaurevoir line. But the hero of the day was 2nd Lieut. E. Roughley, who gained a footing with his men in the front trench of the main system. He won the Military Cross. Durhams also held a trench running back from the before-mentioned road to Mortho Wood.

All these gains were held during the 7th and at

The Last Campaign, 1918

1 a.m. on the 8th, under a heavy barrage, the Fifteenth went forward in the darkness, with the K.O.Y.L.I. on their left, and burst into the Beaurevoir defences. The German resistance was soon overcome though one machine-gun post held out for a time. Capt. R. Purvis and 2nd Lieut. A. A. Tuffs went on to Angles Château and took it with its garrison of 30 Germans. But others lurked in the woods around the building and there were no British troops on the flanks of this party of Durhams, who now numbered no more than 30. The officers judged it prudent to withdraw to a convenient sunken road where reinforcements eventually reached them. At 6 a.m., after another struggle, the château was occupied again, but the grounds were mined and repeated explosions compelled a second retirement. Later in the morning came the final capture of the building which was then held as the right of the line occupied by the Fifteenth. Both Capt. Purvis and 2nd Lieut. Tuffs were awarded the Military Cross.

On the evening of the 8th the East Yorkshires took Warlincourt and the British line was pushed still farther forward, so that on the 10th the Durhams were billetted in this village which was almost untouched by shell fire and contained many furnished houses. The breaking of the Beaurevoir line had cost the Fifteenth 213 casualties, besides Capt. Purvis and 2nd Lieuts. C. C. Cuthbert, D. Barker, V. W. Schmidt, and C. P. Metcalf, all wounded.

The last of the elaborate defensive zones constructed by the Germans had now been won, and beyond lay open, rolling, cultivated country—well wooded and watered. The 17th Division had passed through into this promised land and for nine days the Fifteenth stayed at Walincourt. Then they moved north-eastward to Montigny in the track of the advance and so on to the sugar factory on the Cambrai road below Inchy. The battalion arrived here on October 22nd and moved out at 5 p.m. to relieve the 9th Duke of Wellington's Regt. in position east of Amerval, beyond the Selle river. The K.O.Y.L.I. were to attack on the right, the East Yorkshires on the left. Two companies of Durhams were to follow the right battalion to the second objec-

The Durham Forces in the Field

tive and then extend and take a portion of the third objective which was the road running south from Vendegie-au-Bois. The other two companies were to assist the East Yorkshiremen in " mopping up " the village of Ovillers, which lay in a hollow, and were then to come forward and join the rest of the battalion. The 110th Brigade, on the left of the 64th, were rather heavily shelled during the assembly, but all was quiet on the right. At 2 a.m. on October 23rd the infantry attacked and the Durhams, following hard on the heels of the East Yorkshires, were soon in Ovillers. Beyond the village the Yorkshiremen halted, as arranged, while the Fifteenth crossed a small stream and were fighting their way into Vendegie-au-Bois before half-past seven. There was some close work here before the German resistance weakened, but eventually many of the enemy, including a regimental commander and his staff, yielded themselves prisoners. In the houses were found many of the French inhabitants.

The Fifteenth took over the whole of the brigade front during the morning, while tanks were pushing forward, the other battalions forming a defensive flank to the right where the advance had not progressed so far. The 62nd Brigade soon came through the Fifteenth in order to carry on the attack and by the evening the line was established north-east of the village. Heavy shell and machine-gun fire prevented any further movement that day, but operations were resumed on October 24th.

The K.O.Y.L.I. were again upon the right and the Fifteenth on the left joined with the 62nd Brigade. While assembling for the attack gas shells caused many casualties, but before 4 a.m. the line went forward under a barrage which did not cow the German machine-gunners. These were tackled with the bayonet and the Durhams swept on. Capt. John Sedgwick, M.C., leading his men with great gallantry and resolution. The enemy fought hard in the village of Poix-du-Nord and here Colonel Neeves was wounded. Capt. Sedgwick—who won a bar to his Cross—succeeded him and, though the hostile shell fire was increasing, the village was taken together with many prisoners. A German battery, firing over open sights, combined with terrific machine-

The Last Campaign, 1918

gun fire to prevent further progress. It was now nearly 11 A.M., and high explosive and gas shells streamed into Poix-du-Nord, slaughtering and torturing many of the civilian population. At four in the afternoon the East Yorkshires came up on the right and the whole line went forward again. There was no further check and the Ghissignies-Englefontaine road was reached that evening, though considerable casualties were sustained. 2nd Lieut. V. R. Chapman, who had done particularly well during the fighting of the previous day, was wounded, but led his platoon until the end and supervised the consolidation of the line before giving up. He was awarded the Military Cross.

Before dawn of the 25th the battalion had greatly strengthened their position and at 5 A.M. a German counter-attack was repulsed with loss along the whole front. In the evening the 110th Brigade came in and the Fifteenth withdrew to Vendegie-au-Bois. Casualties in the ranks amounted to 246, and 2nd Lieut P. Hodkinson had been killed. Lieut.-Col. H. H. Neeves, D.S.O., M.C., 2nd Lieuts. L. W. Lund, R. Dozford, J. C. Fitzsimmons, and W. R. Chapman, M.C., were all wounded, and 2nd Lieut. E. Frankland was wounded and missing. Sergt. H. Osborne, M.M., and Pte. J. Horan were both awarded the Distinguished Conduct Medal and the Military Medal was won by Sergts. W. G. Rowney and E. J. Magee; Lance-Sergts. G. Oxford, C. Stannard, and H. Taylor; and Ptes T. W. Elliott, D. Hardy, and J. N. Wilson.

The Fifteenth moved to Inchy for training and reorganisation on October 26th and three days later came up to Vendegie-au-Bois again. Here Lieut.-Col. A. C. Barnes, D.S.O., arrived and assumed command, while drafts received amounted to 11 officers and 158 men and included Capt. A. M. Lascelles, V.C., M.C. After ten days' rest the Fifteenth followed up the British advance. On November 5th the battalion moved eastwards through the forest of Mormal, where the 62nd Brigade had met with no opposition. In the early morning of the 7th the River Sambre was crossed by a pontoon bridge at Berlaimont and the way then led through Aulnoye and Bachant. The 110th Brigade had

The Durham Forces in the Field

been checked nearly half a mile west of the stream called Rau Grimour, so the Fifteenth deployed behind one of the Leicester battalions at 8.15 a.m. and, with the East Yorkshires on the right, advanced to the attack nearly half an hour later. Artillery and machine-guns disputed the advance which was enfiladed from the left where the British troops had not yet made good the crossings of the Sambre. But the Fifteenth persevered and after repulsing a counter-attack on the left flank crossed the stream and approached the western outskirts of Limont-Fontaine. Capt. A. E. Owles won the Military Cross for his gallant leadership and Sergt. G. Holborn, of Sunderland, who took command of a company when his officers had fallen, was awarded the Distinguished Conduct Medal.

In the afternoon, when it was decided to take Limont-Fontaine and the higher ground beyond, the Fifteenth had the K.O.Y.L.I. on their right. The British guns put down a barrage and the Yorkshires and Durhams streamed forward into the village, where they fought the Germans hand to hand and routed them. 2nd Lieut. F. Walkington, D.C.M., who led his men with great dash, was once surrounded by the enemy in his eagerness to get forward. He was awarded the Military Cross and 2nd Lieut. A. A. Tuffs, M.C., won a bar to his decoration. He led three platoons through the northern part of the village and forward over the ground beyond, where the whole line was eventually established. D company, indeed, could, and would, have gone on further, but were ordered to stand fast for relief that night. Early next morning the Fifteenth withdrew to Bachant and Berlaimont. The battalion had fought their last battle in the war, losing 124 men most of them wounded. Of the officers Capt. A. M. Lascelles, V.C., M.C., and Lieut. R. C. M. Gee were killed and 2nd Lieut. A. Rae, M.C., was wounded.

Military Medals were won by Sergts. A. Tuldy, W. Beale, and J. Morgan; Corpl. S. F. Harrison; and Ptes. J. F. Williams, W. Sollett, J. McMahon, R. Gelson, R. Jenkins and J. Burnand.

The Fifteenth were still at Berlaimont when on November 11th came the news of the Armistice.

The Last Campaign, 1918

The Fifteenth take pride of place in this story of the final campaign seeing that they started in the advance from the Ancre in August and were in action until the end, encountering a full share of the stoutest opposition offered by the Germans in retreat. But the Thirteenth arrived from Italy in time to bear an honourable and arduous part in this drive north-eastward towards Maubeuge.

On the reduction of infantry brigades to a three-battalion establishment each brigade of the three British divisions in Italy sent a battalion to France. These troops formed the reconstituted 25th Division. The Thirteenth arrived at St. Riquier from Italy on September 18th and 19th, marching to billets at Millancourt. The battalion, with the 9th Yorkshire Regt. and 11th Sherwood Foresters—old comrades of the 23rd Division—now formed the 74th Brigade. Training proceeded in rather unfavourable weather until September 27th, when the Thirteenth went by train to Albert and, eventually, by way of Ribémont, Maricourt, and Noislains, reached Ronssoy on October 3rd. On this date the 25th Division replaced Australian troops on the battle front with the 74th Brigade in support to the 7th. The Thirteenth only halted for half an hour at Ronssoy, marching on to Mont St. Martin, south of le Catelet, where they prepared for battle. There were 11 casualties from shell fire on this day.

On October 4th the 7th Brigade attacked the high ground north of Beaurevoir as a preliminary to the capture of the village, but could make no impression on the elaborate defences. At 1 o'clock next morning the Thirteenth moved up to assembly positions beyond Prospect Hill, east of le Catelet, and five hours later the 74th Brigade advanced to the attack. The Thirteenth had the Yorkshiremen on the right and the Foresters on the left. In spite of the artillery preparation heavy machine-gun fire met the attack and caused many casualties. Lieut.-Col. D. H. Clarke, D.S.O., M.C., was soon badly wounded and Capt. L. M. Greenwood, M.C., succeeded him in command of the battalion. Every effort was made to push on and the Durhams reached the sunken road running from Guisancourt

The Durham Forces in the Field

Farm south-eastward of Beaurevoir. In front was a maze of trenches which gave considerable trouble, but even these were captured and the Villers-Outréaux road was crossed. The Thirteenth now found themselves further forward than the other battalions and under fierce shrapnel and machine-gun fire. The position was untenable without support on the flanks and they withdrew reluctantly to the sunken road. Heavy machine-gun fire compelled a further retirement and the battalion eventually dug in about 400 yards forward from the old front line. They had lost heavily, especially in officers. Lieuts. H. P. Hart and W. Golder; 2nd Lieuts. P. C. Smith and P. Dodds were all killed. Capt. C. R. Chapman; Lieuts. A. E. Hales, E. O. Cutter, and F. L. F. Bees, M.C.; and 2nd Lieuts. A. E. Forrest, R. W. Robinson, N. H. Willis, M.C., R. I. Aikenhead, T. Bolton and J. D. Inches were wounded; and 2nd Lieut. C. Audas was missing.

Manchesters of the 7th Brigade, with two tanks, got into Beaurevoir during the day, but could not clear the village which fell to the 75th Brigade in the evening. There was now some prospect of a successful advance north of Beaurevoir and at 4 A.M. on October 6th the British artillery opened a heavy bombardment of the German positions. Ten minutes later the Thirteenth went forward again with the Sherwood Foresters on the left. The latter seized and held Guisancourt Farm; the Thirteenth got beyond the sunken road from Villers-Outréaux and dug in across the high ground facing south-east. 2nd Lieuts. R. W. Dewar, W. Bannerman, and E. H. Callow were wounded before the battalion were relieved on the early morning of the 8th and, although casualties in this position were not numerous despite the hostile shell fire, the losses on October 5th had left the Thirteenth very weak in numbers. But there was not much time to rest. After replenishing battle stores at Lormisset the battalion marched up in pursuit of the still advancing British line during the small hours of the 9th. Orders to attack were received on the way and a brief halt was made at Serain Farm on the cross-roads south-east of the village of that name. The 75th Brigade had advanced in the fog and reached Maretz

The Last Campaign, 1918

and the road running south-east from it, so it was now the task of the 74th to go through and attack the high ground north-east of Honnechy. The Thirteenth marched eleven miles on this morning before coming into action. The Sherwood Foresters led the brigade and at first there was no opposition, but on approaching the railway cutting south-east of Honnechy there came machine-gun fire from the north and east. The cutting was strongly held by the Germans, but the three weak battalions of the 74th Brigade drove them out and established a line behind it, with the Thirteenth in reserve. Cavalry had appeared and the enemy resistance weakened, but, unfortunately, the Lewis gun carts had not been able to keep up on the march, so proper toll could not be taken of the Germans in retreat. The advance was now resumed and the division reached the objective without much opposition, though the Thirteenth lost a good officer in Capt. I. Bewley, M.C., who was killed during the day.

At 5.30 a.m. on October 10th the Thirteenth led the 74th Brigade in touch with troops of the 75th on the left. There was no barrage, but each brigade had a field battery attached. The intention was to reach the high ground north-east of le Cateau, but at ten o'clock the Thirteenth were held up by machine-guns south-west of the village of St. Benin. The American troops advancing on the right had been checked west of St. Souplet, so the 74th Brigade were ordered to carry St. Benin at once. Major L. M. Greenwood, M.C., took the Thirteenth forward through a heavy hostile barrage at 2.30 p.m. There was some hand-to-hand fighting, but the village was taken in an hour and a line established beyond the river Selle in touch with the Americans on the right. During the night the enemy bombarded St. Benin and the valley to the south-west with gas shells, but he was not so active next day. Orders to advance again were cancelled and at night the 2nd Royal Munster Fusiliers relieved the Thirteenth who withdrew to Honnechy. Losses since the beginning of the month had reached the total of 21 officers and 428 men, mostly sustained in the heavy fighting at Beaurevoir. Major Greenwood, having led the battalion gallantly and well

The Durham Forces in the Field

since October 5th, was awarded the Distinguished Service Order. The Military Cross was won by 2nd Lieuts. W. Dewar, R. H. Farrier, and W. Bannerman for gallant leadership as company commanders and initiative in dealing with German machine-gun posts. 2nd Lieut. Bannerman had continued to direct operations after being wounded. During the four days' fighting many N.C.O.s and men had done particularly devoted and gallant work, sergeants, corporals and even privates replacing fallen officers and directing the advance. Lewis gunners, runners, signallers, and stretcher-bearers are also represented among C.-S.-M. I. Hammond; Sergt. H. Heatherington; Lance-Corpls. I. W. Barron and J. W. Smith; Ptes. I. Crossley, G. Russell, S. Powell, A. E. Shelley, J. Beatie, W. Horne, F. Dyer, and G. Bews—recipients of the Military Medal. Pte. J. Clark, M.M., was a stretcher-bearer who won a bar to his decoration.

On October 12th the battalion marched to billets at Prémont, where the French people, just freed from the German occupation, welcomed the troops warmly. Drafts were received and the work of reorganising and training went on. Major L. N. Greenwood, D.S.O., M.C., was removed to hospital on the 13th. Ill with influenza he had continued on duty throughout the operations, refusing to leave the Thirteenth with whom he had served almost from the time of their formation. This very gallant officer died of pneumonia soon afterwards. Lieut.-Col. P. F. Hone, D.S.O., M.C., arrived on October 16th and assumed command. Two days later the battalion moved up to Maretz and then to Honnechy, where another big draft was received and the companies were trained in open warfare. The Lewis gunners were able to get on the range here and the Thirteenth were in good fettle when on the night of October 22nd they moved up and halted about a mile north-west of le Cateau ready to attack again.

At 1.20 a.m. on October 23rd the 74th Brigade followed the rest of the division, who had liberated the village of Pommereuil. The direction was still north-east, the wood called Bois l'Evêque being in the path of the advance.

The Last Campaign, 1918

East of le Cateau in the valley of the Richemont stream the Thirteenth, with the Sherwood Foresters, came under slight machine-gun fire. Still advancing, the Durhams passed through troops of the 75th Brigade on the western edge of the wood and, swinging to the right, reached the road to the north of it, due west of Rue du Pont. Here two strong belts of wire confronted the battalion and the brigade line rested in the evening along the north edge of the wood. 2nd Lieut. C. H. Bishop, M.C., was mortally wounded on this day. At four next morning the attack was resumed, the Thirteenth on the left of the Yorkshires going for the Rue du Pont position, called by the Germans the Hunding Stellung. Losses were heavy, for the German wire was untouched by the British artillery, but the Thirteenth were not to be denied and the line was taken by half-past seven. In this fighting Lieut. R. S. F. Mitchell, M.C., who led his company with great dash through the German wire and later was prominent in directing the consolidation of the captured position, won a bar to his decoration. Lieut.-Col. P. H. Hone, D.S.O., M.C., wounded here by a sniper while making a personal reconnaissance, was awarded a bar to his Order and 2nd Lieut. J. W. Willey, who was acting as adjutant, received the Military Cross for his good service in preparing for the resumption of the attack. This took place at 2 P.M. under a creeping barrage, the brigade making a successful advance eastwards through le Faux to a line on the high ground beyond. The Thirteenth, now very weak in numbers, were represented by two companies led by Lieut. R. S. F. Mitchell, M.C., and 2nd Lieut. H. Gardner—afterwards awarded the Military Cross. 2nd Lieuts. A. Holmes and H. C. Geipel were wounded on this day and the former officer died. Major H. G. Faber arrived to command the battalion.

The 74th Brigade, with the 9th Yorkshires and the Thirteenth in line from right to left, were now in enclosed country on the outskirts of Landrecies. Movement forward was difficult, for the German machine-gunners commanded roads, paths and gaps in the hedges and observed the movements of our troops from vantage

The Durham Forces in the Field

points in houses. Nevertheless, patrols were busy day and night and a Lewis gun post was established in a favourable position. The German artillery engaged in a vindictive gas-shelling of the liberated villages in rear causing cruel suffering to the unprotected French inhabitants. At 5 A.M. on August 29th two platoons were pushed out on each flank to establish forward posts, but met with deadly rifle and machine-gun fire. On the left the Durhams were practically surrounded, but fought their way back under 2nd Lieut. I. A. B. Allison who had previously done good work, and was awarded the Military Cross. 2nd Lieuts. W. E. Walker and W. Bannerman, M.C., were wounded on this day, before the end of which the Sherwood Foresters relieved the Thirteenth who withdrew into support at Rue du Pont. A further advance was contemplated, but on October 31st the battalion moved back to camp near St. Benin. The week's fighting had cost 285 casualties in the ranks, most of them incurred in the breaking of the Hunding Stellung. The Military Medal had been won by C.-S.-M. G. Thomson, D.C.M.; Sergts. I. B. Walton and J. Killeen; and Ptes. C. Jackson, G. Poulter, and J. Robinson. C.-S.-M. I. S. Hammond, M.M., was awarded a bar to his medal.

After resting and reorganising the Thirteenth marched forward to Pommereuil on November 3rd. Next day the 75th Brigade attacked and the 74th followed with the Sherwood Foresters in the van. The Sambre canal was crossed about 400 yards south-west of Landrecies and at four o'clock the brigade passed through the 75th. A position was occupied astride the Maroilles road with the Thirteenth in support to the two other battalions. Abandoned big guns and field batteries were numerous, for the enemy resistance had at last reached breaking-point and it was only a question of pushing him hard in retreat. When the advance was resumed at 6.15 A.M. on November 5th a troop of the 12th Lancers led the way and cyclists and armoured cars were in evidence. Soon after midday the advance guard crossed the Petite Helpe river, where one bridge was still intact, cleared Maroilles and reached Rue du Faux, east of that village. Here some

The Last Campaign, 1918

groups of German machine-gunners disputed the way for a time. The Thirteenth were not required for outpost duty and spent the night in billets north of Maroilles.

On the 6th the infantry of the advance guard were drawn from the 9th Yorkshires. The lancers were stopped by machine-gun fire west of Marbaix and the attached field battery had to come into action before the advance could be resumed. Meanwhile the Thirteenth moved round through Taisnières to attack Marbaix from the north-west, but the village was entered without much opposition during the afternoon. The outpost line for the night ran 500 yards beyond.

It was the turn of the Thirteenth to provide the advance guard next day, but the 75th Brigade came through early on November 7th and the 74th concentrated at Maroilles. The Durhams had sustained only 14 casualties during these four days. On the morrow they marched back to Bousies, south-west of the forest of Mormal, where work was commenced on the repair of the roads in the vicinity. Here news of the Armistice arrived.

A few more honours have still to be recorded. Sergt. A. Sledge, M.M., and Lance-Corpl. R. Bell each received the Distinguished Conduct Medal and Pte. F. Malloy was awarded the Military Medal.

The Eleventh, working in the line which gripped Lens on its western and southern sides and extended southwards to Fresnoy, continued their tasks during September. The monotony of labour on the communication trenches in the forward area was broken by heavy gas shell bombardments, to which the British guns made adequate reply, while quantities of gas were projected upon the German positions. On September 4th and 5th Avion and its vicinity was heavily drenched with mustard gas shell. Towards the end of the month the 20th Division captured the enemy trenches south-west of Acheville.

When, on October 6th, the division was relieved the Eleventh, who had always kept three platoons training, moved to Estrée Cauchie and did nothing

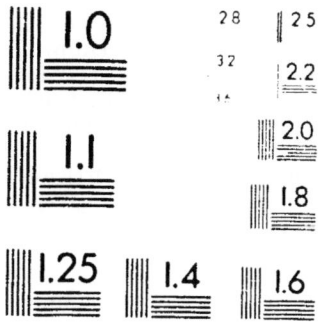

The Durham Forces in the Field

else till the end of the month. On the 31st the battalion reached Frémicourt by train, and were taken by bus to Cambrai. Two days' rest followed and then they moved north-eastward in the track of the advance through Rieux, Monsécourt, Sepmeries and Jenlain; then on to St. Waast-la-Vallée, where they arrived on November 9th. The 20th Division were about to relieve the 24th in the line between Maubeuge and Mons, but on November 11th, when the Pioneers were marching forward to Feignies, came the order to "stand fast on the line reached at 11 A.M." The Eleventh went to work at once upon repair of the roads north of Maubeuge.

CHAPTER II

IN the advance through Flanders made by French and Belgian troops and part of the British Second Army, under the supreme command of the King of the Belgians, the Eighteenth, Nineteenth, Twentieth and Twenty-Ninth were concerned.

First came the German withdrawal from the Lys salient. The line taken over by the Eighteenth on August 22nd consisted for the most part of a series of rifle pits, and the Durhams set to work, under continuous shell fire, to improve the defences. Two days later the battalion moved to the north, their left flank then resting just south of the St. Jan's Cappel-Bailleul road. Wet weather now caused much discomfort. The right of the Eighteenth was relieved on August 27th which left a frontage of two companies who, on the 29th, straightened the line by pushing forward and establishing posts. Many fires had been observed behind the German lines and it was no matter for surprise to see the enemy retiring at dawn next day. There were now few hostile guns in action and the Eighteenth followed up without difficulty, patrols of D company entering deserted Bailleul, where much damage had been wrought. On the southern outskirts

The Last Campaign, 1918

of the town men of A company got in touch with the 1st K.O.S.B. near the railway station. C company came through and were ordered to take Mont de Lille, an isolated hill about 1,500 yards south-east of Bailleul, which had been attacked unsuccessfully by a party of Borderers earlier in the day. Major D. E. Ince conducted a reconnaissance and at 7 p.m. the company went forward and obtained a footing on the lower slopes. Later in the evening the whole hill was taken and a Lewis gun recovered. C company dug in here, while A and B companies pushed ahead on the right and D company kept touch on the left flank with the 15th West Yorkshires, who had reached the lunatic asylum outside the town to the north-east. The troops encountered various booby traps in dug-outs and shelters as they advanced, but had had warning of what to expect and there were no casualties in the Eighteenth.

The 63rd Brigade had to take up a line running nearly a mile east of Mont de Lille and on the left the 36th Division were to take good the high ground known as le Ravelsberg, which continues eastward to Neuve Eglise. August 31st dawned in rain and mist. C company of the Eighteenth, on Mont de Lille, could see the troops of the 36th Division coming south-eastwards down the slopes of le Ravelsberg about half-past six. This advance had squeezed out the West Yorkshires, and the Eighteenth now held the whole brigade front, in touch on the right with the 29th Division who had experienced some difficulty with German machine-guns near la Crèche, north of Steenwerck station. A and B companies of the Eighteenth advanced in artillery formation, with scouts ahead, and, although they met with some sniping and machine-gun fire from houses and trees, they reached their allotted position and dug in with D company in support. It company, on the right, had to form a defensive flank until touch was obtained with the Borderers of the 29th Division in the evening.

Hostile artillery fire, both shrapnel and high explosive, had now grown in volume. The Eighteenth were still in touch with the retreating enemy, who

The Durham Forces in the Field

was burning houses as he withdrew; but the converging advance of the divisions on the flanks was pinching out the 93rd Brigade. About midnight, in heavy rain, the 1st Border Regt. began to relieve the Eighteenth whose casualties amounted to 12.

The Durhams moved to camp between Meteren and Bailleul, where they had to supply parties for clearing and repairing roads. On September 5th the battalion moved east of Bailleul. An observation balloon in the vicinity of this camp attracted shell fire which caused many casualties. When the Eighteenth moved up to reserve positions south-east of Neuve Eglise on September 12th, the German bombardment caused the distribution of the companies over a wide area. D company were located about La Pernisse Farm, which lay in the direction of Nieppe, and on the night of September 15th a hurricane burst of mustard gas shells caught 40 of the sleeping men before they could be roused. Fortunately few proved to be seriously affected. On September 18th the battalion returned to their old camp east of Bailleul where, on arrival, C company sustained 18 casualties from an 8-inch shell.

On September 27th the Eighteenth left their training and salvage work and took over the right of the 92nd Brigade line, north of Ploegsteert village.

In the attack next day two battalions of the 92nd Brigade were to clear Ploegsteert Wood from the north, while the Eighteenth attacked from the west to create a diversion and make what progress was possible. September 28th was very wet. The Durham men advanced on a line from Ploegsteert village to Hyde Park Corner at 3 P.M. in shallow columns, with scouts in front. There was confused fighting in the wood as groups of men, struggling forward through the mud, strove to work round and rush the German machine-guns from the rear. Sergt. E. C. Powell, of St. Neot's, who handled his platoon with exceptional courage and ability on this day, won the Distinguished Conduct Medal. On the right C company, under 2nd Lieut. Perry, M.C., took Maison 1875 and the farm called Touquet Berthe by the road east of Ploegsteert village.

The Last Campaign, 1918

On the left D company, led by 2nd Lieut. Bryson, found progress more difficult, for the British attack from the north was stoutly resisted. Still, the afternoon was, on the whole, a satisfactory one for the Eighteenth, thanks largely to the direction of operations by Lieut. E. I. Weddell, who was awarded the Military Cross. Six prisoners and two light machineguns were captured and many Germans had been killed and wounded. The Eighteenth had 15 casualties. About 7 p.m. C company lost Touquet Berthe, which was heavily shelled and mortared by the enemy.

The attack was resumed next morning, and the enemy finally ejected from the wood, the Eighteenth reaching a line well east of Touquet Berthe without being heavily engaged. Losses amounted to 13, nearly all wounded. On the left touch was established with the East Yorkshiremen of the 92nd Brigade, while the right flank was thrown back to join with the 40th Division, who had not advanced. That night, in darkness and rain, the battalion moved to a new position east of the wood in readiness to attack next morning towards the River Lys south of Deulemont. This advance was over muddy, open ground and D company, on the right, were held up by machine-gun fire; but in the centre B company went all the way and pushed patrols still further. One light machine-gun was taken by A company.

On October 1st the right of the line had to swing forward to the river bank in conjunction with the division further south; but the latter did not move and B and D companies, who carried out their task at a cost of 3 killed and 4 wounded, had to provide for a defensive flank to the right. The day proved to be fine and the good visibility resulted in heavy hostile shell fire later, which killed 12 men of the Eighteenth and wounded 16 more. At night the battalion were relieved and returned to the 93rd Brigade at a camp between Neuve Eglise and Mount Kemmel.

On October 4th the Eighteenth were in the line again, relieving a battalion of York and Lancasters and one company of the Twenty-Ninth. Between Deulemont and Warneton patrols were active, but

The Durham Forces in the Field

could not find a bridge over the River Lys. Germans were seen in some strength on the east bank, but on October 6th the line was handed over to the 12th Royal Scots Fusiliers and ten days of training in divisional reserve followed. When, on the 16th, the battalion moved up again and crossed the Lys by a single duckboard bridge north of Deulemont, the British line had passed far ahead. On the morning of October 18th the battalion were advancing over undevastated country and at mid-day halted at the village of Bondues, on the Lille-Tourcoing road, where the delighted inhabitants gave them a hearty welcome. The night was spent in Tourcoing and next day the march was through Roubaix to Lannoy, during which the enthusiasm of the people reached its height. Refreshments of all kinds and little presents were pressed upon the men and the billets at Lannoy were luxurious.

On October 20th the Eighteenth moved up to Leers Nord, another battalion of the brigade now holding the front, which was west of the river Scheldt (Escaut). Leers Nord was found to be within range of the German shrapnel, but company training was carried on here. Lieut.-Col. F. Walton, M.C., from the 1/6th Durham Light Infantry, arrived on October 22nd to take temporary command. On October 26th the battalion went back to Mouscron—which is north-east of Tourcoing and just inside the Belgian border—and two days later to Steenbrugge. On November 3rd the Eighteenth moved west to continue training at Roncq in divisional reserve. By the time that the battalion came up to Märcke on the 8th there was much talk of the coming Armistice. Next day they marched forward to Sweveghem, the division having taken over a sector further north. It was intended that the Eighteenth should participate in an attack across the Scheldt to capture the wooded high ground beyond Ruyen; but the Germans had retired and the battalion waited on the west bank of the river while the engineers constructed a duckboard bridge. The night was spent at Ruyen and the 92nd Brigade were still ahead when, at 10 A.M. on November 11th, the

The Last Campaign, 1918

Eighteenth resumed their march. The transport had crossed the river by pontoon bridge at daybreak and followed in rear of the battalion. There was another warm welcome for the Durhams at Renaix, where the news of the coming Armistice had been received with deep thankfulness.

On the morning of the fateful November 11th the Eighteenth moved east about four miles to the village of Quesnau.

The Nineteenth marched northward from Lerdeghem to Herzeele on September 2nd and on the 4th when the 35th Division completed the relief of the 30th American Division in the Comines canal sector south of Ypres—the battalion moved to a reserve position east of Poperinghe. It was not till September 12th that the Durhams took over the front line. Next morning at dawn a post under Lance-Corpl. Cranney captured 5 Saxons, 2 of whom were wounded. During the day the Nineteenth moved northwards, so that their left rested on the south edge of Zillebeke Lake.

This marked the extreme left of the divisional line which was advanced 1,000 yards two days later under cover of an effective artillery barrage. On the right of the Nineteenth 2nd Lieut. Reid's platoon went forward. The ground had been patrolled the night before and found clear of Germans, but the enemy had pushed out posts since and these obstinately contested the advance. 2nd Lieut. Reid was hit and was never seen again; the men lost the precise direction, but advanced as far as a ruined building where, with the assistance of the support company, a post was subsequently established. Next in the line were 2nd Lieut. H. Shepley's platoon, who also encountered a strong resistance. After reaching the objective the Durhams were forced back, but afterwards regained the ground and held it. Here most of the casualties occurred and most of the prisoners were taken, many Germans being killed and wounded. 2nd Lieut. Shepley was awarded the Military Cross. Further north Lieut. Dales got his platoon forward without being engaged. On the extreme left 2nd Lieut. G. S. Leach's platoon also carried out the task without hindrance, but this officer then led a small raid which yielded 8 prisoners and two light machine-guns, and won him the Military Cross. The whole affair resulted in 25 Saxons being taken, including those hiding in shell-holes and places where they were afterwards found by patrols. Of the Nineteenth 4 men were killed and 12 wounded.

The battalion were relieved on the 16th and came into the line again eight days later, under a heavy barrage which caused some casualties.

Then, on September 28th, British, French and Belgians began to roll back the German armies in Flanders. At 5.25 a.m. there opened an intense bombardment of the enemy positions and five minutes later the infantry advanced. The Nineteenth were on the left of the 18th Lancashire Fusiliers, the 104th Brigade being in the centre of the divisional line. The German barrage was not heavy and the Durhams having taken the tortured mass of earth still called Hill 60, swept on, while Bavarians came forward through the mist and smoke to surrender. At Klein Zillebeke C.-S.-M. W. G. Walker, of Salford, won the Distinguished Conduct Medal by disposing of some German snipers. The ridge was won but 2nd Lieut. F. W. Blake, who had been partially gassed before the fight began, pushed forward with patrols beyond the objective, capturing a machine-gun and still more prisoners. He won the Military Cross.

The 17th Lancashire Fusiliers came through at a quarter to ten in the morning, and had to carry on the attack without artillery support, as it was impossible to get the guns forward quickly enough through the mud. The Fusiliers were checked on Basseville Beek by machine-gun fire from the rise on which the remains of the village of Zandvoorde stood. Here the line remained for the night, rations, water and ammunition being brought up by pack animals. The Nineteenth had suffered little and many prisoners and field guns, trench-mortars and machine-guns of light and heavy calibre, large quantities of ammu-

The Last Campaign, 1918

nition, signalling gear, range finders and a searchlight were among their trophies of the day.

Zandvoorde fell to the 105th Brigade on the afternoon of September 29th and the Nineteenth took over positions on the ridge near the village in the evening. Capt. E. A. Parke, who accomplished fine work as adjutant during these days, and Lieut. J. Sharp, a company commander whose gallantry and initiative were very marked, were each awarded the Military Cross.

The 104th Brigade took up the advance on the evening of September 30th. The Nineteenth marched through Tenebrielen and deployed at America cabaret, half-way between Wervicq and the Menin road. With the 18th Lancashire Fusiliers on the right, they advanced to pierce the strong and well-defended switch line running north-east to Gheluwe, on the Menin road, but uncut wire and machine-guns held up both battalions soon after the start. Darkness fell and Lancashires and Durhams stayed where they were for the night.

At dawn another attempt was made, but the Germans, in "pill-boxes" and behind stoutly wired defences, were too strong. All that could be done was to throw forward little groups of men to establish advanced posts and thus about 200 yards were gained.

The German shell fire grew worse now and increased to a heavy bombardment when the Nineteenth were relieved by the 17th Lancashire Fusiliers in the evening. By October 3rd the Durhams had reached Zillebeke to rest and refit. Since the beginning of the operations 2 officers had been wounded, and losses in the ranks amounted to 141. Sergt. R. Stoddart, of Medowsley, had commanded a platoon with marked ability since the first attack. He accounted for one German machine-gun detachment single-handed and on another occasion helped to get in the wounded under heavy shell fire. For this good work he received the Distinguished Conduct Medal.

On October 5th the 104th Brigade relieved troops of the 36th Division in front of Terhand, but the Nineteenth, being reserve battalion, were only required to

The Durham Forces in the Field

move W and X companies up to the vicinity of Becelaere. On the 11th the battalion concentrated here on their way up for the next attack and, while reconnoitring the ground next day, Capt. K. Smith was wounded.

The 104th Brigade assembled near the road running northward to Roiders from Menin on the night of the 13th and were shelled next morning before the attack was launched. Advancing behind a creeping barrage, the 17th Lancashire Fusiliers led the way until a line running south from Moorzeele was reached. Then the Nineteenth and 18th Lancashire Fusiliers came through on the left and right respectively to take the high ground south of Gulleghem which overlooked the crossings of the river Lys. The morning was fine, but the troops had to advance in a thick fog which made it difficult to keep direction. X and Y companies led the Nineteenth and, in the face of considerable shell and machine-gun fire, the objective was reached on the line of the hamlets Poeselhoek, Schoon Water and Kappelhoek, where a few Belgian inhabitants were found. 2nd Lieut. H. Chadwick, who commanded one of the support platoons, led his men forward with great dash through a hostile barrage and reinforced the line where men were badly needed. He received the Military Cross. Sergt. J. R. Robertson, M.M., of Trimdon Colliery, distinguished himself on this day by leading an attack upon a troublesome machine-gun and sniper's post. Though the Durham men were greatly outnumbered, the machine-gun and 3 Germans were captured and the remainder put to flight, the sergeant winning the Distinguished Conduct Medal. In this advance many abandoned field guns were found, together with some transport and machine-guns uncountable. The Nineteenth lost 2nd Lieut. H. W. Jordan, M.C., Lieut. H. W. Dales, and the chaplain, Capt. A. H. Streeten, wounded, and casualties in the ranks amounted to 90 in all.

The line was now consolidated, and strong patrols went forward in the direction of Bisseghem. Next morning another little advance took piece in order to make good the spurs south-east of Poeselhoek and

The Last Campaign, 1918

Schoon Water. Sergt. R. Stoddart, D.C.M., always a doughty fighter, led an attack on two farms and carried them. He had been chiefly responsible for the capture of three troublesome machine-guns during the previous day's advance and now retired severely wounded, having won a bar to his decoration.

On the morning of October 16th the 106th Brigade came through and advanced the line to the western bank of the Lys river by clearing Bisseghem of the enemy. The 104th Brigade came forward again on October 18th. On that night the 106th made good the crossings of the Lys and established posts 1,000 yards beyond the river. At 11 p.m. pontoon bridges were in position and the Nineteenth crossed with the rest of the 104th Brigade and assembled in order to attack at dawn. At 5.30 a.m., in thick mist, all three battalions went forward under the usual creeping barrage, the Nineteenth being on the left. The Durhams reached the Aelbeke-Courtrai road without much opposition and advanced eastward, meeting many French and Belgian civilians. Later, shrapnel and machine-gun fire caused many casualties, but before noon W company had patrols in Courtrai. These were the first British troops to enter the city. Some Germans were taken there but no fighting occurred and later in the day Z company established a post in the Grande Place.

The advance was resumed at 7 a.m. next day towards the ridge south-west of Sweveghem. There was no general artillery preparation, but each battalion had two field guns and some Vickers guns attached. Progress was slow as the gunners had to be called upon to deal with the enemy batteries and with farms which harboured machine-guns. It was half-past six in the evening before the battalion reached its appointed line. On the extreme left Lieut. W. Iley found a row of houses not yet cleared by the troops on that flank of the Nineteenth. He led a successful assault which routed the enemy and made good the line, for which service he received the Military Cross.

Early on October 21st troops of the 41st Division advanced and the battalion soon withdrew to billets at Courtrai to refit.

The Durham Forces in the Field

2nd Lieut. W. E. Lannard, whose task as signalling and intelligence officer during the advance was of peculiar difficulty and danger, was awarded the Military Cross for his good work; 2nd Lieut. James Murray, who had proved himself a company commander of great gallantry and resource, received the same decoration.

While at Courtrai drafts to the number of 183 arrived, and Lieut.-Col. H. R. McCullagh left the battalion for a tour of duty in England. He was succeeded by Major B. C. H. Keenlyside, of the 18th Lancashire Fusiliers.

The British line was now near the river Scheldt and the Nineteenth came in north of Avelghem on the evening of October 29th. They were on the right when the advance was resumed in the early morning of October 31st. Some 6-inch howitzers had been brought up to Avelghem, and opened fire at the German positions on the east bank of the Scheldt less than a mile away. This close-range bombardment must have been very demoralising, while an effective smoke barrage further assisted the advance of the infantry. Still, there were Germans who fought stoutly before the Nineteenth took Rugge, Trappelstraat, and Wiermaerde. 2nd Lieut. R. Wood won the Military Cross for heading a determined rush under heavy machine-gun and artillery fire on some farm buildings where 30 Germans and three machine-guns were taken. At 8.45 A.M. a fresh barrage came down and the success was exploited to the very bank of the river. Major Keenlyside, though wounded, went on with his men until the final limit of the advance was reached, his courage and devotion gaining him the Military Cross. Lieut. W. R. Brute and 2nd Lieut R. Shield were also wounded on this day, 2nd Lieut. F. W. Blake, M.C., was killed, and casualties in the ranks amounted to 98 killed and wounded. The brigade captured nearly 300 Germans, including 6 officers, and several field guns, fifty-eight machine-guns, nine trench mortars and two ambulance cars full of enemy wounded.

The task of the Nineteenth was now nearly ended. On November 1st the battalion were relieved by part of the Twentieth and some of the Queen's and withdrew

The Last Campaign, 1918

to Sweveghem and then to Courtrai. Lieut.-Col. W. Rigby, D.S.O., Royal Irish Rifles, assumed command on November 3rd.

The brigade concentrated at Staceghem, on the canal east of Courtrai, four days later and on November 8th moved off to follow the retiring enemy. The line of the Scheldt had been abandoned by the Germans and the Nineteenth crossed on this day and spent the night at Berchem. The 104th Brigade now led the division and the march was resumed at 7 A.M. on November 10th, by which hour the transport and a field battery had crossed the river. The principal roads were rendered impassable for vehicles by reason of the huge craters of mines blown by the Germans and detours by bad side roads led to further difficulties; but good progress was eventually made.

At Louise-Marie the troops were received with joy and thankfulness. Before evening the 18th Lancashire Fusiliers occupied an outpost line well beyond that village, which held the Nineteenth and the rest of the brigade. The cyclists, who led the advance, had encountered a few German horsemen, but there had been no fighting.

The line of the River Dendre was ordered to be secured before the cessation of hostilities on November 11th and the march was therefore resumed in the morning. Cyclists held the bridge-head at Grammont before 11 A.M. and at that hour were beginning to get into touch with the enemy. The infantry arrived later and the Nineteenth went into billets at Everbecq.

R.-S.-M. W. C. Mason, of Shildon, a veteran with a record of almost continuous active service since August, 1914, was afterwards awarded the Distinguished Conduct Medal. On many occasions he had displayed great gallantry under fire and was a pattern of all the soldierly virtues.

On the Kemmel front the Germans withdrew on August 30th and by 7 o'clock next evening our patrols were on the Vierstraat switch line between Kemmel village and Neuve Eglise. As support battalion the Twentieth were not engaged, but they relieved the

The Durham Forces in the Field

1 105th Americans in the switch line north of Vierstraat on the night of September 2nd, Lieut. G. H. Johnson and two others being wounded in the process. The Americans had little idea of the enemy's dispositions, but in the early morning of September 4th the Twentieth had to take part in an attack which was intended to reach the Wytschaete-Voormezeele road. There was no time for a proper reconnaissance and the

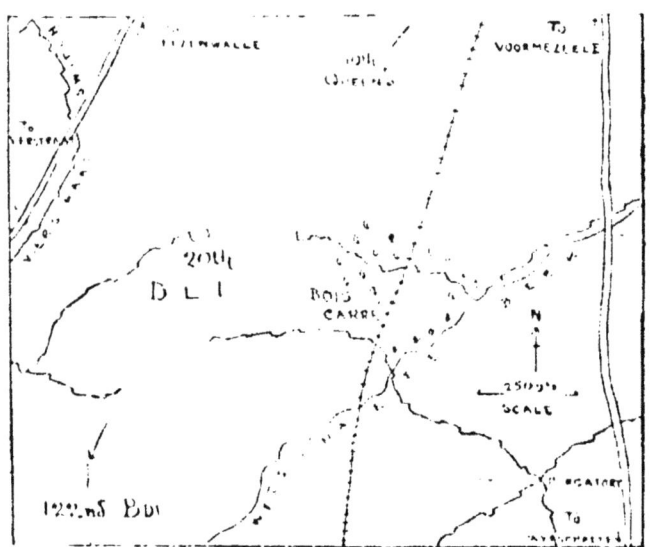

battalion were further handicapped by a delay in the issue of orders. A preliminary bombardment had been dispensed with and the two assault companies of the Wearsiders were forming up west of the light railway when the shrapnel and machine-gun barrage came down.

In the hurried advance which followed the right company swung too much to the south and suffered heavily from enfilade fire on their left flank. All the officers and most of the N.C.O.s had been killed or wounded when the Germans delivered a counter-attack

The Last Campaign, 1918

and Sergt. H. Ebbs, of King's Lynn, who reorganised the company, was obliged to conduct a retirement across the railway. 2nd Lieut. F. Wood brought up two platoons of the company in support and succeeded in carrying the line forward again, though losses were severe. The men hung on doggedly in shell holes between the railway and the trench junction called Purgatory. Here 15 Germans were taken before orders came to withdraw.

Meanwhile Capt. N. W. Turnbull had got forward rapidly with the left company but was not in touch with the Queen's on that flank. The Germans counter-attacked down a trench with bombs and a withdrawal became necessary, but the support company pushed up reinforcements so that a defensive flank could be formed through Bois Carré to the railway. Hostile machine-gun fire was so deadly that nothing more could be done.

On the right flank no touch could be obtained with the 122nd Brigade and another advance about 9 a.m. by two platoons of the reserve company failed to cross the railway.

In this action 2nd Lieuts. E. Russell and J. S. Wails were killed, and Capt. W. R. Eppstein was mortally wounded; 2nd Lieut. P. T. Conrath was wounded and missing; Lieut.-Col. A. V. A. Gayer, D.S.O., was partially gassed; and 2nd Lieuts. T. H. Bassett, C. G. Lowell, W. R. Maclaren, and Lieut. F. Brunt were all wounded. Losses in the ranks amounted to 124.

Capt. N. W. Turnbull and 2nd Lieut. F. Wood were awarded the Military Cross. The Distinguished Conduct Medal was won by Sergt. Ebbs and also by Sergt. J. W. Sherriff, of Elamo Lane, for his work as platoon commander. Corpl. J. G. Wilkinson, of Bishop Auckland, who got a Lewis gun into action at a critical time and continued to fight it till both his legs were broken, received the same decoration.

Major C. Pannall, M.C., now assumed command of the Twentieth, who were relieved at night and moved back to Dickebusch. Training was interrupted here by bad weather and working parties on the Vierstraat switch line suffered nightly from gas shelling. On September 15th the Wearsiders withdrew to Lumbres

The Durham Forces in the Field

and afterwards to Bonnigues, near the forest of Tournehem, for musketry and tactical training. They came forward again in time for the great advance of September 28th, when the 124th Brigade attacked with the 26th Royal Fusiliers and the 10th Queen's. A, B, and C companies of the Twentieth had to guard the right flank of the advance along the Comines canal to Kortewilde. All went well in spite of the bad weather and though 2nd Lieut. Lax was gassed the Wearsiders had few casualties.

The next stage included the capture of the ground south of Kortewilde, in conjunction with which Houthem was to be taken and the crossing over the canal made good. All this was done next morning when D company of the Twentieth cleared the Germans from Houthem taking 30 prisoners, ten machine-guns and a quantity of stores. There were some casualties, including Capt. A. I. Browne killed and 2nd Lieut. Parker wounded. On this day the Nineteenth were on Zandvoorde ridge, not far to the north.

On September 30th the 124th Brigade continued the advance to a line west of the Comines and Wervicq railway. The Twentieth were still in support, but C company moved up on the right to a position near Hospital Farm, west of the canal. Losses were slight, but the rain made the advance a trying one. The brigade were now well forward of the troops on either flank and there was no move on the following day. On October 2nd the advance of the 41st Division was directed due eastwards, the other brigades attacking the German line south of the Menin road. This was the Gheluwe switch, which the Nineteenth had already failed to carry, and progress was still slow. The Wearsiders did not come into action, but had Lieuts. G. Atkinson and Blair wounded by shell fire and 4 casualties in the ranks.

In the evening of the next day they relieved the 1st K.O.S.B. of the 29th Division at Gheluwe and handed over to a battalion of the 34th Division in the early hours of the 5th. The battalion were now due to leave the line and they reached billets near Abeele on October 8th, where training for the next attack was

352

The Last Campaign, 1918

carefully carried out over the country towards Poperinghe. On October 13th the Twentieth came up by light railway and bivouacked at Clapham Junction on the Menin road; at 11 p.m. they began to assemble on tapes laid by an advanced party. The attack was to move forward north of Menin until the line of knolls to the north-east of that town was reached and taken. This position was a continuation of that carried on the same day by the Nineteenth and the rest of the 104th Brigade operating on the left of the 41st Division.

The 124th Brigade had the Twentieth on the right and the Fusiliers on the left, the Queen's being in support. Until the second lift of the barrage the 122nd Brigade led the attack; then the 124th were to go through. There was a thick mist at 5.35 a.m. on October 13th when the infantry advanced. The enemy put down a barrage which contained much smoke so that it was extremely difficult to maintain touch and direction, but section commanders got their men on in excellent style, though for a time one could not see more than five yards ahead. When the Durhams and Fusiliers took the lead soon after 8 o'clock heavy machine-gun fire from farm buildings and German field guns firing over open sights at point-blank range hindered the advance. But the two eighteen-pounders attached to each battalion dealt with the German gunners and the farms were gradually outflanked. Progress became much quicker as the mist cleared and D company then had to extend the line on the right of C company. At about 11 a.m., under the personal direction of Major C. Pannall, M.C., this operation, involving a fresh attack, was successfully carried out and by 4 p.m. the whole of the objectives had been taken, the enemy leaving nine field guns and three howitzers in this part of the field. While the battalion dug in patrols pushed forward over the Courtrai road towards the river Lys, 2nd Lieut. F. B. Davison accomplishing daring and effective work.

Next morning B company came forward and cleared the ground in front, despite considerable machine-gun fire. This operation, in which 2nd Lieut. Davison was again to the fore, made good the west bank of the Lys as far as Wevelghem on the left.

The Durham Forces in the Field

The Twentieth were withdrawn from the line in the evening of October 15th, having lost Capt. F. Brant, Lieut. G. Goodley, and 2nd Lieut. W. J. Scott, all wounded, and 2nd Lieut. J. Foster who died of his wounds. Casualties in the ranks amounted to 71 wounded. Major Pannall was awarded the Distinguished Service Order and 2nd Lieut. Davison the Military Cross; Lieut. L. W. Shepherdson, M.C., who had done particularly good and gallant service as signalling officer, added a bar to his decoration.

While the battalion rested in farms between Moorzeele and Gulleghem the 123rd Brigade carried on the advance across the Lys. When the Wearsiders marched on October 20th through Gulleghem to Märcke and on to Marionetteberg it was to assist in taking forward the British line to the left bank of the Scheldt.

Early on the morning of the 21st the Wearsiders were in position on the road leading from Belleghem to Sweveghem with the right of the battalion on the main road near Belleghem; on the left were the 10th Queen's, the Fusiliers being in support. The advance was to be south-eastward from the line reached by the 35th Division. There was no barrage, but a section of eighteen-pounders, two Vickers guns and two Stokes mortars accompanied each attacking battalion. The showery weather made heavy-going across the ploughed fields, but the Durhams on the right met with no opposition till after the hamlet of Brockenhock was reached. Then heavy machine-gun and artillery fire brought the British gunners into action, but the Wearsiders, whose losses were very small, took Bavegeiknok and crossed the railway.

This last advance linked up with the troops on the right, but on the left the Queen's had had trouble in negotiating the Courtrai-Bossuyt canal. The bridges and locks of this waterway had been destroyed by the enemy, who put up a stout resistance at the railway tunnel. The Fusiliers were put in on the right of the Queen's, but there was still a large gap on the left of the Twentieth, so Major Pannall moved A company forward and assisted in closing the line, Fusiliers and

The Last Campaign, 1918

Durhams establishing posts on the left defensive flank west of the canal. The advance had only cost the Twentieth 2 men wounded, but heavy shell fire now did considerable damage, D company being troubled by a trench mortar in the wooded grounds of the château at Bossuyt just in front of their position. Before the end of the day 2nd Lieut. J. W. Armstrong and 2 men had been killed and 2nd Lieuts. J. Wood and S. W. Warwick and 45 others wounded.

During the two following days, while the other battalions of the brigade strove to get forward on the left, the Twentieth improved their positions and pushed out patrols to locate the enemy posts for the benefit of the British gunners. On the night of October 23rd the 1/7th Cheshires came up in relief and the battalion moved back for a day's rest. The 124th Brigade then took over a portion of the line to the north, relieving troops of the 29th Division, and in the early morning of the 25th the Twentieth relieved the 10th Queen's on the right of the line, which ran along the western slopes of the ridge near the hamlet of Kattestraet. On the crest were the Germans, who had to be driven off and followed eastwards down to Avelghem and the western bank of the Scheldt. Four minutes before 9 A.M. the British barrage came down almost on the front line in order to deal with any German posts which might have been thrust forward. The enemy retaliated with a counter-barrage which caused many casualties before the attack was fairly started. There was stubborn fighting on this day: every farm contained machine-gunners and the slow progress of the troops on the right of the Twentieth brought galling enfilade fire from that flank. When the advance had reached the vicinity of Vierkeerhoek losses were so heavy that A and B companies were replaced by C and D companies from the support line. The Twentieth were then able to get on down hill till the hamlets of Driesch and Bosch were reached, but the enemy resistance did not weaken and the line remained here for the night. The Wearsiders had lost 2nd Lieuts. W. Hebron and D. Lax and 22 men killed, while Capt. R. Wilkinson, 2nd Lieuts. J. Appleton, F. Wood, and J. Donnelly, M.C., D.M., M.M., and 111 others were

The Durham Forces in the Field

wounded. The Queen's came up on either flank to strengthen the line.

During the night patrols pushed forward on the left and the attack was resumed next morning. Belgian civilians reported that the enemy was retiring and at 10 A.M. a patrol entered Avelghem. By the afternoon the Twentieth were holding the Tournai-Audenarde road with the right on Avelghem. When the Queen's came up at night to take over, patrols had pushed on almost as far as Rugge which eventually fell to the Nineteenth some days later.

The remainder of the month was spent on the southern outskirts of Courtrai, which was not badly damaged though all bridges across the Lys had been destroyed. Some shops were open and a German cinema hall, abandoned intact, was used for the entertainment of the troops. On November 1st the battalion took over a portion of the line on the left bank of the Scheldt, near Kerkhove, among the troops relieved being two companies of the Nineteenth. On the way Lieut.-Col. A. V. A. Gayer, D.S.O., arrived from England and resumed command.

The 41st (French) Division were found to be on the left in front of Elseghem. On the night of the 2nd a patrol of the Wearsiders succeeded in crossing the Scheldt by a broken bridge: it was not an easy passage, and the patrol had to be withdrawn at daylight, but it is believed that these were the first British troops to cross the river. The enemy was not very active during these days, but at dawn and dusk he put down a barrage on the Tournai-Audenarde road and drenched the surrounding country with mustard gas and tear shells. On the night of the 4th the Twentieth, having lost 4 killed and 15 wounded, were relieved and spent several days in reorganising and also practising for an attack which was to force the passage of the Scheldt.

At 3 A.M. on November 9th came the news that the Germans had retired from the river and the battalion moved forward to Meersche, crossing the Scheldt by a foot-bridge at Kerkhove while the transport used a pontoon bridge near by. Next day the march was resumed, but a delay was caused by a crater in the road

The Last Campaign, 1918

which necessitated a detour. The night was spent at Schoorisse, where French troops were already talking of the Armistice. On the morning of November 11th C and D companies acted as advance guard, the brigade having passed through the 123rd Brigade. At about 9.30 a.m. Colonel Gayer announced that an Armistice had been signed and came into force at eleven o'clock. When hostilities ceased the Twentieth were about a mile and a quarter west of Nederbraket and the march was continued through this little town to billets beyond.

The Twenty-Ninth continued to provide working parties for the Ypres defences until September 5th, when they moved back by light railway to the vicinity of Poperinghe. Training continued here, and working parties were still required, but on the 13th the battalion took over a sector of the Ypres defences south of the Menin road. Energetic patrolling was necessary as the Germans were suspected to be about to retire.

At dawn on the 17th patrols of the battalion got into touch with several enemy posts and were forced to withdraw under close machine-gun fire and a bombing attack; but 2nd Lieut. A. Dean handled his men well and got in with only 6 casualties, bringing back all the wounded. This officer received the Military Cross and Lance-Corpl. A. Woombs and Pte. H. Birch the Military Medal. At about the same time a covering party, in a moment of enthusiasm, tried to rush a hostile post, but the enterprise failed and several men did not return.

On the night of September 19th the Twenty-Ninth moved back to continue training at Winnizeele, northeast of Cassel. About a week later came a move to Reninghelst, where the Durhams were in reserve when the 14th Division attacked south of Ypres on the opening day of the final advance. On October 1st the Twenty-Ninth moved up to take over the line east of Messines ridge and running roughly north-east from Warneton. The battalion had a long and tiring march over bad roads much congested with traffic and the transport, by some mistake, was sent forward to the eastern slopes of the ridge, where it came under the German harassing fire. The enemy artillery shelled the forward area in this part of the line unceasingly, having excellent observation posts in the churches of Wervicq and Comines. In spite of this and of the mud the Twenty-Ninth settled in and strove to improve the trenches. Patrols were active and the line of forward posts gained ground, although the enemy was on the alert.

On October 4th 2nd Lieut. W. Thompson made a daring reconnaissance to the banks of the Lys, near Warneton. Under machine-gun fire the whole time, he brought in his patrol safely and delivered a valuable report. 2nd Lieut. C. A. Carter did similar good work, shooting a German and bringing in important identifications. Both these officers received the Military Cross. On October 5th two sections of No. 8 platoon were blown up in a dug-out, presumably by a delayed action mine, and 17 men were killed. The battalion were relieved that night and spent four days in support positions, still living in the mud under the heavy fire of the enemy.

On October 10th, when the Twenty-Ninth came forward again, fires in Wervicq and the random shooting of his artillery pointed to the retirement of the enemy. Patrols were pushed out at once, but found the Germans on the alert. Many machine-guns and trench mortars were discovered in position on the north outskirts of Comines and west of the town a post of the Twenty-Ninth was rushed and captured by the enemy in the mist soon after daybreak on the 12th.

On October 14th the 30th Division on the left attacked, the Twenty-Ninth—now very tired and dirty, but still keen—being ordered to send patrols across the Lys if the enemy opposition weakened. At 9.30 A.M. the Germans were still holding farms on the right bank of the river south-west of Comines. Later in the morning the troops of the 30th Division reached Wervicq and patrols of the Twenty-Ninth made for the river at a point north-east of Comines, and also further east near Godshuis. These patrols reached the river bank un-

The Last Campaign, 1918

molested, and inspected the broken bridges. Hostile shelling and machine-gun fire, active the day before, had practically ceased and it appeared as though the enemy had withdrawn from the town. To verify this it was necessary for the sappers to bridge the river so that patrols could cross. Colonel Ridley got the trench mortars to open on the wire which could be seen on the right bank and, after an hour's bombardment, patrols, preceded by scouts, approached the remains of the railway bridge opposite the distillery and also the broken bridge at Codshuis. At the latter place the ground gave no cover and the crossing had to take place in full view of the enemy, if he were still there. A Lewis gun team on the north bank covered the sappers, who came down and commenced to erect a single duckboard bridge thirty inches wide. Before the engineers had completed their task the Lewis gunners crossed the river, but as they established themselves on the south bank heavy machine-gun fire opened from the front and both flanks. Yet two more sections were passed over and another platoon were ready to follow. It was about 2 P.M. when heavy artillery fire opened on the place of crossing, which was then shelled unceasingly for three hours. The Lewis guns of the Twenty-Ninth replied valiantly, but no more men crossed the river. Eventually all troops had to be withdrawn under shelter of the houses on the north bank of the Lys and by his gallant work in assisting to cover the retirement Pte. W. Allen, of Desford, won the Distinguished Conduct Medal. The new bridge stood, still undamaged by the enemy shells.

At the bridge by the distillery two Lewis guns covered the operations of the sappers by fire from the railway embankment north of the river. Casualties here became heavy as the German fire increased during the afternoon and 2nd Lieut. C. A. Carter, who led his platoon very gallantly, was killed. At half-past three operations were suspended, with the bridge not quite completed.

No further attempt to cross the Lys was made that night, but a patrol reached the island formed by the Norte-Lys channel and the river, and sustained several

The Durham Forces in the Field

casualties from German machine-guns, including 2nd Lieut. A. Dean, M.C., who was killed.

It was not till 3 A.M. on October 15th that the German fire slackened. The Twenty-Ninth had orders to advance at 5.30 A.M., a difficult task as matters stood for there was only the Godshuis bridge available. The reserve company and two platoons of the left company were to cross here and advance south-eastwards behind a barrage. Another platoon were to make the passage at the railway bridge, while an advance over Norte-Lys was to endeavour to clear the German machine-gunners from the houses on that side of the town.

But the enemy had withdrawn and by 11 A.M. the tired Twenty-Ninth occupied the line of the railway south of Comines and the road to Wervicq-Sud on the left. The troops on the flank were not yet over the river and so further advance was delayed until the 33rd Londons got forward on the right and the 30th Division followed suit on the left. The battalion line was then adjusted accordingly. In the evening the 16th Manchesters relieved the Twenty-Ninth, who were taken back by bus as far as Wulverghem, where wet weather made a morass of the camp and living under canvas was very uncomfortable. The Twenty-Ninth had had more than a fortnight of digging, patrolling, fighting and advancing in mud and bad weather, mostly under heavy fire. Colonel Ridley, M.C., who had been a great source of inspiration to his tired men and had handled the situation with great skill on October 14th, was awarded the Distinguished Service Order; 2nd Lieut. C. J. Jeffrey, a company commander who did particularly well on that day, received the Military Cross.

On October 18th the Twenty-Ninth came up by lorry to billet in Hazebrouck factory. On the next day, when patrols of the Ninteenth entered Courtrai, the Twenty-Ninth moved up to Roncq.

The next ten days were spent in training at Luinghe, near Mouscron, whose inhabitants proved to be very hospitable. On October 31st the 41st Brigade took over the line and the Twenty-Ninth moved to brigade reserve at Dottignies. The enemy shelled the eastern side of

The Last Campaign, 1918

this village and on the night of November 2nd D company lost 3 killed and 3 wounded in billets. Three days later the battalion took over a portion of the front on the west bank of the river Scheldt, near Helchin. After three days spent in rain and mud under considerable shell fire the Durhams were relieved and moved to Herseaux, near the French border, where news of the Armistice reached them.

THE VICTORY IN ITALY, 1918

Early in October, 1918, the Italian *Comando Supremo* began to contemplate an offensive and a general plan of attack was soon decided upon. General the Earl of Cavan was offered the command of a mixed Italian-British army, with which it was intended to force the line of the Piave river. The advance was then to continue to the Livenza, where a defensive flank would be formed to protect the Italian Eighth and Twelfth Armies as they drove northward. At the same time an offensive was to be undertaken both in the Mount Grappa and in the Asiago sectors.

The Twelfth moved to Arzignano on October 6th and continued training there till the 14th, when they entrained at Vicenza for Mestre and reached billets at Mirano that evening. The 7th and 23rd Divisions were now concentrating in the vicinity of Treviso for the coming operations. On October 22nd the Twelfth reached Treviso and marched northward to Catena next day.

The British troops were to force the Piave almost due east of Spresiano, where the river bed was over a mile wide and contained many islands. The chief of these, the Gravi di Papadopoli, was beyond the main channel and was held as an advanced position by the Austrians. Papadopoli was taken by troops of the 7th Division on the nights of October 23rd and 24th—a brilliant operation, in which the assistance of the Italian boat men was invaluable.

On the night of October 24th the Twelfth moved up towards the river and bivouacked in fields, hedges being used, as far as possible, to conceal the troops from aerial observation. Next day Major E. Borrow, D.S.O., went forward with a small party to locate the place for the passage of the Piave and the first assembly point for the battalion. Rain fell in torrents during this reconnais-

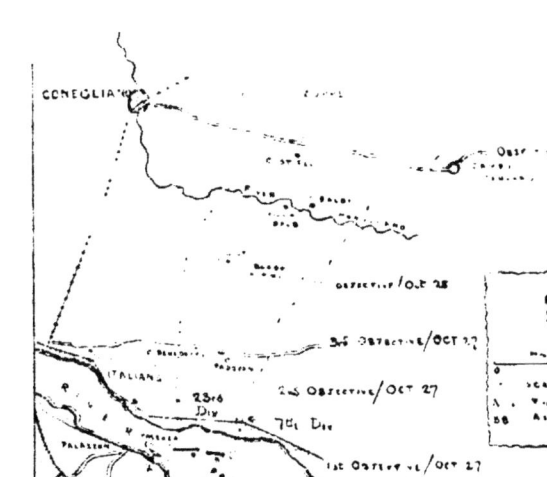

The Durham Forces in the Field

sance. In the evening the Twelfth were guided to the point of passage, only to find that the river had risen so much that the operations were postponed. The Durhams returned whence they came and waited during the following day.

No bridges were yet in position from the right bank of the Piave to Papadopoli—the current was too strong—but in the evening of the 26th a foot-bridge was constructed on the left, where the 68th Brigade were to cross. This afforded passage to Cosenza island over one deep stream, but another, equally unfordable, had to be crossed by boats before Papadopoli was reached. All the attacking British troops used this route on the night of October 26th, though other bridges were ready for use soon afterwards.

The Twelfth despatched a good deal at their assembly position on the south bank and Major Borrow took his party ahead as before to receive the battalion and to indicate their forming-up place on the island. The Austrian fire was very heavy, shrapnel and 8-inch and 11-inch shells falling near the crossings, but all went well. Two battalions made the passage before the turn of the Durhams came and at 11.30 p.m., when the Allied bombardment opened, not one of the Twelfth had arrived on the island. At two o'clock on the morning of the 27th Colonel Holford appeared at the head of two companies and the others followed an hour later.

The 23rd Division were on the left of the 7th and the 68th Brigade formed the extreme left of the British line with the 11th N.F. on that flank and the Twelfth next. The 10th N.F. had to form a defensive flank as the advance proceeded.

By 3.30 a.m. the infantry were ready. They had to cross several streams, which it was hoped were fordable, and then attack an earthen bund, in some places as much as 12 feet high, which rose steeply from the river bed and was defended by uncut wire and machine-gun posts. The creeping barrage came down at 6.45 a.m. and the Durhams went forward. While wading through the water machine-gun fire killed and wounded half the leading company, who then arrived before the Austrian

GENERAL VIEW OF THE PIAVE

THE MONTICANO RIVER

The Victory in Italy, 1918

wire. Capt. Charles Gibbens, M.C., D.C.M., headed a party who cut a passage through, but all the men were killed and he was wounded. Pte. G. Brown and Sergt. O'Hara lent gallant assistance and C company were masters of the first objective soon after half-past seven. D company passed through and advanced over fairly open ground towards the next position. The enemy infantry showed little spirit, but his machine-gunners were of sterner stuff and fought skilfully in their concrete posts till rushed or surrounded. The second objective was won before 9 A.M. and A and B companies pushed on towards the next position, the road between C. Padovan and C. Benedetti. This cultivated country —enclosed land with hedges and buildings—was all in favour of the defence, but the skilled fighters of the Twelfth would not be denied. A and B companies reached their goal before eleven o'clock and consolidated the position. On the right the Durhams were in touch with the 69th Brigade and in the afternoon they took over part of the line of the 11th N.F. on the left. This success had cost the Twelfth 2nd Lieuts. J. Hodgson and Fisher and 27 men killed; Capt. C. Gibbens, M.C., D.C.M., 2nd Lieuts. Smith and Wade and 111 others wounded; and 11 missing. Major H. St. J. Carr West, serving with the 69th Brigade, was killed while rallying troops on the right of the Twelfth. Several hundred prisoners were taken by the battalion and many machine-guns, together with three guns of heavy calibre, two heavy trench mortars, and two tank guns. The plight of the wounded—carried back across the fiercely shelled Piave by Austrian prisoners who, from sheer fright, sometimes dropped the stretchers into the swift-flowing current—was not enviable.

The advance was resumed at 12.30 P.M. next morning, when the 10th N.F. had gone in on the left of the Durhams. Some of the Austrian rearguards fought obstinately and machine-gun nests were always a trouble, one party of the Twelfth capturing a strong point after a fight which lasted three-quarters of an hour. Here 40 Austrians were taken and three anti-aircraft guns. The desired objective, Borgo Pin to C. Guiot, was reached and held by C and D companies, who established an outpost line, and casualties only amounted to 3 killed and 30 wounded on this day.

At midnight A company, under Lieut. Wiley, with a mobile 6-inch trench mortar section, pushed out and seized a crossing over the Monticano river, north-east of Mareno, a difficult and dangerous piece of work which helped the advance considerably next day.

The objective on October 29th was the Conegliano-Campo Cervaro road. Starting at 8.30 A.M. rapid progress was made at first, but the country was difficult and direction hard to maintain. The Austrians were strongly posted on the far bank of the Monticano and it was not till 1 P.M. that A company, supported by two platoons of C company, forced a passage near C. Balbi. Further to the left D company and the remainder of C company were still held up near Villa Balbi, so B company were ordered to follow A, change front, and clear the north bank from the right. This operation was not successful until the arrival on that flank of the 11th N.F., now commanded by Major Borrow, who had succeeded Lieut.-Col. St. Hill, in action. Every farmhouse, hedge and ditch held some of the enemy and progress was still slow, but the whole brigade front was cleared by 6.30 P.M. The Italian inhabitants rushed forth from the houses to welcome the British troops.

A company and the two platoons of C company had pushed ahead and reached the battalion objective. They numbered less than 120 bayonets, and were completely isolated. Attacked by greatly superior numbers they fell back 300 yards, when the battalion headquarters came up on the left and were forced to withdraw again under close-range machine-gun fire. But B company were now in touch and when darkness fell about 6 P.M. a line was established about 200 yards short of the objective. Here C and D companies came into position. Casualties on this day numbered 28, Lieut. W. N. Blenkinsop being fatally wounded. The enemy machine-gunners had again fought well; one gun was discovered with four Austrian officers lying dead around it.

By 3.30 A.M. on October 30th the whole of the Twelfth were in position close to the Conegliano-Campo

The Victory in Italy, 1918

Cervaro road on which posts were established. So roughly had the Austrians been handled that they withdrew before dawn, abandoning a very strong position and a battery of 5.9 guns. Italian cavalry and cyclists now came through and the 70th Brigade replaced the 68th, who sat down and discussed the rations which had at last arrived. The Twelfth, who had sustained 6 more casualties, now followed the advance by Cse. S. Felice and Zoppe to billets in Orsago, reached at 8 P.M. This was a long, tiring march over bad roads, but no one fell out—a surprising performance when it is remembered that all ranks had been wet through since crossing the Piave, had lain out in the open in the frost and had been fighting for three successive days.

At 10.30 A.M. next day the Twelfth were called upon for a further effort, the 70th Brigade being held up near Sacile. In half an hour the Durhams moved off, but found all opposition had been overcome. They billetted at Sacile and remained there for two days.

In this final victorious advance the Twelfth had captured four 6-inch howitzers, four 5.9 guns, two anti-aircraft guns, two heavy trench mortars, two anti-tank guns, forty-six machine-guns, seven wagons, eighteen horses and 1,020 Austrians, besides vast quantities of stores and ammunition. Many honours were won by the battalion. For his fiery courage, which always led him into the thick of the fight, Lieut.-Col. J. H. E. Holford, D.S.O., added a bar to his Order; Capt. Gibbens, whose prowess has been recorded, received the Distinguished Service Order; Capt. W. L. Hughes, M.C., won a bar to his cross for his fine leadership throughout the advance. He led the final assault on the troublesome strong point captured on October 28th. The Military Cross was conferred upon Capt. John Wilson, who was specially prominent in the first attack across the Piave. Pte. G. Brown, who has already been mentioned, received the Distinguished Conduct Medal, as did Lance-Corpl. G. Nelson, M.M., for gallantry under fire during the critical moments of October 29th. Lance-Corpl. R. Defty, Corpl. W. F. Showell, Pte. W. Lewins, Sergt. W. Littlewood and Sergt. (a C.-S.-M.) W. Monk were each awarded a bar to his Military

The Durham Forces in the Field

Medal. Sergts. A. E. Richardson, G. Ritchie, and J. W. Starkings; Corpls. W. Patterson and S. Parkin; Lance-Corpls. T. Moses, J. McVean, and W. Newman; and Ptes. T. Kisby, N. Maudlin, J. Nichol and S. Gerry won the Military Medal.

The Italian decorations conferred included the Silver Medal for Valour to Colonel Holford and Major Borrow; the Bronze Medal for Valour to Lance-Corpl. G. Nelson, D.C.M., M.M., and the *Croce di Guerra* to Capt. J. Wilson, M.C., 2nd Lieuts. W. T. Colville, and T. Smithson; Major and Qr.-Mr. Clements, O.B.E.; C.-S.-M. W. Woodhead, M.M., and Lance-Corpl. R. Defty, M.M.; and Ptes. S. Gerry, M.M., and N. Maudlin, M.M.

The Twelfth moved from Sacile to Talponedo on November 3rd, and the Armistice with the Austrians came into effect at 3 p.m. on the following day.

CONCLUSION

This record of the Service Battalions of Durham may well conclude at 11 A.M. on November 11th, 1918, when the fighting on the Western Front came to an end. The Armistice proclaimed the complete overthrow of the German armies, which meant that the purpose for which the New Armies had been raised was at last fulfilled. Nearly forty-three months had passed since the Tenth, the first of our Service Battalions, arrived in France; thereafter Durham had sent battalion after battalion into the battle line. Her men had fought, endured, toiled, and died in the long months of monotonous trench warfare; on the battlefields of the Somme, Arras, Ypres and Cambrai; in the German Offensive when their sacrifice averted disaster; and during the final victorious advance.

Their survivors and successors in France and Belgium did not greet the Armistice in the fashion that prevailed at home. They simply saw their arduous task come slowly and surely to an end made possible by the sacrifice of those who went before.

There is no need to follow the Battalions through the succeeding months—during the tedious time of demobilisation when the ranks grew thinner and thinner until at last the cadre of each unit came home as quietly, and almost as secretly, as the original battalion had crossed to France to fight.

An honoured relic of each Service Battalion of the Durham Light Infantry is a Union flag—their King's Colour. On November 11th, 1920—the second anniversary of the granting of the Armistice to Germany the Colours of the Tenth, the Eleventh, the Twelfth, the Thirteenth, the Fourteenth, the Fifteenth, the Twenty-Second, the Twenty-Ninth, the 51st, and the 52nd are being laid up, with due ceremony, in the Chapter House of Durham Cathedral. The Colours of

The Durham Forces in the Field

the Eighteenth and the Nineteenth already hang there; that of the Twentieth is in proud possession of the Parish Church of Bishopwearmouth, Sunderland.

No Service Battalion of Durham were among the troops who marched to the Rhine, but early in January, 1919, the Twentieth went by train to Germany and joined the Army of Occupation. They were afterwards brigaded with the 51st and 52nd Durham Light Infantry, forming the 3rd Northern Brigade of the 3rd Northern Division of the British Army of the Rhine.

The 52nd Durham Light Infantry were at Catterick Camp at the beginning of March, 1919, and entrained on the 2nd for Dover. They crossed next day to Dunkerque and were conveyed by rail to Cologne, which was reached on the 6th. Two days later they took over the military guards of the city, being the first of the young battalions to perform this duty. On March 10th General Plumer inspected the guards, whom he pronounced "very clean, and smart, and soldierly."

The 51st Battalion, travelling by the same route, arrived in Cologne two days after the 52nd and took over the guards from the latter on March 11th. The two battalions and the Twentieth then performed this duty in rotation.

On April 4th Lieut.-Col. J. A. Tupman was succeeded in the command of the 51st by Lieut.-Col. B. J. Curling, D.S.O., and Lieut.-Col. J. B. Muir, D.S.O., commanding the 52nd, was replaced by Lieut.-Col. C. W. Frizell, D.S.O., M.C.

The 53rd Battalion arrived from England on April 9th, but were at once reduced to cadre strength, 13 officers and 217 men joining the 51st and 14 officers and 205 men going to the 52nd Battalion.

These young soldiers who served in the garrison of the occupied territory well maintained the reputation of the British Army in circumstances which could not be otherwise than difficult. Durham has every reason to be proud of them.

SENTRY OF THE 51st DURHAM LIGHT INFANTRY
HOHENZOLLERN BRIDGE, COLOGNE

INDEX

10th (S.) Bn. the Durham Light Infantry

Arras battle, 132, 148
— raid, 106
— sector, 27, 105
Brigade, composition of, 7
Cameron Covert line, 193
Casualties, Arras battle, 133, 134, 149
— Arras raid, 106
— Arras sector, 27, 106
— Cameron Covert line, 193
— Chérisy sector, 167
— Delville Wood, 67, 68, 70, 79
— Gapaard sector, 208
— Goudberg sector, 239
— Gueudecourt, 79, 82
— Hooge, 14-17
— Inverness Copse, 181
— Oct., 1915, to end of, 25
— Pilckem sector, 26
— Wieltje sector, 26
Cavalry at Arras battle, 133
Chérisy sector, 167
Colour, King's, 369
Command and changes in same, 1, 16, 27, 239
Complimented by G.O.C. Bde., 208
— by G.O.C. Div., 240
Delville Wood, 67
Disbandment, 240
Embarkation for France, 14
Farewell of Col. Morant, 240

Formation, 1
France, arrival in, 14
Gapaard sector, 208
German Retreat, 1917, 107
Goudberg sector, 239
Gueudecourt, 79
Honours, Albert Medal, 25
— Arras battle, 134
— Arras raid, 106
— Delville Wood, 69
— Gueudecourt, 82
— Hooge, 15, 17
— Inverness Copse, 181
— Pilckem sector, 26
— various, 26, 27
Hooge, 14-17
Invasion warning, 8
Inverness Copse, 177
Pilckem sector, 26
Raid, Arras, 106
St. Eloi sector, 25
Somme battle, 67, 79
Song on the march, 241
Tanks, 133, 178, 179
Training at home, 7
Trenches, first tour in, 14
Vendeuil sector, 240
Wancourt line, 118
Wieltje sector, 25
Ypres, 3rd battle, 177, 192

11th (S.) Bn. the Durham Light Infantry (Pioneers)

Armistice, 338
Cambrai battle, 218
Carnoy, 108
Casualties, Cambrai battle, 219-223

Casualties (continued)
— German Offensive, March, 1918, 271
— German Retreat, 1917, 150
— Guillemont, 71, 74

Index

11th (S.) Bn. the Durham Light Infantry (Pioneers)
(continued)

Casualties *(continued)*
— Lens, 397
   Lesbœufs, 79
— le Transloy, 92
— Noreuil sector, 150
— Wieltje sector, 29, 107
— Ypres, 3rd battle, 205, 207
Cavalry at Gouzeaucourt, 222
Colour, King's, 369
Command and changes in same, 8, 27, 221, 267, 270, 285, 307
Complimented by G.O.C. Div., 150
D company, German Offensive, March, 1918, 268
Embarkation for France, 17
Fleurbaix sector, 28
Formation, 1
France, embarkation for, 17
Gas attacks, Lens, 307
German Offensive, March, 1918, 264
   Retreat, 1917, 109
Gheluvelt sector, 211
Gouzeaucourt, 221
Guillemont, 71
Ham-Noyon sector, arrival in, 242

Hebuterne sector, 107
Honours, German Offensive, March, 1918, 265, 270, 271
— Italian, 109
— Ypres, 3rd battle, 207
Jee's detachment, German Offensive, March, 1918, 267
Langemarck, 205
Laventie sector, 17, 28
Lens sector, 307, 337
Lesbœufs, 78
le Transloy, 79, 91
Maubeuge, move towards, 338
Mézières, 270
Morval sector, 108
Noreuil sector, 150, 167
Pilckem sector, 28
Pioneers, reorganised as, 8
Reorganised as Pioneers, 8
— in 3 companies, 242
Sailly-Saillisel sector, 109
Somme battle, 70, 78, 91
Tanks, 206, 218, 219, 222
Training at home, 8
Trenches, first tour in, 18
Wieltje sector, 28, 107
Ypres, 3rd battle, 204

12th (S.) Bn. the Durham Light Infantry

Armentières, sector N. of, 110
— sector S. of, 18, 29
Armistice, Austrian, 368
Asiago sector, 252
Austrian Armistice, 368
— Offensive, 253
Bailiff Wood, 54
Brigade, composition of, 9
Calonne sector, 29
Casualties, Armentières, sector N. of, 110
— Armentières, sector S. of, 29
— Austrian Offensive, 256

Casualties *(continued)*
— Bailiff Wood, 54, 57
— Klein Zillebeke raid, 168
— le Sars, 102
— Martinpuich, 90, 91
— Menin Road, 190
— Messines battle, 162, 163
— Piave battle, 365-7
— Pozières, 62
— Rœutel line, 191
— Somme battle (additional), 67, 90
— Zillebeke sector, 111, 152
Colour, King's, 369

Index

12th (S.) Bn. the Durham Light Infantry

Command and changes in same, 9, 30, 111, 209, 252
Complimented by G.O.C. Bde., 63
— by G.O.C. Div., 63
Estaires, 19
Formation, 1
France, arrival in, 18
Ghelpac gorge, 251
Hill 60, 151
Honours, Austrian Offensive, 257
— Bailiff Wood, 56
  French, 111, 152
  Hill 60, 152
  Italian, 368
  K.L. in Zillebeke raid, 168
  le Sars, 103
  Menin Road, 188, 190
- - Messines battle, 163
- Piave battle, 367
- Pozières, 63
- Somme battle (additional), 67, 110
- various, 31, 111, 152, 209
- - Zillebeke sector, 151

Light Infantry (*continued*)

Italy, arrival in, 231
Klein Zillebeke sector, 168
le Sars, 100
Martinpuich, 90
Menin Road, 188
Messines battle, 161
Montello sector, 231-6
Mountains, departure from, 259
  — move to, 259
Piave battle, 362
Pozières, 61
Raid, Klein Zillebeke, 168
Reutel line, 191
Riviera, reception on, 230
Somme battle, 53, 61, 67, 90, 100
Song on the ———h, 211
Souchez sect
Tank, 100
Training at home, 9
Trenches, first tour in, 4
Ypres, 3rd battle of, 188, 191
Zillebeke sector, 119, 151

13th (S.) Bn. the Durham Light Infantry

Armentières, sector N. of, 111
— sector S. of, 18, 31
Armistice, 337
Asiago sector, 252
Austrian Offensive, 253
Bailiff Wood, 57
Beaurevoir Line, 331
Brigade, composition of, 9, 331
Calonne sector, 32
Casualties, Armentières, sector S. of, 18, 31, 32
— Asiago sector, 252
— Austrian Offensive, 256
  Bailiff Wood, 57, 58
— Calonne sector, 32, 33
— German raid near Hill 60, 151

Casualties (*continued*)
— High Wood, 90
  Klein Zillebeke sector, 168
  Last Campaign, 331-3, 335, 336
  le Sars, 103
  March, 1918, total to, 32
  Menin Road, 186, 187
- Messines battle, 164
  Montello sector, 232, 234
  Munster Alley, 64-66
  Pozières, 63
- Reutel line, 195, 196
- Souchez sector, 33
Colour, King's, 369
Command and changes in same, 9, 33, 34, 65, 111, 209, 250, 252, 331, 334, 335

Index

13th (S.) Bn. the Durham Light Infantry *(continued)*

Complimented by artillery, 33rd Div., 188
Estaires, 19
Formation, 1
France, arrival in, 18
— return to, 259
High Wood, 88
Hill 60, German raid, 152
Honnechy, 333
Honours, Armentières, sector S. of, 31, 32
— Austrian Offensive, 257
— Bailiff Wood, 58
— Belgian, 236
— German raid, Hill 60, 153
— High Wood, 89
— Last Campaign, 334-7
— le Sars, 104
— Menin Road, 187, 195, 235
— Messines battle, 165
Munster Alley, 64, 66, 67
Royal Humane Society, 19
Somme battle (additional), 63
Souchez raid, 34
— various, 34, 112, 153, 235
Hunding Stellung, 335
Italy, arrival in, 231
Kenny, Pte. T., V.C., 31

Klein Zillebeke sector, 168
Landrecies, 335
Last Campaign, 334
le Sars, 104
Menin Road, 185
Messines battle, 164
Montello sector, 232
Mountains, move to, 250
Munster Alley, 63, 67
Pozières, 63
Raid, Armentières, 32
— German, Hill 60, 152
— Klein Zillebeke, 168
— Mt. Sorrel, 153
— Souchez, 33
Reorganisation of 25th Div., 331
Reutel line, 195
Riviera, reception on, 230
St. Benin, 333
Somme battle, 57, 63, 88, 100
Souchez sector, 33
Tanks, 186, 332
Training at home, 9
Transfer to 74th Bde., 25th Div., 331
Trenches, first tour in, 18
Youens, 2nd Lieut. F., V.C., 168
Ypres, 3rd battle, 185, 195
Zillebeke sector, 111

14th (S.) Bn. the Durham Light Infantry

Armentières sector, 34
Arras battle, 137
Brigade, composition of, 10, 31
Cambrai battle, 225
Cambrin sector, 113
Cantaing, 225
Casualties, Arras battle, 140
Cambrai battle, 225, 226, 228
Cambrin sector, 114
— Ginchy-Lesbœufs road, 77
Hamel sector, 113
— Lens sector, 210, 211

Casualties *(continued)*
Lesbœufs line, 78
le Transloy, 93, 95
Loos battle, 21
Loos sector, 115, 151, 153, 170, 210
Quadrilateral, 76
six months to June 30th, 1916, 36
Wieltje sector, 35
Cavalry at Cambrai battle, 225
Colour, King's, 369
Command and changes in same, 10, 36, 78, 113, 114

Index

14th (S.) Bn. the Durham Light Infantry (continued)

Complimented by G.O.C. Div., 229
Disbandment, 243
Dynamite Magazine, 139
Embarkation for France, 20
Formation, 2
France, arrival in, 20
Gas attack, Wieltje sector, 35
Hamel sector, 112
Honours, Arras battle, 140
— Cambrai battle, 225, 228
    Cambrin raids, 113, 114
    le Transloy, 94
    Loos raids, 170
    various, 36, 111, 115
    Wieltje sector, 35
Lascelles, Capt. A. M., V.C., M.C., 229
Lens sector, 210
le Transloy, 93

Loos battle, 20
— sector, 111, 154, 169, 210
Louveral, trenches near, 243
Marcoing, 226
Noreuil sector, 242
Novel Alley, etc., 139
Pilckem sector, 30
Ploegsteert sector, 31
Quadrilateral, 74
Raid, Hamel, 113
Raids, Cambrin, 113, 114
— German, 210
    Loos, 169, 170
Somme battle, 74, 93
Tanks, 224, 225
Training at home, 10
Transfer to 18th Bde., 6th Div., 34
Trenches, first tour in, 34
Wieltje sector, 35, 112

15th (S.) Bn. the Durham Light Infantry

Armentières sector, 37
Armistice, 330
Arras battle, 131, 140
— sector, 115
Banner, St. Cuthbert's, 115
Bazentin-le-Petit Wood, 58
Beaurevoir Line, 326
Brigade, composition of, 10, 244
Bullecourt sector, 242
Cambrin sector, 115, 116
Casualties, Armentières sector, 37
— Arras battle, 137, 142
— Arras sector, 115
— Bazentin-le-Petit Wood, 59
— Cambrin sector, 115
— Epéhy sector, 244
— German Offensive, March, 1918, 263
— German Offensive, April, 1918, 285
— German Offensive, May, 1918, 303
— Gueudecourt, 84, 86

Casualties (continued)
— Hamel sector, 308
— Last Campaign, 323, 325-7, 329, 330
    Loos battle, 21, 23, 24
    Reutel, 192
— Reutel line, 196, 197
    Somme battle (July 1st), 17, 18
Cauroy, 300
Chapel Hill, 260, 324
Colour, King's, 369
Command and changes in same, 10, 46, 48, 115, 116, 191, 243, 244, 261, 263, 302, 322, 325, 326, 328, 329
Complimented by G.O.C. Div., 323
Embarkation for France, 20
Epéhy sector, 243
Fontaine sector, 155
Formation, 2
France, arrival in, 20

373

Index

15th (S.) Bn. the Durham Light Infantry (*continued*)

Ficourt sector, 38
German Offensive, March, 1918, 260
    Offensive, April, 1918, 285
    Offensive, May, 1918, 298
    raid, 211
Gueudecourt, 83
Hamel sector, 308
Heaviside, Pte. M., V.C., 112
Hervelou ridge, 302
Honours, Armentières sector, 37
    Arras battle, 135, 137, 143
    Belgian, 244
    Chapel Hill, 260, 261
    French, 137, 308
    Ficourt sector, 38
    — German Offensive, March, 1918, 260, 261, 288
    German Offensive, May, 1918, 303
    — German raid, 211
    Gueudecourt, 83
    Last Campaign, 323-30

Honours (*continued*)
    - Reutel, 191, 192
    Reutel line, 197
    - Somme battle (J'y 1st), 48
Last Campaign, 321
Limont-Fontaine, 330
Locre sector, 285
Loos battle, 20
Luisenhof Farm, 321
Miraumont, 321
Poix-du-Nord, 328
Raid, German, 211
Reutel, 190
Reutel line, 196
Sensée sector, 170, 211
Somme battle, 15, 58, 83
Tanks, 85, 86, 141, 328
Training at home, 10
Trenches, first tour in, 36
Vendegies-au-Bois, 328
Villers-Guislain, 325
Ypres, 3rd battle, 190, 196

16th (R.) Bn. the Durham Light Infantry

Formation, 4

17th (R.) Bn. the Durham Light Infantry

Formation, 4

18th (S.) Bn. the Durham Light Infantry (1st County)

Armistice, 313
Arras battle, 143
Ayette ridge, 284
Beaumont Hamel sector, 42
Brigade, composition of, 11, 245
Casualties, First Garde Stellung, 121
    Gavrelle, 146-8
    German Offensive, March, 1918, 284
    German Offensive, April, 1918, 290, 291

Casualties (*continued*)
    German raid, 117
    Hartlepools bombardment, 11
    Hébuterne sector, 118
    - Last Campaign, 340, 341
    Plate Becque, 310, 311, 314
    Somme battle, 52
Colour, King's, 370
Command and changes in same, 10, 117, 245, 246, 282-4, 312
Dogs, messenger, 311
Egypt, 39

Index

18th (S.) Bn. the Durham Light Infantry (1st County)
(continued)

Embarkation for Egypt, 39
— for France, 41
Festhubert sector, 117
First Garde Stellung, 119
Formation, 2
France, arrival in, 41
Gavrelle, 143, 171
German Offensive, March, 1918, 284
— Offensive, April, 1918, 288
— raid, 117
— Retreat, 1917, 119
Givenchy sector, 117
Hartlepools bombardment, 11
Hébuterne sector, 118
Honours, First Garde Stellung, 121
— German Offensive, March, 1918, 283
— German Offensive, April, 1918, 290, 291
— German Offensive, 1918, 309
— German raid, 117
— Gommecourt raid, 118
— Last Campaign, 340, 341
— Plate Becque, 310, 311, 314, 315

Hunter-Weston's message, 52
Last Campaign, 338
Meteren, 309, 316
Middlesboro', 11
Moyenneville, 283
Neuve Chapelle sector, 116, 117
Outtersteene, 288
Plate Becque, 309–15
Ploegsteert Wood, 310
Raid, German, 117
— Gommecourt, 118
Reorganisation of brigade, 245
— of division, 245
Serre sector, 42
Somme battle, 48
Song on the march, 241
Suez Canal defences, 40
Training at home, 11
Transfer to 93rd Bde., 31st Div., 11
Trenches, first tour in, 42
Vimy line, 171, 212, 244
Voyage to Egypt, 39

19th (S.) Bn. the Durham Light Infantry (2nd County)

Armistice, 349
Arras sector, 122
" Bantam " standard, 3
— standard abolished, 122
Brigade, composition of, 12, 246
Casualties, Arras sector, 122
— German Offensive, March, 1918, 276, 277
— German Offensive, April, 1918, 293, 294
— German raid, 172
— Gillemont Farm, 215
— Last Campaign, 344–6, 348
— Les Trois Sauvages, 156
— Locre sector, 317

Casualties *(continued)*
— Longueval, 60
— Martinsart sector, 316
— Somme battle, 61, 70
— Ypres, 3rd battle, 198, 199
Colour, King's, 370
Command and changes in same, 3, 12, 60, 122–4, 198, 246, 316, 348, 349
Courtrai entered, 347
Embarkation for France, 42
Favières Wood, 275
Festhubert sector, 43
Fleurbaix sector, 43
Formation, 3
France, arrival in, 42

Index

Bn. the Durham Light Infantry (2nd County)
(continued)

..., 157, 171
... March, 1918,
April, 1918, 293
, 172
1917, 123
orm, 211
ector, 171
man Offensive, March,
'6
aid, 172
Road raid, 247
paign, 343-9
ector, 123
d, 317
ke, 314
7
ign, 343
tor, 43
auvages, 156

Lihons sector, 123
Lorre sector, 316
Longueval, 60
Malzhorn ridge, 70
Martinsart sector, 316
Montauban, 59
Omignon river sector, 155
Poelcappelle, 198, 246
Raid, Houthulst Road, 217
— Locre, 347
— Martinsart, 316
Raids, Arras, 122
— German, 122, 172
Richebourg-St. Vaast sector, 43
Somme battle, 59, 70
Training at home, 12
Transfer to 104th Bde., 246
Trenches, first tour in, 43
Treux, 277
Ypres, 3rd battle, 197

0th (S.) Bn. the Durham Light Infantry

sector N. of, 44, 124
357
350
5
mposition of, 13, 238
Armentières, sector N.
125
Offensive, March, 1918,
1
Offensive, April, 1918, 296
57
mpaign, 351, 352, 354-6
battle, 160, 164, 165, 166
sector, 125, 126
berg sector, 318, 319
battle, 87, 88, 89, 100
rd battle, 174-6, 184
g's, 370
and changes in same, 3,
124, 177, 237, 354, 356

Complimented by Artillery, 93rd
  (A) Bde., 281
— by G.O.C. Bde., 281
— by G.O.C. Div., 41
Embarkation for France, 43
Flers, 87
Formation, 3
France, arrival in, 13
— return to, 238
German Offensive, March, 1918, 278
— Offensive, April, 1918, 295
Germany, arrival in, 370
Hill 35, 295
— 60 sector, 157
Honours, Armentières, sector N.
  of, 44, 125
— French, 157
— German Offensive, March, 1918,
  278, 280
— Italy, 237

Index

20th (S.) Bn. the Durham Light Infantry (continued)

Honours (continued)
— Last Campaign, 351, 354
— Messines battle, 160
— Somme battle, 86, 99, 100
— various, 157
— Ypres, 3rd battle, 176, 216
Houthem, 352
Italy, arrival in, 236
Last Campaign, 349
Messines battle, 159, 165
Montello sector, 236
Nieuport Bains sector, 215

Raids, Armentières, sector N. of, 44, 124
St. Eloi sector, 125, 157
Scheldt, first across, 356
Scherpenberg sector, 318
Somme battle, 86, 98
Lower Hamlets, 182
Training at home, 12
Transfer to 124th Bde., 238
Trenches, first tour in, 44
Ypres defences, 295, 317
— 3rd battle, 174, 182

21st (R.) Bn. the Durham Light Infantry

Formation, 4

22nd (S.) Bn. the Durham Light Infantry (3rd County) (Pioneers)

Absorbed by 1/7th Durham Light Infantry, 306
Bois des Buttes, 304
Bouchavesnes, 128
Cambrin sector, 126
Casualties, Bouchavesnes, 130
— Cambrin sector, 126
— German Offensive, March, 1918, 273, 274
— German Offensive, April, 1918, 297, 298
German Offensive, May, 1918, 305
— la Boisselle, 53
— le Transloy, 96, 98
— Ploegsteert sector, 216
— Somme battle, 53, 98
— Ypres, 3rd battle, 202, 204
— Zillebeke sector, 172, 173
Colour, King's, 369
Command and changes in same, 4, 13, 273, 296
Complimented by C.E., 8th Corps, 248

Complimented (continued)
— by C.-in-C., 203
— by G.O.C., 23rd Bde., 204
Embarkation for France, 44
Formation, 3
France, arrival in, 44
German Offensive, March, 1918, 271
— Offensive, April, 1918, 296
— Offensive, May, 1918, 304
— Retreat, 1917, 131
Gernicourt, 304
Hannebeck bridged, 203
Harbonnières, 273
Honours, Belgian, 248
— Bouchavesnes, 131
— German Offensive, March, 1918, 272-5
— German Offensive, April, 1918, 297, 298
— various, 218
— Ypres salient, 203
le Transloy, 95
— sector, 127

Index

) Bn. the Durham Light Infantry (3rd County) (Pioneers) (*continued*)

, 199
ector, 216
;tor, 127
on in 3 companies, 219

Somme battle, 53, 95
Training at home, 13
Ypres salient, 158, 172, 217, 247
— 3rd battle, 199

3rd (R.) Bn. the Durham Light Infantry

4

(Works) Bn. the Durham Light Infantry

5

9th (S.) Bn. the Durham Light Infantry

51
Last Campaign, 357,
's, 369
d changes in same,

Embarkation for France, 319
Formation, 319
France, arrival in, 319
Godshuis, 359
Honours, Last Campaign, 357, 360
Last Campaign, 357
Ypres defences, 320, 357

1st (G.) Bn. the Durham Light Infantry

's, 369
hange in, 370

Germany, arrival in, 370
Origin, 5

nd (G.) Bn. the Durham Light Infantry

's, 369
hange in, 370

Germany, arrival in, 370
Origin, 5

rd (Y.S.) Bn. the Durham Light Infantry

rival in, 370

Reduction, 370

General

System, 1
battle, 166
s, to Nation, 2
ppeal for recruits, 1
, 2
ary Committee, 3

Song on the march, 241
Spirit of the recruits, 7
Training, character of, 7
— difficulties, 6

Y CASSELL & COMPANY, LIMITED, LA BELLE SAUVAGE, LONDON, E C 4

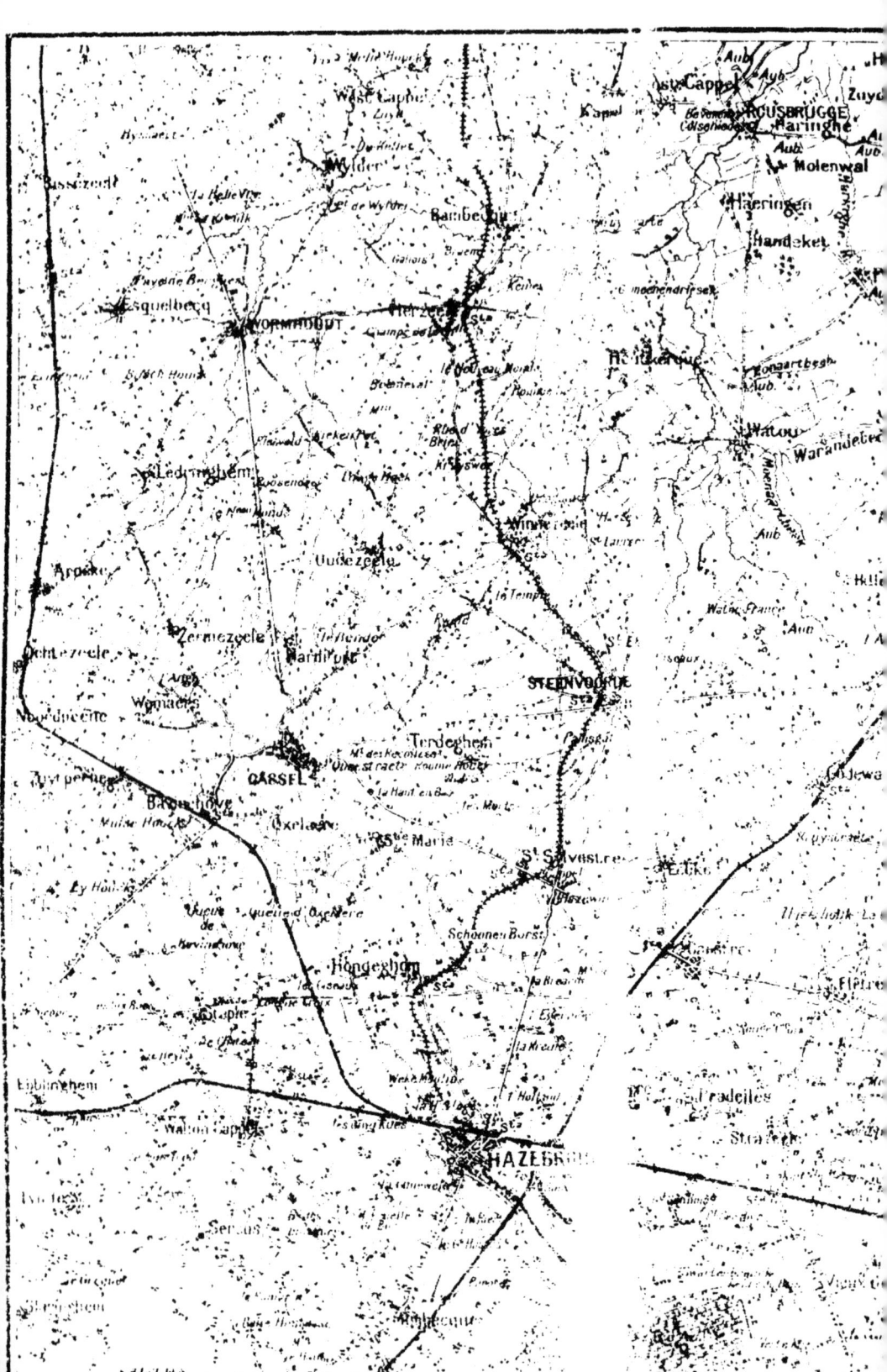

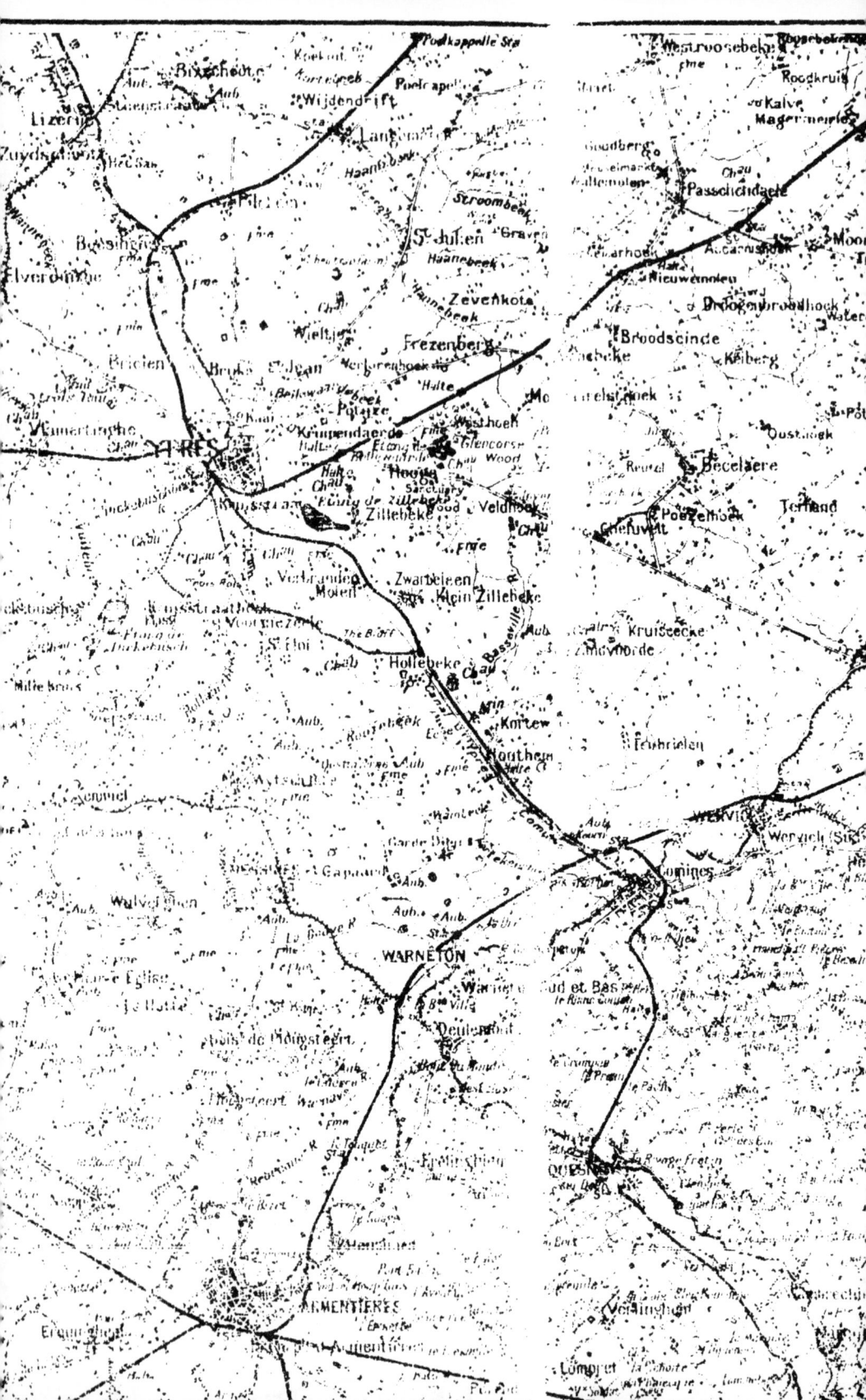

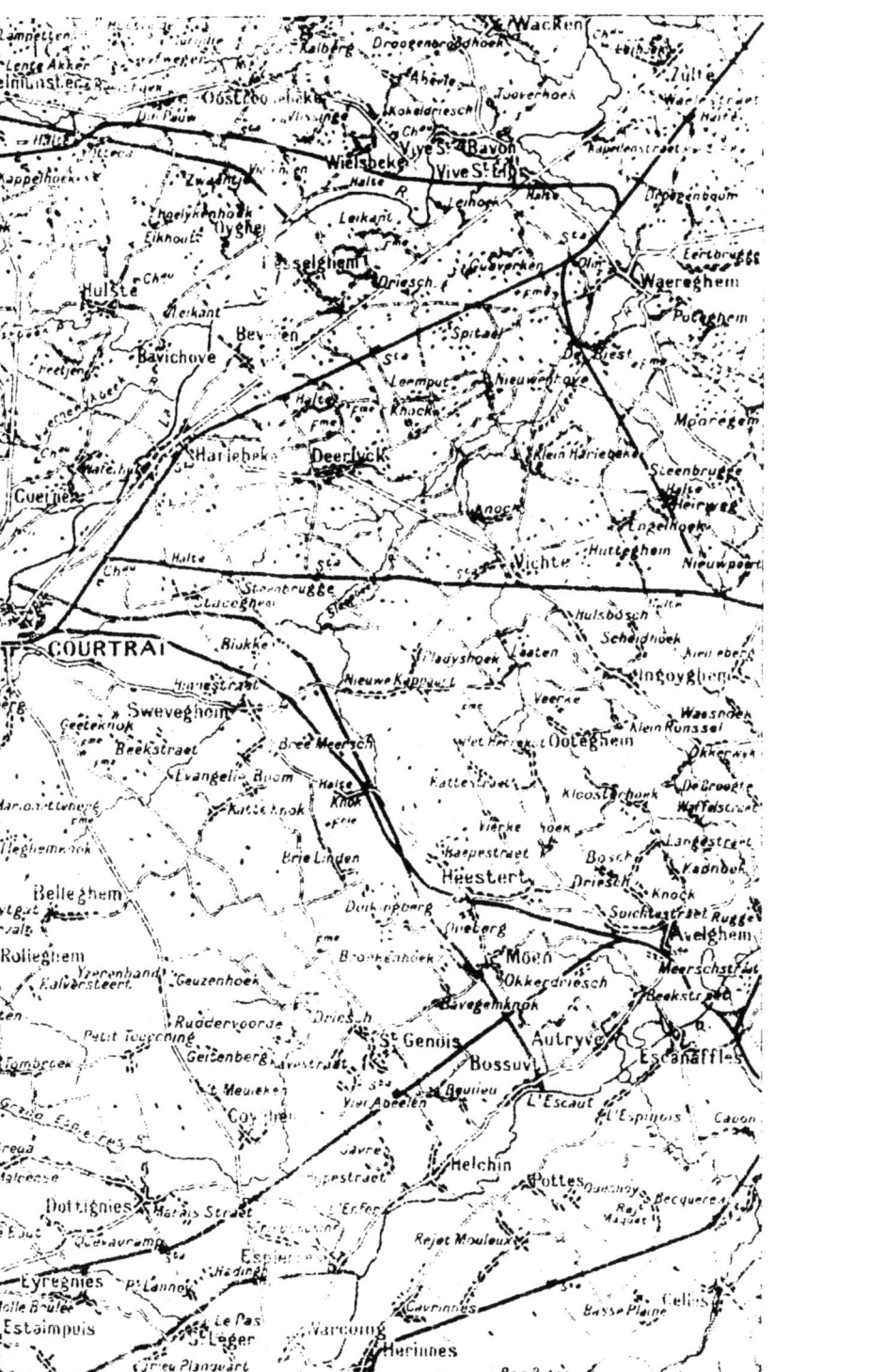

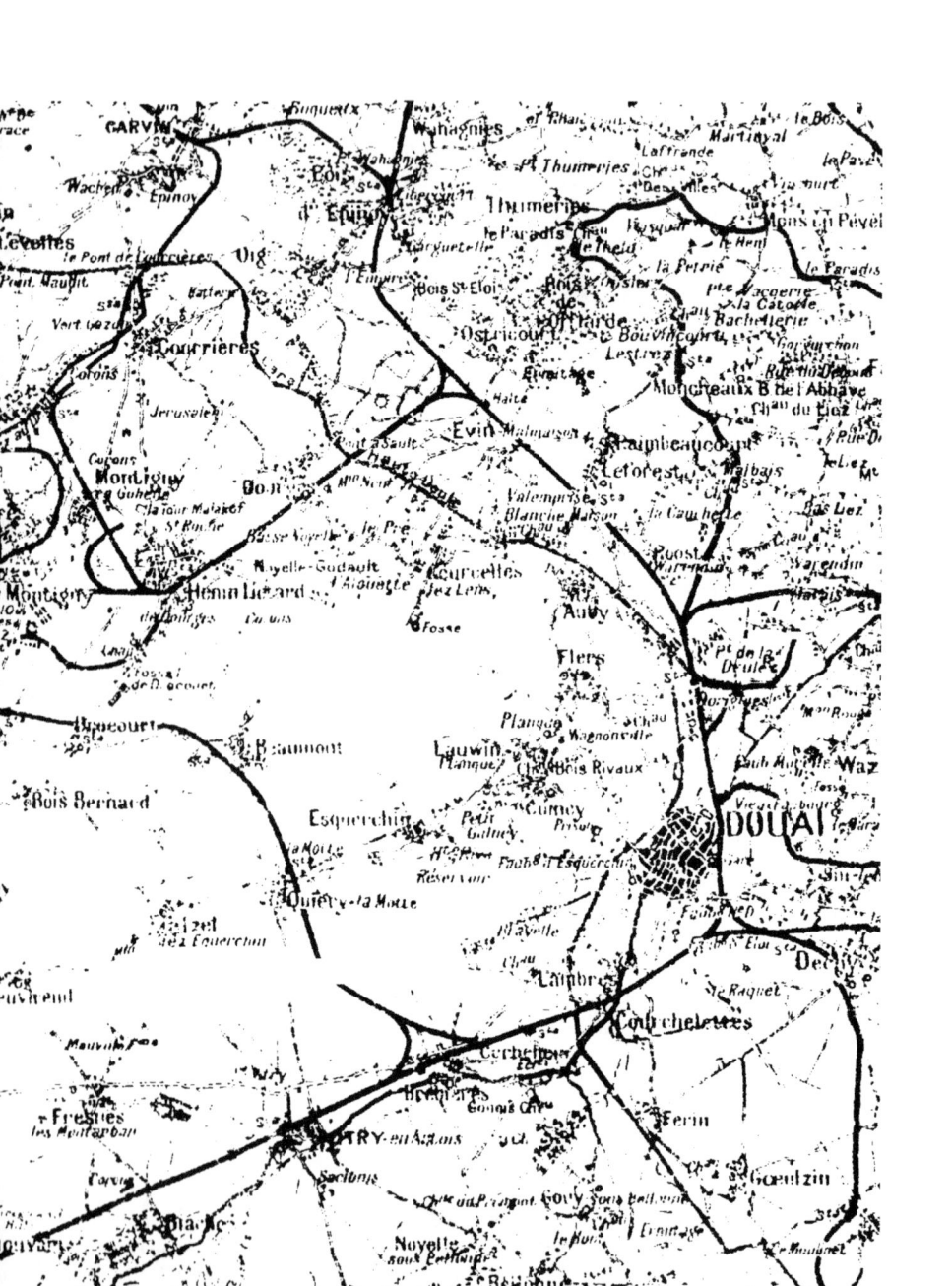

Map 2

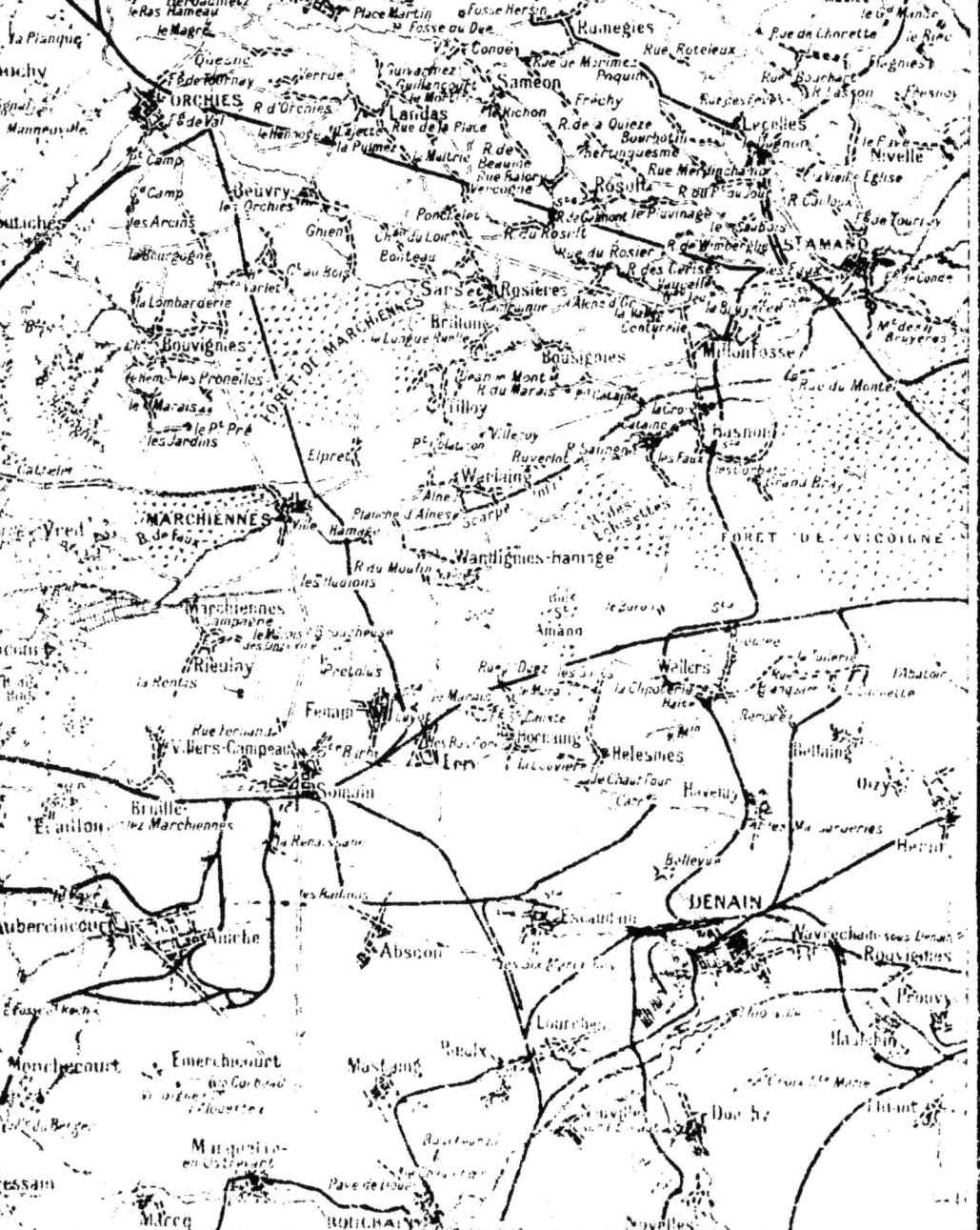

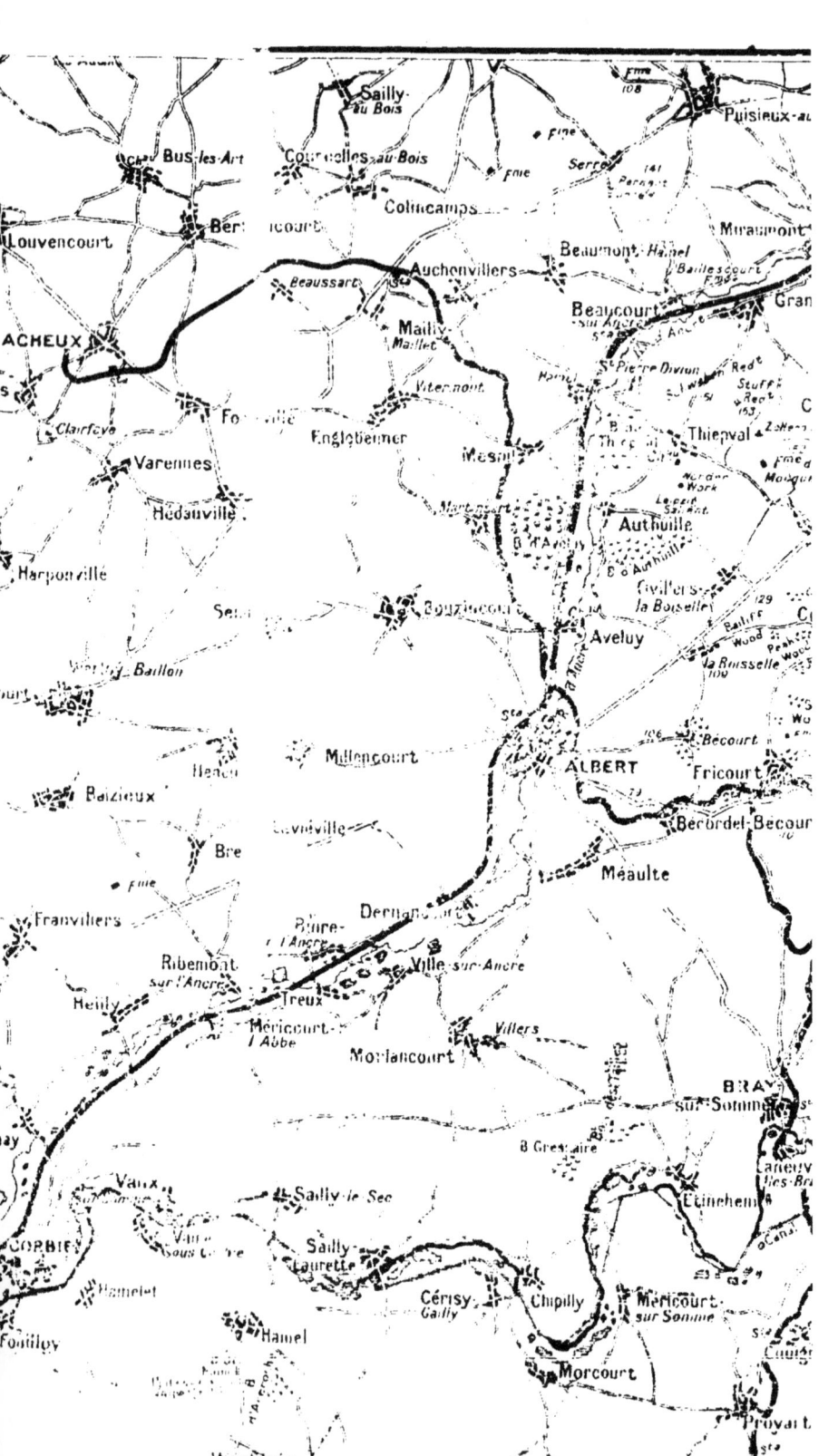

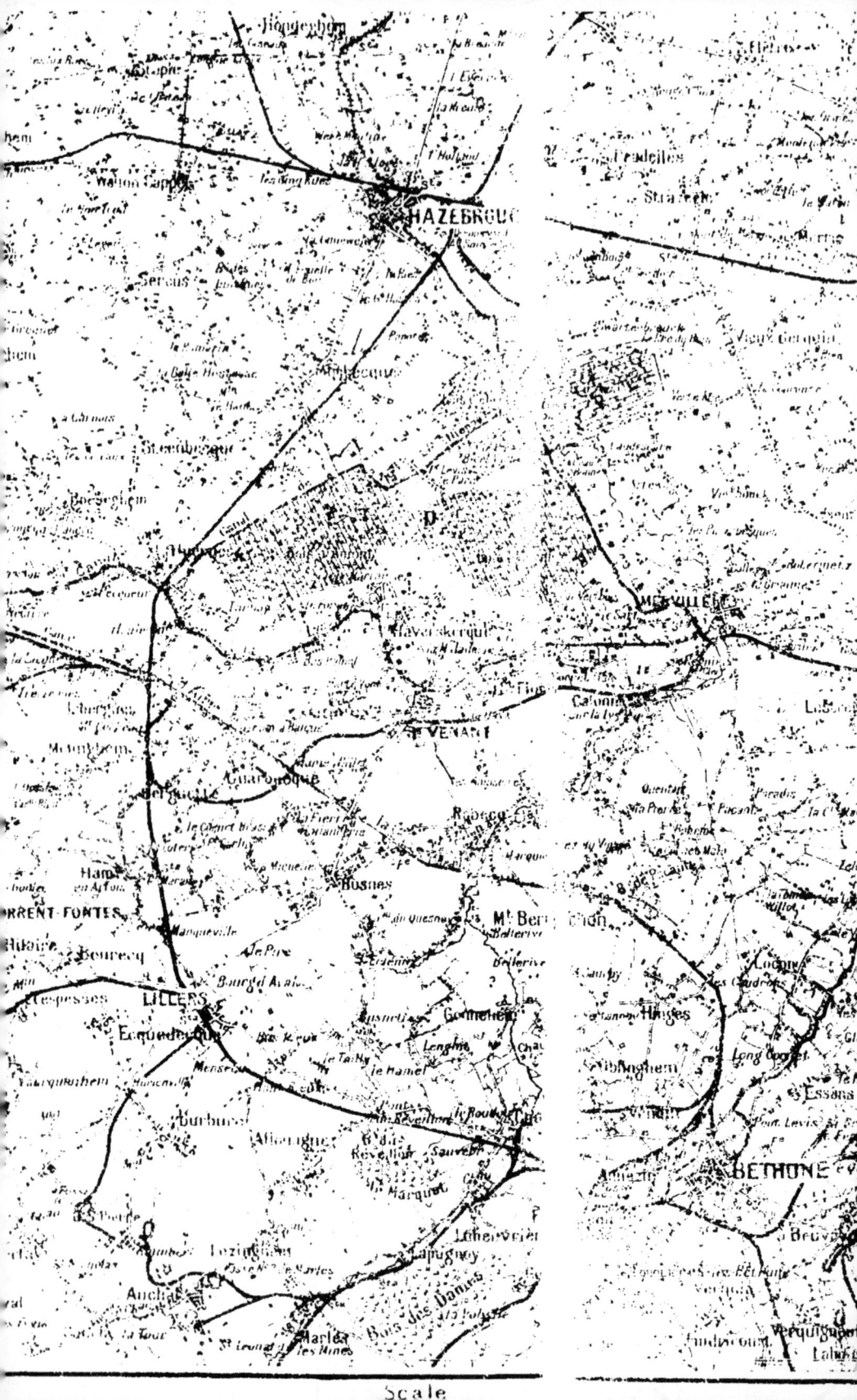

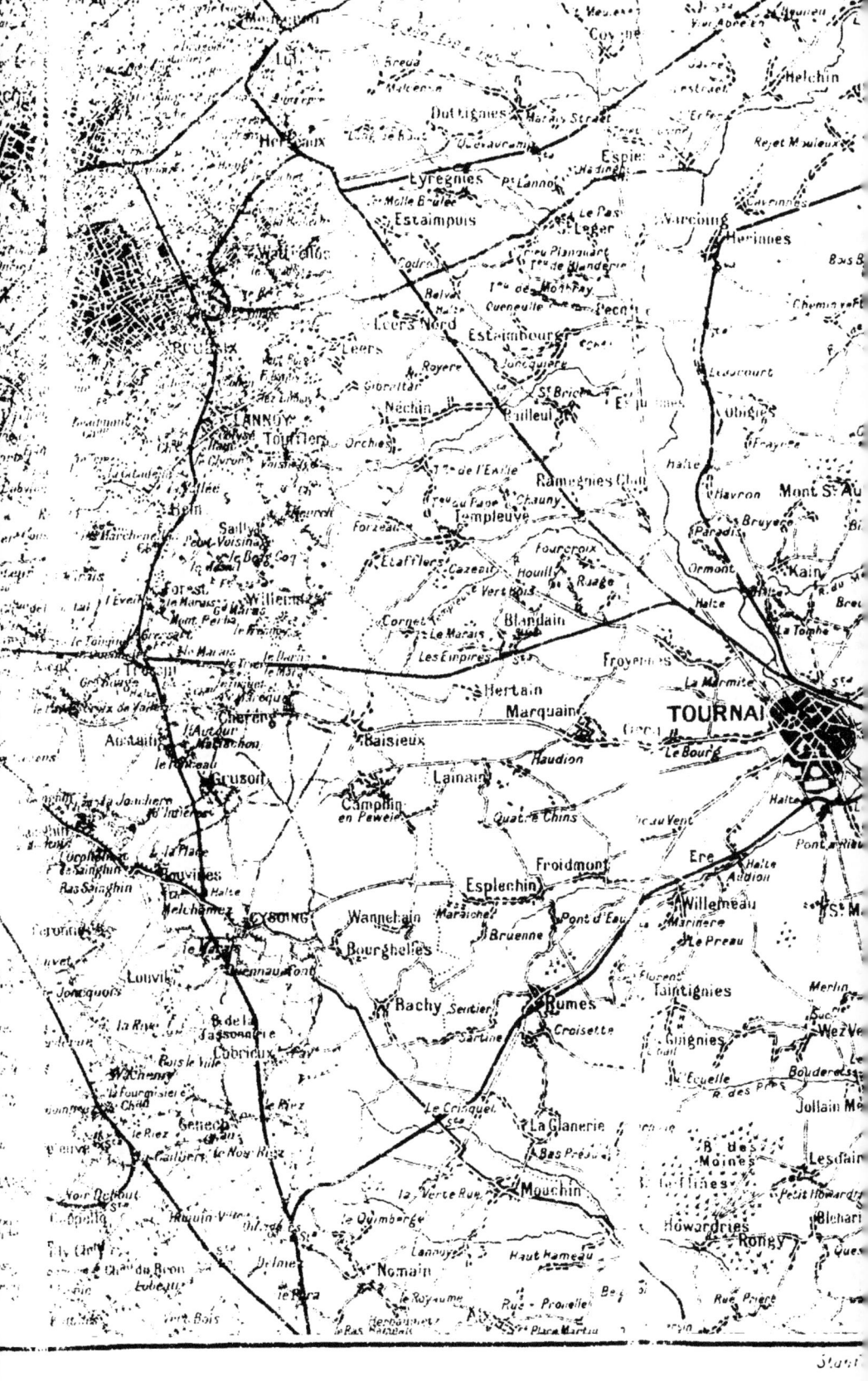

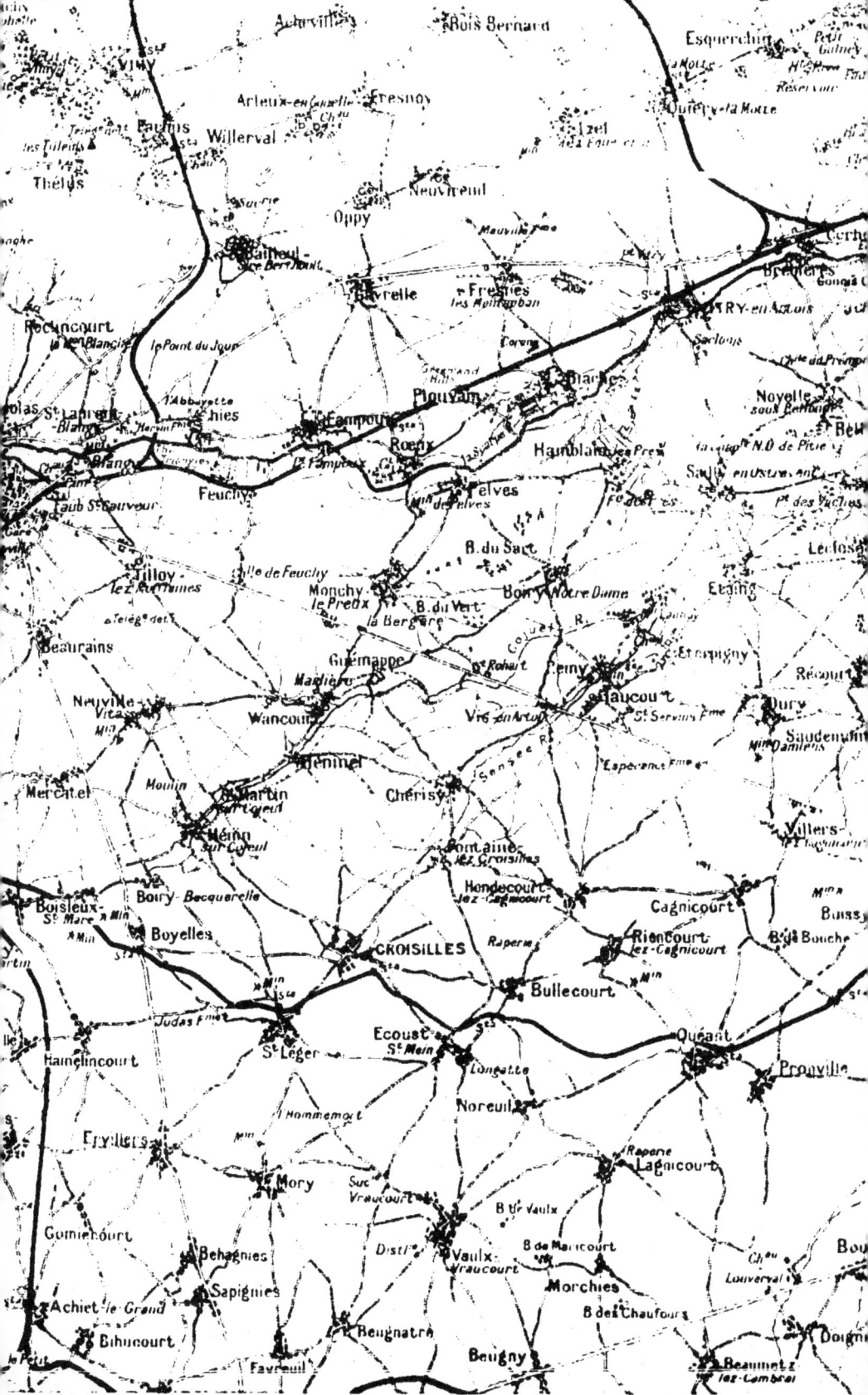

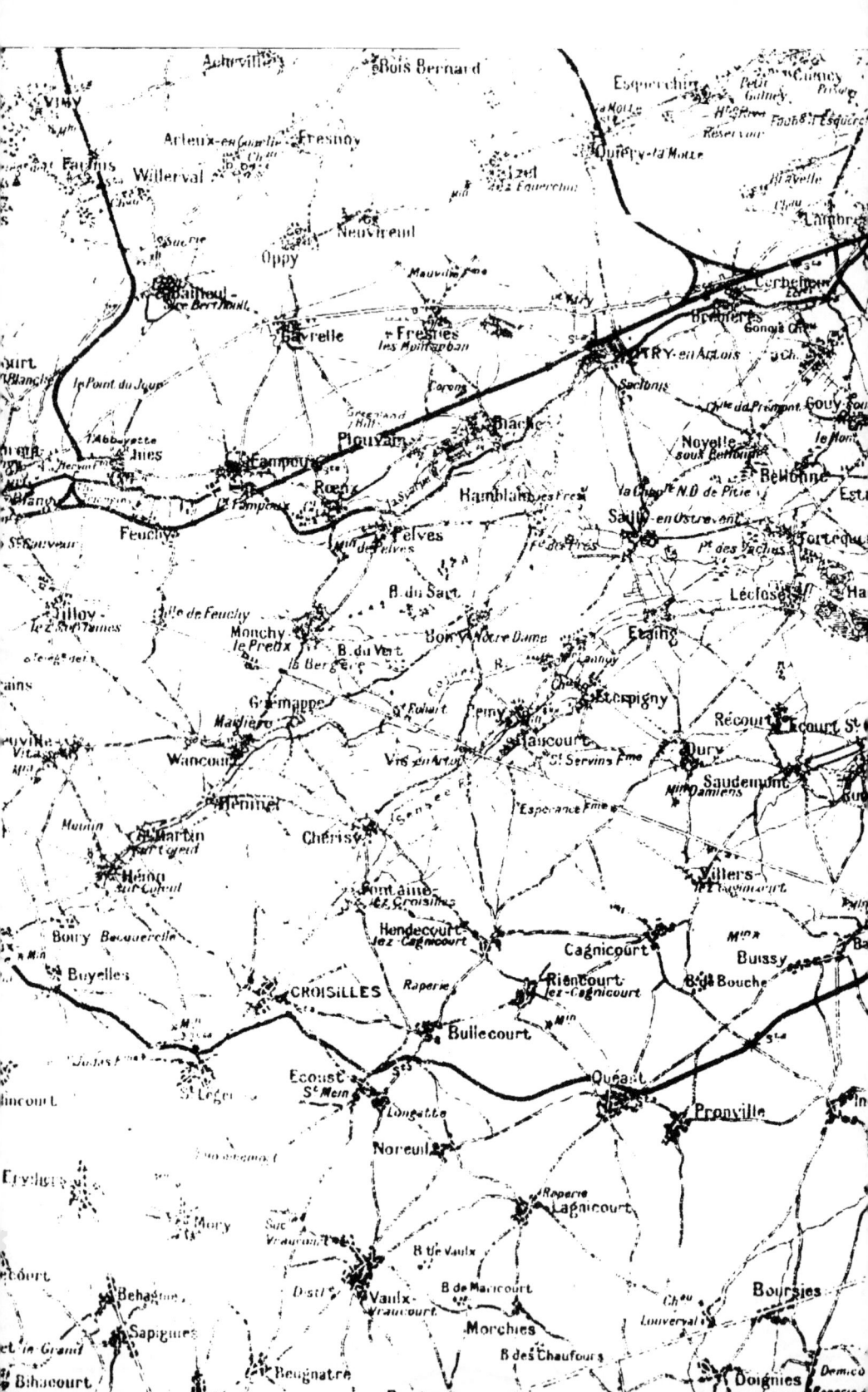

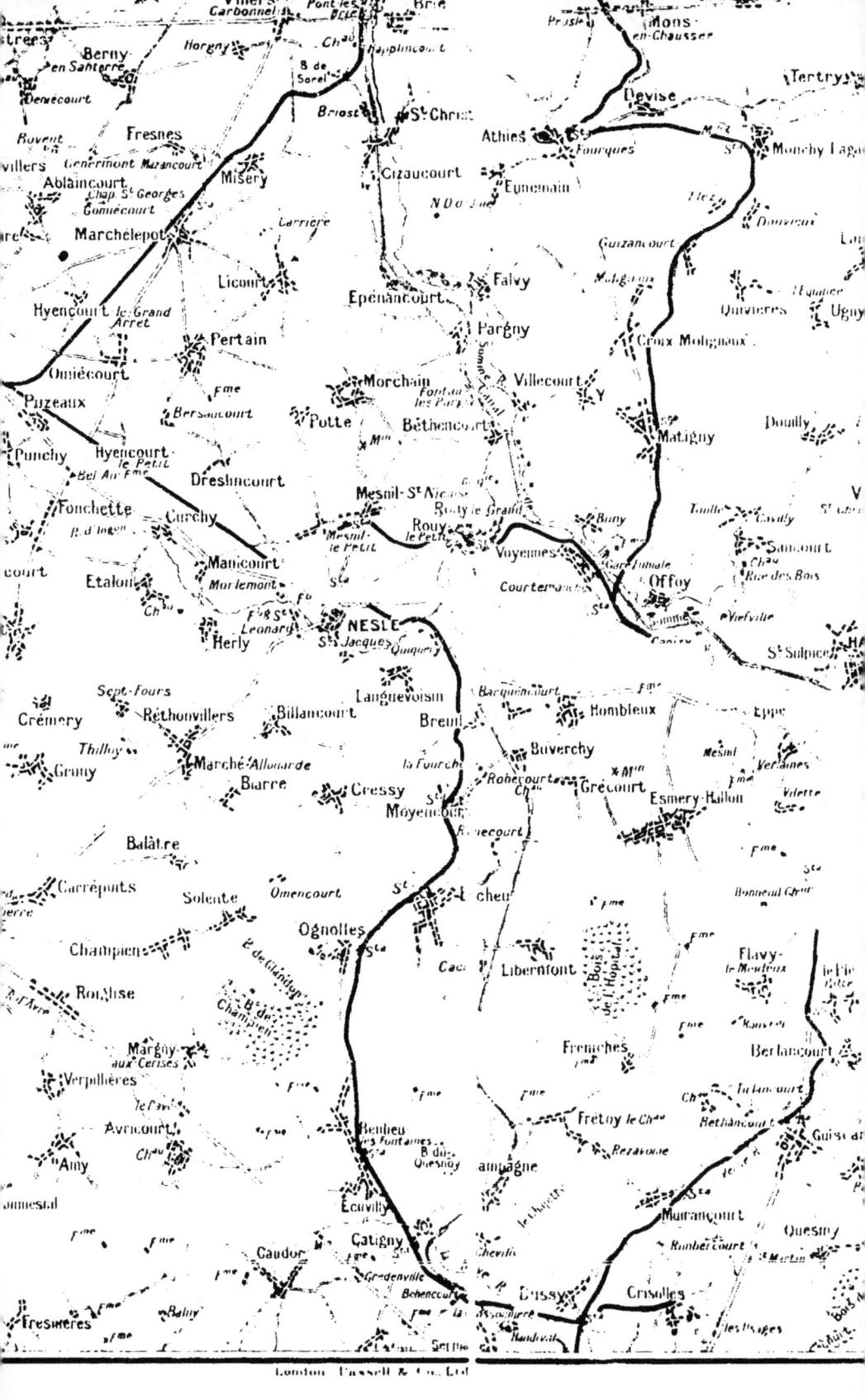

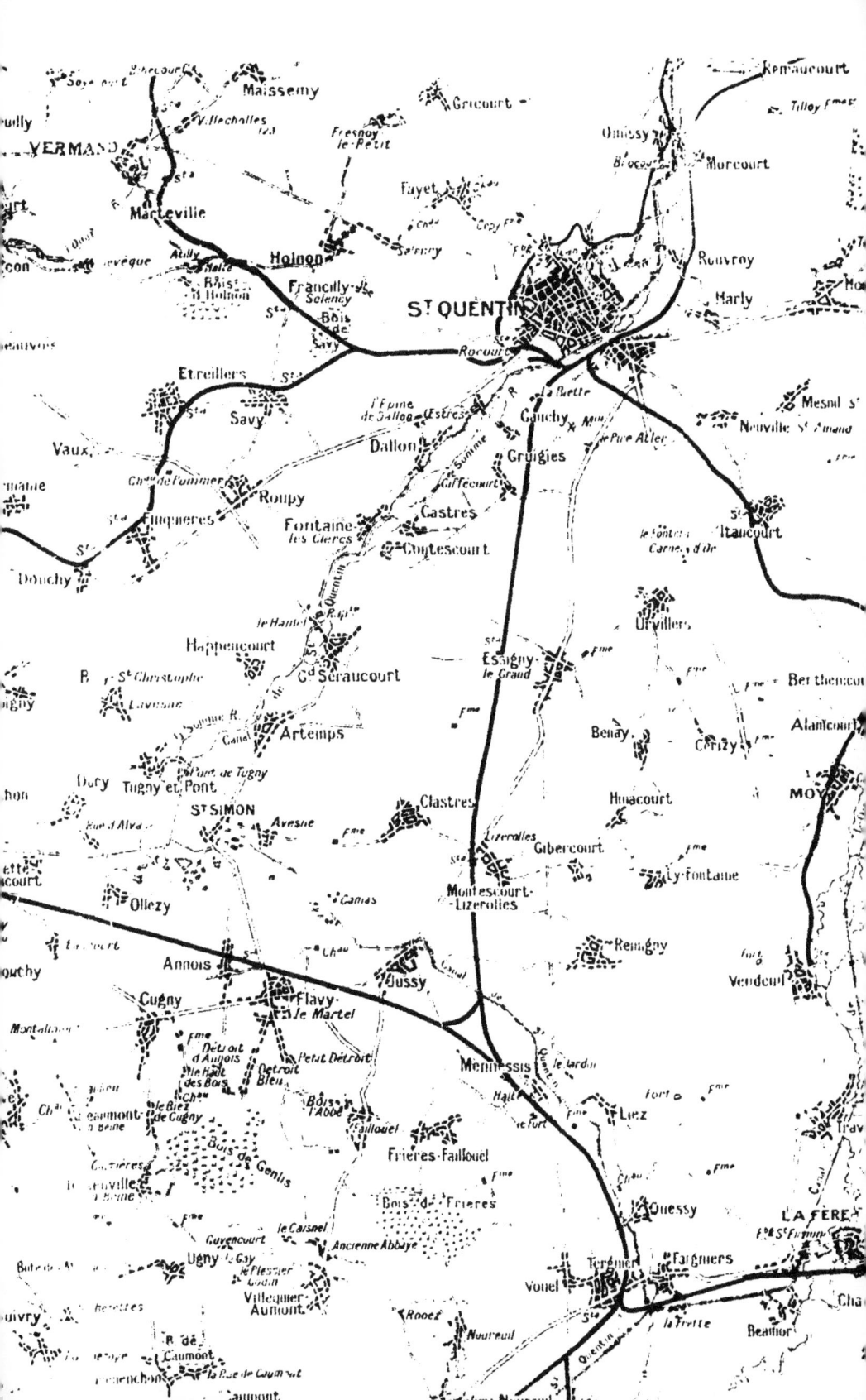

WS - #0037 - 230226 - C0 - 229/152/25 [27] - CB - 9780666830920 - Gloss Lamination